JUDGING EUROPE'S JUDGES

After successive waves of EU enlargement, and pursuant to the entry into force of the Lisbon Treaty, the European Court of Justice finds itself on the brink of a new era. Both the institution itself and the broader setting within which it operates have become more heterogeneous than ever before. The issues now arriving on its docket are also often of great complexity, covering an unprecedented number of fields. The aims of this volume are to study the impact of these developments, examine the legitimacy of the Court's output in this novel context and provide an appraisal of its overall performance. In doing so, specific attention is paid to its most recent case law on four topics: the general principles of EU law, external relations, the internal market and Union citizenship.

Featuring contributions by Maurice Adams, Henri de Waele, Johan Meeusen and Gert Straetmans, Koen Lenaerts, Ján Mazák and Martin Moser, Stephen Weatherill, Jukka Snell, Michael Dougan, Daniel Thym, Eileen Denza, Michal Bobek and JHH Weiler.

Judging Europe's Judges

The Legitimacy of the Case Law of the European Court of Justice

Edited by
Maurice Adams
Henri de Waele
Johan Meeusen
and
Gert Straetmans

• HART •
PUBLISHING
OXFORD AND PORTLAND, OREGON
2013

Published in the United Kingdom by Hart Publishing Ltd
16C Worcester Place, Oxford, OX1 2JW
Telephone: +44 (0)1865 517530
Fax: +44 (0)1865 510710
E-mail: mail@hartpub.co.uk
Website: http://www.hartpub.co.uk

Published in North America (US and Canada) by
Hart Publishing
c/o International Specialized Book Services
920 NE 58th Avenue, Suite 300
Portland, OR 97213-3786
USA
Tel: +1 503 287 3093 or toll-free: (1) 800 944 6190
Fax: +1 503 280 8832
E-mail: orders@isbs.com
Website: http://www.isbs.com

British Library Cataloguing in Publication Data
Data Available

ISBN: 978-1-84946-335-5

Typeset by Hope Services, Abingdon
Printed and bound in Great Britain by
TJ International Ltd, Padstow

Preface

The contributions in this volume were originally prepared for an expert seminar that was organised at the University of Antwerp (Belgium) on 3 and 4 November 2011, entitled 'Judging Europe's Judges – The Legitimacy of the Case Law of the European Court of Justice in a Union Transformed'. Most of the contributors were presented at the seminar and underwent substantial modifications subsequently, following the lively discussions among the authors and participants. Some were composed at a later stage, in order to address particular issues that emerged repeatedly over the course of the debates.

The editors of this volume invited Professor Koen Lenaerts, Vice-President of the Court of Justice of the European Union, to deliver the seminar's key-note lecture. This way, an insider's view – based of course upon all pertinent legal and academic sources and references – introduced all participants to the legitimacy theme and its importance for the ECJ and invited them to engage in further debate. Lenaerts's lecture, which now serves as the book's opening chapter, broadly explored various fields of EU law; the other speakers were asked to focus their contribution on more specific fields. The seminar was concluded with considerations on the various lectures and debates by Professor JJH Weiler; his contribution now serves as the book's epilogue.

The seminar in Antwerp concluded a larger research project on the democratic legitimacy of the role of the Court of Justice in the European Union, which ran from 2007–11. This project was funded by the Research Foundation – Flanders (FWO), and purported to explore the possibility of establishing the European Court of Justice as a democratic institution. The project resulted in a series of publications, largely inspired by the work of Hans Kelsen. These were followed up by the aforementioned seminar, which brought together experts from all over Europe and across the Atlantic to engage in a broader reflection on the different conceptions of legitimacy in the European legal order – and in particular, to examine the legitimacy of the case law of the EU's Court of Justice. Hence the theme of the seminar, which is in turn reflected in the title of this volume.

The editors would like to express their sincere gratitude to Dr Christine Janssens and Dr Sven Braspenning (both of the University of Antwerp) for their much appreciated assistance in the editing of this book and the preparation of the seminar.

Maurice Adams, Henri de Waele, Johan Meeusen and Gert Straetmans

Antwerp/Tilburg, July 2013

Table of Contents

Preface v
About the Authors ix

Introduction: Judging Europe's Judges 1
Maurice Adams, Henri de Waele, Johan Meeusen and Gert Straetmans

1. The Court's Outer and Inner Selves: Exploring the External and Internal Legitimacy of the European Court of Justice 13
Koen Lenaerts

2. Adjudication by Reference to General Principles of EU Law: A Second Look at the *Mangold* Case Law 61
Ján Mazák and Martin Moser

3. The Court's Case Law on the Internal Market: 'A Circumloquacious Statement of the Result, Rather than a Reason for Arriving at It'? 87
Stephen Weatherill

4. The Legitimacy of Free Movement Case Law: Process and Substance 109
Jukka Snell

5. The Bubble that Burst: Exploring the Legitimacy of the Case Law on the Free Movement of Union Citizens 127
Michael Dougan

6. Towards 'Real' Citizenship? The Judicial Construction of Union Citizenship and its Limits 155
Daniel Thym

7. Placing the European Union in International Context: Legitimacy of the Case Law 175
Eileen Denza

8. Of Feasibility and Silent Elephants: The Legitimacy of the Court of Justice through the Eyes of National Courts 197
Michal Bobek

Epilogue: Judging the Judges – Apology and Critique 235
JHH Weiler

Index 255

About the Authors

Maurice Adams is Professor of General Jurisprudence and 'vfund' Professor of Democratic Governance and the Rule of Law at Tilburg University, and Visiting Professor at the Universities of Antwerp and Leuven.

Michal Bobek is Professor of European Union Law at the College of Europe, Bruges and Research Fellow at the Oxford University Institute of European and Comparative Law.

Eileen Denza is formerly Legal Counsellor, Foreign and Commonwealth Office, Counsel, EC Committee, UK House of Lords and Visiting Professor, University College London.

Henri de Waele is Senior Lecturer in European Law at the Radboud University Nijmegen and Guest Professor of European Institutional Law at the University of Antwerp.

Michael Dougan is Jean Monnet Chair and Professor of European Union Law at the University of Liverpool.

Koen Lenaerts is Judge and Vice-President of the Court of Justice of the European Union and Professor of European Law at the University of Leuven.

Ján Mazák is Professor of European Union Law at Masaryk University, Brno and a former Advocate General at the Court of Justice of the European Union.

Johan Meeusen is Vice-Rector and Professor of European Union Law and Private International Law at the University of Antwerp and former holder of a Jean Monnet Chair *ad personam*.

Martin Moser is *référendaire* at the Court of Justice of the European Union (Cabinet of Judge Siniša Rodin; formerly inter alia, Cabinet of Advocate General Ján Mazák).

Jukka Snell is Professor of European Law at the University of Turku and Professor of EU Law at Swansea University.

Gert Straetmans is Professor of European Economic and Commercial Law at the University of Antwerp and Visiting Professor at the Rheinische Friedrich-Wilhelms-Universität Bonn.

Daniel Thym is Chair of Public, European and International Law and Co-Director of the Research Centre on Immigration and Asylum Law at Konstanz University.

Stephen Weatherill is Jacques Delors Professor of European Law, Deputy Director for European Law at the Institute of European and Comparative Law at the University of Oxford and a Fellow of Somerville College.

JHH Weiler was University Professor and Joseph Straus Professor of Law and European Union Jean Monnet Chaired Professor at New York University School of Law. As of 1 September 2013, he is President of the European University Institute, Florence.

Introduction: Judging Europe's Judges

MAURICE ADAMS, HENRI DE WAELE, JOHAN MEEUSEN AND GERT STRAETMANS

I. DYNAMIC ADJUDICATION

DISCUSSIONS ON THE proper role of adjudicators are as old as the proverbial way to Rome: *Quis custodiet ipsos custodes*? In recent times, especially in the context of the functioning of international and supranational courts, these discussions have acquired a new momentum.[1] Moreover, the debate appears to elicit much stronger sentiments than ever before, with hardened pleas for placing fetters on tribunals that are external to the nation state emerging with ever-increasing frequency.[2] Quite paradoxically, this occurs at a moment when the globalisation process seems to have reached cruising speed, with the intertwining of legal orders and multiplication of spheres of governance becoming a nigh irreversible process.[3]

Naturally, the functioning of courts in international and supranational settings raises countless questions. Their adjudicatory task as such, however, might be considered by and large the same when compared with that of national courts, since they are all expected to apply the law. Correspondingly, in the opening chapter of this volume, Koen Lenaerts emphasises that courts must not intrude into the political process, as the borderline between law and politics is of vital importance for a court's legitimacy, and intends to preserve a legal system's checks and balances. Yet, when applying the law, courts must also determine what the law is, and thus interpret it. This is (also according to Lenaerts) 'risky business' – for in doing so, they are in fact drawing the borderlines of their own legitimacy.

[1] See recently, eg A von Bogdandy and I Venzke (eds), *International Judicial Lawmaking* (Berlin, Springer, 2012); J Christoffersen and MR Madsen (eds), *The European Court of Human Rights between Law and Politics* (Oxford, Oxford University Press, 2011); G Conway, *The Limits of Legal Reasoning and the European Court of Justice* (Cambridge, Cambridge University Press, 2012).

[2] Consider, eg the remarks by Lord Hoffman in his Judicial Studies Board Annual Lecture regarding the European Court of Human Rights: 'The Universality of Human Rights', 19 March 2009: 'Even if the Strasbourg judges were omniscient, knowing the true interests of the people of the United Kingdom better than we do ourselves, it would still be constitutionally inappropriate for decisions of the kind which I have been discussing to be made by a foreign court'.

[3] AM Slaughter, *A New World Order* (Princeton NJ, Princeton University Press, 2005).

That courts must apply the law can therefore not mean that they are denied all interpretative manoeuvring space, or that they should behave as the imaginary – legalistic – mouth of the law.[4] That would be quite impossible because, although judicial decisions should be grounded in an elaboration of relevant legal texts, the precise meaning and relevance of those texts are themselves subject to debate. In addition, adjudication has nowadays become more challenging than ever before, since the law is increasingly interlinking different sets of interests, so as to address ever more complex societal problems and issues. As a result, in individual cases, courts can no longer confine themselves to applying the legal rules as established by the legislator. Rather, they are increasingly expected to weigh and reconcile the relevant interests themselves. Also, on ever more frequent occasions, courts must derive appropriate standards from the available rules – ie, principles of proper administration and good governance, demarcations of responsibility, etc – which may then serve as benchmarks for assessing the extent to which conflicting interests should be protected. For that reason, the process of adjudication will necessarily have to be dynamic – at least, if the law itself is to remain a valued means for channelling social developments.

II. THE EUROPEAN COURT OF JUSTICE: A DYNAMIC ADJUDICATOR IN A UNION TRANSFORMED

The above holds in particular for the European Court of Justice (ECJ), which finds its origin in the tribunal established more than 60 years ago by the European Coal and Steel Community Treaty, concluded by the then six Member States. Over time, the legal and political landscape wherein the ECJ operates has undergone a spectacular transformation, a process which reached its provisional apogee with the entry into force of the Lisbon Treaty in December 2009. For one thing, as a result of successive rounds of enlargement, the territorial scope of EU law expanded ever further, nearly doubling the number of Member States and citizens to be adjudicated. In addition, there is the expansion of the Court's jurisdiction *ratione materiae*, which nowadays covers an unprecedented number of fields. As a result, it finds itself having to rule on issues such as terrorist listings, the rights of aircraft passengers and the permissibility of using human embryos for industrial or commercial purposes.[5]

As such, the ECJ can count on relatively strong support within the scholarly community, where it is still generally regarded as the principal guarantor of the rule of law within the Union. Admittedly, it has in the past been repeatedly accused of overstepping the limits of the conferred mandate. Yet, such allega-

[4] Montesquieu's famous metaphor, which informed many of the previous discussions about the role of the judiciary (usually also in terms of 'judicial activism' versus 'judicial restraint').

[5] See eg Joined Cases C-402/05 P and C-415/05 P *Kadi and Al Barakaat International Foundation v Council and Commission* [2008] ECR I-6351; Joined Cases C-402/07 and C-432/07 *Sturgeon v Condor* and *Böck v Air France* [2009] ECR I-10923; Case C-34/10 *Brüstle v Greenpeace*, Judgment of 18 October 2011, not yet reported.

tions have invariably received quick rebuttals in legal doctrine.[6] In the past few years, criticism of supposed faux pas hardly displays a structural trend, but mostly emerges ad hoc, in editorials, the margins of case notes or articles mainly devoted to other themes.[7] Still, the renewed attention in academia for the role and function of the judiciary, in particular in international and supranational settings, justifies a comprehensive inspection of the ECJ's performance. For that purpose, we invited a select number of scholars to engage in a contemporary assessment of the legitimacy of its case law. Significantly, the Court is recognised as a dynamic adjudicator in almost every contribution included in this volume. Thus, in their chapter on the judicial development of the general principles of EU law, Ján Mazák and Martin Moser confirm that interpretation always involves a process of understanding that can, as such, not be turned into a mathematical formula (see chapter two). According to them, this especially holds true when dealing with EU rules and provisions, which incorporate myriad variables, including the broadly formulated Article 19 TEU that explicitly entrusts the Court to 'ensure the observance of the law'.

In chapters three and four, in their discussion of the breadth and ambiguity of the Treaty provisions on the internal market, Stephen Weatherill and Jukka Snell acknowledge as well that the interpretation exercise is a highly demanding one. Weatherill draws specific attention to the ambiguity of the internal market rules, asserting that they leave open a 'host of vital questions' and 'delegate much interpretative autonomy to the Court'. This brings him to conclude that the ECJ's case law in this domain carries vital implications for the vertical and horizontal distribution of competences in the EU – yet the Court does not refrain from using 'troublingly imprecise words and phrases'. In Weatherill's view, it is precisely the evasive quality of the Treaty provisions establishing the guiding concepts that lies at the root of the problem. Snell, in his contribution, indicates how much more controversial the free movement case law has become. Recent rulings have had a much more direct effect on national economic models, impacting on labour relations and regulating the business and governance of corporations. As long as the focus was essentially on the free movement of goods, national economic models were only challenged indirectly. With the coming of age of the internal market however, this has all changed drastically, with the interpretative choices to be made not getting any easier. In a similar vein, Michael Dougan and Daniel Thym survey the interesting yet complex challenges currently facing the

[6] For the indictments, see H Rasmussen, *On Law and Policy in the European Court of Justice. A Comparative Study in Judicial Policy-Making* (Dordrecht, Martinus Nijhoff Publishers, 1986); P Neill, *The European Court of Justice: A Case Study in Judicial Activism* (London, European Policy Forum, 1995); TC Hartley, 'The European Court, Judicial Objectivity and the Constitution of the European Union' (1996) 112 *LQR* 95. For the rebuttals, see, inter alia, JHH Weiler, 'The Court of Justice On Trial' (1987) 24 *CML Rev* 555; T Tridimas, 'The Court of Justice and Judicial Activism' (1996) 21 *ELRev* 199; A Arnull, 'The European Court and Judicial Objectivity: A Reply to Professor Hartley' (1996) 112 *LQR* 411.

[7] Or the occasional newspaper; *cf* R Herzog and L Gerken, 'Stoppt den Europäischen Gerichtshof!' *Frankfürter Allgemene Zeitung* (8 September 2008).

ECJ's citizenship case law (chapters five and six). This case law also illustrates the increasing entanglement of economic and non-economic free movement rights, which has prompted the Court to take a new turn on fundamental concepts such as the general principle of non-discrimination, the notion of restrictions to movement, the required cross-border dimension and the import/export of goods divide. Hence, here as well, dynamic adjudication is the name of the game.

The institutional complexity of the multilayered European legal system too leads to certain issues being more strongly present than is generally the case in a purely national context. One of the particular headache dossiers concerns the proper allocation of powers between the various levels, a topic abundantly addressed in this volume. In chapter one, for example, Koen Lenaerts expounds how in its case law, the Court defers to both the Union legislator (horizontal allocation of powers) and the Member States (vertical allocation of powers). In chapter seven, Eileen Denza notes that in delineating the EU and the international legal order, the Court is similarly deferential to external tribunals. The prime importance of this theme is equally underscored in the contributions by Stephen Weatherill and Jukka Snell, as well as those by Michael Dougan and Daniel Thym. They all confirm that the distribution of powers in a given field influences – or should indeed influence – the outcome and legitimacy of the Court's decisions.

III. ON GAUGING LEGITIMACY

The tectonic shifts flagged above appear to justify an in-depth examination of the challenges facing the Court, and merit a renewed appraisal of its output in order to determine how it has been coping so far. Our enquiry aims to gauge the legitimacy of its functioning in light of the transformations the EU has undergone in a relatively short period of time. Yet of course, as Michal Bobek asserts in chapter eight, in the realm of notions, legitimacy is one of the troubling ones. Indeed, though frequently employed in scholarly discourse, there exists no common understanding on its exact content.[8] Legitimacy may thus, inter alia, be explored from a legal, political, sociological or moral point of view.[9]

Notwithstanding these different angles from which legitimacy may be approached, it has become an established practice to separate input from output legitimacy. From the input perspective, legitimacy presupposes mechanisms or procedures that link political decisions with citizens' preferences. From the output perspective, it refers (generically put) to the fact that the citizens are will-

[8] *cf* RL Abel, 'Redirecting Social Studies of Law' (1980) 14 *Law and Human Behaviour* 805, 825: 'The concept of legitimacy has neither a precise definition nor a clear behavioral correlative'.

[9] N Huls, 'Introduction: From Legitimacy to Leadership' in N Huls, M Adams and J Bomhoff (eds), *The Legitimacy of Highest Courts' Rulings: Judicial Deliberations and Beyond* (The Hague, TMC Asser Press, 2009) 13–18.

ing to support the decisions made.[10] The two may be positively correlated, with output legitimacy resulting from input legitimacy. However, the judiciary constitutes a special case here, as the prior involvement of the public in its decision-making is weak – even when members of representative assemblies are sometimes implicated in the recruitment and selection of judges.

It is therefore interesting to note here that, according to Bobek, the posture of national courts should serve as a main yardstick for measuring the legitimacy of the Court's judicial activity. In his contribution, he does not look at how the case law of the ECJ is received by citizens, but by domestic courts. Since it lies within the Court's competence to supply guidance on what EU law means and how it is to be applied by national courts, Bobek reflects on whether the decisions of the Court can be applied by ordinary domestic judges – something he refers to as the 'feasibility' of the Court's rulings. Thus, he prefers to adopt a notion of *functional* legitimacy. In an alternative and equally original approach, Koen Lenaerts opts to distinguish between external and internal legitimacy, examining the interaction between the Court and the EU legislator on the one hand, and between the Court and the Member States on the other.

Another distinction that seems useful in the study of adjudication is the one that separates substantive from procedural legitimacy. According to the substantive view (new) rules or interpretations may be considered legitimate when they are perceived to embody proper ends and standards, and when their addressees regard them as the most appropriate solutions to the problems in the given context.[11] In the procedural view, the main question is whether or not the rule or interpretation stems from the rightful source of authority, and whether those addressed by a (new) rule or interpretation believe that it has come into being and operates in accordance with general accepted principles of due process.[12] Examples of the procedural legitimacy approach abound in this volume, in which some of the Court's most controversial judgments of the last decade (for example, *Viking*, *Laval*, *Förster* and *Mangold*) are scrutinised. While some of these cases are discussed by more than one author, it is interesting to see how their opinions sometimes converge and sometimes diverge on different aspects of the legitimacy issue. For example, whereas in chapter three, Stephen Weatherill expresses his unease with the cryptic 'substance of rights' doctrine established in *Ruiz Zambrano*, in chapter five, Michael Dougan appears to regard it as curious, but not principally flawed.

The multiplicity of definitions notwithstanding, most of the existing characterisations of the legitimacy concept are informed by two elements: acquiescence and/or obedience. Courts could therefore be said to possess the power of

[10] *cf* FW Scharpf, *Governing in Europe: Effective or Democratic?* (Oxford, Oxford University Press, 1999) 7–10.

[11] I Clark, *Legitimacy in International Society* (Oxford, Oxford University Press, 2005) 18.

[12] TM Franck, *The Power of Legitimacy among Nations* (New York, Oxford University Press, 1990) 19. This harks back to a conception of legitimacy of the German sociologist Niklas Luhmann ('*Legitimation durch Verfahren*').

legitimacy if they are able to command acceptance, mainly from the members of the community they are meant to serve, so as to render the use of force unnecessary.[13] Phrased in these terms, the aforementioned 'output perspective' clearly and prominently re-enters the debate. Indeed, in an increasingly complex environment such as the EU this is of seminal importance, since it translates to an ECJ that manages to secure the continued willingness of other actors to comply with its rulings, even when that does not correspond with those actors' immediate self-interest. At the same time, Bobek rightfully cautions that mere silence or absence of open resistance does not necessarily come down to acceptance.

In order to gauge legitimacy in this setting, one could undertake to investigate the level of popular support for the Court's judgments across the Union, or the support existing in the individual Member States and among their governments, etc. Such socio-empirical research has been conducted in the past, but requires a methodology with which most lawyers are insufficiently acquainted.[14] As will have become clear, this volume rather proceeds along an alternative path, electing to have the performance of the ECJ assessed by seasoned scholars that engage in wide-ranging legal analyses of the Court's rulings in various fields of law. In so doing, a tentative link is forged between the legitimacy concept and the normative, interpretative and institutional specificities of EU law. All the same, whereas there can be no doubt that the support for its output matters to any institution, we refrain from identifying a single actor whose acquiescence or obedience can serve as the sole, decisive measuring rod.

IV. THE RELEVANCE OF INSTITUTIONAL DESIGN

In their judgments, the Union's judges must maintain a delicate balance between substantive legal 'correctness' on the one hand, and procedural aspects (securing majorities within chambers, deciding within a reasonable time, managing workload) on the other.[15] For that reason, any appraisal of the Court's case law must acknowledge the relevance of its institutional structure, composition and modus operandi. Arguably, the high number of judgments to be rendered on an annual basis, coupled with the prohibition on the publication of dissenting opinions, leaves an unmistakable imprint, and produces a typical style of reasoning.[16] For

[13] LR Helfer and AM Slaughter, 'Towards a Theory of Effective Supranational Adjudication' (1997) 107 *Yale Law Journal* 273, 278.

[14] See eg GA Caldeira and JL Gibson, 'The Legitimacy of the Court of Justice in the European Union: Models of Institutional Support' (1995) 89 *American Political Science Review* 356. Studies conducted from a quantitative angle often neglect the value-oriented nature of the concept of legitimacy. For an incisive review see J Kocken, 'Questioning Legitimacy or Why Social Scientists Find Legitimacy Where None Exists' (2008) 29(3) *Recht der Werkelijkheid* 7.

[15] Huls, above n 9, 25.

[16] On this, from a comparative point of view, see M Lasser, *Judicial Deliberations. A Comparative Analysis of Judicial Transparency and Legitimacy* (Oxford, Oxford University Press, 2004).

one thing, the ECJ regularly resorts to employing sophisticated judicial formulas that suggest continuity and an overriding rationale.[17]

Furthermore, it is essential to recognise that the Court operates (in the words of Koen Lenaerts) as a 'constitutional umpire in a multilayered system of governance'. This setting, which also manifests itself in a truncated system of judicial protection, probably explains the argumentative style that generally characterises the ECJ's pronouncements. After all, it has to suit several legal traditions at once. Thereby, as is more generally the case in adjudication, its jurisprudence seems marked by a fuzzy logic, leading to decisions that are neither 'true' nor 'false' in an empirically verifiable way. Nevertheless, this does not mean that overly opaque judgments should become the standard. In some quarters, decisions of that type seem to be readily acceptable – for example, at the Cour de cassation in France, where only a small in-crowd is able to embrace the message, however terse or enigmatic it may be. Despite being based on a French model, the Union's judiciary might ponder whether it can still content itself with such a practice when it entails that its dicta can only be fathomed by pundits. Even if those decisions continue to fit in with the overall narrative of European integration, it is rendered vulnerable to critique when that story becomes less compelling.

Evincing the backgrounds and preferences of the various authors, appraisals of the Court's contemporary style of reasoning are made in many of the following chapters. Thereby, the classic discussion on the merits of introducing dissenting opinions in the ECJ is revisited by several contributors. Stephen Weatherill, for example, comes out strongly in favour of such a move, arguing that the quality of the reasoning in hard cases would be opened up to scrutiny and development. In vivid contrast, however, Michal Bobek is much less convinced of their added value, believing that they would merely invite new bewilderment, rather than increasing the accessibility of the Court's decisions.

V. JUDGING JUDGMENTS, IMPROVING QUALITY

As known, the ECJ originally wallowed in 'benign neglect from the powers that be and the mass media'.[18] Initially, the judges had to feel their way, and they did so by deriving basic rules from the multitude of technical provisions, interpreting these rules in light of the objectives set out in the Treaties, slowly developing a system of case law on that foundation.[19] Their adjudicatory practice was dynamic from the very beginning, with a wholesome array of fundamental rights, a firmly entrenched internal market and a defiantly autonomous legal order constituting some of the most salient achievements. The Court strenuously sought to deliver

[17] L Azoulai, 'The Court of Justice and the Social Market Economy: The Emergence of an Ideal and the Conditions for its Realization' (2008) 45 *CML Rev* 1335, 1339–40.

[18] E Stein, 'Lawyers, Judges, and the Making of a Transnational Constitution' (1981) 75 *AJIL* 1.

[19] T Koopmans, *Courts and Political Institutions. A Comparative View* (Cambridge, Cambridge University Press, 2003) 274.

judgments that fit in with the European integration narrative, and while attention for its work was gradually expanding, in society-at-large, few saw a need for questioning that direction. From this point of view, its case law has been superbly effective. Yet, effectiveness is not necessarily a proxy for legitimacy, nor does it suffice for a wholehearted scholarly endorsement. All in all, the opinions prevailing in academia, while maybe not decisive, surely count for something, for they could vindicate the judicial achievements – or precipitate their demise. Moreover, comments on certain rulings that are strongly adverse might also be indicative of a lukewarm reception among the wider audience. This justifies once again an enquiry into the current state of play.

Ultimately of course, legitimacy is not a binary thing but something that comes in gradations. Bearing that in mind, the individual authors were left considerable discretion to formulate their own benchmarks for legitimacy, and apply a specific frame of analysis if they so preferred. Their contributions cover specific domains and seek to ascertain, inter alia, whether the judgments display sufficient consistency, whether the outcomes were well founded, whether the results were reasonably predictable and whether the ECJ defers to the EU legislator and the Member States whenever appropriate. While some are patently more optimistic than others, concerns with regard to the quality of the Court's reasoning (flowing from such overarching exigencies as transparency, coherence and persuasiveness) run like a red thread through the chapters. Fortunately, many authors do not limit themselves to voicing discontent, but venture to proffer solutions as well. At the end of the day, it is to be hoped that all chapters collected in this volume will, in one way or the other, contribute to improving the legitimacy of the case law of the European Court of Justice.

VI. A CONCISE OVERVIEW OF THE CONTRIBUTIONS

In chapter one, Koen Lenaerts explores the Court's external and internal legitimacy when it interacts with the Union's legislature, the Member States and national courts. With regard to the external dimension, Lenaerts first explains – pointing to a series of recent judgments – how the ECJ displays due deference to the policy choices of the EU legislator (*Test-Achats*; *Sturgeon*), and how it is the Court's role neither to anticipate nor to pre-empt policy choices that fall within the purview of the EU legislator (C-211/08 *Commission v Spain*). Lenaerts subsequently demonstrates how the ECJ strives to find an equilibrium between national and EU interests, and that it maintains an open ear for national interests even in the presence of harmonising measures (*Mesopotamia Broadcast*). He furthermore draws attention to the importance of constitutional principles embedded in national law, and illustrates how the ECJ welcomes 'value diversity' (*Omega*; *Sayn-Wittgenstein*). Lenaerts also stresses, however, that national policy choices are bound by consistency requirements (*Placanica*; *Hartlauer*; *Blanco Pérez*). As to the internal legitimacy of the Court's case law, he recalls that the ECJ operates under the principle of collegiality, and that its judgments are necessarily based on consensus. To his mind, precisely this fact explains why the argumentative discourse of the ECJ is limited to the very essential and why – in particular in hard cases of constitutional importance – the argumentative discourse is built up progressively, in a 'stone-by-stone approach' (as illustrated by *Rottman*, *Ruiz Zambrano*, *McCarthy* and *Dereci*). Lenaerts concludes that as a constitutional umpire, the ECJ has taken its role seriously, constantly endeavouring to strike a balance between the different interests at stake in a multilayered system of governance.

In the next chapter, Ján Mazák and Martin Moser discuss the legitimacy of the use of general principles of EU law in a string of recent cases, with particular attention to the *Mangold* and *Kücükdeveci* judgments (and their siblings). Mazák and Moser choose to focus on the quality, soundness and coercive pull of the Court's judicial reasoning, rather than on substantive acceptance or societal response. Prior to evaluating the Court's manoeuvrings in *Mangold* and *Kücükdeveci*, they consider the nature and foundations of the general principles in Union law. While they do not dispute that developing Union law on the basis of general principles lies within the judicial competence conferred by Article 19 TEU, they do criticise the way in which the Court discovered and employed the general principle of non-discrimination on grounds of age in *Mangold* and *Kücükdeveci*. From the legitimacy point of view, the authors identify two main problems. First, to their mind, the reasoning as to the foundation of the general principle prohibiting discrimination on grounds of age is quite feeble. Second, the ostensible awarding of horizontal direct effect to general principles in *Mangold* raises problems of legal certainty and consistency, besides muddling the constitutional allocation of powers within the European legal order. For that reason, Mazák and Moser conclude that with the *Mangold* case law, the ECJ may have reached the limits of legitimate adjudication.

Chapters three and four are devoted to recent case law on the internal market, and contain meticulous examinations of how the Court has been fine-tuning the Treaties' free movement provisions. The central theme of Stephen Weatherill's contribution is the constitutionally significant, yet strikingly ambiguous wording in several pronouncements on the scope and content of the internal market rules, such as for instance 'a *considerable* influence' with regard to Article 34 TFEU (*Mickelsson and Roos*), 'a *serious* inconvenience' with regard to Article 21 TFEU (*Runevič-Vardyn*), or 'the *substance* of rights' with regard to Article 20 TFEU (*Ruiz Zambrano*). His main argument is that at the heart of the problem lies not so much the Court's case law, but rather the internal market itself. Weatherill masterfully elaborates how the ambiguity and breadth of the internal market provisions further complicate already difficult questions with regard to determining the outer limits of EU law. Similarly, regarding harmonisation measures, he explains how the ECJ's nebulous tests are an inevitable consequence of the wording of Article 114 TFEU. The judgments Weatherill discusses (C-376/98 *Germany v Parliament*; *Vodafone, O2 et al v Secretary of State*; *Alliance for*

National Health v Secretary of State for Health; C-301/06 *Ireland v Parliament and Council*) illustrate that the Treaty actually denies the ECJ a useful operational role in establishing the boundaries of Article 114 TFEU. Definitional precision remains elusive. Consequently, a case-by-case examination is required, which delegates considerable power to the relevant institution (the judiciary as far as Article 34 TFEU is concerned; the legislature where it concerns Article 114 TFEU). Finally, Weatherill muses on whether the ECJ could have done a better job. He concludes that at a micro-level, this is probably so, but that at a macro-level, the Court largely follows the logic of the Treaty when it develops internal market law.

To a considerable extent, the views of Jukka Snell dovetail with Weatherill's conclusion – ie, that the final verdict on the legitimacy question should not be overly harsh. Nevertheless, he follows a different 'plan of attack', and discusses numerous other judgments. Snell opts to study the Court from a dual angle, namely, first, as a judicial institution and, second, as an EU institution. With regard to the judicial angle, his point of departure is that 'power must be kept in check', and that legitimacy should be examined on the basis of three main standards: sources, consistency and reasoning. He then applies these criteria to the Court's free movement case law, and finds that the legitimacy of this case law has been weakened by insufficiently reasoned (*Smits and Peerbooms*; *Fidium Finanz*; *Säger*) and inconsistent judgments (C-110/05 *Commission v Italy*, and *Mickelsson and Roos* vis-a-vis *Keck*; *Kerckhaert* vis-a-vis *Cassis de Dijon*; *Gysbrechts* vis-a-vis *Alpine Investments*). Regarding the Court as an EU institution, Snell's main argument is that it should ensure that it does not excessively interfere with national economic models (referring to *Viking*; *Laval*; *Centros*; *Volkswagen*) nor with areas that the Treaties allocate to Member States (for example, direct taxation; health care; education). His main concern here is that the Court has proceeded too much on an ad hoc basis, and failed to adopt a principled, consistent approach, thus neglecting to spell out the basic foundations in its legal reasoning.

Chapters five and six focus on the Court's case law on EU citizenship. Michael Dougan's contribution is essentially divided into an analysis of judgments delivered before 2008, and judgments delivered after 2008. He starts off with a critical reading of the case law from 1998 to 2008 (*Sala*; *Grzelczyk*; *Baumbast* and *Collins*) and then moves on to discuss the post-2008 instalments, drawing attention to the technique of 'indirect judicial review' (*Förster*; *Vatsouras*), the 'personal circumstances' assessment (*Förster*; *Wolzenburg*; *Sayn-Wittgenstein*; *Rottman*; *Gottwald*) and the 'substance of rights' test (*Ruiz Zambrano*; *McCarthy*; *Dereci*). While Dougan acknowledges that, since 2008, the outcome of a citizenship case has become highly unpredictable, he declines to appraise this evolution by subscribing to constitutional anxieties about judicial activism. His main argument is rather that the 'second generation' case law on EU citizenship must be seen as an interactive, two-way dialogue between judges and politicians about how best to balance the construction of a meaningful form of Union citizenship on the one hand, against the need to respect the social competences and financial concerns of the Member States on the other – while at the same time remaining sensitive to relevant changes in the broader European integration landscape.

In chapter six, Daniel Thym offers another examination of the legitimacy of the citizenship case law, by gauging the case law's impact on, and acceptance by, the EU legislator and the Member States. Thym first examines the case law on access to social benefits (*Martínez Sala*; *Grzelczyk*; *Baumbast*; *Collins*; *Bidar*; *Förster*; *Vatsouras*; *Teixeira*; *Ibrahim*) in order to verify whether a dialogue with the EU legislator indeed takes place, and whether (sufficient) deference is shown towards the Member States. Hereafter, he assesses the quality of the Court's reasoning, profoundly deploring the lack of clarity and coherence in a number of recent judgments. Thym subsequently looks into the Court's case law on third- country national family members, with particular emphasis on the *Ruiz Zambrano* judgment and the Court's much-debated 'substance of rights' test. According to him, constitutional legitimacy requires this test to be interpreted in light of the federal vertical balance of power and the horizontal dialogue with the EU legislator. Thym concludes that the latest directions in the ECJ's case law have moved EU citizenship into a new era, but that when exploring this novel frontier, some hard choices will have to be made.

Chapters seven and eight are devoted to the position of the EU/ECJ vis-a-vis other legal orders and other courts and tribunals. Eileen Denza, reflecting on the Union's international context, starts off with a succinct analysis of the Court's mandate under the Treaties. Immediately hereafter, she takes a closer look at the case law on conflicts between international obligations and EU legislation (*Intertanko*; *Air Transport Association of America*; *Kadi*). This is followed by an analysis of the reception of customary international law (*Air Transport Association of America*). Next, she addresses the relationships the ECJ maintains with other international courts, in particular with the European Court of Human Rights (*ERT*), in order to ascertain whether this case law can be considered legitimate. Denza's discussion is not limited to an assessment of legitimacy in terms of deference to other (international) legal orders, but extends to explaining how the Court's case law is legitimate in terms of being protective of the Union's own legal system (*Kadi*; Opinion 1/09; C-459/03 *Commission v Ireland*).

In chapter eight, Michal Bobek adopts the perspective of national courts, developing what he calls a 'functional legitimacy' or 'legitimacy as feasibility' approach. In his eyes, the crucial question is not whether the Court's decisions are legitimate *in se*, but whether the judicial output is feasible in the eyes of national courts. Are national courts actually satisfied with the Court's decisions once they receive them? Do national courts consider the Court's decisions as authoritative? And do national courts in practice take heed of the ECJ's pronouncements in other cases? After plumbing the depths of these questions, Bobek draws several surprising conclusions. One of these pertains to the Court's standard of reasoning in individual judgments (in general, according to Bobek, the current standard does not raise too much cause for concern). Another relates to the presumed acceptance of, and faithful compliance with the ECJ's case law in the domestic legal orders, which seems to convey a false sense of security (for silence should not necessarily be understood as a national embracing of the European judicial mandate). Last but not least, Bobek highlights some institutional and procedural opportunities for the Court to generate legitimacy, which are, in his view, far from sufficiently exploited.

In his epilogue, JHH Weiler engages particularly with the opening chapter by Koen Lenaerts. He means to demonstrate thereby that the legitimacy issue is far more complex than Lenaerts's text and conclusions would suggest. As a result, as Weiler himself puts it, Lenaerts's chapter stands as one bookend to this volume, and his epilogue as the other.

We hope that this volume sparks off a fresh debate on the role and functioning of the ECJ. There would seem to be good reason for this, not least because the topics dealt with in each of the contributions do not, in Weiler's words, 'deal with trivia'. . .

1

The Court's Outer and Inner Selves: Exploring the External and Internal Legitimacy of the European Court of Justice

KOEN LENAERTS*

JUDICIAL LEGITIMACY MAY be examined from two different, albeit complementary, perspectives.

Externally, the legitimacy of the judiciary and its role in democratic societies are deeply intertwined, as it is only by defining what courts should do (and what they should refrain from doing) that one may determine whether they enjoy legitimacy. To that effect, one must first define 'what the law is', and only then appraise whether courts are limiting themselves to 'interpreting and applying the law'. If courts go beyond their duty of saying 'what the law is', they lack legitimacy as they intrude into the political process. By drawing the borderline between law and politics, courts in fact are drawing the contours of their own legitimacy. The imperative need for courts to stand behind that line is by no means a novel question, but it has accompanied them ever since constitutionalism was born. As Chief Justice Marshall famously articulated more than two hundred years ago, in *Marbury v Madison*,[1] whilst '[i]t is emphatically the province and duty of the Judicial Department to say what the law is', acts of a political nature 'can never be examinable by the Courts'.[2] Drawing the line between law and politics may be seen as a manifestation of the principle of separation of powers which seeks to prevent courts from undermining the prerogatives of the political branches of government and thus, to preserve the 'check and balances' set out by the Founding Fathers.

* All opinions expressed are strictly personal to the author.

[1] *Marbury v Madison*, 5 U.S. (1 Cranch) 137 (1803).

[2] ibid.

Internally, legitimacy looks at the quality of the judicial process. In systems such as the EU where the judicial function is shared between the EU and the national judiciaries – ie, where that function is vertically integrated – legitimacy requires judicial power to be allocated in accordance with the Treaties. This means that judicial legitimacy is conditioned upon those two types of courts acting with mutual respect and deference. An EU court will be deprived of its legitimacy, not only if it intrudes into the political sphere, at either EU or national level, but also if it encroaches upon the prerogatives of national courts. The same applies for the latter in relation to the prerogatives of EU courts.[3] In a broader sense, given that no legal order operates in isolation, but interacts with other legal orders in a bilateral or multilateral context, courts may not impinge upon the competences that have been transferred to supranational or international tribunals. Hence, in multilayered systems of governance, the notion of 'comity'[4] – understood as a means of guaranteeing a constructive judicial dialogue among different courts – becomes of paramount importance to determine whether a given court enjoys legitimacy.[5]

In addition, internal legitimacy looks at courts as 'rational actors', by focusing on the soundness of their legal reasoning.[6] The question whether courts enjoy legitimacy thus amounts to examining whether their rationale is sufficiently transparent and easy to understand or whether it is cryptic; whether the grounds of judgment are strong enough to be convincing and adequately meet the arguments put forward by the parties; whether the court's rulings are coherent with the existing case law and based on impartial criteria known in advance or whether they are simply unpredictable and arbitrary.

External and internal judicial legitimacy complement each other: the line between law and politics must be drawn in accordance with the institutional capacities of the judicial department: ie, the lack of judicially manageable standards implies that some decisions are not fit for judicial deliberations but are better left in the hands of the political process.

The European Court of Justice (the ECJ) strives to enjoy both external and internal legitimacy. As a result of the 'constitutionalisation of the Treaties', which transformed the European Union from an international organisation into 'a composite legal order', the ECJ has continuously been called upon to uphold the 'rule

[3] See Opinion 1/09 *Draft Agreement on the European and Community Patents Court*, 8 March 2011, not yet reported, para 85 (holding that 'the tasks attributed to the national courts and to the [ECJ] respectively are indispensable to the preservation of the very nature of the law established by the Treaties').

[4] See E Chemerinsky, *Federal Jurisdiction* (New York, Aspen Publishers, 2007) 39 (who defines 'comity' as 'the deference owed to [S]tate courts as those of another sovereign').

[5] See eg FG Jacobs, 'Judicial Dialogue and the Cross-Fertilization of Legal Systems: The European Court of Justice' (2001) 38 *Texas International Law Journal* 547.

[6] See generally J Bengoetxea, *The Legal Reasoning of the European Court of Justice: Towards a European Jurisprudence* (Oxford, Clarendon Press, 1993).

of law' as provided for by Article 19 TEU. As I mentioned 20 years ago, one may distinguish three historical strands in the ECJ's jurisprudence.[7]

First, at the beginning of European integration, the ECJ was confronted with the following problem: although the original version of the EC Treaty commanded the ECJ to 'ensure that in the interpretation and application of [the Treaties] the law is observed', it did not provide a definition of 'the law'. In order to honour that constitutional mandate in a self-referential and, in that sense, autonomous legal order, the ECJ could not limit itself to a formalistic understanding of the rule of law. Accordingly, it had no choice but to complete the constitutional lacunae left by the authors of the Treaties. In so doing, the ECJ was well aware of the fact that in order not to put at risk the legitimacy of an incipient Union, EU law could not break away from the constitutional traditions of the Member States. Thus, it took a leading role in setting the founding principles of the EU legal order by having recourse to the general principles of law which provide a material constitutional content to the 'law' of the EU.[8] The paradigmatic example of the gap-filling function of the ECJ is the incorporation of fundamental rights into the EU legal order as general principles of EU law. Furthermore, by virtue of the principles of primacy and direct effect, individuals are entitled to have the rights which EU law bestows upon them enforced by national courts and, where appropriate, have conflicting provisions of national law set aside by them. For those rights to become more than empty promises, their enforcement had to become a reality. To that end, the ECJ first developed the principles of equivalence and effectiveness, which require national law on remedies not to discriminate against the enforcement of EU rights and not to make the exercise of those rights virtually impossible or excessively difficult.[9] However, these two principles only seek to neutralise the effect of national rules of procedure which hamper the proper enforcement of EU law, but are incapable of guaranteeing an effective protection of EU rights where national law does not provide sufficient injunctive or monetary relief. Hence, in a further development of its case law, the ECJ decided to enhance the effective protection of EU rights by creating new remedies, this time grounded in EU law itself.[10]

Second, the ECJ aimed to safeguard the core of European integration set out in the Treaty by providing solutions to problems that were expected to be tackled by the EU political institutions, but were not in practice, as the latter could

[7] K Lenaerts, 'Some Thoughts about the Interaction between Judges and Politicians' (1992) 93 *University of Chicago Legal Forum* 100.

[8] K Lenaerts and JA Gutiérrez-Fons, 'The Constitutional Allocation of Powers and General Principles of EU Law' (2010) 47 *CML Rev* 1629, 1632 et seq.

[9] See, to that effect, Case 33/76 *Rewe* [1976] ECR 1989, paras 5 and 6; Case 45/76 *Comet* [1976] ECR 2043, para 13. See K Lenaerts, 'National Remedies for Private Parties in the Light of the EU Law Principles of Equivalence and Effectiveness' (2011) 46 *Irish Jurist* 13.

[10] In relation to interim relief, see Case C-213/89 *Factortame I* [1990] ECR I-2433. In relation to state liability in damages, see Joined Cases C-6/90 and C-9/90 *Francovich and Others v Italian State* [1991] ECR I-5357; Joined Cases C-46/93 and C-48/93 *Brasserie du Pêcheur and Factortame III* [1996] ECR I-1029.

not reach the then necessary consensus. It thus allowed interest-driven litigation to overcome the political deadlock that prevented the completion of the internal market, as free movers sought to tear down barriers to trade that could have been eliminated by EU harmonisation. The principle of mutual recognition defined in *Cassis de Dijon* best encapsulates this line of jurisprudence.[11] It in turn set the stage for the Commission's action plan for adopting a 'new approach' to remove obstacles to interstate trade,[12] which, with the adoption of the Single European Act (the SEA), was no longer governed by intergovernmental dynamics given that Member States gave up their right to veto (ex Article 100a EEC, now Article 114 TFEU). Member States thus accepted that EU internal market legislation could be passed against their will and yet be binding upon them. As a consequence, the establishment and functioning of the internal market became an objective to be attained by both positive and negative integration techniques; ie, on the one hand, legislative measures adopted by the Union political process and on the other, enforcement by the ECJ of the prohibitions laid down in the Treaties themselves to erect barriers to interstate trade. The EU legislator and the ECJ are not in a competing relationship when pursuing that objective; they are rather to be seen as joining efforts.

Last, but not least, once the constitutional foundations of the EU legal order were put in place and the establishment and functioning of the internal market secured, the ECJ moved onto a new paradigm. As the constitutional court of a more mature legal order, it now tends to be less assertive as to the substantive development of EU law. It sees its role primarily as one of upholding the 'checks and balances' built into the EU constitutional legal order of states and peoples, including the protection of fundamental rights.[13] This does not, however, prevent the ECJ from taking a more proactive stand in some areas of EU law, yet overall it displays greater deference to the preferences of the EU legislator or, as the case may be, to those of the Member States.[14] The ECJ thus favours both continuity of its role as a constitutional umpire and change in the substantive EU law achieved by the traditional interaction between the political and judicial processes.

One could look at those three strands through the prism of the 'activism v self-restraint' divide.[15] A quick glance at them might suggest that the first two

[11] Case 120/78 *Rewe-Zentral v Bundesmonopolverwaltung für Branntwein* [1979] ECR 649.

[12] See Commission White Paper, 'Completing the Internal Market', of 14 June 1985, COM (85) 310 final.

[13] Lenaerts, 'Some Thoughts about the Interaction between Judges and Politicians', above n 7, 95.

[14] In the context of the law on remedies, Tridimas refers to that approach as 'selective deference'. See T Tridimas, *The General Principles of EU Law* (Oxford, Oxford University Press, 2006) 418–22.

[15] See eg P Neill, 'The European Court of Justice: A Case Study in Judicial Activism', Evidence submitted to the House of Lords Select Committee on the European Communities, Subcommittee on the 1996 Inter-Governmental Conference, Minutes of Evidence, House of Lords, 18th Report (Session 1994–95) 218 et seq, and the reply given by D Edward, 'Judicial Activism – Myth or Reality?' in AIL Campbell and M Voyatzi (eds), *Legal Reasoning and Judicial Interpretation of European Law* (Hampshire, Trenton Publishing, 1996) 29 et seq. See also TC Hartley, 'The European Court, Judicial Objectivity and the Constitution of the European Union' (1996) 112 *LQR* 95 and the

are characterised by an activist ECJ, whereas the third reveals an ECJ more committed to judicial self-restraint. However, a critical observer may also argue that in none of those three strands did the ECJ really engage in judicial activism as it limited itself to doing what the Treaties required it to do: ie, to uphold 'the rule of law'.[16] In my view, this shows that the 'activism v self-restraint' discourse is misconceived and does not lead to a productive discussion, unless one first solves the following question: what should the role of the ECJ be? In other words, how can the ECJ enjoy external and internal legitimacy?

Hence, the purpose of the present contribution is to explore the external and internal legitimacy of the ECJ when the latter interacts with the EU legislature, the Member States, and national courts. Based on the study of recent case law, this contribution supports the contention that, as a constitutional umpire, the ECJ takes its role seriously, that is, it is seeking to strike the balance imposed by the rule of law among the different interests at stake in a multi-layered system of governance. This type of analysis does not aim to shield every ECJ judgment from criticism as to its outcome and/or reasoning but serves to highlight that the ECJ strives to achieve overall consistency in judicial decision-making as a basis of its legitimacy.

I. EXTERNAL LEGITIMACY

Part I of this contribution is devoted to examining how the ECJ draws the line that divides the judicial process from the realm of politics. Whilst section A looks at the interactions between the ECJ and the EU legislator, section B explores how the ECJ strives to accommodate, as far as possible, national interests. That is so not only in the absence of EU harmonisation, but also where the EU legislator has adopted secondary EU legislation.

A The ECJ and the EU Legislator

When the ECJ interprets EU legislation, it must ensure that the latter complies with primary EU law. However, in so doing, it may not replace the choices made by the legislature with its own. The ECJ is called upon to uphold simultaneously the principles of hierarchy of norms and of separation of powers. If it is not possible to interpret an act of secondary EU law in a way that accommodates those two principles, then the ECJ will have no choice but to annul that act or declare it invalid.

reply given by A Arnull, 'The European Court of Justice and Judicial Objectivity: A Reply to Professor Hartley' (1996) 112 *LQR* 411. More recently, see J Temple Lang, 'Has the European Court of Justice been Involved in "Judicial Legislation"?' (2011) 96 *Svensk Juristtidning* 299.

[16] See eg CWA Timmermans, 'Judicial Activism and Judicial Restraint' in C Baudenbacher and E Busek (eds), *The Role of International Courts* (Stuttgart, German Law Publishers, 2008) 243, 245 et seq.

i Reconciliatory Interpretation: An Example

If an Act adopted by the EU legislator conflicts with the Treaties, the ECJ will have no choice but to annul that Act or declare it invalid. However, in order to safeguard the legitimate objectives pursued by the EU legislator, the ECJ will first do everything within its jurisdiction to interpret secondary EU law in accordance with primary EU law.[17] It follows that, in so far as the ECJ does not interpret secondary EU law in a *contra legem* fashion,[18] the annulment or declaration of invalidity of an Act adopted by the EU legislator operates as the *ultima ratio* in order to uphold the rule of law. The judgment of the ECJ in *Vatsouras* illustrates this point.[19]

Originally, the ECJ ruled in *Lebon*[20] – decided in 1987 – that jobseekers' allowances did not fall within the scope of (then) Community law. However, in *Collins* – decided 17 years later – the ECJ reconsidered its approach. By relying on the Treaty provisions on EU citizenship, it ruled that the principle of non-discrimination on grounds of nationality applies to such allowances.[21] However, access to such allowances is not unconditional, as it is legitimate for the host Member State to subject the grant of jobseekers' allowances to jobseekers having established a 'real link' with the labour market of that state.[22] The ECJ acknowledged that a residence requirement is, in principle, appropriate for the purposes of ensuring a 'real link'. Nevertheless, such a requirement must comply with the principle of proportionality; ie, it must not go beyond what is necessary to establish a 'real link'. The period of residence must not exceed what is necessary in order for the national authorities to be able to satisfy themselves that the person concerned is genuinely seeking work in the employment market of the host Member State; it must also be based on clear criteria known in advance; and provision must be made for access to a means of redress of a judicial nature.[23]

On 29 April 2004, the EU legislator adopted the Citizen's Rights Directive (the CRD),[24] whose Article 24(2) reads as follows:

[17] K Engsig Sørensen, 'Reconciling Secondary Legislation and the Treaty Rights of Free Movement' (2011) 36 *EL Rev* 339, 345 (who considers that reconciliatory interpretation is 'less likely to lead to an inter-institutional conflict and more elegant in resolving the issues without making it necessary to adopt new legislation').

[18] See, by analogy, Case C-212/04 *Adeneler and Others* [2006] ECR I-6057, paras 110–11.

[19] Joined Cases C-22/08 and C-23/08 *Vatsouras and Koupatantze* [2009] ECR I-4585.

[20] Case 316/85 *Lebon* [1987] ECR 2811, para 26. See also Case C-278/94 *Commission v Belgium* [1996] ECR I-4307, paras 39–40.

[21] Case C-138/02 *Collins* [2004] ECR I-2703, para 63; Case C-258/04 *Ioannidis* [2005] ECR I-8275, para 22.

[22] Case C-224/98 *D'Hoop* [2002] ECR I-6191, para 38, *Collins*, above n 21, para 69, and *Ioannidis*, above n 21, para 30.

[23] *Collins*, above n 21, para 72.

[24] Directive 2004/38/EC of the European Parliament and of the Council of 29 April 2004 on the right of citizens of the Union and their family members to move and reside freely within the territory of the Member States amending Regulation (EEC) No 1612/68 and repealing Directives 64/221/EEC, 68/360/EEC, 72/194/EEC, 73/148/EEC, 75/34/EEC, 75/35/EEC, 90/364/EEC, 90/365/EEC and 93/96/EEC, [2004] OJ L158/77.

> [b]y way of derogation from [the principle of equal treatment], the host Member State shall not be obliged to confer entitlement to social assistance during the first three months of residence or, where appropriate, the longer period provided for in Article 14(4)(b).[25]

Arguably, an interpretation of this provision based solely on its wording could suggest that the concept of 'social assistance' laid down therein includes 'benefit[s] of a financial nature intended to facilitate access to employment in the labour market of [the host] Member State'.[26] Such a reading would, however, imply – contrary to *Collins* – that, regardless of the existence of a 'real link' between jobseekers and the labour market of the host Member State, the former would not be entitled to jobseekers' allowances, in spite of the fact that they 'can provide evidence that they are continuing to seek employment and that they have a genuine chance of being engaged' but have not become permanent residents. Bearing in mind that the findings of the ECJ in *Collins* are grounded in primary EU law, such a reading of Article 24(2) of the CRD would be incompatible with that law. That is why, in *Vatsouras*,[27] the referring court called into question the compatibility of Article 24(2) of the CRD with Article 18 TFEU, read in conjunction with Article 45 TFEU, asking whether it was possible to reconcile the 'real link' approach put forward in *Collins* with Article 24(2) of the CRD.

The ECJ replied in the affirmative. At the outset, it confirmed its previous findings in *Collins*, according to which

> nationals of the Member States seeking employment in another Member State who have established real links with the labour market of that State can rely on Article [45(2) TFEU] in order to receive a benefit of a financial nature intended to facilitate access to the labour market.[28]

The ECJ then proceeded to interpret Article 24(2) of the CRD in light of Article 45(2) TFEU, since it considered that a literal interpretation of Article 24(2) of the CRD was over-inclusive and consequently, the concept of 'social assistance', understood in its natural and ordinary meaning, needed to be narrowed down. Hence, benefits of a financial nature intended to facilitate access to employment in the labour market of the host Member State fall outside the scope of that provision.[29] This includes not only jobseekers' allowances, but also any financial benefit whose purpose is 'to promote integration into the labour market'.[30] Thus, in relation to jobseekers' allowances, Article 24(2) of the CRD does not apply. It is for the national court to determine, in light of *Collins*, whether a

[25] Art 14(4)(b) of the CRD refers to the period during which 'the Union citizens can provide evidence that they are continuing to seek employment and that they have a genuine chance of being engaged'.

[26] *Collins*, above n 21, para 63.

[27] *Vatsouras*, above n 19.

[28] ibid, para 40.

[29] ibid, para 45.

[30] Opinion of AG Ruiz-Jarabo Colomer in *Vatsouras*, above n 19, para 57.

jobseeker has established sufficient connections with the society of the host Member State.

ii Primary EU Law and the Objectives Pursued by the EU Legislator

Moreover, the ECJ strives to provide a solution which accommodates both the objectives pursued by the EU legislator and primary EU law. For example, if the challenged provision of secondary EU law not only conflicts with primary EU law but is also inconsistent with the objectives pursued by the EU legislator, then the ECJ will have fewer difficulties in annulling or invalidating such provision. On the contrary, if by interpreting secondary EU law in light of primary EU law, the ECJ manages to enhance the objectives pursued by the EU legislator, then it will tend to follow such reconciliatory interpretation rather than to annul or invalidate the challenged act of secondary EU law. These two different outcomes are highlighted by comparing the ruling of the ECJ in *Test-Achats*[31] with that in *Sturgeon and Others*.[32]

In *Test-Achats*, the referring court asked the ECJ whether Article 5(2) of Directive 2004/113[33] was valid in light of the principle of equal treatment between men and women. Article 5(1) of Directive 2004/113 implements that principle in relation to 'actuarial factors'. It provides that the differences in premiums and benefits arising from the use of sex as a factor in the calculation thereof must be abolished by 21 December 2007 at the latest. By way of derogation, the second paragraph of Article 5 of Directive 2004/113 stated that it was permitted for Member States to introduce proportionate differences in individuals' premiums and benefits where the use of sex was a determining factor in the assessment of risk based on relevant and accurate actuarial and statistical data.[34] If a Member State made use of that option before 21 December 2007, its decision had to be reviewed five years after that date, with account being taken of a Commission report.

At the outset, the ECJ stressed that Directive 2004/113 expressly refers to Articles 21 and 23 of the Charter. Accordingly, the validity of Article 5(2) of Directive 2004/113 had to be determined in light of those two provisions. Next, the ECJ looked at the Treaty provisions which define the principle of equal treatment between men and women as a social objective to be attained by the European Union, namely the second sub-paragraph of Article 3(3) TEU and Articles 8, 19(1) and 157(1) TFEU. In this regard, it pointed out that '[i]n the

[31] Case C-236/09 *Association Belge des Consommateurs Test-Achats ASBL and Others v Conseil des Ministres*, Judgment of 1 March 2011, not yet reported.

[32] Joined Cases C-402/07 and C-432/07 *Sturgeon and Others* and *Böck v Air France* [2009] ECR I-10923.

[33] [2004] OJ L373/27. Directive 2004/113 implements the principle of equal treatment between men and women in the access to and supply of goods and services.

[34] This meant, for example, that national law could allow car insurance companies to impose higher premiums on men than on women given that, in accordance with statistical data, men have a higher risk of causing a car accident than women.

progressive achievement of that equality, it is the EU legislature which . . . determines when it will take action, having regard to the development of economic and social conditions within the European Union'.[35] This meant, for example, that since the use of actuarial factors related to sex was a widespread practice in the Member States, it was permissible for the EU legislator to provide for the appropriate transitional period. This was actually the rationale underpinning Article 5(1) of Directive 2004/113 which sets 21 December 2007 as the deadline for the implementation of the principle of equal treatment between men and women in relation to actuarial factors. By contrast, Article 5(2) contained a derogation from that principle, which was subject to no temporal limitation. '[G]iven that Directive 2004/113 is silent as to the length of time during which those differences may continue to be applied', the ECJ observed, 'Member States which have made use of the option are permitted to allow insurers to apply the unequal treatment without any temporal limitation'.[36]

The Council supported the validity of Article 5(2) of Directive 2004/113, arguing that, in the context of certain branches of private insurance, the respective situations of male and female policyholders may not be regarded as comparable, given that, in light of statistical data, the levels of insured risk may be different for men and for women. However, the ECJ took a different view. According to Recitals 18 and 19 of Directive 2004/113, the latter favoured the application of rules of unisex premiums and benefits. Accordingly, 'Directive 2004/113 is based on the premise that [. . .] the respective situations of men and women with regard to insurance premiums and benefits contracted by them are comparable'.[37]

For the ECJ, Article 5(2) of Directive 2004/113 which

> enables the Member States in question to maintain without temporal limitation an exemption from the rule of unisex premiums and benefits, works against the achievement of the objective of equal treatment between men and women, which is the purpose of Directive 2004/113, and is incompatible with Articles 21 and 23 of the Charter.[38]

Consequently, that provision was held to be invalid upon the expiry of an appropriate transitional period, ie, 21 December 2012.[39]

[35] *Association Belge des Consommateurs Test-Achats and Others*, above n 31, para 20.

[36] ibid, para 26.

[37] ibid, para 30. Of course, one could call into question whether that premise was well founded. See, in this regard, P Watson, 'Equality, Fundamental Rights and the Limits of Legislative Discretion: Comment on *Test-Achats*' (2011) 36 *EL Rev* 896. Be that as it may, this was not the question that the ECJ was asked to examine in *Test-Achats and Others*.

[38] ibid, para 32. *Association Belge des Consommateurs Test-Achats and Others*, above n 31, para 32. See, in this regard, C Tobler, 'Case Note on Case C-236/09, Association belge des Consommateurs Test-Achats and Others' (2011) 48 *Common Market Law Review* 2041, at 2060 (who observes that '[t]he [ECJ]'s finding in *Test-Achats* in essence implies a criticism of the legislative decisions made by the Council in adopting Directive 2004/113').

[39] 21 December 2012 is the date on which the decision to derogate from the principle of equal treatment between men and women laid down in Art 5(2) of Directive 2004/113 was to be reviewed by the Member State concerned.

In *Sturgeon and Others*, the ECJ was asked whether Regulation 261/2004[40] confers a right to compensation upon airline passengers in the event of delay. The wording of Regulation 261/2004 does not expressly create a right to compensation for those passengers whose flights are delayed, as opposed to passengers whose flights are cancelled, on whom such a right is explicitly conferred. Can this legislative silence be read as denying compensation to this category of passengers? The ECJ replied in the negative. It began by observing that, in light of its objectives, Regulation 261/2004 does not exclude awarding compensation to passengers whose flights are merely delayed. Nor does Regulation 261/2004 rule out the possibility that, for the purposes of recognition of the right to compensation, both categories of passengers can be treated alike.[41] Next, the ECJ noted that, in accordance with a general principle of interpretation, 'a [Union] act must be interpreted in such a way as not to affect its validity'.[42] This means that a Union act must be interpreted in compliance with superior rules of EU law, including the principle of equal treatment. Hence, where passengers whose flights are cancelled and passengers whose flights are delayed are in a comparable situation, Regulation 261/2004 must be interpreted in such a way as to treat both categories of passengers equally. To this effect, the ECJ noted that both categories of passengers suffer similar damage, consisting of a loss of time. In particular, the situation of passengers whose flights are delayed is comparable to that of passengers who are informed upon arrival at the airport that their flight is cancelled and subsequently re-routed in accordance with Article 5 of Regulation 261/2004. Since Article 5(1)(c)(iii) of Regulation 261/2004 only provides for a right to compensation where the cancellation of a flight and its subsequent re-routing entail a loss of time equal to or in excess of three hours, the same should apply in the event of delay.[43] Therefore, the ECJ ruled that in order for Regulation 261/2004 to comply with the principle of equal treatment, it had to be interpreted so as to grant a right to compensation to passengers whose flights are delayed and who reach their final destination three hours or more after the arrival time originally scheduled by the air carrier.[44] Finally, the ECJ recalled that air carriers are not

[40] Regulation No 261/2004 of the European Parliament and of the Council of 11 February 2004 establishing common rules on compensation and assistance to passengers in the event of denied boarding and of cancellation or long delay of flights, and repealing Regulation (EEC) No 295/91, [2004] OJ L46/1.

[41] *Sturgeon and Others*, above n 32, para 46.

[42] ibid, para 47.

[43] ibid, para 57.

[44] The approach followed by AG Sharpston is somewhat different. She concurred with the ECJ in acknowledging that if compensation to passengers whose flights are delayed were excluded, then it would be impossible to reconcile Regulation No 261/2004 with the principle of equal treatment. Yet, in contrast to the ECJ, the Advocate General did not provide a particular time-limit after which passengers whose flights are delayed enjoy a right to compensation. In her view, 'the actual selection of a magic figure is a legislative prerogative'. See Opinion of AG Sharpston in *Sturgeon and Others*, above n 32, paras 93–94. However, the ECJ deployed another argument in order to counter this 'separation of powers' objection. It invoked Recital 15 in the Preamble of Regulation No 261/2004, whereby 'the legislature . . . linked the notion of "long delay" to the right to compensation'. Thus,

obliged to pay compensation where they manage to prove that cancellations and delays are caused by extraordinary circumstances.[45]

More recently, in *Nelson and Others*,[46] several airlines, the International Air Transport Association (IATA) and the UK called into question the validity of Articles 5 and 7 of Regulation 261/2004, as interpreted by the ECJ in *Sturgeon and Others*, on the ground that that judgment was at odds with the principles of legal certainty and proportionality. They urged the ECJ (Grand Chamber) to depart from its findings in *Sturgeon and Others* (a ruling given by a chamber of five judges).

As to the principle of legal certainty, they posited that the method of interpretation followed by the ECJ in *Sturgeon and Others* was incompatible with paragraph 76 of the *IATA and ELFAA* judgment. In the latter case, the ECJ conceded that Recitals 14 and 15 of the Preamble of Regulation 261/2004 gave,

> the impression that, generally, operating air carriers should be released from all their obligations in the event of extraordinary circumstances, and it accordingly gives rise to a certain ambiguity between the intention thus expressed by the [EU] legislature and the actual content of Articles 5 and 6 of Regulation No 261/2004 which do not make this defence to liability so general in character.

'However', the ECJ added, 'such an ambiguity does not extend so far as to render incoherent the system set up by those two articles, which are themselves entirely unambiguous'.[47] For the applicants, this meant that, in *Sturgeon and Others*, the ECJ should not have relied upon Recital 15 of Regulation 261/2004 with a view to modifying the meaning of the relevant provisions of that Regulation. The ECJ, nonetheless, took a different view: 'as regards [. . .] the relationship between the judgments in *IATA and ELFAA* and *Sturgeon and Others*, it is apparent [. . .] that there is no tension between those two judgments, the second judgment applying the principles laid down by the first'.[48] As

the ECJ did not encroach upon the prerogatives of the EU legislator but simply limited itself to clarifying a legislative choice already contained in Regulation No 261/2004, namely the distinction between 'delay' (inferior to three hours) and 'long delay' (equal to or in excess of three hours). Whilst the latter gives rise to compensation, the former does not. See *Sturgeon and Others*, above n 32, para 62.

[45] *Sturgeon and Others*, above n 32, para 67 (extraordinary circumstances are defined as those which 'are beyond the air carrier's actual control').

[46] Joined Cases C-581/10 and C-629/10 *Nelson and Others*, Judgment of 23 October 2012, not yet reported.

[47] Case C-344/04 *IATA and ELFAA* [2006] ECR I-403.

[48] *Nelson and Others*, above n 46, para 64. In para 45 of *IATA and ELFAA*, above n 47, the ECJ found that the authors of the Convention for the Unification of Certain Rules for International Carriage by Air, concluded in Montreal on 28 May 1999, signed by the European Community on 9 December 1999 and approved on its behalf by Council Decision 2001/539/EC, [2001] OJ L194/38 ('the Montreal Convention') did not intend 'to shield air carriers from any form of intervention other than those laid down by those provisions, in particular action which could be envisaged by the public authorities to redress, in a standardised and immediate manner, the damage that is constituted by the inconvenience that delay in the carriage of passengers by air causes, without the passengers having to suffer the inconvenience inherent in the bringing of actions for damages before the courts' (See *Nelson and Others*, above n 46, para 46). Stated differently, the Montreal Convention

explained by AG Bot, a distinction should be drawn between the question of interpretation raised in *IATA and ELFAA* and that raised in *Sturgeon and Others*. In the former case, the ECJ explained that the ambiguity which may arise on reading Recitals 14 and 15 of the Preamble of Regulation 261/2004 could not call into question the fact that the body of that Regulation made clear that the defence of extraordinary circumstances is not a general rule, but applies only to the obligation to pay compensation. Conversely, in *Sturgeon and Others*, the question whether long delays may give rise to compensation could not be answered by looking at the relevant provisions of Regulation 261/2004. Thus, the ECJ was right to examine Recital 15 of the Preamble thereof.

In relation to the principle of proportionality, the applicants argued that, as interpreted by the ECJ in *Sturgeon and Others*, Regulation 261/2004 would impose an excessive burden on air carriers as they would have to provide compensation to passengers suffering a loss of time equal to or in excess of three hours. They also pointed out that the financial cost brought about by that compensation would be passed on to passengers by means of an increase in fares or a reduction in the number of flights from local airports and services to outlying destinations.[49] Whilst acknowledging that that compensation may entail certain financial consequences to air carriers, the ECJ found that 'those consequences cannot be considered disproportionate to the aim of ensuring a high level of protection for air passengers'.[50] First, not all delays may give rise to compensation, but only long delays.[51] Second, provided that the conditions laid down in Article 7(2)(c) of Regulation 261/2004 are met, the amount of compensation may be reduced by 50 per cent.[52] Third, compensation is excluded where the delay in question is caused by 'extraordinary circumstances' as defined by the case law of the ECJ.[53] Fourth, air carriers having paid compensation to passengers suffering long delays may seek to recover that amount from any person who caused the delay.[54] Fifth, statistics show that 'the proportion of flights for which delay confers entitlement to the compensation provided for under Regulation No 261/2004 is less than 0.15%'.[55] Sixth, applicants failed to provide evidence

does not prevent public authorities from redressing, in a standardised and immediate manner, the damage that is constituted by the inconvenience that delay in the carriage of passengers by air causes. In *IATA and ELFAA*, above n 47, the ECJ ruled that 'the assistance and taking care of passengers envisaged by Article 6 of Regulation No 261/2004 in the event of a long delay to a flight constitute such standardised and immediate compensatory measures' (*See IATA and ELFAA*, above n 47, para 46). In the same way, in *Sturgeon and Others*, the compensation envisaged by Art 7 of Regulation No 261/2004 in the event of a long delay to a flight also constitutes such a standardised and immediate compensatory measure which the Montreal Convention does not oppose (See *Nelson and Others*, above n 46, para 48).

49 *Nelson and Others*, above n 46, para 73.

50 ibid, para 76.

51 ibid, para 77.

52 ibid, para 78.

53 See *Sturgeon and Others*, above n 32, para 67. More recently, see Case C-12/11 *McDonagh*, Judgment of 31 January 2013, not yet reported.

54 *Nelson and Others*, above n 46, para 80.

55 ibid, para 82.

showing that 'the payment of compensation in the event of long delays to flights would give rise to an increase in fares or a reduction in the number of flights from local airports and services to outlying destinations'.[56] Most importantly, recalling its previous ruling in *Vodafone and Others*,[57] the ECJ held that 'the importance of the objective of consumer protection, which includes the protection of air passengers, may justify even substantial negative economic consequences for certain economic operators'.[58]

As a result, the ECJ held that '[c]onsideration [of the questions referred for a preliminary ruling] has disclosed no factor of such a kind as to affect the validity of Articles 5 to 7 of Regulation 261/2004'.[59]

The problems with which the ECJ was confronted in *Test-Achats* and *Sturgeon and Others* are, to some extent, similar. First, in both cases, the ECJ had to review the compatibility of an act of secondary EU law with the principle of equal treatment. Second, in both cases, the alleged incompatibility of the challenged EU act resulted from a lacuna contained therein. In *Test-Achats*, Directive 2004/113 was silent as to whether the derogation laid down in Article 5(2) was subject to a temporal limitation. In the same way, in *Sturgeon and Others*, the wording of Regulation 261/2004 does not expressly create a right to compensation for those passengers whose flights are delayed. However, in *Test-Achats* the ECJ declared Article 5(2) of Directive 2004/113 invalid, whereas in *Sturgeon and Others* it decided to construe Regulation 261/2004 so as to award a right to compensation to passengers whose flights are delayed for more than three hours. How can these two different outcomes be explained? Did the ECJ engage in judicial activism in these cases?[60] In my view, the approach followed by the ECJ in both *Sturgeon and Others* and *Test-Achats* is not only consistent,

[56] ibid, para 83.

[57] Case C-58/08 *Vodafone and Others* [2010] ECR I-4999, paras 53 and 69.

[58] *Nelson and Others*, above n 46, para 81.

[59] ibid, para 60.

[60] See eg J Balfour, 'Airline Liability for Delays: The Court of Justice of the EU Rewrites EC Regulation 261/2004' (2010) 35 *Air and Space Law* 71, 75 (who argues that '[t]he disregard of clear provisions of EU regulations and rewriting of them by the [ECJ] raises serious concerns about the rule of law in the EU that [go] far beyond the interests of just airlines and passengers. It would be regrettable if this deeply unsatisfactory judgment was allowed to stand unchallenged'). But see Temple Lang, above n 15, 309 (who posits that '[i]t is understandable that neither the [ECJ] nor the Advocate General wished to declare the Regulation invalid because it was discriminatory, because that would have deprived many airline passengers of a right to compensation'); C van Dam, 'Air Passenger Rights after *Sturgeon*' (2011) 36 *Air and Space Law* 260, at 265 (who posits that '[t]he airlines may be right to point out that, also in *Sturgeon*, the principle of legal certainty was at stake. However, even though the [ECJ] did not explicitly refer to this principle, it will probably have concluded that, in the context of the questions referred by the national courts, it had to give way to the principle of equal treatment. Legal principles do not have an absolute value and often conflict with each other. It is one of the [ECJ]'s tasks to reconcile them or to give way to one to the detriment of the other') and S Garben, 'Sky-high Controversy and High-flying Claims? The *Sturgeon* Case Law in Light of Judicial Activism, Euroscepticism and Eurolegalism' (2013) 50 *CML Rev* 15, at 45 (who argues that '[w]e have seen that although there are good reasons to be critical of the ruling, especially with regard to the poor quality of legal reasoning, the outcome of the case can be defended. The [ECJ] has rightly taken a forceful approach in the protection of European consumers, providing a necessary counterbalance to the EU-induced privatization of the air travel sector').

but more importantly, it is deferential to the policy choices of the EU legislator. Indeed, a close reading of *Sturgeon and Others* and *Test-Achats* reveals that the ECJ limited itself to applying the principle of equal treatment so as to enhance the objectives pursued by the EU legislator.

It is worth noting that, in *Sturgeon and Others*, Regulation 261/2004 seeks primarily to ensure a high level of protection for all passengers who suffer from similar serious trouble and inconvenience connected with air transport.[61] As an act of judicial deference to the EU legislator, the ECJ sought not to call into question that level of protection, whilst at the same time ensuring compliance with the principle of equal treatment. This meant, in essence, that Regulation 261/2004 had to be construed so as to expand the categories of passengers benefiting from those rights, rather than inviting the EU legislator to revisit the entire scheme set out in this Regulation. A joint reading of the principle of equal treatment and the objectives pursued by Regulation 261/2004 favoured pushing the bounds of interpretation to the utmost (though not beyond the limits of *contra legem*) in order not to adversely affect the high level of protection already put in place by the EU legislator. By contrast, in *Test-Achats*, the challenged provision of Directive 2004/113 was a derogation from the objectives pursued by that Directive, namely the application of rules of unisex premiums and benefits. Article 5(2) was thus inconsistent with the objectives pursued by Directive 2004/113. Just as it does in testing the compatibility of national measures with EU law,[62] the ECJ required in *Test-Achats* that there should be no internal inconsistencies in secondary EU law, when it verifies the validity of that law in light of primary EU law.

iii Judicial Deference to Legislative Choices

When the ECJ is called upon to interpret secondary EU law, it must respect the framework laid down by the EU legislator. Hence, contrary to primary EU law, which must be interpreted as a 'living constitution' capable of coping with societal changes, the ECJ must refrain from rewriting secondary EU law, even if the latter is outdated or no longer fulfils the objectives it pursues. The role of the ECJ is indeed neither to anticipate nor to pre-empt policy choices that fall within the purview of the EU legislator. The ruling of the ECJ in *Commission v Spain* illustrates this point.[63]

One should briefly recall that an EU citizen has the right to receive 'cross-border' health care services under two coexisting regimes. On the one hand,

[61] See eg *Sturgeon and Others*, above n 32, paras 44–45 (where the ECJ held that 'it is apparent from Recitals 1– 4 in the Preamble, in particular from Recital 2, that the regulation seeks to ensure a high level of protection for air passengers regardless of whether they are denied boarding or whether their flight is cancelled or delayed, since they are all caused similar serious trouble and inconvenience connected with air transport'. Hence, the ECJ ruled that 'the provisions conferring rights on air passengers, including those conferring a right to compensation, must be interpreted broadly').

[62] For further discussion, see I.B.i of the present contribution.

[63] Case C-211/08 *Commission v Spain*, Judgment of 15 June 2010, not yet reported.

there is Regulation 883/2004[64] which entered into force on 1 May 2010, replacing Regulation 1408/71.[65] Regulation 883/2004 lays down a system of prior authorisation. On the other hand, there are the Treaty provisions on the freedom to provide (or receive) services as interpreted by the ECJ. It is worth noting that the case law of the ECJ under these Treaty provisions has been largely codified by the recently adopted Directive 24/2011 (the Patient's Rights Directive, the PRD).[66] In relation to cases of 'scheduled treatment', it may happen that the coverage of a treatment is lower in the Member State of stay than in the Member State of affiliation. For such a situation, the ECJ held in *Vanbraekel* that:

> Article [56 TFEU] is to be interpreted as meaning that, if the reimbursement of costs incurred on hospital services provided in a Member State of stay, calculated under the rules in force in that State, is less than the amount which application of the legislation in force in the Member State of registration would afford to a person receiving hospital treatment in that State, additional reimbursement covering that difference must be granted to the insured person by the competent institution.[67]

This is known as the 'Vanbraekel reimbursement'.

In *Commission v Spain*, the ECJ held that the 'Vanbraekel reimbursement' does not apply to people who travel to other Member States for purposes other than receiving medical care, ie, persons who claim the reimbursement of the health care incurred in the Member State of stay under Article 22 (1)(a) Regulation 1408/71 (now Article 19 of Regulation 883/2004). First, it stressed that, unlike scheduled treatment, national legislation denying the 'Vanbraekel reimbursement' in cases of unscheduled treatment 'cannot be regarded as having any restrictive effect on the provision of hospital treatment services by providers established in another Member State',[68] given that the unexpected character of that type of treatment does not induce the insured person to cancel his or her trip. Second, the ECJ found that the contested legislation could not, in general terms, be regarded as restricting the freedom to provide hospital treatment services, tourist services or educational services, since it appears too uncertain and indirect to consider that the person insured in the Member State of affiliation would be induced not to leave that Member State or to return there early in order to receive medical treatment.[69] Finally, the ECJ ruled that its interpretation of Article 56 TFEU was consistent with 'the principle of overall compensation of risks' laid down in Articles 22 (1)(a) and 36 of Regulation 1408/71 (now Articles 19 and 35 of Regulation 883/2004). In accordance with

[64] Regulation No 883/2004 of the European Parliament and of the Council of 29 April 2004 on the coordination of social security systems, [2004] OJ L166/1.

[65] Regulation No 1408/71 of the Council of 14 June 1971 on the application of social security schemes to employed persons and their families moving within the Community, [1986] OJ L266/39 (English special edition).

[66] Directive 2011/24/EU of the European Parliament and of the Council of 9 March 2011 on the application of patients' rights in cross-border healthcare, [2011] OJ L 88/45. The deadline for transposing that Directive is 23 October 2013.

[67] Case C-368/98 *Vanbraekel and Others* [2001] ECR I-5363, para 53.

[68] *Commission v Spain*, above n 63, para 65.

[69] ibid, para 72.

that principle, cases in which the hospital treatment provided for in the Member State of stay is of a higher financial cost than that offered in the Member State of affiliation are offset by cases in which the hospital treatment provided for in the Member State of stay is of a lower cost.[70] Otherwise, the ECJ reasoned, the Member State of affiliation would be systematically exposed to the highest financial burden.

According to Van der Mei,[71] the ruling of the ECJ in *Commission v Spain* has been superseded by Article 7(4) of the PRD, since the latter does not distinguish between scheduled and unscheduled treatment. Indeed, that provision states that:

> [t]he costs of cross-border healthcare shall be reimbursed or paid directly by the Member State of affiliation up to the level of costs that would have been assumed by the Member State of affiliation, had this healthcare been provided in its territory without exceeding the actual costs of healthcare received.

Van der Mei relies on this occurrence with a view to criticising the ruling of the ECJ in *Commission v Spain*. After looking at the legislative process that led to the enactment of the PRD, he observes that, in relation to Article 7(4) thereof, 'no objections were raised, and no amendments were proposed'. Indeed, ever since it was included in the original 2008 Commission proposal, Article 7(4) of the PRD remained unchanged. Hence, the EU legislator (including the Member States) appeared not to be opposed to the application of the 'Vanbraekel reimbursement' to unscheduled hospital treatment. In his view, *Commission v Spain* gave rise to a 'unique and reverse situation, in which the Member States prove to be more "patient-friendly" than the overly conservative [ECJ]'.[72]

Even if one were to assume that Article 7(4) of the PRD applies to unscheduled treatments, which is far from being clear,[73] I cannot agree with such criticism. By qualifying the ECJ as a 'patient-friendly' or as an 'overly conservative' court, one embarks onto the wrong debate. Those two adjectives refer to policy considerations and should therefore be reserved to the appraisal of the work done by the political process. In *Commission v Spain*, the ECJ limited itself to examining the compatibility of Spanish legislation with Article 56 TFEU; it found that Article 56 TFEU does not require Member States to award the 'Vanbraekel reimbursement' to unscheduled hospital treatment. In so doing, it effectively held that the awarding of such reimbursement in the event of unscheduled hospital treatment was a matter for the EU legislator alone to determine, as it involved policy choices concerning financial tradeoffs in the health care budgets of the Member States, as the money spent on moving

[70] ibid, paras 78 and 79.

[71] AP van der Mei, 'Cross-border Access to Healthcare and Entitlement to Complementary "Vanbraekel Reimbursement"' (2011) 36 *ELRev* 431.

[72] ibid, 439.

[73] See 28th Recital of the PRD, which states that '[the PRD] should not affect an insured person's rights in respect of the assumption of costs of healthcare which becomes necessary on medical grounds during a temporary stay in another Member State according to Regulation (EC) No 883/2004'.

patients is not being spent on other patients' needs. Thus, it is wrong to say that the ECJ was not 'patient-friendly' or 'overly conservative'. One can only infer from *Commission v Spain* that the ECJ is seriously committed to leaving policy choices in the hands of the EU legislator, where they actually belong if the EU is to be seen as a system based on representative democracy.[74]

B The ECJ and the Member States

The ECJ strives to strike the balance imposed by the rule of law between national and EU interests. In the absence of EU harmonising measures, the ECJ strikes that balance where a Member State relies on national identity or public health considerations, with a view to derogating from the Treaty provisions on free movement and EU citizenship. By contrast, when EU harmonising measures have been adopted, the ECJ weighs national interests against the objectives pursued by the EU legislator.

i In the Absence of EU Harmonisation

a The Importance of Constitutional Principles Embedded in National Law

In the absence of EU harmonisation, and in so far as there are no national measures producing a protectionist effect (or having a protectionist intent), Member States enjoy a broad leeway to safeguard national interests which are deemed fundamental to their identity. Beyond a core nucleus of shared values where the ECJ must ensure uniformity, EU law cannot disregard the cultural, historical and social heritage that is part and parcel of national constitutional traditions. In other words, beyond that core nucleus, the ECJ welcomes 'value diversity'.[75] The rulings of the ECJ in *Omega* and *Sayn-Wittgenstein* illustrate this approach.[76]

In *Omega*, the Bonn police authority prohibited Omega from offering games involving the simulated killing of human beings on the ground that they infringed human dignity. Given that Omega had entered into a franchise contract with a British company, it argued that the ban was contrary to the freedom to provide services embodied in ex Article 49 EC (now Article 56 TFEU). Thus, the ECJ was called upon to strike a balance between ex Article 49 EC and human dignity, as understood by a national authority. After noting that the ban constituted a restriction on the freedom to provide services which, nevertheless,

[74] See Case 220/83 *Commission v France* [1986] ECR 3663; Case 205/84 *Commission v Germany* [1986] ECR 3755; Case 252/83 *Commission v Denmark* [1986] ECR 3713; Case 206/84 *Commission v Ireland* [1986] ECR 3817. See also Case C-513/04 *Kerckhaert and Morres* [2006] ECR I-10967, paras 22–24 (holding that the fundamental freedoms do not require the elimination of double taxation resulting from the parallel exercise by the Member States concerned of their respective powers of taxation. This required a political solution to be adopted by the EU legislator or through double tax conventions concluded by the Member States).

[75] Lenaerts and Gutiérrez-Fons, above n 8, 1663.

[76] Case C-36/02 *Omega Spielhallen* [2004] ECR I-9609 and Case C-208/09 *Sayn-Wittgenstein*, Judgment of 22 December 2010, not yet reported.

pursued a legitimate objective – the protection of human dignity – the ECJ ruled that, for the purposes of applying the principle of proportionality,

> [i]t is not indispensable [. . .] for the restrictive measure issued by the authorities of a Member State to correspond to a conception shared by all Member States as regards the precise way in which the fundamental right or legitimate interest in question is to be protected.[77]

Thus, the fact that a Member State other than Germany had chosen a system of protection of human dignity less restrictive of the freedom to provide services did not imply that the German measure was contrary to the EC Treaty. Given that the ban satisfied the level of protection required by the German Constitution and did not go beyond what was necessary to that effect, the ECJ considered that it was a justified restriction on the freedom to provide services. Thus, *Omega* demonstrates that the ECJ did not seek to impose a common conception of human dignity, nor did it embrace the national conception prevailing outside Germany, which was more protective of free movement. Instead, it endorsed a model based on 'value diversity', where national constitutional traditions are not in competition with the economic objectives of the Union, but form an integral part of them.[78]

The ECJ followed the same approach in *Sayn-Wittgenstein*. The facts of the case were as follows. In 2003, the Austrian Constitutional Court delivered a judgment in which it interpreted the Law on the abolition of the nobility, which enjoys a constitutional status as it implements the principle of equal treatment in this field. It held that the Law on the abolition of the nobility prohibits Austrian citizens from bearing titles of nobility, including those of foreign origin. This meant for Ilonka Fürstin von Sayn-Wittgenstein – an Austrian national residing in Germany who took the name of her German stepfather – that all official documents delivered by Austrian authorities could no longer contain the noble elements 'Fürstin von', ie, her surname could only be registered as 'Sayn-Wittgenstein'. The latter, who had been using the prefix 'Fürstin von' both personally and professionally in Germany for more than 15 years, argued that the Law on the abolition of the nobility hampered her rights to free movement. By contrast, the Austrian Government stressed the importance of the Law on the abolition of the nobility which, as a matter of public policy, 'went hand in hand with the creation of the Republic of Austria'.[79] Hence, the referring court asked, in essence, whether Article 21 TFEU may authorise a Member State to rely on reasons of a constitutional nature in order not to recognise all the elements of a name obtained by one of its nationals in another Member State. The ECJ began by finding that the refusal by Austrian authorities to recognise the noble elements of Ms Sayn-Wittgenstein's surname constituted a restriction on her rights to free movement. Such refusal may cause Ms Sayn-Wittgenstein

[77] *Omega*, above n 76, para 37.
[78] Tridimas, *The General Principles of EU Law*, above n 14, 341.
[79] *Sayn-Wittgenstein*, above n 76, para 32.

> 'serious inconvenience' within the meaning of *Grunkin and Paul*[80] result[ing] from having to alter all the traces of a formal nature of the name 'Fürstin von Sayn-Wittgenstein' left in both the public and the private spheres, given that her official identity documents currently refer to her by a different name.[81]

Indeed, the discrepancy in names may dispel doubts as to Ms Sayn-Wittgenstein's identity and the authenticity of the documents she submits, or the veracity of their content.[82] As to the justification, the ECJ held that, as a matter of public policy, a Member State may restrict the right to free movement in order to protect an element of its national identity.[83] Although public policy had to be interpreted strictly, the ECJ noted that, since 'the concept of public policy may vary from one Member State to another and from one era to another [,] [t]he competent national authorities must therefore be allowed a margin of discretion within the limits imposed by the Treaty'.[84] Next, the ECJ recognised as legitimate the objective pursued by the Law on the abolition of the nobility, which 'seeks to ensure the observance of the principle of equal treatment as a general principle of law',[85] enshrined in Article 21 of the Charter. As to the principle of proportionality, the ECJ recalled its findings in *Omega*:

> It is not indispensable for the restrictive measure issued by the authorities of a Member State to correspond to a conception shared by all Member States as regards the precise way in which the fundamental right or legitimate interest in question is to be protected and that, on the contrary, the need for, and proportionality of, the provisions adopted are not excluded merely because one Member State has chosen a system of protection different from that adopted by another State.[86]

Hence, the ECJ ruled that the refusal by Austrian authorities to recognise the noble elements of the surname of a national of that State was compatible with Article 21 TFEU.

Moreover, in order to strengthen its approach, the ECJ for the first time, though in passing, referred to Article 4(2) TEU, according to which 'the [EU] is to respect the national identities of its Member States, which include the status of the State as a Republic'.[87] This is an important development which suggests that Article 4(2) TEU is to be interpreted as protecting 'national identity' understood as the fundamental constitutional principles of the Member States. However, the fact that the ECJ mentioned Article 4(2) TEU in the context of the principle of proportionality implies that 'national identity' is not absolute, but must be weighed against the fundamental values of the EU.[88] This means that

[80] Case C-353/06 *Grunkin and Paul* [2008] ECR I-7639.
[81] *Sayn-Wittgenstein*, above n 76, para 67.
[82] ibid, para 69.
[83] ibid, paras 83 and 84.
[84] ibid, para 87.
[85] ibid, para 89.
[86] ibid, para 91.
[87] ibid, para 92.
[88] See A von Bogdandy and S Schill, 'Overcoming Absolute Primacy: Respect for National Identity under the Lisbon Treaty' (2011) 48 *CML Rev* 1417, 1420 (arguing that '[n]ational identity

where fundamental constitutional values of the Member States are at stake, but no core value of the Union is in danger, then 'value diversity' will prevail over uniform application of EU law. Conversely, where the national measure at issue threatens values of essential importance to the very existence of the Union (such as the prohibition of discrimination on grounds of nationality), the Member State concerned will not be able to rely on Article 4(2) TEU. The approach followed by the ECJ in *Omega* and *Sayn-Wittgenstein* is fully consistent with this reading of Article 4(2) TEU. Where the contested national measure has nothing to do with protectionism;[89] ie, where no core value of the Union is at stake, the ECJ seeks to respect 'value diversity' by applying a 'proportionality test' which leaves to the Member States the level at which constitutional principles of fundamental importance are to be protected.

b The Importance of Consistency

The way in which the ECJ applied the principle of proportionality in *Omega* and *Sayn-Wittgenstein* is not limited to national measures protecting fundamental constitutional principles. The ECJ has equally favoured 'value diversity' where a national measure pursues a legitimate objective in relation to which EU law does not require Member States to adopt the same level of protection. For instance, this is the case where, in the absence of EU harmonisation, non-discriminatory national measures constituting obstacles to free movement aim to protect public health or public morality. Needless to say, this approach does not apply where the core values of the Union are put at risk.

However, the fact that the ECJ recognises considerable leeway to the Member States when they establish the level at which national interests are protected, does not exclude that it will examine the consistency of the national legislation as a whole aiming to protect that interest. As the ECJ held in *Placanica*:[90]

> With regard to the [objective of reducing gambling opportunities], it is clear from the case law that although restrictions on the number of operators are in principle capable of being justified, those restrictions must in any event reflect a concern to bring about

. . . does not enjoy absolute protection under EU law, but has to be balanced against the principle of uniform application of EU law; implementing this duty is a task of both the ECJ and national constitutional courts as parts of a system of composite constitutional adjudication').

[89] *cf* Case C-438/05 *International Transport Workers' Federation and Finnish Seamen's Union* [2007] ECR I-10779. In relation to that case, I have argued that trade unions sought protectionist measures by struggling to keep jobs at home. Whilst it is in principle legitimate for trade unions to seek to protect workers from social dumping, it is equally true that trade unions are not entitled to shield local labour markets from competition coming from Member States with low average wages. For this reason, the ECJ may have felt that granting a margin of appreciation to trade unions in such a broad way, as if they were Member State authorities, was inappropriate. Otherwise, the ECJ might have tilted the balance in favour of a 'social Europe' that arguably excludes a large part of its new citizens. Trade unions could easily engage in social protectionism, leading to retaliatory measures and eventually to the fragmentation of social groups across Europe. See Lenaerts and Gutiérrez-Fons, above n 8, 1666.

[90] Joined Cases C-338/04, C-359/04 and C-360/04 *Placanica and Others* [2007] ECR I-1891.

> a genuine diminution of gambling opportunities and to limit activities in that sector in a consistent and systematic manner.[91]

After *Placanica*, the ECJ has continuously stressed the importance of consistency of the national rules on gambling in order to secure their compatibility with the Treaty provisions on free movement. Though Member States enjoy a wide margin of discretion in deciding the level of protection at which they wish to ban behaviour of dubious morality such as gambling,[92] the ECJ is committed to verifying that those national rules are free from internal and external contradictions.[93] The contested national rules often set up a public monopoly or restrict market access for private operators so as to fight crime and/or prevent individuals from becoming addicted to gambling. However, the ECJ engages in a joint reading of the national rules at issue and the national legislation as a whole. If that reading shows inconsistencies revealing that the objective of combating crime and/or game addiction is 'illusory', whilst the national legislation's true purpose appears to be to increase public revenue, the contested national rule will not be justified.[94]

The ECJ went on testing the consistency of the justifications put forward by the Member States in other areas of the law, such as the provision of health care services.[95] For example, in *Hartlauer*,[96] the ECJ examined the compatibility of the Austrian system of prior authorisation for the setting up and operation of outpatient dental clinics with EU law. In order to better understand the case, it is worth pointing out that the Austrian social security system is mixed. On the one hand, it is based on a system of benefits in kind when health care services are provided by establishments belonging to the social security institutions or by establishments or independent practitioners contracted to sickness funds ('contractual practitioners').[97] On the other hand, if an insured patient wishes to hire the services of a non-contractual practitioner, he or she has a right to reimbursement by the social security system up to a ceiling of 80 per cent of the sum that would have been charged by a contractual practitioner. Austrian legislation conditioned the setting up and operation of non-contractual outpatient dental clinics upon obtaining a prior authorisation which could not be granted if demand for dental services within a given province was already satisfied by the

[91] ibid, para 53.

[92] See Case C-42/07 *Liga Portuguesa de Futebol Profissional* [2009] ECR I-7633, para 57 (holding that 'the legislation on games of chance is one of the areas in which there are significant moral, religious and cultural differences between the Member States. In the absence of [EU] harmonisation in the field, it is for each Member State to determine in those areas, in accordance with its own scale of values, what is required in order to ensure that the interests in question are protected').

[93] See S Van den Bogaert and A Cuyvers, '"Money for Nothing": The Case Law of the EU Court of Justice on the Regulation of Gambling' (2011) 48 *CML Rev* 1175.

[94] See eg Joined Cases C-316/07, C-358/07, C-359/07, C-360/07, C-409/07 and C-410/07 *Stoß*, Judgment of 8 September 2010, not yet reported, para 106; and Case C-46/08 *Carmen Media Group*, Judgment of 8 September 2010, not yet reported, para 68.

[95] See eg Case C-500/06 *Corporación Dermoestética* [2008] ECR I-5785.

[96] Case C-169/07 *Hartlauer* [2009] ECR I-1721, para 55.

[97] See Opinion of AG Bot in *Hartlauer*, above n 96, paras 30–32.

existing dental service providers. Hartlauer, a German company which had unsuccessfully applied for a licence to open an outpatient dental clinic in Vienna, challenged that negative decision before the Austrian courts. It alleged that the Austrian legislation was contrary to the freedom of establishment. However, in recalling the case law of the ECJ regarding patient mobility and hospital care,[98] Austria argued that, even if there was a restriction of the freedom of establishment, it could be justified on the ground that there was a general interest in planning the number of outpatient dental clinics so as to avoid wastage of financial, technical and human resources, whilst ensuring a sufficient and permanent access to a high-quality dental treatment. Accordingly, in order to preserve health care planning, the system of prior authorisation was necessary. In addition, an open access to non-contractual practitioners would drive contractual practitioners to disappear from the market, since the former would focus on the profitable part of the market, rendering sickness funds incapable of covering their costs ('cream-skimming').

Although the ECJ recognised the objective pursued by Austria as legitimate,[99] it noted that no authorisation was required for 'group practices' which, unlike outpatient dental clinics, take the legal form of a for-profit partnership comprising partners with an independent entitlement to practise and who are personally liable.[100] But given that 'the premises and equipment of group practices and those of outpatient dental clinics may have comparable features and that in many cases the patient will not notice any difference between them' and that 'group practices generally offer the same medical services as outpatient dental clinics and are subject to the same market conditions',[101] the ECJ found that the contested Austrian legislation contained a clear inconsistency: group practices could also upset the organisation and planning of the provision of care in an area.[102]

More recently, the ruling of the ECJ in *Blanco Pérez*[103] provides a good example which shows how the ECJ combines a soft application of the proportionality test with the requirement of consistency. In that case, the ECJ examined the compatibility of Austrian legislation (Spain) which conditioned the opening of new pharmacies upon obtaining a prior authorisation, the award of which had to comply with geographical and demographical limits.[104] Those limits were as follows:

[98] See eg Case C-385/99 *Müller-Fauré and van Riet* [2003] ECR I-4509; Case C-372/04 *Watts* [2006] ECR I-4325.

[99] *Hartlauer*, above n 96, para 52.

[100] ibid, para 59.

[101] ibid, paras 57 and 58.

[102] ibid, para 60.

[103] Joined Cases C-570/07 and C-571/07 *Blanco Pérez and Chao Gómez*, Judgment of 1 June 2010, not yet reported.

[104] In addition, the ECJ also examined the selection criteria for licensees for new pharmacies which, in essence, gave preference to pharmacists with professional experience obtained within the Autonomous Community of Asturias. The ECJ found those criteria to be discriminatory and that they could not be justified by the need to maintain a level of quality in the pharmaceutical service, given that pharmacists falling within the scope of Directives 85/432 – [1985] OJ L353/34 – and 2005/36 – [2005] OJ L255/22 – were deemed to be sufficiently qualified to provide services of a high quality. *Blanco Pérez*, above n 103, para 115 et seq.

- in each pharmaceutical area, a single pharmacy may be opened, as a general rule, per unit of 2 800 inhabitants [(the '2800 inhabitants' rule)];
- a supplementary pharmacy may not be opened until that threshold has been exceeded, that pharmacy being established for the fraction above 2000 inhabitants; and
- each pharmacy must be a minimum distance away from existing pharmacies, that distance being, as a general rule, 250 metres [(the '250 metre' rule)].[105]

Hence, the contested national measure limited the number of pharmaceutical service providers according to economic and social needs. Although the contested national measure was applicable without discrimination on grounds of nationality,[106] the ECJ found that it was liable to hinder or render less attractive the exercise by EU nationals of the freedom of establishment, since a system of prior authorisation caused undertakings to bear additional administrative and financial costs, and prevented the undertakings not satisfying the predetermined requirements from carrying out a self-employed pharmaceutical activity[107]

Next, the ECJ held that the contested measure could be justified on grounds of public health, given that it sought to distribute the number of pharmacies within a given geographical area evenly, so as to ensure adequate access to pharmaceutical services as well as to improve the reliability and the quality of the provision of medical products to the public.[108]

As to the principle of proportionality, the ECJ first recalled that

> it is for the Member States to determine the level of protection which they wish to afford to public health and the way in which that level is to be achieved. Since the level may vary from one Member State to another, Member States should be allowed [a margin] of discretion.[109]

Accordingly, as the ECJ held in *Omega* and *Sayn-Wittgenstein*, 'the fact that one Member State imposes more stringent rules than another in relation to the protection of public health does not mean that those rules are incompatible with the Treaty provisions on the fundamental freedoms'.[110] Second, the ECJ examined whether the contested legislation was appropriate to the aim pursued. It noted that the '2800 inhabitants' rule was capable of preventing both a 'surplus' of pharmacies in densely populated areas which might be perceived as very profitable, and a 'deficit' of pharmacies in geographically isolated or disadvantaged areas.[111] The ECJ further observed that the '2800 inhabitants' rule may not be sufficient to ensure adequate access to pharmaceutical services. Indeed, such demographical limit does not prevent the establishment of a high concentration of pharmacies within one and the same pharmaceutical area, generating a duplication of structures in some parts of that area, whilst other parts of the

[105] ibid, para 52.
[106] ibid, para 62.
[107] ibid, para 54.
[108] ibid, para 78.
[109] ibid, para 44.
[110] ibid, para 68.
[111] ibid, para 72.

same area might suffer from a lack of pharmacies. That is why the ECJ also upheld the '250 metres' rule. In addition, in referring to its previous ruling in *Hartlauer*,[112] it ruled that

> it is also essential that the way in which that legislation pursues that objective is not inconsistent. According to the case law of the [ECJ], the various rules – and the national legislation as a whole – are appropriate for ensuring attainment of the objective relied upon only if they genuinely reflect a concern to attain that objective in a consistent and systematic manner.

For the case at hand, this meant that the '2800 inhabitants' rule and the '250 metres' rule contained in the contested legislation had to be readjusted so as to take into account areas with special geographical and demographical features. For example, for rural, mountainous or tourist areas, the limit of 2800 inhabitants per pharmacy could be inappropriate to ensure adequate access to pharmaceutical services. Likewise, in densely populated areas, a minimum distance of 250 metres per pharmacy could bring about a shortage in the supply of pharmaceutical services.[113] Accordingly, the ECJ held that it was for the referring court to ascertain whether those two basic rules could be adapted in accordance with the special features of certain pharmaceutical areas. Finally, after stressing again that the Member States enjoy a broad margin of discretion in relation to the protection of public health, the ECJ rejected that the contested measure went beyond what was necessary to attain the aim pursued.[114]

Cases like *Placanica*, *Hartlauer* and *Blanco Pérez* show that the ECJ endeavours to find the true purpose underpinning the national measure in question. In so doing, it focuses on the contextual aspects of the proportionality principle. In other words, the principle of proportionality is not applied in an abstract fashion, 'but as a part of the legal and factual context in which the [contested] measure operates'.[115] In order to ensure that there is no protectionist objective behind the contested national measure, judicial deference in relation to the 'necessity' prong of the principle of proportionality is compensated by incor-

[112] See *Hartlauer*, above n 96.

[113] *Blanco Pérez*, above n 103, paras 99–102.

[114] In so doing, it found that the Member State concerned was entitled to consider that a 'minimum number' system was less effective than the scheme set out by the contested legislation. According to that alternative system, a 'licence for setting up a new pharmacy would be issued . . . in areas where there was already an adequate number of pharmacies, until each of the specific geographical zones had the minimum number of pharmacies required. However, as soon as each of those areas had the minimum number of pharmacies, the opening of new pharmacies would be possible' (ibid, para 105). Indeed, given that Spain had decided to transfer to the Autonomous Communities the organisation of the distribution of pharmacies and that it was a national objective to channel pharmacists towards areas where there were no pharmacies, in whatever region, the ECJ observed that the 'minimum number' system could actually hinder that objective: 'it is possible [, the ECJ reasoned,] that the pharmacists concerned would tend to swell the numbers of pharmacists in regions where the minimum number has already been reached – and where, as a consequence, there are no restrictions on the opening of pharmacies – instead of setting up in areas where there are no pharmacies, in the regions where the minimum number has not been reached'; ibid, para 111.

[115] G Mathisen 'Consistency and Coherence as Conditions for Justification of Member State Measures Restricting Free Movement' (2010) 47 *CML Rev* 1021, 1040.

porating the 'consistency' test into the 'suitability' prong of the same principle. In so doing, the ECJ enhances the legitimacy of its legal reasoning: verifying the absence of contradictions in the justifications put forward by the Member States is a strong way for the ECJ to dismiss arbitrary criteria when assessing the compatibility of national measures with EU law.

ii *In the Presence of EU Harmonisation*

In the presence of EU harmonising measures, it is not sufficient for national law to comply with primary EU law. Additionally, Member States must comply with the way in which the EU legislator has struck the balance between the substantive law of the Union and national interests. The normative yardstick determining the compatibility of national law with EU law is then also constituted by secondary EU law. It follows that the margin of manoeuvre enjoyed by national authorities, if any, is limited by the legislative framework put in place by the EU legislator. This does not mean, however, that, within that framework, the ECJ will never be in a position to accommodate national interests. The recent ruling of the ECJ in *Mesopotamia Broadcast* illustrates this point.[116]

Before explaining the facts of the case, an overview must be given of the way in which the EU legislator has sought to remove obstacles to the freedom to provide broadcasting services within the EU. Directive 89/552[117] (as amended by Directive 97/36)[118] encapsulates 'the principle of the originating Member State' whereby 'it is necessary and sufficient that all broadcasts comply with the law of the Member State from which they emanate'.[119] It is for the authorities of that Member State to check whether television broadcasts emanating therein comply with the rules on broadcasting thereof. In accordance with Article 2a of Directive 89/552, only exceptionally and provisionally may the receiving Member State suspend the retransmission of a televised broadcast emanating from other Member States, in so far as such a broadcast is in breach of Article 22(1) or (2) and/or Article 22a of that Directive. The latter provision states that 'Member States shall ensure that broadcasts do not contain any incitement to hatred on grounds of race, sex, religion or nationality'. Moreover, Article 2a of Directive 89/552 lays down additional requirements for suspension.[120] It follows

[116] Joined Cases C-244/10 and C-245/10 *Mesopotamia Broadcast*, Judgment of 22 September 2011, not yet reported.

[117] Council Directive 89/552/EEC of 3 October 1989 on the coordination of certain provisions laid down by Law, Regulation or Administrative Action in Member States concerning the pursuit of television broadcasting activities [1989] OJ L298/23.

[118] Directive 97/36/EC of the European Parliament and of the Council of 30 June 1997 amending Council Directive 89/552/EEC on the coordination of certain provisions laid down by law, regulation or administrative action in Member States concerning the pursuit of television broadcasting activities, [1997] OJ L202/60.

[119] Opinion of AG Bot in *Mesopotamia Broadcast*, above n 116, para 9.

[120] Art 2a of Directive 89/552 provides: '2. Member States may, provisionally, derogate from paragraph 1 if the following conditions are fulfilled: (a) a television broadcast coming from another Member State manifestly, seriously and gravely infringes Article 22(1) or (2) and/or Article 22a; (b)

that, in areas coordinated by Directive 89/552, the receiving Member State may only suspend a broadcast in compliance with Article 2a.

Mesopotamia Broadcast is a holding company incorporated under Danish law which owns several Danish broadcasting licences and operates, inter alia, the broadcaster Roj TV. Roj TV's programmes are produced mainly in Kurdish and broadcasted via satellite throughout Europe and the Middle East. In 2006 and 2007, convinced that Roj TV supported the objectives of the PKK, which the EU has classified as a 'terrorist' organisation, Turkey lodged a complaint with the Danish Television Committee. However, those complaints were dismissed on the grounds that Roj TV had violated neither Article 22 nor Article 22a of Directive 89/552. In 2008, the German Federal Ministry of Interior took a different view, prohibiting Mesopotamia Broadcast from carrying out, through the agency of Roj TV, any activities falling within the scope of the German law governing associations (the '*Vereinsgesetz*'). It also precluded Roj TV from undertaking its activities in Germany. Its decision was based on the fact that Roj TV supported the use of violence to achieve the political aims of the PKK and in relations between Turks and Kurds, thus infringing the constitutional 'principles of international understanding' for the purposes of the *Vereinsgesetz*. Mesopotamia Broadcast and Roj TV challenged that decision before the competent German court. They argued that the decision of the German authorities was in breach of Directive 89/552 as it was for Danish authorities alone to exercise control over their broadcasting activities. Moreover, they posited that the German decision was in breach of Article 2a of that Directive. Conversely, the German Federal Government argued that Directive 89/552 did not prevent Member States from applying their general rules on criminal or police matters or the *Vereinsgesetz*, even if those rules were capable of adversely affecting television broadcasting activities.

At the outset, the ECJ stressed that Directive 89/552 has a non-exhaustive character, and accordingly,

> with regard to areas relating to public order, public morality or public security [. . .] a Member State is free to apply to the activities carried out by broadcasters on its territory generally applicable rules concerning those fields, in so far as those rules do not hinder retransmission.[121]

during the previous 12 months, the broadcaster has infringed the provision(s) referred to in (a) on at least two prior occasions; (c) the Member State concerned has notified the broadcaster and the Commission in writing of the alleged infringements and of the measures it intends to take should any such infringement occur again; (d) consultations with the transmitting Member State and the Commission have not produced an amicable settlement within 15 days of the notification provided for in (c), and the alleged infringement persists. The Commission shall, within two months following notification of the measures taken by the Member State, take a decision on whether the measures are compatible with Community law. If it decides that they are not, the Member State will be required to put an end to the measures in question as a matter of urgency. 3. Paragraph 2 shall be without prejudice to the application of any procedure, remedy or sanction to the infringements in question in the Member State which has jurisdiction over the broadcaster concerned'.

[121] *Mesopotamia Broadcast*, above n 116, para 37.

Next, it examined whether the activities carried out by Roj TV fell within the meaning of 'any incitement to hatred' as provided for by Article 22a of Directive 89/552. The ECJ replied in the affirmative. In light of the literal, systematic and teleological interpretation of Article 22a, it defined 'incitement to hatred' as a concept 'designed to forestall any ideology which fails to respect human values, in particular initiatives which attempt to justify violence by terrorist acts against a particular group of persons'.[122] Hence, since the activities of Roj TV stirred up the violence between Turks and Kurds in Turkey and intensified the tensions between those two groups in Germany, that behaviour was covered by the concept of 'incitement to hatred'. This meant that German authorities were precluded from hindering Roj TV's retransmissions, unless they did so in accordance with Article 2a of Directive 89/552. The fact that the risk of confrontation between those two groups was more likely in Germany than in Denmark was of no relevance.[123]

However, referring to its previous ruling in *De Agostini*,[124] the ECJ recalled that a distinction had to be drawn between, on the one hand, national measures which constitute an obstacle to retransmission per se and, on the other, national measures with the general aim of protecting public policy. Whilst the former type of measure must comply with Article 2a of Directive 89/552, the latter type falls outside the scope of coordination of that Directive and must only comply with primary EU law. This meant for the case at hand that Directive 89/552 did not prohibit Germany from adopting a measure which 'pursue[d] a public policy objective without however preventing retransmission per se, on its territory, of television broadcasts from another Member State'.[125] Hence, Germany could, for example, prohibit Roj TV from producing broadcasts and organising public events within its territory. The ECJ deferred to the national court the determination of the types of activities which were contrary to the principles of international understanding as provided for by the *Vereinsgesetz* but did not prevent the retransmission per se in Germany of Roj TV's broadcasts.

Mesopotamia Broadcast is a positive development which confirms that, in interpreting EU harmonising measures, the ECJ takes national interests seriously. Thus, the fact that the EU legislator has harmonised an area of law does not automatically rule out that national interests may be taken into account. On the contrary, *Mesopotamia Broadcast* shows that the ECJ seeks to strike the balance intended by EU law taken as a whole, between the objectives pursued by the EU legislator and the interests of the Member States. On the one hand, the ECJ ruled that Germany was precluded from exercising a double control on the broadcasting activities of Roj TV. The exercise of such control would run counter to the principle of the originating Member State. This meant that German

[122] ibid, para 42.

[123] ibid, para 45.

[124] Joined Cases C-34/95 to C-36/95 *De Agostini and TV-Shop* [1997] ECR I-3843 (in that case, the national measures at issue sought to protect consumers from misleading advertising).

[125] *Mesopotamia Broadcast*, above n 116, para 50.

authorities had either to trust the decision adopted by their Danish counterparts or to follow the procedure laid down in Directive 89/552 in order to oppose that decision. On the other hand, the ECJ stressed that Directive 89/552 could not be interpreted so as to deprive the receiving Member State, namely Germany, of its police powers. Germany could control the activities of Roj TV which took place within its territory. For example, a public event organised by Roj TV could be banned, even if that implied that such event could no longer be broadcast.

II. INTERNAL LEGITIMACY

So far, the present contribution has primarily focused on examining whether the ECJ is committed to standing behind the line that divides 'law' from 'politics'; ie, it has focused on the external aspects of judicial legitimacy. By contrast, part II of this contribution aims to determine whether the judicial function in the EU legal order is exercised in a way that guarantees a high-quality judicial process. To this end, section A examines whether the ECJ is committed to respecting the allocation of judicial powers provided for by Article 267 TFEU. Section B then looks into the question whether the ECJ operates as a 'rational actor' ensuring that the outcome it reaches is based on convincing grounds. It thus assesses the persuasiveness of the ECJ's legal reasoning.

A The ECJ and National Courts

One of the key elements explaining the success of European integration lies in that, from the very beginning, the ECJ brought national courts on board. The relationship between the ECJ and national courts has been portrayed as a 'dialogue'.[126] This means that, although there are some hierarchical elements in that relationship,[127] mutual cooperation and empowerment is at its centre. The principles of direct effect and primacy in conjunction with the preliminary reference procedure gave to national courts a leading role in the legal construction of Europe.[128] Those two constitutional principles and Article 267 TFEU somehow shifted powers from the national legislature and executive to the national judiciary as well as from higher courts to lower courts.[129] The lowest court of the national judicial pyramid may indeed have to set aside national law breach-

[126] See Opinion 1/09, above n 3, para 84.

[127] See eg RB Ahdieh, 'Between Dialogue and Decree: International Review of National Courts' (2004) 79 *New York University Law Review* 2029; J Komárek 'Federal Elements in the Community Judicial System: Building Coherence in the Community Legal Order' (2005) 42 *CML Rev* 9.

[128] See Opinion 1/09, above n 3, para 66 (holding that '[a]s is evident from Article 19(1) TEU, the guardians of that legal order and the judicial system of the European Union are the [ECJ] and the courts and tribunals of the Member States').

[129] T Tridimas, 'The European Court of Justice and the Draft Constitution: A Supreme Court of the Union?' in T Tridimas and P Nebbia (eds), *European Law for the Twenty-First Century: Rethinking the New Legal Oder,* Vol 1 (Oxford, Hart Publishing, 2004) 114.

ing EU law, even if that implies departing from the case law of the supreme or constitutional court.[130]

Additionally, the relationship between the ECJ and national courts may be assessed in terms of allocation of powers. Unlike other federal systems, the EU rests on an integrated judiciary,[131] in which judicial power as to the enforcement of EU law is shared between EU and national courts.[132] First, regarding judicial review of EU measures, EU courts enjoy the monopoly to declare secondary EU law invalid.[133] Accordingly, in order to ensure compliance with the rule of law, access to these courts must be guaranteed. Where private applicants do not enjoy direct access to EU courts, the ECJ has held, and now the Treaty itself suggests,[134] that national rules of procedure must provide indirect means of challenging those measures.[135] Second, under the preliminary reference procedure, the ECJ has jurisdiction only to interpret EU law, not national law,[136] so that it may not declare a national measure to be incompatible with EU law.[137] The interpretation of EU law is indeed a task for the ECJ to undertake, whereas its application to the case at hand is for the national courts alone to carry out.[138]

Just as happens with national law, it is often difficult, if not impossible, to draw the dividing line between interpretation and application of EU law. Sometimes the ECJ will provide a ruling of general application,[139] whilst in others the answer will be adapted to 'the specific circumstances of the [. . .] case' at

[130] See eg Case C-314/08 *Filipiak* [2009] ECR I-11049, para 84; C-409/06 *Winner Wetten*, Judgment of 8 September 2010, not yet reported, para 60.

[131] D Halberstam, 'Comparative Federalism and the Role of the Judiciary' in K Whittington, D Kelemen and G Caldeira (eds), *The Oxford Handbook of Law and Politics* (Oxford, Oxford University Press, 2008) 142.

[132] See Opinion 1/09, above n 3, para 69.

[133] See eg Case 314/85 *Foto-Frost* [1987] ECR 4199; Case C-461/03 *Gaston Schul Douane-expediteur* [2005] ECR I-10513.

[134] See Art 19 (1) TEU which states: 'Member States shall provide remedies sufficient to ensure effective legal protection in the fields covered by Union law'. See also K Lenaerts, 'Le Traité de Lisbonne et la Protection Juridictionnelle des Particuliers en Droit de l'Union' (2009) 46 *Cahiers de Droit Européen* 711.

[135] K Lenaerts, 'The Rule of Law and the Coherence of the Judicial System of the European Union' (2007) 44 *CML Rev* 1625.

[136] See eg Case 27/74 *Demag* [1974] ECR 1037, para 8; Case C-347/89 *Eurim-Pharm* [1991] ECR I-1747, para 16; and Case C-246/04 *Turn- und Sportunion Waldburg* [2006] ECR I-589, para 20. More recently, see Case C-515/08, *dos Santos Palhota and Others*, Judgment of 7 October 2010, not yet reported, para 18 (holding that 'Article 267 TFEU is based on a clear separation of functions between national courts and tribunals and the [ECJ], and the latter is empowered to rule only on the interpretation or the validity of the acts of the European Union referred to in that article. In that context, it is not for the [ECJ] to rule on the interpretation of national laws or regulations or to decide whether the referring court's interpretation of them is correct').

[137] This is different under Arts 258 to 260 TFEU.

[138] See eg Case C-54/07 *Feryn* [2008] ECR I-5187, para 19 (holding that Art 267 TFEU 'does not empower the [ECJ] to apply rules of [EU] law to a particular case, but only to rule on the interpretation of the Treat[ies] and of acts adopted by [EU] institutions').

[139] See eg Case C-101/08 *Audiolux and Others* [2009] ECR I-9823, para 64 (holding that '[EU] law does not include any general principle of law under which minority shareholders are protected by an obligation on the dominant shareholder, when acquiring or exercising control of a company, to offer to buy their shares under the same conditions as those agreed when a shareholding conferring or strengthening the control of the dominant shareholder was acquired').

hand.[140] This flexibility is of paramount importance for the proper functioning of the preliminary reference procedure. It allows the ECJ to accommodate its answers to different factors. First, the degree of precision with which the referring court sets out the facts of the case and interprets the relevant parts of national law, determines the generality or specificity of the answer provided by the ECJ. When the order for reference is very precisely drafted there is a bigger chance of the ECJ giving a tailor-made answer as to the EU law implications of the case. Second, where the ECJ has already rendered several rulings in a given area of EU law so that the questions referred to it are neither of great complexity nor raise novel issues, it may limit itself to recalling previous case law. This should be seen as a sign of maturity of the EU legal order whereby the ECJ trusts national courts as to the daily application of EU law. Third, in matters which raise national sensitivities, the ECJ will opt for answering the questions referred to it in such a way as to take into account the concerns put forward by the Member States.[141] Last, but not least, in some cases, the ECJ simply provides the EU law framework within which the referring court must take its decision. This is done in cases involving questions of fact or national law that still have to be determined by the referring court. The ECJ then clarifies the several possible ways under EU law to go about the case, leaving it to the national court to select the correct one after assessing the facts and aspects of national law. The ruling of the ECJ in *Bressol* and its implementation by the Belgian Constitutional Court provide an excellent illustration in this regard.

In *Bressol*,[142] the ECJ was asked by the Belgian Constitutional Court to examine the compatibility of the decree of the French Community ('the 2006 decree'), which regulated the number of students in certain programmes in the first two years of undergraduate studies in higher education, with the Treaty provisions on EU citizenship. The system of higher education of the French Community is based on free access to education; ie, there are no entry exams. However, in recent years, French students who had failed to pass the entry exams in France have gone to study at the Universities of the French Community. The number of students having become too large, in particular in medical and paramedical courses, the authorities of the French Community thought that, considering the budgetary, human and material resources available to the teaching institutions concerned, such an influx of students was jeopardising the quality of teaching – and, because of the nature of the programmes at issue, public health. Accordingly, in relation to nine medical or paramedical programmes,[143] the French Community adopted the 2006 decree which provided a *numerus clausus*

[140] Case C-145/09 *Tsakouridis*, Judgment of 8 June 2010, not yet reported.

[141] See eg Joined Cases C-483/09 and C-1/10 *Gueye and Others*, Judgment of 15 September 2011, not yet reported.

[142] Case C-73/08 *Bressol and Others*, Judgment of 13 April 2010, not yet reported.

[143] Those nine programmes were: Bachelor in physiotherapy and rehabilitation; Bachelor in veterinary medicine; Bachelor of midwifery; Bachelor of occupational therapy; Bachelor of speech therapy; Bachelor of podiatry-chiropody; Bachelor of physiotherapy; Bachelor of audiology; Educator specialised in psycho-educational counselling.

for enrolment by non-resident students who were selected by the drawing of lots, whilst resident students continued to enjoy free access to the courses referred thereto. In order to qualify as a resident student, a double condition had to be fulfilled. Essentially, residents were 'persons who both [had] their principal residence in Belgium and [had] a right of permanent residence in Belgium'.[144] Moreover, the number of non-resident students in those courses could not exceed a 30 per cent threshold. Mr Bressol and other students, most of them French nationals, brought an action before the Belgian Constitutional Court contesting the constitutionality of the 2006 decree. They posited that that decree violated the principle of equality by treating resident and non-resident students differently, for no valid reason.

At the outset, the ECJ stressed that EU law does not detract from the Member States the power to organise their education systems and vocational training. A Member State is free to opt for a system based on free access or for a system which lays down a *numerus clausus* of students. However, in so doing, it must comply with EU law, in particular with the Treaty provisions on EU citizenship.[145] Next, the ECJ found that the 2006 decree put non-resident students at a disadvantage vis-a-vis resident students, since only the latter continued to enjoy free access to any of the nine medical or paramedical courses referred to. Since the condition of residence was more easily met by Belgians than by students of other nationalities, the 2006 decree created a difference in treatment indirectly based on nationality that needed to be justified.[146]

As to the justification of the 2006 decree, the Belgian Government argued that it sought to counter the excessive burdens on the financing of higher education brought about by non-resident students. However, observing that the financing of higher education did not depend on the total number of students but was based on a system of a 'closed envelope', the ECJ dismissed that justification.[147]

In addition, the Belgian Government posited that the 2006 decree aimed to ensure the quality and continuing provision of medical and paramedical care within the French Community. It argued that the large numbers of non-resident students were likely ultimately to reduce the quality of teaching in medical and paramedical courses which require a significant amount of hours of practical training. In the same way, those large numbers may also bring about a shortage of qualified medical personnel throughout the territory which would undermine the system of public health within the French Community, given that after completing their studies, non-resident graduates tend to return to their country of origin to exercise their profession there, whilst the number of resident graduates remains too low in some specialities.[148] The ECJ recognised as legitimate the public health concerns raised by the Belgian Government. However, it pro-

[144] Opinion of AG Sharpston in *Bressol*, above n 142, para 25.
[145] *Bressol*, above n 142, paras 28 and 29.
[146] ibid, para 46.
[147] ibid, para 50.
[148] ibid, para 58.

vided a detailed framework of analysis that the referring court had to follow in order to determine whether there were genuine risks to the protection of public health and thus, whether the 2006 decree complied with EU law.

First, in assessing those risks, the referring court had to take into consideration

> the fact that the link between the training of future health professionals and the objective of maintaining a balanced high-quality medical service open to all is only indirect and the causal relationship less well established than in the case of the link between the objective of public health and the activity of health professionals who are already present on the market.[149]

Second, the ECJ pointed out that, whilst the Member State concerned does not have to wait for the risks to the protection of public health to materialise, it must, however, show that those risks actually exist. Third, the ECJ held that, for each of the nine courses covered by the 2006 decree, the analysis undertaken by the referring court had to determine the maximum number of students who can be trained at a level which complies with the desired training quality standards, as well as the number of graduates which is necessary to ensure adequate public health services. In determining those numbers, the analysis may not focus on one or the other group of students but it must take into account the number of non-resident students who decide to practise in Belgium, the number of resident students who decide to work in a Member State other than Belgium and the number of health care service providers who may come to work in Belgium.

As to the proportionality of the contested measure, the ECJ held that the referring court had to verify whether a system of *numerus clausus* for non-resident students can really bring about an increase in the number of graduates ready to ensure the future availability of public health services within the French Community. As to the necessity of the measure, the ECJ ruled that it was for the referring court to ascertain whether there were less restrictive means of encouraging students who study in the French Community to establish themselves there. Finally, the ECJ compelled the referring court to verify whether the system of selection for non-resident students (based on chance rather than on merits) was necessary to attain the objectives pursued.

Three months after the ECJ delivered its ruling, the Belgian Constitutional Court addressed six questions to the Government of the French Community. The purpose of those questions was to obtain the relevant information with a view to implementing the framework of analysis laid down in *Bressol*. After obtaining a reply, the Belgian Constitutional Court examined thoroughly each of the nine programmes referred to in the 2006 decree,[150] and found that only three of them satisfied the requirements laid down by the ECJ, namely Bachelor in physiotherapy and rehabilitation, Bachelor of physiotherapy and Bachelor in veterinary medicine. In relation to the first two, it found that there was a real

[149] ibid, para 69.

[150] Belgian Constitutional Court, *Bressol and Others*, Judgment of 31 May 2011, No 89/2011. Available in French, Dutch and German at: www.const-court.be.

risk to the protection of public health, as physiotherapy services currently suffer from a significant shortage in the French Community, which might even worsen with the increase in demand for those services and with the incoming retirement of the baby boomers. Data were also provided showing that the number of new graduates necessary to ensure a high quality of physiotherapy services was of 323 per year. As to the suitability of the 2006 decree, the Belgian Constitutional Court found that, in light of statistical data submitted, a reduction in the number of non-resident students had helped to increase the number of resident students.[151] It also observed that between 61 and 70 per cent of nationals of a Member State other than Belgium who have studied physiotherapy in the French Community do not establish themselves in the latter Member State. As to the necessity of the 2006 decree, the Belgian Constitutional Court examined whether the French Community could have adopted a less restrictive measure, such as giving incentives to non-resident students to stay in Belgium, or encouraging physiotherapists having studied abroad to come to that Member State whilst limiting the number of physiotherapy students. As to the first alternative measure, the Belgian Constitutional Court found that it was not financially viable, since Belgium would suffer from a double burden: namely, paying for the studies of non-resident students and for their initial stay in Belgium. As to the second alternative, it ruled that such a radical solution might run the risk of diminishing the quality of health care services in the French Community. Finally, owing to the fact that the organisation of entry exams for non-residents would impose administrative and financial burdens on the Universities of the French Community, the Belgian Constitutional Court considered that the system of selection for non-resident students by the drawing of lots was the less controversial. It also guaranteed social equality between the applicants. As to the programme on veterinary medicine, the Belgian Constitutional Court reached the same conclusion. The only difference was that the risk to the protection of public health did not come from a possible shortage in veterinary services but from the influx of non-resident students which could jeopardise the quality of the education veterinary students receive. In relation to the other six, the French Community had failed to provide sufficient evidence in support of the 2006 decree. Hence, in relation to the latter courses, the 2006 decree was annulled.

B The Persuasiveness of the ECJ's Legal Reasoning

It is often argued that the legal reasoning of the ECJ is not elaborated enough; that it is closer to a mathematical formula than to a clear and well articulated

[151] eg, prior to the adoption of the 2006 decree, there were 880 non-resident students, whilst the number of resident students was 334. By contrast, in the academic year 2008–09, the situation was reversed: the number of non-resident students was 366, whilst that of resident students was 734. The Belgian Constitutional Court also noted that the number of applications lodged by non-resident students had not stopped increasing: in the academic year 2006–07, the number of non-resident applicants was 457, whilst in the academic year 2010–11 it was 611.

statement of reasons; and that, more often than not, some parts of its argumentative discourse are missing, have been skipped or jumped through. For example, Weiler has urged the ECJ to abandon its 'Cartesian discourse', in favour of a more 'Anglo-Saxon-oriented' deliberation.[152] He posits that, 'especially in its [c]onstitutional jurisprudence, it is crucial that the [ECJ] demonstrate[s] . . . that national sensibilities were fully taken into account. And it must amply explain and reason its decisions if they are to be not only authoritarian but also authoritative'. Most importantly, Weiler stresses that 'the Cartesian style, with its pretence of logical legal reasoning and inevitability of results, is not conducive to a good conversation with national courts'.[153]

There is undeniably great merit in those observations, but they fail to grasp the fact that the ECJ operates under the principle of collegiality. In light of the latter principle, reaching an outcome based on consensus is of paramount importance for the daily inner workings of the ECJ. Accordingly, for the sake of consensus, in hard cases the discourse of the ECJ cannot be as profuse as it would be if dissenting opinions were allowed. As consensus-building requires bringing on board as many opinions as possible, the argumentative discourse of the ECJ is limited to the very essential. In order to preserve consensus, the ECJ does not take 'long jumps' when expounding the rationale underpinning the solution given to novel questions of constitutional importance. On the contrary, the persuasiveness of its argumentative discourse is built up progressively, ie, 'stone-by-stone'. This means that, in order to fully apprehend the approach of the ECJ in an area of EU law, a critical observer should not limit him or herself to studying the 'groundbreaking' case, but he or she should also read the relevant case law predating as well as postdating that case. This idea is illustrated by the recent developments in the case law relating to the Treaty provisions on EU citizenship.

Ruiz Zambrano is a landmark case in the law on EU citizenship.[154] In that case, the ECJ ruled that, even in the absence of a cross-border element, 'Article 20 TFEU precludes national measures which have the effect of depriving citizens of the Union of the genuine enjoyment of the substance of the rights conferred by virtue of their status as citizens of the Union'.[155] In so doing, the ECJ was sending a clear message: the Treaty provisions on EU citizenship are not limited to being a 'fifth freedom' which operates under the dynamics of free movement law. The rights attaching to the status of citizen of the Union may be relied upon, even in the absence of a cross-border element, against any national measure causing the deprivation of those rights.

For the case at hand, this meant that Mr Ruiz Zambrano – a Colombian national staying illegally in Belgium – had, as the father of two Belgian minors, a derivative right to reside and to work in Belgium, in spite of the fact that his

[152] JHH Weiler, 'Epilogue: The Judicial Après Nice' in G de Búrca and JHH Weiler (eds), *The European Court of Justice* (Oxford, Oxford University Press, 2001) 215.

[153] ibid, 225.

[154] Case C-34/09 *Ruiz Zambrano*, Judgment of 8 March 2011, not yet reported.

[155] ibid, para 42.

children had never left that Member State. The ECJ reasoned that if Mr Ruiz Zambrano were to leave the territory of the Union because of his irregular immigration status (or because a work permit was not issued to him), his children would be obliged to do the same. As a result, 'those citizens of the Union would . . . be unable to exercise the substance of the rights conferred on them by virtue of their status as citizens of the Union'.[156] Interestingly, in contrast to the extensive Opinion of AG Sharpston,[157] the ECJ's legal reasoning is contained in ten paragraphs,[158] out of which only six concerned Article 20 TFEU.[159] Explaining such an important development in only six paragraphs may, for some, show that the argumentative discourse of the ECJ is laconic, cryptic and even minimalist. However, the ruling of the ECJ in *Ruiz Zambrano* did not come 'out of the blue', but it draws on the previous ruling of the ECJ in *Rottmann*. As a matter of fact, in the key passage of *Ruiz Zambrano*, ie, paragraph 42, the ECJ itself refers to *Rottmann*.

C The Founding Stone

Rottmann thus set the founding stone that paved the way towards the emancipation of EU citizenship from the limits inherent in its free movement origins. The facts of the case are as follows. Whilst being the subject of judicial investigations in Austria, Dr Rottmann, an Austrian national, moved to Germany in 1995. Two years later, Austria issued an arrest warrant against him. In February 1999, he acquired German nationality by naturalisation, which meant simultaneously losing his Austrian nationality. However, in August 1999, Austria informed Germany of the arrest warrant issued against Dr Rottmann. Taking the view that by withholding that information Dr Rottmann had obtained German nationality by deception, Germany revoked that nationality and, since the original nationality did not revive, Dr Rottmann became stateless. Dr Rottmann challenged that decision before the German courts. In essence, the referring court asked the ECJ whether, in a situation such as that of Dr Rottmann, it was contrary to Article 20 TFEU for a Member State to withdraw from a citizen of the Union the nationality of that state acquired by naturalisation and obtained by deception inasmuch as that withdrawal deprived the person concerned of the status of citizen of the Union and of the benefit of the rights attaching thereto by rendering him stateless,

[156] ibid, para 44.

[157] Opinion of AG Sharpston in *Ruiz Zambrano*, above n 154, which contains 178 paragraphs. Eg, it is worth noting that, unlike the Opinion of AG Sharpston, the ECJ did not address the issue of reverse discrimination. Perhaps, once it held that the situation of Mr Ruiz Zambrano was not purely internal; the ECJ reasoned that it was no longer necessary to determine the role played by reverse discrimination in the context of EU citizenship.

[158] ibid, paras 36–45.

[159] The other four concern the reformulation of the questions referred by the Belgian court (ibid, para 36), the observations of the parties (ibid, paras 37 and 38) and an explanation as to why Directive 2004/38, [2004] OJ L158/77, does not apply to the situation of Mr Ruiz Zambrano (ibid, para 39).

acquisition of that nationality having caused that person to lose the nationality of his Member State of origin. In the key passage of the judgment, the ECJ held that

> [i]t is clear that the situation of a citizen of the Union who, like the applicant in the main proceedings, is faced with a decision withdrawing his naturalisation, adopted by the authorities of one Member State, and placing him, after he has lost the nationality of another Member State that he originally possessed, in a position capable of causing him to lose the status conferred by Article [20 TFEU] and the rights attaching thereto falls, by reason of its nature and its consequences, within the ambit of [EU] law.[160]

In reaching that conclusion, the ECJ stressed once again that 'citizenship of the Union is intended to be the fundamental status of nationals of the Member States'.[161] With a view to transforming this postulate into a living truth, the ECJ places weight on the status of a citizen of the Union as such rather than on free movement. In light of *Rottmann*, even in the absence of any physical movement between Member States, national measures which deprive an individual of his or her status of citizen of the Union, and thereby of the rights attaching to that status, fall within the scope of application of the Treaty provisions on EU citizenship.

Accordingly, reading *Ruiz Zambrano* in light of *Rottmann*, one may conclude that the former is actually endorsing and developing the approach followed in the latter: even in the absence of a cross-border element, Article 20 TFEU opposes a national measure which does not formally deprive an individual of the rights attaching to his or her status as an EU citizen but, in practical terms, produces the same effect.

i The Three Unsolved Questions after Ruiz Zambrano

After *Ruiz Zambrano*, three important questions were left open. First, the ECJ did not clarify how, in the absence of a cross-border element, Articles 20 and 21 TFEU interact. Second, neither did it specify under which circumstances a national measure may 'have the effect of depriving citizens of the Union of the genuine enjoyment of the substance of the rights conferred by virtue of their status as citizens of the Union',[162] or when does a national measure produce a 'deprivation effect'? It was thus left to future cases to decide whether the ECJ would opt for a restrictive or a broad interpretation. On the one hand, in accordance with a restrictive interpretation, a national measure would only produce a

[160] Case C-135/08 *Rottmann*, Judgment of 2 March 2010, not yet reported, para 42.

[161] ibid, para 43. In so doing, the ECJ sought to stress the fact that EU citizenship is more than a fifth freedom which protects the rights of free movement of economically inactive citizens. This can be seen by contrasting the Opinion of AG Poiares Maduro in this case with the ruling of the ECJ. Unlike the Advocate General, the ECJ 'disregard[ed Dr Rottmann's] earlier move and look[ed] exclusively to the future effects that withdrawal of German citizenship would have by rendering [Dr] Rottmann stateless.' See the Opinion of AG Sharpston in *Ruiz Zambrano*, above n 154, para 42.

[162] *Ruiz Zambrano*, above n 154, para 42.

'deprivation effect' when it brings about, de jure or de facto, the loss of the rights attaching to the status of citizen of the Union. In order to produce such an effect, the national measure at issue would have to cause more than a mere hindrance on – namely a serious inconvenience to – the rights attaching to the status of citizen of the Union. On the other hand, according to a broad interpretation, a measure producing a 'deprivation effect' would be tantamount to a measure which is 'liable to hinder or make less attractive the exercise of [rights attaching to the status of citizen of the Union] guaranteed by the Treaty'.[163] Last, but not least, the ECJ had also to clarify whether fundamental rights, especially the right to respect for a person's private and family life, had to be taken into account for the purposes of determining the existence of a deprivation effect.

Since those three questions were not addressed right away but their resolution was postponed for future cases, did *Ruiz Zambrano* adversely affect the internal legitimacy of the ECJ? In my view, it did not. First, providing answers to those three questions was not necessary to solve the case at hand. The ruling of the ECJ in *Ruiz Zambrano* gave sufficient guidance to the referring court. It made crystal clear that Mr Ruiz Zambrano had a derivative right to reside with his children and to have access to the employment market in Belgium. Second, under the preliminary reference procedure laid down in Article 267 TFEU, the ECJ operates as the court of both first and last resort. This means that the ECJ cannot benefit from the 'percolation' effect known in relation to the US federal judiciary. There are no EU Circuit Courts of Appeals that could adopt diverging approaches on an important question of EU law, after which the ECJ would settle the matter by undertaking a comparative study of the advantages and disadvantages of each approach. The preliminary reference procedure does not operate in such a way, as there are no EU lower courts that can be used as 'laboratories' until the discussion among these courts is mature enough for the ECJ to decide. Hence, in cases such as *Ruiz Zambrano*, where the ECJ is drawing the external contours of the Treaty provisions on EU citizenship, it must be sure of the steps taken, of the direction in which it goes and of the consequences of its decisions. In the procedural setting of preliminary references, judicial prudence counsels in favour of limiting the argumentative discourse of the ECJ to the questions which are really to be answered in order to solve the case at hand. A concise ruling is then preferable to one that rests on assumptions of an excessively general and abstract nature which are likely to be subsequently reconsidered in view of concrete questions raised by new cases. It would undoubtedly be more damaging to the internal legitimacy of the ECJ to send 'mixed signals' than to design an argumentative discourse that, though not as extensive as some would like it to be, appears to be sound and likely to gain momentum and strength as the case law develops.

[163] That expression is commonly used by the ECJ in the context of the Treaty provisions on free movement. See eg Case C-19/92 *Kraus* [1993] ECR I-1663, para 32.

ii The 'Stone-by-Stone' Approach

As mentioned above, the fact that the argumentative discourse in *Ruiz Zambrano* left important questions unanswered is no less and no more than a sign of judicial prudence. It is not that the ECJ decided to avoid answering difficult, complex and politically sensitive questions; on the contrary, it is simply that those questions would only be addressed when the cases at hand required it. This is actually what the ECJ did in *McCarthy* and subsequently in *Dereci*.[164]

a McCarthy: Drawing the Distinction Between the 'Impeding Effect' and the 'Deprivation Effect'

Mrs McCarthy, a dual Irish and UK national, was born and had always lived in the UK; ie, she had never exercised her right of free movement. She married a Jamaican national who lacked leave to remain in the UK in accordance with that Member State's immigration laws. In order to prevent his deportation, she and her husband applied to the Secretary of State for a residence permit and residence document under European Union law as, respectively, a Union citizen and the spouse of a Union citizen. However, their application was rejected on the grounds that Mrs McCarthy was neither economically active nor self-sufficient, as she was a recipient of state benefits. The referring court asked, in essence, whether Article 21 TFEU applied to a situation such as that of Mrs McCarthy. To this effect, the ECJ held that

> no element of the situation of Mrs McCarthy, as described by the national court, indicates that the national measure at issue in the main proceedings has the effect of *depriving* her of the genuine enjoyment of the substance of the rights [attaching to] her status as a Union citizen, or of *impeding* the exercise of her right to move and reside freely within the territory of the Member States, in accordance with Article 21 TFEU.[165]

Indeed, the failure by UK authorities to take into account Mrs McCarthy's Irish nationality had in no way affected her right to move and reside freely within the EU.

Next, the ECJ went on to distinguish the facts of the case at hand from those in *Ruiz Zambrano* and *Garcia Avello*. In contrast to *Ruiz Zambrano*, the ECJ observed that the national measure at issue in the main proceedings did not have the effect of obliging Mrs McCarthy to leave the territory of the Union.[166] As to *Garcia Avello*, the ECJ explained that what mattered in that case was not whether the discrepancy in surnames was the result of the dual nationality of the persons concerned, but the fact that that discrepancy was liable to cause serious inconvenience for the Union citizens concerned that constituted an obstacle to freedom of movement that could be justified only if it was based on

[164] See Case C-434/09 *McCarthy*, Judgment of 5 May 2011, not yet reported, and Case C-256/11 *Dereci*, Judgment of 15 November 2011, not yet reported.

[165] *McCarthy*, above n 164, para 49 (emphasis added).

[166] ibid, para 50.

objective considerations and was proportionate to the legitimate aim pursued.[167] The ECJ thereby in effect ruled that dual nationality is not in itself a sufficient connecting factor with EU law.[168]

Accordingly, the ECJ decided that the situation of a person such as Mrs McCarthy had no factor linking it with any of the situations governed by EU law and was thus confined in all relevant respects within a single Member State.

After *McCarthy*, one may argue that a combined reading of Articles 20 and 21 TFEU suggests that in order for a national measure to fall within the scope of EU law, the latter must produce either a 'deprivation effect' or an 'impeding effect'. The 'impeding effect' refers to the traditional line of case law according to which the application of the Treaty provisions on EU citizenship requires the existence of a cross-border link, not however that the national measure in question causes the loss, in practice, of the rights attaching to the status of citizen of the Union. As *Garcia Avello* shows, it suffices that the national measure at issue is liable to cause 'serious inconveniences' to a right attaching to the status of citizen of the Union. By contrast, as *Ruiz Zambrano* made clear, the 'deprivation effect' does not depend on the existence of such a link, but focuses on the rights attaching to the status of EU citizen. In other words, the 'deprivation effect' does not require a cross-border link but requires the national measure to cause more than 'serious inconveniences'. That effect requires a de facto loss of one of the rights attaching to the status of citizen of the Union.

It follows from the foregoing that the 'impeding' and 'deprivation' effect are subject to different requirements which are not, however, mutually exclusive: it is still possible for a national measure which applies in a cross-border context to cause the loss of the rights attaching to the status of EU citizen, thus producing both types of effect. Hence, the ECJ opted for a restrictive interpretation when defining a national measure capable of producing a 'deprivation effect'.

Furthermore, it is worth noting that the ECJ did not expressly refer to *Zhu and Chen*. However, that silence should not be interpreted as a sign of inconsistency. On the contrary, a close reading of *Zhu and Chen* reveals that the latter judgment is entirely consistent with *McCarthy*. The application of the national measure in question in *Zhu and Chen* would have caused a 'deprivation effect': just like the children of Mr Ruiz Zambrano, the deportation of Mrs Chen would have forced her infant child, Catherine Zhu, to leave the territory of the Union. The deportation of her mother would indeed have had 'the effect of depriving her of the genuine enjoyment of the substance of the rights attaching to her status as a Union citizen'. Hence, her Irish nationality provided a sufficient connecting factor with EU law, not because she was an Irish national living in the UK, but owing to the fact that her Irish nationality allowed her to benefit from the rights attaching to her status as an EU citizen. Accordingly, since the national measure at issue caused the de facto loss of a right attaching to her

[167] ibid, para 52 (referring to *Grunkin and Paul*, above n 80, paras 23, 24 and 29).
[168] ibid, para 54.

status as an EU citizen, namely her right to move, that measure fell within the scope of Article 21 TFEU.[169]

Moreover, it is true that in *Ruiz Zambrano*, instead of having recourse to Article 21 TFEU, the ECJ grounded the 'deprivation effect' in Article 20 TFEU. However, given that Article 21 TFEU limits itself to giving expression to a right already laid down in Article 20(2)(a) TFEU, one may argue that Article 21 TFEU also opposes a national measure which has 'the effect of depriving a Union citizen of the genuine enjoyment of the substance of [the right to move]'.[170]

b *Dereci*: The Scope of Application of Fundamental Rights

In *Ruiz Zambrano*, the referring court asked, as a third question, whether fundamental rights, in particular Articles 21, 24 and 34 of the Charter, had to be taken into account for the purposes of determining the compatibility of the national measure in question with the Treaty provisions on EU citizenship. However, since Article 20 TFEU by itself opposed that national measure, there was no need for the ECJ to answer the delicate question concerning fundamental rights. In *McCarthy*, the ECJ implicitly did not take fundamental rights into account for the purposes of determining the existence or absence of a 'deprivation effect', as the deportation of Mr McCarthy would adversely affect the private and family life of his wife. But this was not conclusive, since the ECJ clearly found that 'no element of the situation of Mrs McCarthy, as described by the national court, indicates that the national measure at issue in the main proceedings has [either a deprivation or an impeding effect]'.[171] By contrast, in *Dereci*, the ECJ considered that the time was right to address that question directly.

The facts of that case are as follows. Just as in the case of Mr Ruiz Zambrano, Mr Dereci is a third-country national (of Turkish nationality) residing illegally in a Member State of which his children are nationals, namely Austria. Just as the children of Mr Ruiz Zambrano, those of Mr Dereci are still minors and have never exercised their right to free movement. After recalling its main findings in *Ruiz Zambrano*, the ECJ clarified what is to be understood by a national measure producing a 'deprivation effect'. Such effect may only take place where 'the Union citizen has, in fact, to leave not only the territory of the Member State of which he is a national but also the territory of the Union as a whole'.[172] Consequently, the impact that the deportation of family members of an EU citizen who do not have the nationality of a Member State may have on the family life or on the economic well-being of that EU citizen 'is not sufficient in itself to support the view that [the EU] citizen [concerned] will be forced to leave [the]

[169] Today, an EU citizen in the same situation as that of Catherine Zhu would fall within the scope of Art 3(1) of Directive 2004/38, as that person, unlike Mrs McCarthy, would only have the Irish nationality. Hence, he or she would be an Irish national challenging an administrative decision adopted by UK authorities.

[170] *Ruiz Zambrano*, above n 154, para 42.

[171] *McCarthy*, above n 164, para 49.

[172] *Dereci*, above n 164, para 66.

territory [of the EU] if such a right is not granted'.[173] Put simply, fundamental rights are not taken into account for the purposes of determining the existence or absence of a 'deprivation effect'; ie they are not relevant for the purposes of determining the scope of application of the Treaty provisions on EU citizenship in situations such as those of Mr Ruiz Zambrano, Ms McCarthy or Mr Dereci. Otherwise, the ECJ would be relying on fundamental rights in order to expand the substantive scope of application of EU law beyond the competences conferred on the EU, contrary to Articles 6(1) TEU and 51(2) of the Charter. Only after having established that the national measure in question produces, in the factual circumstances of the case, a 'deprivation effect' may the restriction brought about by that measure be examined in light of the Charter, in particular Article 7 thereof. Conversely, if the national measure in question does not produce such an effect, then that measure does not fall within the substantive scope of application of EU law. This does not mean, however, that the fundamental rights of the persons concerned are deprived of any protection. As the ECJ clearly stated, in such cases, it is for the national courts and, as the case may be, for the European Court of Human Rights (ECtHR) to judicially enforce Article 8 of the European Convention on Human Rights (ECHR).[174]

c *Iida*: Purely Hypothetical Impediments to Free Movement

In the aftermath of *McCarthy* and *Dereci*, some scholars criticised the fact that the ECJ failed to take into account 'the impediments to prospective movements'.[175] They posited that the ECJ itself appears to acknowledge in paragraph 49 of the *McCarthy* judgment that the traditional line of case law applied to the situation of Mrs McCarthy. Contrary to the views of the ECJ, the deportation of Mr McCarthy was liable to 'deter' or 'dissuade' Mrs McCarthy from exercising her right of free movement. They argued, in light of *Carpenter*,[176] that as the mother of three children and the primary carer of her disabled son, Mrs McCarthy would have no prospects of exercising her right to move if her husband were deported.[177] However, those criticisms appear to be grounded in a set of facts which differ from those described by the referring court.[178] The factual

[173] ibid, para 68.

[174] ibid, paras 72 and 73.

[175] See eg N Nic Shuibhne, 'Case Note on *McCarthy* and *Dereci*' (2012) 49 *CML Rev* 349, 366 (holding that the ECJ failed to examine 'prospective movement rights').

[176] Case C-60/00 *Carpenter* [2002] ECR I-6279. See also Case C-1/05 *Jia* [2007] ECR I-1.

[177] Nic Shuibhne, above n 175, 370.

[178] According to settled case law, it is for the referring court to describe the factual scenario of the case at hand. In that regard, the ECJ has consistently held that Art 267 TFEU 'is based on a clear separation of functions between the national courts and the [ECJ], the latter is empowered only to give rulings on the interpretation or the validity of [an EU] provision on the basis of the facts which the national court puts before it'. See, inter alia, Case 104/77 *Oehlschläger* [1978] ECR 791, para 4, and Case C-435/97 *WWF and Others* [1999] ECR I-5613, para 31. Logically, this means that factual lacunas are not for the ECJ to fill. Moreover, at the hearing, parties may, if they deem it necessary, complete the factual scenario described by the referring court. Hence, D Kochenov and R Plender, 'EU Citizenship: From an Incipient Form to an Incipient Substance? The Discovery of the Treaty

scenario of the case, as described by the ECJ and the Advocate General, does not suggest that Mrs McCarthy sought to exercise her right to move. Thus, in my view, *Carpenter* is not the appropriate comparator. Of course, had the referring court stated that Mrs McCarthy envisaged to work in (or to move to) a different Member State and that Mr McCarthy would be in charge of taking care of the children in her absence, then the ECJ would have undoubtedly followed the same rationale as that endorsed in *Carpenter*. However, as mentioned above, the prospects of Mrs McCarthy exercising her right to move were not mentioned at all by the referring court. Thus, in *McCarthy*, there were no 'prospective impediments to the right to move'. Those impediments were, if anything, purely hypothetical and as such, fell outside the scope of the Treaty provisions on EU citizenship.[179] This was made clear by the ECJ in *Iida*.[180]

In that case, Mr Iida, a third-country national residing legally in Germany, sought to obtain a residence permit as the spouse and father of two EU citizens. The purpose behind such a request was to improve his immigration status as his residence permit was to expire on 2 November 2012, subsequent extension being discretionary. However, German authorities rejected his application on the ground that his spouse and daughter, two German nationals, no longer lived with him in Germany but had moved to Austria. Before determining whether the Treaty provisions on EU citizenship applied to a situation such as that of Mr Iida, the ECJ examined whether Directive 2003/109[181] and the CRD were applicable to the case at hand.

At the outset, the ECJ noted that Mr Iida was, in principle, entitled to a residence permit as provided for by Directive 2003/109.[182] However, since Mr Iida had voluntarily withdrawn his application, a residence permit could not be granted on the basis of that Directive.[183] As to the CRD, its provisions apply to 'beneficiaries' who are defined as 'all [EU] citizens who move to or reside in a Member State other than that of which they are a national, and to their family

Text' (2012) 37 *ELRev* 369, 389–90 who argue that the ECJ 'closed its eyes to the essential elements of the McCarthy family situation which were able to shed some light on what was actually going on. Three children, one of them severely disabled and in need of constant care, went unreported', are not accounting for a proper functioning of the preliminary reference procedure. In addition, even assuming that in the factual setting of the case at hand, a real issue of protecting the fundamental right to family life of the persons concerned arises, this does not automatically turn that issue into a matter of EU law. This will only be so if a substantive nexus to the latter law is present, such as the 'impeding effect' or the 'deprivation effect' of the national measure in question.

179 See S Adam and P Van Elsuwege, 'Citizenship Rights and the Federal Balance between the European Union and its Member States: Comment on Dereci' (2012) 37 *ELRev* 176, 183.

180 Case C-40/11 *Iida*, Judgment of 8 November 2012, not yet reported.

181 Council Directive 2003/109/EC concerning the status of third-country nationals who are long-term residents, [2003] OJ L16/44.

182 First, the ECJ found that none of the cases mentioned in Article 3(2) of Directive 2003/109 was applicable to the case at hand. Second, Mr Iida was a third-country national who had resided legally and continuously in Germany for five years prior to the submission of the relevant application. Third, because of his employment, he was able to provide for himself and had sickness insurance in respect of all risks normally covered in Germany. Lastly, he was not a threat to public policy or public security. See *Iida*, above n 180, paras 41 et seq.

183 ibid, para 48.

members as defined in Article 2(2) who accompany or join them'.[184] In this regard, the ECJ examined whether Mr Iida could be regarded as a 'family member' for the purposes of Article 2(2) thereof. Regarding direct relatives in the ascending line, the CRD limits the concept of 'family members' to those who are dependent on the EU citizen concerned. For Mr Iida, this meant that he could not be considered to be a family member of his daughter within the meaning of that provision, as he did not depend on her.[185] In addition, whilst qualifying as a 'family member' of his spouse, Mr Iida could not be regarded as a 'beneficiary' for the purposes of the CRD owing to the fact that 'Article 3(1) [thereof] requires that the family member of the [EU] citizen moving to or residing in a Member State other than that of which [she] is a national should accompany or join [her]'.[186] Stated simply, in order to benefit from the provisions of the CRD, Mr Iida should have moved with his wife to Austria. Thus, neither Directive 2003/109 nor the CRD was applicable to the case at hand.

Regarding the Treaty provisions on EU citizenship, the ECJ went on to examine whether the refusal to grant Mr Iida a residence permit could be liable to deny his spouse and daughter 'the genuine enjoyment of the substance of the rights associated with their status of Union citizen or to impede the exercise of their right to move and reside freely within the territory of the Member States'.[187] The ECJ replied in the negative. First, it observed that, unlike the situation of Mr Ruiz Zambrano, Mr Iida did not seek to obtain a residence permit in the Member State where his spouse and daughter lived. Second, the refusal of German authorities to grant a right of residence under EU law to Mr Iida had not discouraged his spouse or daughter from exercising their right of free movement, as the fact that they had moved from Germany to Austria demonstrates. Finally, the ECJ found that Mr Iida enjoyed a right of residence in Germany which was, prima facie, renewable and, in any event, he was entitled to a residence permit as a long-term resident within the meaning of Directive 2003/109. Most importantly, the ECJ recalled that purely hypothetical prospects of exercising the right of free movement do not fall within the scope of the Treaty provisions on EU citizenship. Accordingly, '[t]he same applies to purely hypothetical prospects of that right being obstructed'.[188]

Furthermore, *Iida* confirmed the approach developed by the ECJ in *Dereci*. The compatibility of the national legislation at issue with fundamental rights could not be examined as a matter of EU law, given that, as applied to Mr Iida, such legislation was not intended to implement a provision of EU law. Indeed, as mentioned above, neither the Treaty provisions on EU citizenship nor Directive 2003/109 nor the CRD were applicable to the case at hand.

[184] ibid, para 49.
[185] ibid, para 56.
[186] ibid, para 61.
[187] ibid, para 76 (*McCarthy*, above n 164, para 49).
[188] *Iida*, above n 180, para 77.

d *O and S:* Exploring the Notion of Dependency

O and S concerned two joined cases with a similar factual background. The facts of the first case are as follows. In 2008, Mr O, a national of Côte d'Ivoire, married Ms S, a national of Ghana, who held a residence permit and was the mother of an EU citizen of minor age from a previous marriage. In 2009, Mr O and Ms S had a child of Ghanaian nationality in respect of whom they enjoyed joint custody. Mr O applied for a residence permit in Finland on the basis of marriage. However, his application was denied by Finnish authorities on the ground that he did not have sufficient means to provide for himself. Mr O and Ms S challenged that decision before the Finnish courts.

As to the second case, Mr M and Ms L, two Algerian nationals, got married in 2006. Just like Ms S, Ms L held a residence permit and was the mother of an EU citizen of minor age from a previous marriage. In 2007, Mr M and Ms L had a child of Algerian nationality in respect of whom they enjoyed joint custody. Mr M applied for asylum, but his application was unsuccessful. As a result, he was returned to his country of origin in 2006. Ms L then applied for her spouse to be granted a residence permit in Finland on the basis of marriage. However, Finnish authorities rejected her application on the ground that Mr M did not have sufficient means to provide for himself. She then challenged that decision before the Finnish courts.

Accordingly, the referring court asked the ECJ,

> whether the [Treaty] provisions [. . .] on citizenship [. . .] must be interpreted as precluding a Member State from refusing to grant a third-country national a residence permit on the basis of family reunification where that national seeks to reside with his spouse, who is also a third-country national and resides lawfully in that Member State and is the mother of a child from a previous marriage who is a Union citizen, and with the child of their own marriage, who is also a third-country national.[189]

It follows from the foregoing that the factual scenario in *O and S* differs significantly from that in *Ruiz Zambrano*. Unlike Mr Ruiz Zambrano, neither Mr O nor Mr M was respectively the biological father of the EU citizen concerned. Nor did they have the custody of the child.

At the outset, the ECJ observed that the CRD was not applicable to the case at hand, since the EU citizens concerned, both of whom were minors, had never made use of their right of free movement and had always resided in the Member State of which they were nationals, namely Finland.[190] Next, the ECJ went on to examine whether the Treaty provisions on EU citizenship were applicable to the case at hand, ie, whether the national measure in question produced a 'deprivation effect'. In this regard, after recalling its main findings in *Ruiz Zambrano* and *Dereci*, the ECJ provided new guidance relating to the concept of 'depend-

[189] Joined Cases C-356/11 and C-357/11 *O and S*, Judgment of 6 December 2012, not yet reported, para 35.

[190] ibid, para 42.

ency', which was implicitly taken into account in those two judgments for the purposes of determining the existence (or absence) of a 'deprivation effect'. To begin with, the ECJ stated that the question whether a national measure may produce such an effect must be examined by reference to both the law and the facts of the case at hand. Given that both Ms S and Ms L held permanent residence permits in Finland, the ECJ noted that, 'in law, there [was] no obligation either for them or for the [EU] citizens dependent on them to leave the territory of that Member State or of the European Union as a whole'.[191] Regarding the facts of the case, 'it is the relationship of dependency between the [EU] citizen who is a minor and the third-country national who is refused a right of residence', the ECJ wrote, 'that is liable to jeopardise the effectiveness of [EU] citizenship, since it is that dependency that would lead to the [EU] citizen being obliged, in fact, to leave not only the territory of the Member State of which he is a national but also that of the European Union as a whole, as a consequence of such a refusal'.[192] That dependency can be of a legal, financial or emotional nature.[193] In addition, the ECJ rejected that the new approach set out in *Ruiz Zambrano* was limited to situations in which there is a blood relationship between the third-country national who seeks to obtain a residence permit and the EU citizen concerned.[194] As to the situation of Mr O and Mr M, the ECJ held, in light of the information available to it and subject to verification by the referring court, that there was no such dependency.[195] Accordingly, the Treaty provisions on EU citizenship did not preclude Finland from refusing them a residence permit.

However, the ECJ noted that Directive 2003/86 was, in principle, applicable to the case at hand.[196] As Ms S and Ms L were two third-country nationals who held residence permits in Finland, they could be recognised as 'sponsors' within the meaning of Article 2(c) of Directive 2003/86 and apply for family reunification. In this regard, the ECJ held that, subject to compliance with the conditions laid down in Chapter IV of Directive 2003/86 – notably, Article 7(1)(c) thereof which states that the sponsor is required to have stable and regular resources which are sufficient to maintain himself and the members of his family without recourse to social assistance – Finland had the 'positive obligation' to authorise Mr O and Mr M to join their spouses.[197] Whilst in implementing Article 7 (1)(c) of Directive 2003/86 Member States enjoy a 'margin of appreciation', such a margin 'must [. . .] not be used by them in a manner which would undermine the objective and the effectiveness of that [D]irective'.[198] Nor may it be exercised 'in such a manner that its application would disregard the fundamental rights set out in

[191] ibid, para 50.
[192] ibid, para 56.
[193] ibid.
[194] ibid, para 55.
[195] ibid, para 57.
[196] Council Directive 2003/86/EC on the right to family reunification, [2003] OJ L251/12.
[197] *O and S*, above n 189, para 70.
[198] ibid, para 74.

[the] provisions of the Charter',[199] notably Articles 7 and 24(2) and (3) thereof. This meant, in essence, that the Member States are required to strike a balance between the interests of the children concerned and the promotion of family life, and the margin of appreciation enjoyed by national authorities.[200]

O and S is an interesting development in the case law of the ECJ which has two direct implications for the law on EU citizenship. First, it provides further guidance as to what is to be understood by a national measure producing a 'deprivation effect'. Such a national measure must, *either in law or in fact*, force the EU citizen concerned to leave the territory of the EU as a whole. Second, unlike the national measure at issue in *Iida*, in *O and S* the refusal to grant a residence permit to Mr S and Mr M was covered by secondary EU legislation, namely by Directive 2003/86. This meant that the compatibility of those measures with fundamental rights could be examined in light of the Charter. Stated differently, a national measure which neither falls within the scope of the CRD nor produces a 'deprivation effect' but implements other EU measures must pass muster under the Charter.

iii Concluding Remarks

A joint reading of *Rottmann*, *Ruiz Zambrano*, *McCarthy*, *Dereci*, *Iida* and *O and S* shows that the legal reasoning of the ECJ is far from being laconic or cryptic. The sequence of these cases demonstrates that the new approach set out in *Ruiz Zambrano* has been built up progressively, ie, on a 'stone-by-stone' basis. Indeed, in light of *Dereci*, the new approach only operates under exceptional circumstances, namely in so far as the contested national measure forces EU citizens to leave the territory of the Union, depriving them of 'the genuine enjoyment of the substance of the rights conferred by virtue of their status as citizens of the Union'.[201]

If *Ruiz Zambrano* is examined in a vacuum, the discourse of the ECJ in that case was arguably, as Weiler suggests, too Cartesian. However, if those six cases are examined together, the same does not hold true. On the contrary, the way in which the ECJ built up its legal reasoning is rather similar to the way a common law court operates. Indeed, *Rottmann*, *Ruiz Zambrano*, *McCarthy*, *Dereci*, *Iida* and *O and S* show that 'the life of the law [on EU citizenship] has not been logic: it has been experience'.[202] At the outset, the ECJ decided not to answer all the important questions to which the new approach set out in *Ruiz Zambrano* would give rise. Instead, it preferred, for the sake of consensus and as a token of judicial prudence, to answer those questions as and when new cases arrived. The experience gained through the deliberations in *Rottmann* shed light on how to address the issues raised in *Ruiz Zambrano*, in the same way as the latter case

[199] ibid, para 77.
[200] ibid, para 80.
[201] *Ruiz Zambrano*, above n 154, para 42.
[202] OW Holmes, *The Common Law* (Massachusetts, John Harvard Library, 2009) 3.

did to address the issues raised in *McCarthy*, and then in *Dereci*, *Iida* and *O and S* and in cases to come.[203]

Moreover, the 'stone-by-stone' approach followed by the ECJ is not only the right way of building a solid edifice to the rights attaching to the status of citizen of the Union, but it is also entirely consistent with the dynamics of Article 267 TFEU. As mentioned in the previous section, the internal legitimacy of the ECJ requires the latter to honour the role played by national courts during the preliminary reference procedure. The inter-judicial dialogue that takes place under Article 267 TFEU is deeply intertwined with the way in which the ECJ builds up its argumentative discourse. Accordingly, if the ECJ were to follow a model based on 'expository justice' where it would provide exhaustive, albeit abstract, answers based on logic to the points of law raised by the questions referred, it would actually prevent national courts from engaging in a constructive dialogue. When putting forward its legal discourse, the ECJ must strike the appropriate balance between different levels of specificity and generality in its reasoning. It must not be laconic and cryptic, or too abstract, since this would deter national courts from making a reference. In essence, the preliminary reference procedure laid down in Article 267 TFEU being a mechanism of dialogue between courts, the quality of the order for reference will largely determine the drafting style of the answer given in the ECJ's ruling. The latter must indeed constitute, first and foremost, a real contribution to the solution of the case pending before the referring court. Also for this reason, it is best for the ECJ in hard cases of constitutional importance to follow an incremental approach.

III. GENERAL CONCLUSION

It is widely accepted that 'hard cases make bad law', and yet, in my view, cases which put courts at distress, such as those examined in the present contribution, provide good evidence from which one may determine whether the judiciary enjoys legitimacy. Indeed, it is in complex cases that courts often prove what they are (and are not) capable of.

First, cases such as *Vatsouras* and *Sturgeon and Others* demonstrate that, when the validity of secondary EU law is called into question, the ECJ strives to uphold the principle of separation of powers. However, this task is not an easy one as that principle is subject to internal tensions. On the one hand, the ECJ is prevented from rewriting the contested act of secondary EU law. On the other hand, the ECJ must try to avoid inter-institutional conflicts which could arise if the contested act is annulled. Hence, as a means of reconciling those two tensions, the ECJ has recourse to 'reconciliatory interpretation', according to which secondary EU legislation must be interpreted in light of primary EU law in so far as the limit of '*contra legem*' is not overstepped. However, reconciliatory interpretation, as *Test-Achats* reveals, does not take place where the challenged

[203] See eg Case C-86/12 *Alopka and Others* (pending case) and C-87/12 *Ymeraga* (pending case).

provision of an act of secondary EU law is inconsistent with the objectives pursued by that act. In such a case, in order to enhance the objectives pursued by the EU legislator, the principle of separation of powers would actually advise in favour of eliminating such inconsistencies.

Second, cases such as *Omega* and *Sayn-Wittgenstein* show that, where the core values of the Union are not in danger, the ECJ favours 'value diversity'. If, in order to protect a constitutional principle or a legitimate interest (such as public health), a Member State lays down an obstacle to free movement which establishes a higher level of protection than that of other Member States, such a Member State is not acting contrary to the principle of proportionality. However, in order to determine that the Member State is truly pursuing that objective, the ECJ will check whether the contested national measure and the national legislation as a whole are free from contradictions. In addition, as *Mesopotamia Broadcast* illustrates, when interpreting EU harmonising measures, the ECJ does take into consideration national interests. It will strive to interpret EU harmonising measures in a way that accommodates the interests pursued at both national and EU level.

Third, cases such as *Bressol* show that the ECJ is committed to respecting the jurisdiction of national courts, in the same way as the former expects the latter to respect its own. Since, in *Bressol*, the compatibility of the contested legislation depended on data that could only be provided at national level, the ECJ decided to limit itself to laying down a framework of analysis which the Belgian Constitutional Court had to apply. This allocation of judicial functions demonstrates that the preliminary reference procedure operates at its best when it follows 'comity': on the one hand, the Belgian Constitutional Court decided to engage in a dialogue with the ECJ to discuss a sensitive national matter, namely the means the French Community had at its disposal to counter the adverse impact that the exercise of free movement rights by students had on its system of higher education. On the other hand, the reply given by the ECJ must be interpreted as a sign of trust in the referring court: it was ultimately for the latter, in applying the guidelines laid down by the ECJ, to examine the compatibility of the contested legislation with EU law.

Last, but not least, in hard cases of constitutional importance, the legal reasoning of the ECJ follows a 'stone-by-stone' approach. This means that, in order to guarantee consensus and as a token of judicial prudence, the argumentative discourse of the ECJ is limited to answering the legal questions that are necessary to solve the case at hand. As a joint reading of *Rottmann*, *Ruiz Zambrano*, *McCarthy*, *Dereci*, *Iida* and *O and S* demonstrates, the incremental approach followed by the ECJ guarantees a solid and sound evolution of the case law that allows room for the national courts to engage in a constructive dialogue.

The role of the ECJ is that of a constitutional umpire operating in a multilayered system of governance. 'Saying what the law is' often amounts to a risky venture, but one that cannot be avoided if the ECJ is to secure its external and internal legitimacy in pursuing the task conferred on it in Article 19 TEU.

2

Adjudication by Reference to General Principles of EU Law: A Second Look at the Mangold *Case Law*

JÁN MAZÁK AND MARTIN K MOSER*

I. INTRODUCTION

ALLEGEDLY, WHEN MICHELANGELO was asked how he created the magnificent statue of David from a block of stone, he replied that he did not create David from the stone; rather, he saw David in the stone and merely chipped away at the unnecessary pieces until David emerged.

When the Court found in *Mangold*[1] – and subsequently reaffirmed it in *Kücükdeveci*[2] – that a prohibition of discrimination on grounds of age was encased in the general principle of equal treatment – and carved it out as a general principle of EU law which, in addition, can be invoked in private legal relationships – a considerable number of observers in legal as well as political circles made it known that they simply did not buy it: no more than David in the stone, there was no such general principle in EU law which the Court could 'recognise'. It was merely, as the criticism went, a creation, if not a fabrication, of the Court.[3]

The Court had thus conjured up again the recurrent tune of its alleged 'judicial activism', of it adjudicating ultra vires, of the poor reasoning of its decisions and of methodological shortcomings.[4]

* All opinions expressed herein are strictly personal to the authors.

[1] Case C-144/04 *Mangold v Helm* [2005] ECR I-9981.

[2] Case C-555/07 *Kücükdeveci v Swedex* [2010] ECR I-365.

[3] For an overview of the controversy surrounding that ruling, see in particular Editorial Comments: 'The Court of Justice in the Limelight – Again' (2008) 45 *CML Rev* 1571.

[4] For such allegations previously made, see eg H Rasmussen, *On Law and Policy in the European Court of Justice. A Comparative Study in Judicial Policy-Making* (Dordrecht, Martinus Nijhoff Publishers 1986); Editorial Comments: 'Quis Custodiet the European Court of Justice?' (1993) 30 *CML Rev* 899; P Neill, *The European Court of Justice: A Case Study in Judicial Activism* (London, European Policy Forum, 1995); T Tridimas, 'The Court of Justice and Judicial Activism' (1996) 21 *ELRev* 199.

Admittedly, the case law of *Mangold* – which has now become the *Mangold/Kücükdeveci* – attracted criticism from more than just the usual 'Eurosceptic' suspects in the media, academia or political domain. The critical reactions were, in fact, strikingly broad-based, and included, to mention but one, the unusually harsh comment published by the former German President and former President of the Federal Constitutional Court of Germany, Roman Herzog, and others, under the title 'Stop the European Court of Justice'.[5]

However, the *Mangold* history now also records that, in any event, the German Federal Constitutional Court eventually refused to respond to that call. Instead, in its much awaited decision of 6 July 2010 in the case of *Honeywell*, it held that the ruling of the Court in *Mangold* was not ultra vires and that it was therefore not to be declared inapplicable in Germany.[6]

Several Advocates General of the Court have also had the opportunity to comment on *Mangold*. Among them was the Advocate General in charge of the present contribution, who offered in his Opinion in *Palacios de la Villa* – it is no secret – a critical analysis of the controversial judgment.[7] The impression at that time was that, with *Mangold*, the Court in various respects had set foot on a 'very slippery slope'.[8] It is submitted here that the slope remains quite slippery now even after the Court has confirmed – and further elaborated upon – that judgment in *Kücükdeveci*.

It should be noted that the thrust of the criticism voiced[9] – and this applies certainly to the aforementioned Opinion – was generally not directed against the idea per se that there could or should be a ban on discrimination on grounds of age. Rather, the appearance that the Court deemed itself – in the legal frame-

[5] R Herzog and L Gerken, 'Stop the European Court of Justice!', published in German: 'Stoppt den Europäischen Gerichtshof!' in *Frankfurter Allgemeine Zeitung* (8 September 2008); for further criticisms and reactions, see eg M Herdegen, 'General Principles of EU Law – The Methodological Challenge' in U Bernitz, J Nergelius and C Cardner (eds), *General Principles of EC Law in a Process of Development* (The Hague, Kluwer Law International, 2008) 343; D Schiek, 'The ECJ Decision in Mangold: A Further Twist on Effects of Directives and Constitutional Relevance of Community Equality Legislation' (2006) 35 *Industrial Law Journal* 329; M de Mol, 'The Novel Approach of the CJEU on the Horizontal Direct Effect of the EU Principle of Non-Discrimination: (Unbridled) Expansionism of EU Law?' (2011) 18 *Maastricht Journal of European and Comparative Law* 109; by others, however, the ruling was welcomed: see F Fontanelli, 'General Principles of the EU and a Glimpse of Solidarity in the Aftermath of *Mangold* and *Kücükdeveci*' (2011) 17 *European Public Law* 225, 226, and the reactions summarised there in fn 4.

[6] BVerfG, Decision of 6 July 2010 in *Honeywell*, 2 BvR 2661/06.

[7] Case C-411/05 *Palacios de la Villa v Cortefiel Servicios SA* [2007] ECR I-8531, Opinion of AG Mazák, paras 87–97 and 132–38; for critical comments, advocating a restrictive reading of *Mangold*, see also AG Kokott in Case C-321/05 *Kofoed* [2007] ECR I-5795, paras 62–67; AG Geelhoed in Case C-13/05 *Chacón Navas v Eurest Colectividades* [2006] ECR I-6467, paras 46–56; AG Colomer in Cases C-55 to 56/07 *Othmar Michaeler and Others v Amt für sozialen Arbeitsschutz and Autonome Provinz Bozen* [2008] ECR I-3135, paras 14–29.

[8] Opinion of AG Mazák (n 7) para 133.

[9] For an account of the *Mangold/Kücükdeveci* discourse within the Court and in academia, see eg T Papadopoulos, 'Criticising the Horizontal Direct Effect of the EU General Principle of Equality' (2011) *European Human Rights Law Review* 437, 441–44; see also the overview provided by AG Sharpston in Case C-427/06 *Birgit Bartsch v Bosch und Siemens Hausgeräte (BSH) Altersfürsorge GmbH* [2008] ECR I-7245, paras 31–40.

work and on the basis of the reasons provided in *Mangold* – to be in a position to conclude in favour of the existence of a corresponding principle of the Union and to require its application in horizontal circumstances, was perceived by commentators, quite literally, as *a matter of principle*. This raised issues of the limits of the judicial function of the Court and the very legitimacy of its adjudication.

The stakes are indeed high, considering what the recognition by the Court of a normative content as a general principle of Union law implies. Namely, it forms, as primary law, part of the constitutional *acquis* of the Union and is, accordingly, elevated to a rank beyond the reach both of (i) the Union legislature, whose acts have to comply with the general principles of law thus recognised, and (ii) of any national legislation within the scope of EU law, over which it takes precedence according to the principle of primacy of EU law.[10] Moreover (iii), in so far as such a principle gains acknowledgment as a constitutional principle under EU law, it cannot be affected by obligations imposed by an international agreement on the Union.[11] Not least is (iv), which is a lesson to be learned from *Mangold* and *Kücükdeveci*, whereby a general principle may be directly effective in private legal relationships.[12]

The general principles of EU law therefore constitute, without doubt, a powerful judicial instrument in the hands of the Court, to be handled with care and responsibility.

The present chapter reflects on the legitimacy of the use of general principles in the jurisprudence of the Court, with particular regard to the *Mangold* and *Kücükdeveci* case law.

In a first, preliminary part (section II), we present some considerations on the standard or yardstick that we shall take as a basis for that evaluation. In the light of the critiques levelled and the issues raised in relation to the decisions of the ECJ in *Mangold* and *Kücükdeveci*, that case law shall be considered under aspects of what may be termed formal or procedural legitimacy. We shall refer, in essence, to compliance with essential postulates of the legal system as regards – in particular, the proper exercise of the judicial function and its boundaries – rather than legitimacy in the sense of substantive acceptance or sociological response.[13] Any such

[10] See, to that effect, Case C-101/08 *Audiolux SA ea v Groupe Bruxelles Lambert SA (GBL) and Others* and *Bertelsmann AG and Others* [2009] ECR I-9823, para 63; Case C-174/08 *NCC Construction Danmark A/S v Skatteministeriet* [2009] ECR I-10567, paras 42–45. See also T Tridimas, *The General Principles of EU Law*, 2nd edn (Oxford, Oxford University Press, 2006) 50 ff.

[11] See, to that effect, Joined Cases C-402/05 P and C-415/05 P *Kadi and Al Barakaat International Foundation v Council and Commission* [2008] ECR I-6351, paras 282 and 316.

[12] See *Mangold* (n 1) para 77 and *Kücükdeveci* (n 2) para 51.

[13] The former being, however, largely determinative of perceptions in the latter sense. For such a distinction between formal and social legitimacy, see eg S Weatherill, 'Competence and Legitimacy' in C Barnard and O Odudu (eds), *The Outer Limits of European Union Law* (Oxford, Hart Publishing, 2009) 18. There are, however, numerous other, partly overlapping concepts of legitimacy: see the contribution of Koen Lenaerts in this book, referring to internal and external legitimacy, and eg N Huls, 'Introduction: From Legitimacy to Leadership' in N Huls, M Adams and J Bomhoff (eds), *The Legitimacy of Highest Courts' Rulings: Judicial Deliberations and Beyond* (The Hague, TMC Asser Press, 2009) 13 ff; G Conway, *The Limits of Legal Reasoning and the European Court of Justice* (Cambridge, Cambridge University Press, 2012) 94 ff.

evaluation of the legitimacy or 'correctness' of the jurisprudence of the Court – in the absence of a single and universally accepted view about the nature of law, the permitted methods of finding it and, consequently, about the proper exercise of the judicial function – faces the problem of identifying a firm, objective viewpoint from which such an examination could be conducted. It can, in fact, never entirely escape the epistemological dilemma echoed by the notorious '*Quis custodiet custodes?*'.

Subject to that caveat, in the next step we will consider the nature and foundations of the general principles in Union law. To that end, we will briefly place this legal source within the idea of the law and the interpretative paradigms on which the adjudication of the Court, designated by EU law itself as its final arbitrator, appears to be premised (section III). This part is therefore about the contours of the legal context or, linguistically speaking, the 'language game'. Here, the Court has recourse to general principles of law and cannot be disregarded when the justification of the use of general principles in concrete cases is examined. Against that background, we will turn – or, rather, return – to *Mangold* and *Kücükdeveci* and evaluate the approach of the Court and its possible implications (sections IV, V and VI).

II. GETTING TO THE (ARCHIMEDEAN) POINT

The judiciary interprets and applies, but does not make the law; law-making is the domain of a democratically legitimised legislator and the result of a political discourse. Judges translate and integrate the will of the legislator thus expressed in the laws into their case law; thereby, they partake in the chain of democratic legitimation and assert the rule of law rather than their own rule – the infamous '*gouvernement des juges*'.

As widely as those basic propositions about the judicial function and its limits (in any event at that level of generality) may be shared and their observance be legitimately expected, closer inspection in the realm of law reveals the difficulty in identifying an Archimedean point from which an observer could judge, as the title of this book suggests, the judges and their adjudicative performance, in this case of the ECJ.

The role of the Court – as with any court – is intrinsically linked to and defined by the law it must enforce. Accordingly, only by reference to a concept of law can it be determined whether the law was properly interpreted and applied, or whether, conversely, the Court exceeded the limits of the law and of its judicial power.[14] The wider the notion of the law applied, the smaller appear

[14] The notion of law as the decisive premise is also emphasised by Koen Lenaerts in the opening chapter; see also K Lenaerts, 'Some Thoughts about the Interaction between Judges and Politicians in the European Community' (1992) 12 *YEL* 1, 1–3. It is for the very reason that the point regularly remains unconsidered that allegations of 'judicial activism' or, conversely, 'judicial restraint' can – in the absence of a point of reference defining 'normal' judicial activity – be considered as little

legislative lacunae and the further away are shifted the borders to the domains of legislation or politics which a court is supposed not to cross.

There is, however, no litmus test to be administered or microscope to be looked through in order to establish objectively 'what the law is', or more specifically, to verify which interpretation of a legal rule would be legally 'right'. That legal provisions may generally be so determinate as to warrant – as the result of the application of proper interpretative methods – a single, correct interpretation, or that a sharp line could be drawn between interpretation and application of the law on the one hand and judicial law-making on the other, may rather be ascribed to the realm of urban legends of the legal community.[15]

A more realistic view – especially from a legal practitioner's experience – is that interpretation 'always involves a process of understanding which, as such, cannot be turned into a mathematical formula – this is particularly true of [Union] law, with its many variables of interpretation, which themselves include the dynamic evolution of that system of law'.[16] This lies in the nature of law 'which is intrinsically bound by the possibilities of linguistic expression and is therefore as imprecise and imperfect as language itself'.[17]

Accordingly, we have to start from the premise that interpretation and application of the law generally entails, to a greater or lesser extent, the exercise of discretion and an element of creativity.[18] What constitutes the 'correct' interpretation of the law is therefore ultimately only determined – one should add, not merely as a result of a process of cognition but constitutively – by the decision of the court authorised to that effect under the legal system concerned. This, a fortiori, is true in respect of the legal source of the general principles of law, which are not only marked by uncertainty as to their precise normative content, but also as to their very existence.[19]

more than subjective impressions of the beholder: to that effect, inter alia, P Pescatore, 'Jusqu'où le juge peut-il aller trop loin?' in K Thorup and J Rosenlov (eds), *Festskrift till Ole Due* (Copenhagen, GEC Gads Forlag, 1994) 301–02.

[15] To that effect, see H Kelsen, *Reine Rechtslehre. Einleitung in die rechtwissenschaftliche Problematik* (Leipzig-Wien, Franz Deuticke Verlag, 1934) 82–83; see also eg A von Bogdandy and I Venzke, 'Beyond Dispute: International Judicial Institutions as Lawmakers' (2011) 12 *German Law Journal* 979, 983–85; G della Cananea, '*Reaction* – Themis and Dike in the International Arena: Comments on von Bogdandy's and Venzke's 'Democratic Legitimation of International Judicial Lawmaking'' (2011) 12 *German Law Journal* 2059, 2064–67.

[16] AG Stix-Hackl in Case C-495/03 *Intermodal Transports BV v Staatssecretaris van Financiën* [2005] ECR I-8151, para 101 (fns omitted), reflecting on the *CILFIT*-doctrine.

[17] ibid, fn 57; continuing as follows: 'A legal finding is by definition not an "objective finding" in a scientific sense (although, even in a scientific context, that term must be used with caution). Case law is therefore hardly ever a matter of findings alone or a mechanical process of categorisation but also involves an element of decision-making, a fact, moreover, which is very neatly expressed in the judicial formula "hat für Recht erkannt"/ "dit pour droit"'.

[18] See, to that effect, also ECtHR, *SW v United Kingdom* (1995) Series A no 335-B, para 36; von Bogdandy and Venzke, 'Beyond Dispute' (n 15) 985–86. On discretion in the adjudication of the ECJ, see generally J Bengoetxea, 'The Scope for Discretion, Coherence and Citizenship' in O Wiklund (ed), *Judicial Discretion in European Perspective* (The Hague, Kluwer Law International, 2003) 48–74.

[19] *cf* Opinion of AG Mazák (n 7) para 86.

Famously, in the Union legal order, the task of defining the law is entrusted by Article 19 TEU to the ECJ. This Article includes the power to adjudicate on the horizontal and vertical allocation of powers under the Treaties and, thereby, on the limits to its own judicial competence, such as those imposed on it by the principle of conferred powers under Article 5(1) TEU. In this sense, the Court indeed is, qua law, *iudex in re sua*.

That being said, wherever the Court locates the outer borders of EU law and the limits to its judicial function in its adjudication – or where those limits should lie from an external observer's point of view[20] – it is required and of central legitimatory significance that its judicial decisions, in any event, are adequately justified. The question of legitimacy of the case law of the Court shall thus, for present purposes, principally be approached through the prism of the quality and soundness – and, consequently, of the persuasiveness – of the judicial reasoning.[21]

In that regard, it is assumed that judicial decisions should be motivated in a way that they can be perceived as resulting from a proper judicial decision-making process. This therefore – in contrast to policymaking or law-making by the legislature – is guided and bound by an adequate judicial methodology of finding the law. In particular, the reasoning should show those decisions to be rooted in the law which the Court is called upon to apply – in the case of the ECJ, this is in EU law as it is laid down or, in any event, implied in the Treaties.

From a more formal viewpoint, it is of central importance that the argumentation advanced by the Court to that end is coherent. This is necessary both within the individual judgment, and in a wider sense, in view of its case law as a whole and the fundamental premises underlying that jurisprudence about the Union legal order and the allocation of powers it provides.[22]

These requirements in fact are related to a more general requirement lying at the core of the idea of the rule of law which the Court is to uphold: namely, that its adjudication conveys legal certainty. This presupposes, in particular, that the law is judicially interpreted and applied in a way that its meaning, at least in its

[20] On this problematic, see eg C Barnard and O Odudu, 'Outer Limits of European Union Law: Introduction' in C Barnard and O Odudu (eds), *The Outer Limits of European Union Law* (Oxford, Hart Publishing, 2009) 3 f, and the sources cited there in fn 11.

[21] Also in the Opinion in *Palacios de la Villa*, *Mangold* was considered in view of the soundness and conclusiveness of the reasoning on which the Court based its findings (Opinion of AG Mazák (n 7), expressly at para 87). In favour of a legal reasoning approach, see eg J Bengoetxea, N MacCormick and LM Soriano, 'Integration and Integrity in the Legal Reasoning of the European Court of Justice' in G de Búrca and JHH Weiler (eds), *The European Court of Justice* (Oxford, Oxford University Press, 2001) 44 ff; A von Bogdandy and I Venzke, 'On the Democratic Legitimation of International Judicial Lawmaking' (2011) 12 *German Law Journal* 1341, 1344; see also generally Conway (n 13).

[22] See Bengoetxea, MacCormick and Soriano (n 21) 47; O Wiklund, 'Taking the World View of the European Judge Seriously – Some Reflections on the Role of Ideology in Adjudication' in O Wiklund (ed), *Judicial Discretion in European Perspective* (The Hague, Kluwer Law International, 2003) 41–44.

essential contours, remains reasonably predictable to participants in the legal interpretative community.[23]

III. THE GENERAL PRINCIPLES OF EU LAW AS RESULT AND SOURCE OF INTERPRETATION

In the beginning of the general principles of EU law, the earth was without form and void; there was a Treaty in the form of a *traité cadre*, marked by regulatory gaps and substantive vagueness, providing for no more than a framework for a novel and unprecedented legal order.[24]

Certainly, one could just have left it at that, as emptiness does not automatically warrant creation. The Court could have decided to declare a '*non liquet*' every time no express provision could be identified in the Treaties or in secondary legislation which would be applicable to the case before it.

Yet, that was obviously not the vision of its role that the Court embraced. It was already making a decision of principle early in its history when it was asked to adjudicate in *Anomar* on a problem of the revocability of administrative measures for the solution of which the Treaty contained no rules. On the proposal of AG Lagrange, the Court deemed it not only within its judicial powers to decide such cases by reference to general principles, but viewed it as being part of its obligation to provide justice, endowed on it by the authors of the Treaty.[25]

Indeed, by what has now become Article 19 TEU, they had entrusted the Court in a more comprehensive fashion. Its task was to ensure the observance of 'the law' in the interpretation and application of 'the Treaty', implying that the law is expressed in – but in its whole dimension lies behind – the Treaty provisions. Beyond that, it was left to the Court to determine the nature and sources of the law and to spell it out so as to guarantee its rule.[26]

The judicial completion of what is fragmentary in the constituent treaties corresponds and is consequential to a first and essential perception about the nature of EU law to be ascribed to the Court. As David Edward rightly emphasised, it

[23] See Conway (n 13) 5 and 94 ff. Out of the abundant case law of the ECJ on the requirements of legal certainty see, in this context, eg Case 26/69 *Commission v France* [1970] ECR 565, paras 28 and 31; Case 169/80 *Administration des douanes v Société anonyme Gondrand Frères and Société anonyme Garancini* [1981] ECR 1931, para17; Case C-63/93 *Fintan Duff and Others v Minister for Agriculture and Food and Attorney General* [1996] ECR I-569, para 20; Joined Cases C-189/02 P, C-202/02 P, C-205/02 P to C-208/02 P and C-213/02 P *Dansk Rørindustri A/S and Others* [2005] ECR I-5425, paras 218–21; see also the case law of the ECtHR, in particular *SW v United Kingdom* (n 18) paras 35 and 36; *Chapman v United Kingdom*, No 27238/95 ECHR 2001 I, para 70.

[24] Famously noted to that effect by T Tridimas, *The General Principles of EU Law*, 2nd edn (n 10) 18.

[25] Joined Cases 7/56 and 3/57 to7/57 *Algera and Others v Common Assembly* [1957] ECR 39, 55; and the Opinion of AG Lagrange in that case.

[26] *cf* on Art 220 EC (now Art 19 TEU) Tridimas, *The General Principles of EU Law*, 2nd edn (n 10) 19 f; Herdegen (n 5) 344.

constitutes 'a system of law and not just an *ad hoc* collection of rules and diplomatic compromises written down in the treaties'.[27]

The Treaties are thus read and construed under a postulate of coherence, assuming that they are constitutive of a real 'legal order'. The regulatory components disclose their true sense only as part and in view of the whole. That perception – or conception – of the Treaties as embodying a system of law, accordingly, is reflected in the systematic and purpose-oriented interpretative methodology adopted by the Court.[28]

As a consequence, lacunae in the Treaties see themselves narrowed down or in fact transformed from judicial no man's land into resonance chambers where the *ratio contractus* can resound. There, the judge can give a voice to the underlying normative or interpretive premises on which he finds the EU legal order to be based.

Those premises add up today to a whole cascade of normative *topoi* at different levels of generality which inform the interpretation of EU provisions by the Court. This includes, for example, the assumption that EU law is constitutive of an autonomous legal order which is based on the rule of law. It is characterised by primacy and direct effect; or the requirements of effectiveness of EU law – seen both as a whole and as regards the interpretation of individual rules (*effet utile*) – and of its uniform application.[29]

For the very reason that they represent an unwritten, judge-made source of law 'to be sought rather in the Platonic heaven of law than in the law books',[30] the general principles have become the instrument of choice for the Court to introduce and spell out – structurally or substantively – normative standards into and within the EU legal order and to fill gaps left by the Treaties.

In that regard, it is clear from cases like *Brasserie* that the Court views the finding of the law by reference to the fundamental principles of the EU legal system and, where necessary, general principles of the Member States, as belonging to the canon of 'generally accepted methods of interpretation'.[31] It therefore places this method at the heart of the natural powers and tasks of the judiciary.

In order for general principles to be legitimately considered as part of the law, when they are so-to-speak 'made' by the judge, they must remain linked to and

[27] D Edward, 'The Role and Relevance of the Civil Law Tradition in the Work of the European Court of Justice' in D Miller and R Zimmermann (eds), *The Civilian Tradition and Scots Law* (Berlin, Duncker & Humblot, 1997) 316.

[28] See Case C-283/81 *CILFIT v Ministry of Health* [1982] ECR 3415, para 20: 'Every provision of [EU] law must be placed in its context and interpreted in the light of the provisions of [EU] law as a whole, regard being had to the objectives thereof and to its state of evolution at the date on which the provision in question is to be applied'.

[29] All of those aspects and principles thus form the relevant legal context of the interpretation of EU law through the Court, which cannot be excluded when it comes to the question as to whether a principle or rule can indeed be considered as being 'inherent' in the Treaty. When duly taking account of that context, what may appear first as an act of judicial transgression, may well turn out to be sufficiently coupled back to the law and thus inscribed within proper adjudication.

[30] Opinion of AG Mazák (n 7) para 86.

[31] Cases C-46 and C-48/93 *Brasserie du Pêcheur SA v Germany* [1996] ECR I-1029, para 26.

founded in the legal order. Thus, in the case of general principles of Union law, the Court seeks to extract their normative content from the legislative choices contained and expressed in the provisions – or, in any event, the general scheme and spirit – of EU law itself[32] or from those reflected in the laws of the Member States, including instruments of international law to which they adhere.[33] However, the necessary process of induction or deduction, or – as it is commonly labelled in the latter case of principles inspired by the laws of the Member States – the 'evaluative approach' of the Court, in no way amounts to exact mathematics. It again involves an act of judicial law-creation, whereby the Union judge in fact seeks to find a solution which she or he deems to fit best into the specific features and objectives of the EU legal system.[34]

The resulting normative creatures are not sufficiently straightforward to characterise in respect to both their nature and their function.

Indeed, it appears almost obvious to ascribe a 'general, comprehensive character' to general principles of law.[35] Nevertheless, it needs to be added that generality here should be understood as referring to the overarching importance and pertinence, which is – owing to the fact that they express fundamental structures and values underpinning the legal order as a whole and, accordingly, transgress the interest of specific situations – inherent in general principles, rather than to generality or lack of specificity as to their normative content.

In that regard, the concept of a general principle of EU law as a legal source does not necessarily overlap with the commonly known rule/principle divide, where rules apply in an all-or-nothing fashion and allow for syllogistic reasoning, whereas principles are to be weighed against each other and do not as such dictate a specific legal outcome.[36] In fact, as a legal source or type of norm, general principles of EU law, in terms of their normative substance, can occur both either as a fully-fledged legal rule or as a mere principle in the aforementioned sense.[37]

There are plenty of examples of the rule-type general principles in EU law. We can think only of the many detailed and well defined administrative principles

[32] That method is illustrated, even if the existence of the general principle of equal treatment of minority shareholders alleged in that case was denied, by *Audiolux and Others* and *Bertelsmann AG and Others* (n 10) paras 32–52.

[33] See, for the most prominent example, the protection of fundamental rights as general principles of Union law, for which purpose 'the Court draws inspiration from the constitutional traditions common to the Member States and from the guidelines supplied by international instruments for the protection of human rights on which the Member States have collaborated or to which they are signatories. In that regard, the ECHR has special significance': eg, *Kadi and Al Barakaat* (n 11) para 283 and Case C-274/99 P *Connolly v Commission* [2001] ECR I-1611, para 37. The formula is in essence retained in Art 6(3) TEU.

[34] See, on that method, eg AG Maduro in Joined Cases C-120/06 P and C-121/06 P *Fabbrica Italiana Accumulatori Motocarri Montecchio SpA (FIAMM) and Others* [2008] ECR I-6513, para 55; Herdegen (n 5) 345.

[35] *Audiolux* (n 10) para 42.

[36] See eg R Dworkin, *Taking Rights Seriously* (Cambridge, Mass, Harvard University Press, 1977) 22 and 72.

[37] To that effect, see also Opinion of AG Mazák (n 7) para 134.

governing the proceedings before institutions of the Union or the fundamental rights recognised as general principles of Union law on the basis of the European Convention on Human Rights, as interpreted by the European Court of Human Rights (ECtHR).[38]

On the other hand, there are also instances in the case law where general principles of EU law are indeed used in the narrower sense of principles, giving weight or direction rather than indicating, as such, the solution to a legal issue. *Omega* provides a good example in that, in this case, the mere reference to the respect for human dignity as a general principle of EU law – without further specifying what human dignity may normatively entail or require – was in itself sufficient in order to qualify the protection of human dignity as understood under German national law as a legitimate objective in accordance with EU law.[39] Similarly, in the more recent judgment of the Court in *Brüstle*, the principle of respect for human dignity, referred to also by Directive 98/44/EC of the European Parliament and of the Council of 6 July 1998 on the legal protection of biotechnological inventions at issue,[40] had in the Court's reasoning the decisive effect of supporting a wide interpretation of the concept of 'human embryo' within the meaning of that Directive.[41]

That being said, although general principles of law may embody specific legal rules, it follows from their non-written, praetorian nature that they are, as has already been noted,[42] inherently marked by uncertainty. They exist somewhere between the *lex lata* and the *lex ferenda*[43] and until the judiciary has actually defined their contours, 'discussing the concrete content of such a principle can be very much like discussing the shape of a ghost'.[44]

This explains why their application is often accompanied – as in *Mangold* and *Kücükdeveci* – by concerns relating to legal certainty and of the limits of adjudication. For those reasons, at least in the continental legal tradition, adjudication by recourse to general principles of law has usually a somewhat subsidiary character in relation to the application of express legislation, in that it normally comes into play in the absence of such legislation.[45]

The gap, the lacuna, therefore is, so to speak, the 'natural habitat' of general principles of law, and – as we have seen[46] – in the history of the jurisprudence of

[38] eg Joined Cases C-465/00, C-138/01 and C-139/01 *Rechnungshof v Österreichischer Rundfunk and Others* [2003] ECR I-12489, paras 71–90 (right to privacy).

[39] See Case C-36/02 *Omega Spielhallen* [2004] ECR I-9609, paras 34–35.

[40] [1998] OJ L213/13.

[41] See Case C-34/10 *Brüstle v Greenpeace*, Judgment of 18 October 2011, paras 30–34.

[42] See n 19 above.

[43] To that effect, see R Kolb, 'Principles as Sources of International Law' (2006) 53 *Netherlands Intl L Rev* 1, 9.

[44] Opinion of AG Mazák in Case C-47/07 P *Masdar (UK) Ltd v Commission* [2008] ECR I-9761, para 45.

[45] For an overview in that regard, see RG Bono, 'The Development of General Principles of Law at National and Community Level: Achieving a Balance' in R Schulze and U Seif (eds), *Richterrecht und Rechtsfortbildung in der europäischen Rechtsgemeinschaft* (Tübingen, Mohr Siebeck, 2003) 99–101.

[46] See n 25 above.

the Court, the filling of normative gaps, accordingly, is not only the first, but arguably the most natural function of such principles.

The function of general principles of EU law, however, does not stop with gap filling. Once such a general principle has seen the light of the Union legal order, it unfolds its normative force and participates in the transformation of that order, which it starts to shape in its own image.

Legally speaking, this happens in the first place through the obligation of consistent interpretation, whereby both EU law and, within its scope, national law must be interpreted in the light of the general principles of EU law. In the second place, it occurs because general principles have the force and rank of primary EU law,[47] in that they prohibit – EU and national – legislation in the sphere of Union law, to the extent that it is not possible to give such legislation a meaning in conformity with what those principles require.[48]

It is in those functions that the general principles of EU law unveil their fundamental and – as the Court has confirmed in *Audiolux* and *NCC Construction Danmark* – constitutional nature.[49] They constitute, in fact and – as Article 2 TEU suggests – in law, truly constitutional values. Through consistent interpretation and primacy, these values give direction to the innumerable rules and provisions of EU law. In this way, ideally, the narrative of a Union based on the rule of law, fundamental rights, equality etc is continued and unfolded whenever a provision of Union law is to be applied.[50]

In sum, therefore, the general principles of EU law are, and have been, like vehicles at the heart of what can be termed an auto-poetic or self-creational mechanism of legal integration through adjudication. The normative legal ideas and values underpinning the EU legal order as a whole are, by the EU judiciary, translated and crystallised into general principles of EU law which, in turn, inform and determine the interpretation and application of that legal order and of all its normative components.

The question of legitimacy can, of course, already be raised at this fundamental level: does the Court in any way have a mandate to develop EU law on the basis of general principles of law in that way and is that role still within what can be seen as its legitimate judicial powers under the Treaties?

It is submitted that the answer must decidedly be in the affirmative. It appears that such judicial powers are, generally, also conceded to it by the constitutional courts of the Member States.[51] After all, the recognition of general principles of law, in one form or another, is also not uncommon in national legal orders. As

[47] See in more detail already, nn 10 to 12 above.

[48] As to the functions of general principles of EU law, see eg Tridimas, *The General Principles of EU Law*, 2nd edn (n 10) 29–35; see also AG Sharpston (n 9) para 69.

[49] See *Audiolux* (n 10) para 63 and *NCC Construction Danmark* (n 10) para 42.

[50] As to the role of general principles as legal values and catalysts of integration through case law, see generally MK Moser, 'Allgemeine Rechtsgrundsätze in der Rechtsprechung des EuGH als Katalysatoren einer europäischen Wertegemeinschaft' (2012) 1 *ZfRV* 4.

[51] Such as, eg the German Federal Constitutional Court: see eg its decision *Honeywell* (n 6) paras 62–63.

far as EU law is concerned, the Treaties explicitly refer to and endorse this legal source at individual junctures (see Article 6(3) TEU as well as Article 340(2) and (3) TFEU). Moreover, as we have noted, under Article 19 TEU, the Court has been charged broadly with the task of ensuring the observance of the 'law'. The broad wording of Article 263(2) TFEU, including 'infringement of the Treaties or any rule of law relating their application' in the grounds of review, also opens to or even warrants an interpretation whereby the ECJ is empowered to fashion a system of general principles.

In any event, from a pragmatic point of view, in the absence of general principles in the jurisprudence of the Court, EU law would probably have remained – if we think only of the initial absence of a fundamental rights regime in the Treaties – less than an emperor without clothes; namely, 'a mere skeleton of rules, not quite constituting a proper legal "order"'.[52] Such an '*acquis*' arguably would indeed be at odds with the mission by which the Court finds itself bound, to secure observance of a particular legal order and to foster its development with a view to achieving the objectives set out in the Treaties.[53]

The devil lies rather, if at all, in the details and we shall now turn to those of *Mangold* and *Kücükdeveci*.

IV. GENERAL APPROACH OF THE COURT IN *MANGOLD* AND *KÜCÜKDEVECI*

As appears already from the introductory section above, the rulings in *Mangold* and *Kücükdeveci* have essentially two salient features in which some see the 'original sin' of this case law: first is the acknowledgment of the existence of a principle of non-discrimination on grounds of age; second is the conferral on the principle of direct effect in the sense that any contrary national legislation has to be set aside, even in proceedings between private parties.

The facts of those cases need not be recalled in detail for present purposes, but we shall sketch out the essence or general structure of the reasoning of the Court. This will allow greater scrutiny, in the subsequent part, of that reasoning with respect to the aforementioned aspects. A final assessment should then look at the sum of the parts and ask for the further implications of that case law.

It might be recalled that, in *Mangold*, the Court was asked to rule in particular on the issue as to whether Council Directive 2000/78/EC of 27 November 2000 – which established a general framework for equal treatment in employment and occupation[54] and which provided a prohibition of discrimination, inter alia, on grounds of age – precluded a provision of German employment law which allowed workers over the age of 52 to be employed on fixed-term contracts with no restrictions, even where there was no objective reason for this

[52] Opinion of AG Mazák (n 7) para 85.
[53] See Opinion 1/91 of the Court of 14 December 1991, ECR I-6079, para 50.
[54] [2000] OJ L303/16.

fixed-term nature By contrast, under domestic law, such contracts – that is, in respect of workers under the age of 52 – could generally be concluded only if there was an objective justification.

Two factors in the circumstances of the case must be considered as largely determinative of the path the Court would embark on in deciding *Mangold* and thereby establish it as a landmark judgment. First, the issue of the compatibility with the directive at hand was raised in proceedings between private parties – Mr Mangold as employer and Mr Helm as employee – concerning a fixed-term contract of employment, thus in a horizontal legal relationship. Second, although Directive 2000/78 was to be implemented by 2003, under its Article 18(2) Member States were allowed a further three years to do so as far as, inter alia, age was concerned. This meant that, since Germany had made use of this option, the deadline for transposition of the relevant part of the directive had not yet passed at the material time in *Mangold*.

Against that background, in so far as both Advocate General Tizzano[55] and the Court concluded that the terms of Directive 2000/78 indeed were contrary to a national provision as that at issue in *Mangold*, the problematic of the legal consequences to be drawn regarding that finding in the main proceedings and, more generally, the applicability of the directive, was imminent with a view to settled case law of the Court. According to the case law, a directive may – on condition, however, that the deadline for its transposition has passed – be relied on by individuals before national courts as against the state (vertical direct effect)[56] but cannot as such be relied on against an individual in order to have national legislation conflicting with it set aside (horizontal direct effect).[57]

The Advocate General suggested that the Court surmount those obstacles by using, instead of Directive 2000/78, the general principle of equality as its yardstick of interpretation. He argued that it imposed essentially similar requirements as the directive and could, unlike the latter, also be relied on against other private parties with a view to having a national rule disapplied by the national court.[58]

The Court, for its part, in essence embraced the idea to solve the case by reference to general principles of EU law, but in the final analysis took a different, more far-reaching route than that suggested by its Advocate General.

In the first place, with a view to the fact that the period prescribed for transposition into domestic law of Directive 2000/78 had not yet expired, the Court based itself on the *Inter-Environnement Wallonie* case law, pursuant to which Member States, during the period laid down for the transposition of a directive, must refrain from adopting measures liable seriously to compromise the result

[55] *Mangold* (n 1), Opinion of AG Tizzano.

[56] See, inter alia, Case 148/78 *Ratti* [1979] 1629, para 22; Case C-343/98 *Collino and Chiappero* [2000] ECR I-6659, para 22.

[57] See, inter alia, Case C-152/84 *Marshall* [1986] ECR 723, para 48; Joined Cases C-397/01 to C-403/01 *Pfeiffer and Others* [2004] ECR I-8835, para 108. The authors are, however, aware of the diversity of terminological and conceptual approaches to the notion of direct effect.

[58] See Opinion of AG Tizzano (n 55) paras 84 and 101.

prescribed by that directive.[59] That reference, however, in the context of the case in so far, remained somewhat obscure as, according to that case law, national law may, prior to the exhaustion of the time-limit for transposing a directive, have to be interpreted in conformity with it, but can equally not be displaced by the directive in horizontal situations.[60] *Inter-Environnement Wallonie*, in any event, could therefore not serve to support the answer given by the Court in *Mangold* to the effect that the conflicting provision of national law was to be set aside.

That being said, 'in the second place and above all', the Court pointed out that Directive 2000/78 'does not itself lay down the principle of equal treatment in the field of employment and occupation' and acknowledged in this context quite swiftly – we shall return to that reasoning in the following section – the existence of a principle of non-discrimination on grounds of age which must be regarded as a general principle of EU law.[61]

The Court then applied its judgment in *Simmenthal*[62] in order to conclude that it was the responsibility of the national court to guarantee the full effectiveness of the general principle of non-discrimination in respect of age, setting aside any provision of national law which may conflict with EU law 'even where the period prescribed for transposition of that directive has not yet expired'.[63]

It should be noted that it was this ambiguous reference to both Directive 2000/78 and the corresponding general principle of EU law – within this answer to the third question, but also in relation to the answer to the second question – which left some observers wondering which of those sources actually prompted the Court to decide to the effect of an obligation to disapply the national provision at issue; that is, whether it has abandoned its previous stance on the non-horizontal direct effect of directives.[64]

That very issue was consequently also at the heart of the questions referred in *Kücükdeveci*,[65] by which *Mangold* was given – after several years of relative silence; some may even say avoidance as regards *Mangold* in its case law – a full revival by the Court.

Kücükdeveci concerned a provision under the German BGB according to which – for purposes of calculating the statutory notice period which depended on the length of the employment – periods prior to the completion of the employee's twenty-fifth year of age were not taken into account. Again, in the context of a horizontal employment relationship – but this time after the period prescribed for transposition of Directive 2000/78 had expired – the national

[59] Case C-129/96 *Inter-Environnement Wallonie* [1997] ECR I-7411, para 45; see *Mangold* (n 1) paras 67–72.

[60] See in particular Case C-157/02 *Rieser Internationale Transporte GmbH v Autobahnen- und Schnellstraßen-Finanzierungs- AG (ASFINAG)* [2004] ECR I-1477, paras 66–67.

[61] See, to that effect, *Mangold* (n 1) paras 74 and 75.

[62] Case 106/77 *Simmenthal* [1978] ECR 629, para 21.

[63] See, to that effect, *Mangold* (n 1) paras 77 and 78.

[64] *cf* in this context also, Opinion of AG Mazák (n 7) paras 130 and 131.

[65] *Kücükdeveci* (n 2).

court enquired into the compatibility of that national rule with the prohibition of discrimination on grounds of age and wished to know to that effect, in particular, whether the relevant yardstick in this context was primary EU law – thus the general principle of EU law acknowledged in *Mangold* – or Directive 2000/78.

In answering, the Court essentially reaffirmed *Mangold* – with a few refinements and additions – both in respect of the existence of a principle of non-discrimination on grounds of age, which must be regarded as a general principle of EU law, and as regards the obligation imposed on the national court, when hearing a dispute between private parties, of disapplying, if need be, any provision of national law contrary to that principle.[66]

However, the Court did not respond to the call of Advocate General Bot 'to take a more ambitious approach' and to 'accept that a directive intended to counteract discrimination may be relied on in proceedings between private parties in order to set aside the application of national rules which are contrary to the directive'.[67] Instead, the Court confirmed its case law prohibiting the horizontal direct effect of directives and made it clear that the relevant legal source of EU law – by reference to which the question of the compatibility of the national rule at issue was to be examined and to which the direct effect was owed – was the general principle of EU law, not Directive 2000/78 itself.[68]

Interestingly, however, apparently inspired on that point by the suggestion of the Advocate General to the effect that Directive 2000/78 should be used as a substantive yardstick in the examination of the disputed national provision, while the direct legal effect should be produced (or co-produced) by the correlated general principle of EU law,[69] the Court seemed to make a virtue of the ambiguous co-reference to the directive alongside the general principle in *Mangold* and set out to refer throughout its reasoning in *Kücükdeveci* to 'the general principle of European Union law prohibiting all discrimination on grounds of age, as given expression in Directive 2000/78'.[70]

Finally, the Court stated in its reasoning that, in order for that principle to be applicable, the case concerned must fall within the scope of Union law and held that it was Directive 2000/78 itself which had the effect of bringing the national legislation at issue within that scope, as that legislation concerned a matter governed by the directive. In that regard, it distinguished the situation from that

[66] See *Kücükdeveci* (n 2) paras 20–22 and 50–51; a further question was whether the national court was required to make a reference to the Court for a preliminary ruling before it is able to disapply a national provision, which the Court answered in the negative.

[67] *Kücükdeveci* (n 2), Opinion of AG Bot, para 70.

[68] See in particular paras 27 and 56 of the judgment; see more recently Case C-282/10 *Dominguez*, Judgment of 12 January 2012, para 37; to that effect also E Muir, 'Of Ages in – and Edges of – EU Law' (2011) 48 *CML Rev* 39, 53. There appear, though, still to be divergent readings of the *Mangold* case law on that point: see only E Howard, 'ECJ Advances Equality in Europe by Giving Horizontal Direct Effect to Directives' (2011) 4 *European Public Law* 729, 736.

[69] See, to that effect, Opinion of AG Bot (n 67) paras 29–34.

[70] See paras 27, 32, 43, 51, 53 and 56 of the judgment.

underlying *Bartsch*[71] on the grounds that in *Kücükdeveci*, the allegedly discriminatory conduct adopted occurred after the expiry of the period prescribed for the transposition of Directive 2000/78.[72]

V. SELECTED ASPECTS UNDER REVIEW: THE REASONING AS TO THE FOUNDATIONS AND LEGAL EFFECT OF THE GENERAL PRINCIPLE

A As to the Existence of a General Principle of Non-discrimination on the Grounds of Age

The most evident weakness in the reasoning of the Court in *Mangold* probably concerns the foundations of the general principle of EU law prohibiting discrimination on grounds of age. In the key passage of the judgment in that regard, the Court first referred to 'the principle of equal treatment in the field of employment and occupation' which is, as the Court set out, merely expressed but not laid down – one should maybe add, in any event, not constitutively – in Directive 2000/78. It then, in the same passage, described the purpose of that directive, the specific forms of discrimination, including that on the grounds of age, covered by the directive, in order to state that 'the source of the actual principle underlying the prohibition of those forms of discrimination' was to be found, according to the third and fourth recitals in the preamble to the directive 'in various international instruments and in the constitutional traditions common to the Member States'.[73]

In that regard, first of all, while the Court purports in the latter passage to identify a general principle of the prohibition of discrimination on grounds of age on the basis of its commonly recognised comparative law or 'evaluative' method,[74] the sources cited plainly do not support the findings of the Court. Obviously, the international instruments mentioned in the preamble to Directive 2000/78 referred to by the Court in this context[75] certainly enshrine the general principle of equality, but they do not contain any explicit reference to age. Similarly, it appears that in the constitutional orders of the vast majority of the Member States, no recognition was to be found of a specific prohibition of discrimination on grounds of age.[76]

[71] See above (n 9).

[72] See paras 23–25 of the judgment.

[73] *Mangold* (n 1) para 74; see equally *Kücükdeveci* (n 2) para 20; and Case C-147/08 *Jürgen Römer v Freie und Hansestadt Hamburg*, Judgment of 10 May 2011, para 59.

[74] See above (n 34).

[75] The third and fourth recitals in the preamble to Directive 2000/78 include the Universal Declaration of Human Rights, the United Nations Covenants on Civil and Political Rights and on Economic, Social and Cultural Rights and the European Convention for the Protection of Human Rights and Fundamental Freedoms.

[76] It appears that such explicit prohibitions existed only in the constitutions of Finland and – as regards employment conditions – of Portugal: see, inter alia, Opinion of AG Kokott in Case C-550/07 *Akzo Nobel Chemicals* [2010] ECR I-8301, para 96 and fn 78.

Consequently, the Court at most evidenced the existence of the general principle of non-discrimination or equality, whose recognition as a constitutional principle under EU law is, however, long-established and indisputable.

This leads us directly to a further problem underlying that reasoning, which was particularly highlighted in the Opinion in *Palacios de la Villa*[77] and whose potential impact is indeed far-reaching. The concern relates to the fact that the Court seems to have inferred, in a 'short-cut' kind of conclusion from the general principle of equality, the existence of a prohibition of discrimination on specific grounds such as, in the case at hand, age. In that regard, it is to be noted that any specific prohibition of discrimination constitutes a specific expression of the general principle of equality and therefore, conversely, that principle potentially implies a prohibition of discrimination on any grounds which may be deemed unacceptable. Consequently, the express reasoning of the Court, as it has apparently also been distilled into the formula in *Kücükdeveci* 'that the principle of non-discrimination on grounds of age is a general principle of European Union law in that it constitutes a specific application of the general principle of equal treatment',[78] is potentially apt to support the existence of any specific principle of prohibition of discrimination on any grounds. This, in any event, when taken at its face value, would indeed amount to opening a Pandora's box towards the judicial acknowledgment of an unlimited list of specific prohibitions of discrimination.

A decisive premise is hidden and a step omitted in this rationale: namely, an element – entailing at its core, a value judgment – of proof or consideration to the effect that it is specifically age which is to be considered (unless there is another objective reason) to constitute an illegitimate differentiation. If there was an element under consideration which allowed the Court to bridge the gap between the principle of equality and the specific prohibition of age discrimination,[79] it was not mentioned, in any event, in *Mangold*.

In that regard, it is not to be deplored that the Court did not invoke Article 13(1) EC (now Article 19(1) TFEU) as a source and foundation of the prohibition of age discrimination as a general principle of EU law.[80] As it constitutes an enabling legislative provision for the Union legislature to take appropriate action to that effect, one can dispute whether that power has been attributed by the masters of the Treaties to the legislature on the grounds that the prohibition of the forms of discrimination addressed has, in principle, already been recognised or,

[77] See Opinion of AG Mazák (n 7) paras 89–94.

[78] *Kücükdeveci* (n 2) para 50.

[79] It is true that in individual and flagrant cases a differentiation on the grounds of age – as well as other specific grounds – may also be caught by the general principle of non-discrimination or equality (see, to that effect, eg Opinion of AG Sharpston in Case C-227/04 P *Lindorfer v Council* [2007] ECR I-6767); but there is still a notable qualitative difference by comparison to the proposition that there is a self-standing principle prohibiting age discrimination, which thus generally – albeit subject to specific grounds of justification – marks the criterion of age as socially unacceptable and prohibited.

[80] See, however, Opinions of AG Bot (n 67) para 77 and of AG Sharpston (n 9) para 50.

on the contrary, for the very reason that such prohibitions have not yet existed but should be introduced by the legislature. So, which came first, the chicken or the egg? Accordingly, neither Article 13(1) EC (Article 19(1) TFEU), nor Directive 2000/78 itself that emanated from that provision, could be considered as conclusive as regards a pre-existing prohibition of the forms of discrimination to which they refer.[81]

It has also been suggested that the Charter of Fundamental Rights of the European Union (the Charter) in fact supported the findings of the Court as an internal source of inspiration insofar as it prohibits under Article 21(1), inter alia, discrimination based on age and that the Court's reasoning would have been more convincing if it had expressly referred to that source.[82] The argument has its merits, but apart from the fact that, in *Mangold*, the Court simply did not follow that path, the Charter at that time represented a mere, albeit 'solemn', declaration by the political institutions and not yet a binding legal instrument. To base the recognition of the prohibition on age discrimination as a general principle on the Charter would therefore, in itself, have caused further problems,[83] not least in view of the case law of the Court which seems to suggest a stricter standard as far as the recognition of a general principle is concerned, requiring the relevant provisions – in order for them to have indicative value to that effect – to be drafted so as to have binding legal effect.[84]

On the other hand, it is true that a while after *Mangold*, the Court adopted an apparently less cautious approach in that regard and in fact began with *Parliament v Council* to refer, notwithstanding its 'soft law' nature, to the Charter as a source of inspiration for the establishment of general principles, finding support in the preamble to the Charter which presents it as being reflective of a commonly recognised *acquis* of fundamental rights.[85]

Be that as it may, since the entering into force of the Lisbon Treaty on 1 December 2009, the Charter has, pursuant to Article 6(1) TEU, acquired the force of primary EU law and has, as such, expressly been referred to with regard to its Article 21(1) in *Kücükdeveci*, in supplement to the *Mangold* statement on the existence of a principle of non-discrimination on grounds of age.[86] This

[81] Moreover, a different approach on Art 13 may have been inconsistent with *Grant* (see Case C-249/96 *Grant* [1998] ECR I-621, para 48), in which the Court concluded that Community law, as it stood, did not cover discrimination based on sexual orientation: *cf* Opinion of AG Mazák (n 7) para 95.

[82] See, to that effect, inter alia, Herdegen (n 5) 351–52; K Lenaerts and JA Gutiérrez-Fons, 'The Constitutional Allocation of Powers and General Principles of EU Law' (2010) 47 *CML Rev* 1629, 1655; M Dougan, 'In Defence of Mangold?' in A Arnull, C Barnard, M Dougan and E Spaventa (eds), *A Constitutional Order of States? Essays in EU Law in Honour of Alan Dashwood* (Oxford, Hart Publishing, 2011) 221 f.

[83] *cf* also Dougan (n 82) 222.

[84] See, to that effect, Case C-149/96 *Portugal v Council* [1999] ECR I-8395, para 86; Case C-189/01 *Jippes and Others* [2001] ECR I-5689, paras 73 and 74; *Audiolux* (n 10) para 34.

[85] See Case C-540/03 *Parliament v Council* [2006] ECR I-5769, para 38; see also thereafter eg Case C-432/05 *Unibet* [2007] ECR I-2271, paras 37–38; and Case C-450/06 *Varec SA v Belgian State* [2008] ECR I-581, para 48.

[86] See *Kücükdeveci* (n 2) para 21 and, as regards the Charter, para 22.

approach has been confirmed in the more recent judgment in *Prigge*, which concerned age discrimination in the context of the termination of the employment contract of airline pilots.[87] However, it is still unclear whether the Charter must henceforth be regarded as constitutive in view of the recognition of a specific principle of non-discrimination following the *Mangold*-rationale or, rather, as merely an additional authority cited in support of the existence of the principle of non-discrimination on grounds of age thus acknowledged.

In this context, mention should also be made of the judgment of the Court in *Römer*,[88] which can be seen as a first application of *Mangold* to a form of discrimination other than on grounds of age. Although in that case the conditions for the application of that principle were eventually not fulfilled, since the case fell outside the scope of EU law, the judgment must be read so as to imply the recognition of a general principle of non-discrimination on the ground of sexual orientation in analogy with and by reference to *Mangold* and *Kücükdeveci*,[89] which confirms only that the implications of those rulings are obviously not limited to discrimination on grounds of age. Interestingly, however, in this case the Court refrained, in contrast to Advocate General Jääskinen,[90] from referring to Article 21(1) of the Charter which provides also for a prohibition of discrimination on the ground of sexual orientation.

B As to the Legal Effects of the General Principle

A few words should also be specifically devoted to the endowment of a horizontal direct effect on the general principle recognised in *Mangold*.[91] To begin with, there is no reasonable doubt that it is within the jurisdiction of the Court to decide whether general principles of EU law produce such a direct effect,[92] just as the Court had to define in its jurisprudence – including classics such as *Van Gend & Loos*[93] – the legal effects of other EU legal sources, such as Treaty provisions, acts of secondary legislation or international agreements concluded by the Union; the question, however, is whether there is good reason to recognise such an effect in respect of general principles.

It cannot be overlooked that *Mangold* and *Kücükdeveci* provided little explanation on that point in their respective reasoning,[94] which was limited essentially to recalling the case law of the Court according to which it must provide (where a

[87] Case C-447/09 *Reinhard Prigge and Others v Deutsche Lufthansa AG*, Judgment of 13 September 2011, para 38.

[88] *Römer* (n 73).

[89] See, to that effect, *Römer* (n 73) paras 59–60.

[90] Opinion of AG Jääskinen in *Römer* (n 73) paras 124–31.

[91] See already the previous section above at nn 56–58.

[92] Emphasis put on this point by Lenaerts and Gutiérrez-Fons (n 82) 1647.

[93] Case 26/62 *Van Gend & Loos* [1963] ECR 1.

[94] See *Mangold* (n 1) paras 75–77; *Kücükdeveci* (n 2) para 51; for an extensive critique in this regard, see eg de Mol (n 5) in particular at 133.

national rule falls within the scope of EU law, in the framework of a reference for a preliminary ruling) all the criteria of interpretation needed by the national court to determine the compatibility with fundamental rights.[95] It also referenced the need to ensure effective legal protection of individuals under EU law, in accordance with *Simmenthal*.[96] A more profound reasoning would certainly have been welcome, as previous case law had at least been doubtful as to how far general principles are actually capable of applying directly in the private sphere.[97]

Indeed, instances can be found in the case law of the Court where general principles – in particular, the general principle of equal treatment – appear to have been applied in horizontal relationships but concurrently with provisions of EU law (more particularly of the Treaty) which contained specific expressions of the principle and which, above all, were of themselves capable of producing direct effect in the private sphere.[98] On the contrary, previous rulings of the Court have also pointed towards the absence of such a horizontal direct effect of general principles of EU law.[99]

General principles, though, are not by their nature inapt to be ascribed direct effects as far as the requirements of justiciability (clear, sufficiently precise and unconditional) are concerned.[100] If the Court's proposition in *Mangold* is thus far shared so that the prohibition of discrimination on grounds of age indeed constitutes a general principle – and therefore an autonomous source – of EU law, it seems correct that its application in the case cannot as such 'be conditional upon the expiry of the period allowed the Member States for the transposition of a directive'.[101]

Wherever the precise dogmatic foundations and exact limits of the horizontal direct effect according to *Mangold* and *Kücükdeveci* may be found, this effect clearly raises various problems of legal certainty in the light of the judge-made, unwritten nature of general principles.[102] In fact, it makes it almost impossible for private parties to predict where and to what extent a general principle may 'strike' in their horizontal legal relations and to foresee their obligations imposed under EU law.[103]

[95] Case C-442/00 *Rodríguez Caballero* [2002] ECR I-11915, paras 30–32.

[96] *Simmenthal* (n 62) para 21; and Case C-347/96 *Solred* [1998] ECR I-937, para 30.

[97] Accordingly, the reasoning in *Kücükdeveci* cited only *Mangold* as a precedent to the effect that a general principle can be used to displace national rules in horizontal relationships: see *Kücükdeveci* (n 2) para 51.

[98] See eg Case 43/75 *Defrenne II* [1976] ECR 455, para 39; Case C-218/98 *Oumar Dabo Abdoulaye and Others* [1999] ECR I-5723, paras 16–17.

[99] See, inter alia, Case C-2/92 *The Queen v Ministry of Agriculture, Fisheries and Food, ex parte Dennis Clifford Bostock* [1994] ECR I-955, para 24; Case C-60/92 *Otto v Postbank NV* [1993] ECR I-5683, para 16.

[100] *cf* above (n 36); it might *in concreto*, however, be uncertain whether the substance of a general principle is sufficiently precise in order to be directly effective.

[101] *Mangold* (n 1) para 76.

[102] To that effect – and for an overview of that critique – see P Craig and G de Búrca (eds), *EU Law: Text, Cases, and Materials* (Oxford, Oxford University Press, 2011) 213.

[103] In that regard, it does in our view not make a substantial difference – that is, from a perspective of the legitimate expectations of individuals and their right to legal certainty – whether a person's

It also indeed begs the question of how far the judicial accordance of a horizontal direct effect to hazier general principles is coherent with the persisting denial of such an effect of directives. This denial, according to the case law of the Court, is premised, but perhaps not exclusively, on the assumption that the principle of legal certainty prevents directives from creating obligations for individuals.[104]

VI. OVERALL DOGMATIC COHERENCE AND RATIO OF THE *MANGOLD/KÜCÜKDEVECI* RULINGS

While there are, consequently, elements in the argumentation advanced by the Court in *Mangold/Kücükdeveci* which indeed, on closer inspection, turn out to be ill-reasoned or fragmentary, those rulings, when seen individually, remain faithful, in important aspects, to settled case law and fundamental premises underlying the EU legal order. Thus, per se, the Court upheld its settled case law according to which directives cannot displace national law and impose obligations on individuals in horizontal situations. It is, per se, comprehensible that the applicability of a general principle of EU law, as such, cannot be conditioned by the expiry of the period for implementation of a directive.

However, viewed in combination and as a sum of the parts, the approach in those rulings reveals partially paradoxical streaks due to the remarkable – or awkward – relationship between the general principle and the directive on which it seems to be premised. Its inherent logic amounts to a coincidence of opposites whereby the general principle and the directive appear in relation to each other at the same time as separate and mutually dependent, corroborative and undermining, causal and resultant.

On the one hand, the reasoning in *Mangold* and *Kücükdeveci* proceeds on the premise of the autonomy of the general principle of non-discrimination on grounds of age as a legal source in order to draw from its ability to produce direct effects independently of Directive 2000/78, assuming that the latter cannot reduce the effectiveness or temporal scope of the former. It is also implied

legal position is changed – at least for one party of the horizontal legal relationship or dispute concerned, to its detriment – on the grounds that a general principle of EU law merely excludes the application of a national provision (the so-called 'exclusionary' effect, which could also be seen as a mere consequence of the primacy of EU law) or because the general principle is applied fully/in place of a national provision (the 'substitution' effect, sometimes also labelled as 'full direct effect', which could also be seen as a consequence of a narrower notion of direct effect). Admittedly, the *Mangold* and *Kücükdeveci* rulings can be read as implying only an 'exclusionary' horizontal direct effect, but in fact the Court has in its case law never systematically endorsed, in the context of the direct effect of directives, the distinction between 'exclusionary' and 'substitution' horizontal direct effect. There is consequently so far no firm ground to assume that the horizontal direct effect of general principles of EU law would be limited to having provisions of national law set aside and not include the possibility for an individual to directly enforce the substance of a general principle of EU law against another individual.

[104] See, inter alia, Case C-201/02 *Wells* [2004] ECR I-723, para 56.

that the general principle is 'prior' to the directive, both as regards its existence as a norm and, by definition, in terms of its rank in the hierarchy of norms in EU law, the directive being declared to constitute only the expression of the principle, not its source.

On the other hand, and by contrast, the general principle is presented (as follows, in particular, from *Kücükdeveci*),[105] as being, from the bottom up, inextricably tied to and concurrent with the normative substance of Directive 2000/78, in particular Article 6(1) thereof. As a result, the general principle acts as a midwife for the directive in that it brings to bear the substance of the prohibition of discrimination which the directive provides. Meanwhile, it de facto and simultaneously replaces the directive and undermines some of the limitations which are inherent in the nature of this specific legislative act of the Union, notably with regard to horizontal direct effect.

In that regard, insofar as the insistence on the directive as a normative yardstick in this judicial construction is meant to safeguard the prerogatives of the EU legislature and the Member States,[106] it falls short of achieving that objective.[107]

First, Article 19 TFEU reserved to the Council the power, acting in accordance with the procedure provided for under that Article, to take appropriate action to combat, inter alia, discrimination on grounds of age, which it has chosen to do by means of a directive. The application of that prohibition to the private sector was therefore meant to happen through national law and not directly through EU law. Second, according to the legislator, the prohibition of discrimination on grounds of age, as expressed in Directive 2000/78, should become applicable at the end of the period set for its implementation. Therefore, by anticipating the application of the prohibition through the general principle as a vehicle, the legislative choice with regard to the scope *ratione temporis* has been ruled out.

In this respect, the approach in *Mangold/Kücükdeveci* may be contrasted with the respectful recognition of the role of the EU legislature in the more recent judgment *Association Belge des Consommateurs Test-Achats ASBL and Others*. This judgment concerned the principle of equal treatment between men and women, and the Court held, with regard to that same Article 19(1) TFEU on the basis of which Directive 2000/78 has been adopted, that in 'the progressive achievement of that equality, it is the EU legislature which [. . .] determines when it will take action, having regard to the development of economic and social conditions within the European Union'.[108]

Third, it should be noted that the general principle of non-discrimination on grounds of age escapes and transcends the scope *ratione materiae* of Directive

[105] See n 70 above.

[106] See, by implication, Opinion of AG Bot (n 67) para 34; to that effect also A Prechal, 'Competence Creep and General Principles of Law' (2010) 3 *Review of European Administrative Law* 1, 18–19; Lenaerts and Gutiérrez-Fons (n 82) 1647 and 1649.

[107] *cf* on that point also in the following: de Mol (n 5) 132 and Fontanelli (n 5) 239.

[108] Case C-236/09 *Association Belge des Consommateurs Test-Achats ASBL and Others v Conseil des Ministres*, Judgment of 1 March 2011, para 20.

2000/78, as defined under its Article 3. In accordance with the all-pervasive nature of general principles of EU law, it remains, from the moment it comes into existence, not limited to the areas of employment and occupation governed by the directive, but is, in principle, applicable across the entire scope of Union law.[109]

More particularly, general principles apply, when and in so far as a situation or case is covered by a directive – including the directive by which the principle concerned is expressed, on condition that the time limit set for transposing it has expired,[110] but also other directives, not necessarily related in substance to the general principle concerned[111] – or when a situation otherwise falls, on account of a substantive link, within the scope of Union law.[112]

In the light of the foregoing, apart from the question of the foundations of the specific principle of non-discrimination as such, there remains cause for concern as to the constitutional – vertical and horizontal – allocation of powers provided for by the Treaty.[113]

Similar issues of a possibly compromising effect on the constitutional allocation of powers under the Treaties and legal certainty may arise, moreover, in respect of the Charter, which is – pursuant to its Article 51(1) but, more specifically, also in view of the wording of its Article 21(1) – not designed to convey a horizontal direct effect.[114] The limitations on the scope of the Charter in that regard (which have, however, so far not been spelled out in the case law of the Court) could see themselves subverted to the extent that recourse is had in horizontal situations that fall in one way or another within the scope of EU law to general principles of EU law that mirror, in substance – the Charter acting as their source – the fundamental rights laid down therein.[115]

Overall, the reasoning of the Court in *Mangold/Kücükdeveci* conveys a somewhat constructed impression; it is, in various respects, difficult to see how its essentials and underlying premises, when followed to their logical conclusion, add

[109] See, in this context also, *Kücükdeveci* (n 2) para 23 and 53; *Römer* (n 73) para 60. See, to that effect, Fontanelli (n 5) 239; de Mol (n 5) 120; C Favilli, 'The Principle of Non-discrimination from *Grant* to *Kücükdeveci* to *Mangold*' (2011) 2 *European Journal of Social Law* 141, 147 and 149.

[110] See, to that effect, *Kücükdeveci* (n 2) paras 23 and 53; in a way, ironically, the directive triggers in this constellation its own replacement.

[111] See, to that effect, *Mangold* (n 1) itself, para 75.

[112] It is, though, controversial when this is precisely the case. Generally, the scope of Union law embraces situations where the Union institutions are exercising powers conferred by the Treaties, where the Member State is discharging its duty under the Treaties to implement Union law with its own legal system and where the Member State seeks rather to derogate from its binding obligations under Union law: see eg Dougan (n 82) 228–29; see also AG Sharpston in her Opinion in *Bartsch* (n 9) para 69, including the case where 'some specific substantive rule of [EU] law is applicable to the situation'.

[113] See, to that effect, Opinion of AG Mazák (n 7) para 138.

[114] To that effect also, J Kokott and C Sobotta, 'The Charter of Fundamental Rights of the European Union after Lisbon' (2010) 6 *EUI Working Paper* 14.

[115] See, on this problematic, also Dougan (n 82) 238 and 241; X Groussot, L Pech and GT Petursson, 'The Scope of Application of Fundamental Rights on Member States' Action: In Search of Certainty in EU Adjudication' (2011) 1 *Eric Stein Working Paper* 25 ff.

up to a coherent judicial approach. This may be regarded as symptomatic of that jurisprudence being originally result-driven, such as by the – in itself arguably legitimate – objective to reinforce individual rights, which also explains the difficulty in discerning the rationale and the exact boundaries of that case law.

Numerous questions in that regard in fact remain open; for instance:[116] is the *Mangold/Kücükdeveci* ratio limited to the general principle of equality and its specific expressions? Assuming that specific principles of non-discrimination are not freehandedly inferred by the Court from the general principle of non-discrimination, and in so far as the Charter constitutes the true source of the general principle of non-discrimination on grounds of age, must all specific types of discrimination mentioned in Article 21 of the Charter consequently – at least? – be qualified as general principles of EU law? Is there even an objective reason why all of the fundamental rights, as laid down in the Charter, should not be recognised, in parallel, as general principles of EU law? On what conditions can those principles then be relied on against private parties? Assuming that the substance of the fundamental rights laid down in the Charter is, in principle, already by itself sufficiently clear and precise to be justiciable,[117] why should the horizontal direct effect of the corresponding general principles – as sources of primary law – depend on the fact that they are replicated in a secondary law directive? And, as we have concluded above, does a general principle that is expressed in a directive not become automatically applicable – also in horizontal disputes – beyond the scope of the directive in all cases falling for whatever reasons within the scope of Union law?

It will be challenging for the Court – but with a view to legal certainty and other fundamental constitutional requirements necessary – to further spell out the implications of that case law in a conceptually consistent way.

On the other side of the balance sheet, it should be acknowledged that some recent cases may be read as a signal that the Court has no inclination to generally exploit, driven by an expansionist stance, the full potential of adjudication by reference to general principles of EU law that may be laid out in the *Mangold/Kücükdeveci* case law as it currently stands.

In *Audiolux*, the Court refused to acknowledge a specific principle of equal treatment of minority shareholders on the basis of the general principle of equal treatment; although, if there were such a specific principle of non-discrimination, it would undoubtedly constitute a specific expression of the general principle of equal treatment. In that regard, the Court took account of the various choices as to the content of a principle such as that proposed and of the degree of detail by which it would be characterised and the Court

[116] See for discussions of the ratio and implications of those rulings, eg Muir (n 68) 56–60; de Mol (n 5) 129 ff; E Spaventa, 'The Horizontal Application of Fundamental Rights as General Principles of Union law' in A Arnull, C Barnard, M Dougan and E Spaventa (eds), *A Constitutional Order of States? Essays in EU Law in Honour of Alan Dashwood* (Oxford, Hart Publishing, 2011) 215–16.

[117] *cf* also n 38 above.

concluded that such a principle would have to be drafted and enacted by the legislature.[118]

In the same cautionary vein, in *NCC Construction Danmark*, the Court found that for a principle like the principle of fiscal neutrality in VAT law to take effect, it requires legislation to be drafted and enacted, although this principle is indeed intended to reflect, in matters of VAT law, the general principle of equal treatment.[119]

Finally, it should be observed that in *Agafi ei and Others*, the Court remained faithful to the substantive scope of Directives 2000/43 and 2000/78 and found no basis in EU law to address the alleged discrimination on grounds of membership of a socio-professional category or place of work.[120]

VII. CONCLUSION

One thing is certain: *Mangold* has brought the general principles of EU law back to the attention of the legal community and observers of the Court.

The role of general principles of law has been decisive in the judicial laying of the constitutional foundations of the EU legal order; the power of the Court to develop EU law by reference to that judge-made source of law, despite the creative element it entails, as such is legitimate and not generally contested in the Member States.

Yet, the particular way in which the Court found and employed the general principle of non-discrimination on grounds of age in the *Mangold/Kücükdeveci* case law, admittedly, has an evading, transgressing flavour. The judicial reasoning on which it is based exhibits shortcomings and appears not to be guided by a judicial methodology that could be considered as pure in a classical sense. The rulings convey, on the whole, a somewhat constructed picture, apparently rooted in the as such legitimate judicial endeavour of strengthening – in or despite the circumstances of the case – individual rights, and in particular, the effectiveness of the protection from discrimination afforded under EU law. The objective, however, is defeated on another front in so far as individuals can be burdened in their horizontal legal relations by obligations flowing from an unwritten, judicially created general principle, which makes it practically impossible for them to reasonably foresee the rights conferred and obligations imposed on them by the EU legal order. *Mangold* is therefore characterised at its core by a lack of legal certainty – in and of itself a constitutional principle of EU law – and, at least, of collateral damage to the constitutional attribution of powers within the EU legal order.

In that light, there is a case for concluding that, with the *Mangold* case law, the Court, in several respects, is approaching the limits of legitimate judicial adjudication.

[118] See *Audiolux* (n10) paras 59–62.

[119] See *NCC Construction Danmark* (n 10) paras 40–42.

[120] See Case C-310/10 *Agafiţei and Others*, Judgment of 7 July 2011, paras 28–36.

However, it must immediately be added that the *Mangold/Kücükdeveci* rulings leave a whole range of open questions. It is therefore still too early for the precise boundaries and implications of that case law to be assessed. It will be up to the Court to further define those contours in its future case law and thereby to determine its real impact. Legally tenable and coherent lines must be drawn and criteria given in order to adequately frame the vast, expansionist potential inherent in the *Mangold* rationale. In view of the ingredients already provided by that case law, however, a difficult path lies ahead.

It seems that with *Mangold*, the Court has let a genie out of the bottle; he may even grant a few wishes, but it will be as challenging as it is paramount – with a view to the legitimacy of the adjudication of the Court – to keep him within reasonable confines.

3

The Court's Case Law on the Internal Market: 'A Circumlocuacious Statement of the Result, Rather than a Reason for Arriving at It'?

STEPHEN WEATHERILL

I. THE 'LEGITIMACY' OF THE COURT'S CASE LAW: THE PARAMETERS OF THE ENQUIRY

THE THEME OF this volume is enquiring into the legitimacy of the Court's case law. My task in this chapter is focused on the internal market, but the enquiry's ambition deserves to be projected across a much wider narrative, and this calls for a workable broadly applicable set of parameters. In order to bring coherence to an enquiry that is in part devoted to exploring the coherence discoverable in the internal market case law of the Court, I therefore gratefully adopt the approach proposed by the masters of this project. The 'position paper' that framed the original Expert Seminar, incorporated in the introduction to this volume, draws a helpful distinction between substantive and procedural legitimacy. So, according to the substantive view (new) rules or interpretations may be considered legitimate when they are perceived to embody proper ends and standards, and when the addressees of the decision regard them as the most appropriate solutions to the problems in the given context; whereas, under a procedural perspective, the main question is whether or not the rule or interpretation stems from the rightful source of authority, and whether those addressed by a (new) rule or interpretation believe that it has come into being and operates in accordance with general accepted principles of due process.

This helpfully involves two distinct (though connected) strands to the enquiry: the quality of the rule or interpretation chosen and the assessment made of the choice by addressees. Both elements – creation and reception – would readily feature in any enquiry into the legitimacy of judicial decision-making, but there are particular features of the EU legal order that lend a distinctive flavour to the examination of the case law emanating in Luxembourg.

The 'position paper' advised that attention be paid (inter alia) to consistency in the case law, whether arguments progress in an orderly manner, and to coherence. There are internal and external dimensions to this examination of creation: do rulings in a particular area 'fit' with each other and more broadly do they 'fit' the purpose pursued by the provisions in question. At stake is the quality of judgments: whether they are transparent, convincing and coherent. These are questions associated with the preservation of legal certainty; they are also associated with the rule of law. A court does not act 'legitimately' if it strays beyond the proper role of the judge by intruding on the political sphere. It may interpret legislation or other products of the law-making process, but it may not amend them. This is crystal clear in principle – it is fiendishly difficult in practice to reduce to an operationally reliable test by which to separate out what is allowed and what is not. In principle, to move from 'interpretation' to 'amendment' is to pass from light to shade, but that bright line is not so readily recognisably stark in practice. Judges must not be too 'activist' – but this is an invitation to debate, not an objectively verifiable sleight. A court may also stand accused of not acting legitimately by reasoning in ways that are not 'legal'. To decide that whichever party has the bigger feet wins the case is 'reasoning', but it is not 'legal reasoning'. Assessing when a court has so erred demands a benchmark – an understanding of what is the proper role of the judge (not the legislature) and what is legal reasoning (not mere reasoning devoid of proper legal content). For present purposes, I content myself with the pre-planned focus of this project on 'fit' – fit with existing rulings in the area, fit with broader principles. The particular challenge of EU law is the often elusive character of these supposed guiding principles. The Treaty is a spare frame and much interpretative autonomy is delegated to the Court. The internal market provides an appealingly lively testing ground for this proposition.

To move from creation of case law to its reception, judicial decisions may be tested with reference to how they are received: who accepts them, who resists them, how and on what basis? Here there is something distinctive about the institutional environment within which the Court of Justice operates. It is unusually well insulated from the political process. Its judgments on the meaning of EU secondary legislation may be set aside but only after the assembly of the necessary institutional support in the Commission, Council and Parliament, which amounts to a hurdle that is much higher than those typically to be found opposing law reform in national systems. Its judgments on the meaning of provisions of the Treaty are even more aggressively protected, since only revision of the Treaty is apt to make the necessary alteration. Unsurprisingly, this is very uncommon. Nor have periodically aired 'court-curbing' initiatives, such as empowering the Council to overturn Court rulings or establishing a tribunal separate from the Court for dealing with matters of competence, gained traction. As the 'position paper' convincingly maintains, the legitimacy of the

Court's rulings is of enduring importance, since it amounts to the continued willingness of other actors to comply even when that does not correspond with their immediate self-interest. The Court of Justice's interaction with the EU legislature and with the Member States reflects the remarkable level of autonomy conferred on it in the service of making credible long-term commitments in an environment of incomplete contracting. Once delivered, its judgments on the meaning of the Treaty (in particular) have deep roots.

This is especially significant and sensitive given that the Court has – famously, notoriously – a track record in delivering rulings that strain the outer edges of EU law: this is, however one defines the term, an activist court, even if views differ on whether it is *too* activist. Examples abound, but I select only one. The Court has ruled that 'the principle whereby a State must be liable for loss and damage caused to individuals as a result of breaches of Community law for which the State can be held responsible is *inherent in the system of the Treaty*'.[1] In a similar vein, the 'requirement for national law to be interpreted in conformity with Community law is *inherent in the system of the Treaty*'.[2] Both principles – of state liability and of compliant interpretation – are foundationally important in understanding the impact of EU law before national courts. Neither is explicitly envisaged by the Treaty. Both are judicial creations. They are *inherent in the system of the Treaty*. One may deride this as constitutional chutzpah but, short of revision of the Treaty, there is nowhere to go to challenge such interpretative ambition – except to the national courts. It is here that the Court's unusual institutional environment clearly emerges: the scope for setting aside judgments of the Court is strictly limited if one looks only at the process of legislative reform and of Treaty revision, but those judgments are of restricted practical effect if national *courts* of the Member States decline to apply them faithfully. Stripped of the active and willing cooperation of national courts, much of the distance that EU law has put between itself and orthodox public international law is eliminated. There is a compliance pull exerted by judgments of the Court of Justice in the sense that national courts are – in different ways, in different Member States – mandated by domestic law to apply EU law, but there are also plenty of tools available to national judges who wish to curtail the impact at national level of a Luxembourg ruling that they mistrust. Outright defiance based on denial of the constitutional authority of the Court of Justice to make such a judgment (for, most obviously, want of competence or violation of fundamental rights) is highly unusual, but there are more subtle and hard-to-track techniques available for confining the impact of rulings at national level by, for example, reading them in a narrow, fact-specific way. And national courts wishing to avoid a predictably unwelcome ruling in Luxembourg may choose not to make a preliminary reference in the first place. So the Court of Justice

[1] Cases C-6/90 and C-9/90 *Francovich and Others v Italian State* [1991] ECR I-5357, para 35, emphasis added.

[2] Joined Cases C-397/01 to C-403/01 *Bernhard Pfeiffer v Deutsches Rotes Kreuz* [2004] ECR I-8835, para 114, emphasis added.

must ensure the persuasive quality of its judgments, for, under the method of enquiry driving this project, the legitimacy of the Court is in part to be assessed with reference to the reaction of national courts who are by no means simply unthinking agents of the Court of Justice.

One further dimension that marks out the practice of the Court of Justice as distinctive is the single collegiate judgment. At its best, this grants harmonious and vigorous authority to the Court as a single voice. At its worst, it ensures the production of a ramshackle compromise, stripped of principle and reflecting no more than the bare minimum on which the several judges could agree. Rulings of the latter type may try the patience of national courts – or they may be greeted with relief for granting flexible room to manoeuvre at the national level. The internal market provides a rich source of examples of this variation. The single collegiate judgment – which proves to be anything but uniform in style and presentation – is an ambiguous element in securing the Court of Justice's legitimacy.

II. THE CASE LAW ON THE INTERNAL MARKET

The Court's case law on the internal market reveals much about the several matters and themes sketched above. In fixing the scope of application of the rules and in shaping the scope of justification of national rules that fall within the net, the Court is asked to determine how deep EU law reaches into the autonomy of the Member States and the extent to which judicial application of free movement law will advance integration without the need for legislative intervention. Most of all, it reveals a point that is of general application in the design of legal rules: the less precise the mandate on the basis of which a court is asked to operate, the more power is delegated to that court to select among plausible alternatives. And, in consequence, the charge of illegitimate action is correspondingly harder to pin on the judges involved. In the EU, as in many constitutional orders, it is in the nature of the process that fleshing out the system is heavily dependent on judicial choices about open-ended concepts.

As far as questions of 'fit' and coherence are concerned, the law of the internal market is especially intriguing for its absence of precise underpinning definitions. Article 26 TFEU defines the internal market as 'an area without internal frontiers in which the free movement of goods, persons, services and capital is ensured in accordance with the provisions of the Treaties'. But this leaves open all critical questions about the vertical and horizontal allocation of responsibility for the shaping of the internal market. Article 26 TFEU's definition avoids taking any clear position on (i) what sorts of obstacles to trade are attacked and (ii) who should attack them, judicial or legislative institutions. There is nothing fixed about an 'internal market' – Germany has one, the United Kingdom has one, Belgium has one, Canada has one, so does Australia – but the models vary: the patterns of deregulation and of re-regulation which underpin these internal markets are different. So the original 'position paper' informing this project directed that legitimacy in interpretation is tied to embodying *proper ends and standards* – but the EU's Treaties are deficient in establishing a hard-edged superstructure of proper ends and standards. An internal market for the EU needs sufficient regulatory homogeneity to secure an end to internal frontiers and the promotion of the free movement of goods, persons, services and capital in accordance with Article 26 TFEU, but it does not entail the suppression of all local diversity. But where exactly does that dividing line fall? On such matters of detail the Treaty is silent and so the Court is asked to draw the relevant lines. And this chapter is largely about drawing lines.

Woe unto you, Lawyers! is not a book title that conceals its message. Fred Rodell wrote it in 1939.[3] He was a Professor of Law at Yale Law School for 40 years and died in 1980. Fred Rodell, writing in 1939, could not have known anything about the European Union, much less its legal order. But his lament has resonance for students of the law of the EU's internal market:

> A court will solemnly purport to decide that the State of New Jersey may not regulate ticket scalpers – for the reason that the sale of theatre tickets is a business Not Affected With a Public Interest. A court will solemnly purport to decide that the federal government may not supervise wages in the coal industry – on the ground that those wages have only an Indirect Effect on Interstate Commerce; (and then the same court will solemnly purport to decide that the federal government may force a steel company to deal with a union – on the ground that steel wages have a Direct Effect on Interstate Commerce). *As though, in each case, the legal phrase used were anything more than a circumloquacious statement of the result, rather than a reason for arriving at it.* As though, in any case, any abstract legal phrase could conceivably contain the right key – or any key – to the solution of a concrete social or political or human problem. Dealing in words is a dangerous business, and it cannot be too often stressed that what The Law deals in is words (emphasis added).

The allegation that a legal phrase used is merely *a circumloquacious statement of the result, rather than a reason for arriving at it* is temptingly pertinent to some of the Court's leading decisions on the question of when a national measure is sufficiently intrusive to bring the law of the internal market into play. As this chapter will elaborate, in its Article 34 TFEU case law, the Court has ruled that where a national measure has a *considerable* influence on the behaviour of consumers, it falls in principle within the scope of Article 34 TFEU (and requires justification). If the influence is not considerable, the measure escapes the scope of application of Article 34 TFEU. So, the adjective *considerable* carries heavy constitutional weight. In its Article 21 TFEU case law, the Court has ruled that where a national measure is liable to cause a *serious inconvenience* to an affected person, it falls, in principle, within the scope of Article 21 TFEU (and requires justification). If the inconvenience is not serious, the measure escapes the scope of application of Article 21 TFEU. So, the adjective *serious* carries heavy constitutional weight. In

[3] It is available at: constitution.org/lrev/rodell/woe_unto_you_lawyers.htm.

its Article 20 case law, the Court has ruled that where a national measure serves to deprive an individual of 'genuine enjoyment of the substance of the rights conferred by virtue of their status as citizens of the Union', it falls in principle within the scope of Article 20 TFEU. If the deprivation relates to the substance of other rights (or for that matter to the rights conferred by virtue of status as citizens of the Union, but not to the substance of those rights) the measure escapes the scope of application of Article 20 TFEU. But what is the *substance of rights* conferred by virtue of the status of citizen of the Union? In its Article 114 case law, the Court has ruled that where divergent national measures cause an *appreciable* distortion of competition, the matter falls in principle within the scope of Article 114 TFEU and legislative harmonisation by the EU is permitted. If the distortion of competition is not appreciable, the matter escapes the scope of application of Article 114 TFEU. The EU may not intervene to harmonise. So, the adjective *appreciable* carries heavy constitutional weight. Similarly – and finally among this chapter's case studies – where divergent national measures have not yet emerged but are *likely* to emerge, then 'preventive harmonisation' pursuant to Article 114 TFEU is permitted. If emergence is not likely, the matter escapes the scope of application of Article 114 TFEU. The EU may not intervene to harmonise. So, the adjective *likely* carries heavy constitutional weight.

The common theme here is drawing lines. Each of these italicised words represents a dividing line between the application of EU internal market law and the regulatory autonomy of the Member States. If the threshold for the application of EU law is crossed – if a national measure has a *considerable* influence on consumer behaviour, if a measure is liable to cause a *serious* inconvenience, if there is a deprivation of the genuine enjoyment of the *substance of rights*, if regulatory diversity causes an *appreciable* distortion of competition or its *emergence* is likely – then there is a vertical shift in competence. The matter is not simply dealt with at state level: it becomes subject to EU intervention. And the implications are not only vertical, they are horizontal too. If the matter is within the scope of EU competence, there arise matters associated with the (horizontal) allocation of responsibility between the EU's judicial process and the EU's legislative process. The more vigorous the scope of free movement law in striking at national measures that restrict trade, the deeper the (judicially interpreted and applied) incursion into national regulatory autonomy – and the less harmonisation under Article 114 is required. If a measure affecting goods is unlawful within the meaning of Article 34 TFEU, there is no call to resort to harmonisation to promote market integration. The programme of legislative harmonisation is required to address barriers to trade that the Court is prepared to allow to survive the application of the Treaty provisions on free movement. So what is under examination is the interface between judicially-driven and legislature-driven approaches to advancing market integration in the EU – and the balance between (court-driven) deregulation and (legislative) re-regulation.

And yet, these words and phrases – *considerable*, *serious*, *appreciable* – which carry vital implications for the vertical and horizontal distribution of competences and powers are troublingly imprecise. The Court is describing when EU law intrudes into national autonomy, but it is not explaining precisely why. These rulings offer *a circumloquacious statement of the result, rather than a reason for arriving at it.* I am not going to adopt Fred Rodell's words to criticise the Court of Justice. I am going to adopt – or at least adapt – his words to sympathise with the Court of Justice. Given the evasiveness of the Treaty's treatment of the guiding concept of the 'internal market', sometimes the best the Court can do is serve up 'a circumloquacious statement of the result, rather than a reason for arriving at it'.

III. RESTRICTIONS ON USE

Article 34 TFEU is *less* than a charter for general review of Member State economic policy but *more* than a mere anti-discrimination rule. The (in)famous ruling of the Court in November 1993, in *Keck and Mithouard*,[4] was motivated by a concern to separate out national measures that need to be checked against the requirements of the internal market from those that do not. It was inspired by the Court's failure to appreciate that its decisions in the *Sunday Trading* cases in particular[5] represented a step beyond *Cassis de Dijon*[6] by casting the Article 34 TFEU net wide enough to catch measures that applied equally in law and in fact to all products irrespective of their origin. Shrewd litigants, eager for legal instruments apt to attack restraints on commercial freedom, had succeeded in pushing the scope of free movement law far beyond *Cassis de Dijon*'s legitimate subjection of technical standards to judicial control pursuant to Article 34 TFEU in preference to allocating elimination of their trade-restrictive effect solely to the legislative process. From this contamination of the taste of blackcurrant liqueur, the Court chose in *Keck* to retreat.

But realising what the Court was – correctly – trying to achieve is one thing: finding an apt formula is more difficult. *Keck*, widely reckoned to be the tortured product of disagreement among the judges of the Court, did not complete that task, and the Court has now spent almost 20 years trying to pin down with more precision where Article 34 TFEU stops and where national regulatory autonomy begins.

Non-discriminatory rules that do not affect the composition of a product have proved to be illuminatingly tough cases in this project of drawing lines. A ban on *advertising* a product does not involve formal discrimination. Moreover, the product may not be advertised but it may be sold. Advocate General Jacobs famously commented on the 'primordial' importance of advertising in penetrating new

[4] Joined Cases C-267/91 and C-268/91 *Keck and Mithouard* [1993] ECR I-6097.

[5] Case 145/88 *Torfaen BC v B & Q plc* [1989] ECR 765 and its 'follow-up', Case C-169/91 *Stoke on Trent and Norwich City Councils v B & Q plc* [1992] ECR I-6635.

[6] Case 120/78 *Rewe-Zentral v Bundesmonopolverwaltung für Branntwein (Cassis de Dijon)* [1979] ECR 649.

markets in *Konsumentombudsmannen v Gourmet Intenational Products* and accordingly held that an advertising ban is capable of falling within the scope of the Treaty provisions on free movement. The Court agreed.[7] It explained that:

> Even without its being necessary to carry out a precise analysis of the facts . . ., which it is for the national court to do, the Court is able to conclude that, in the case of products like alcoholic beverages, the consumption of which is linked to traditional social practices and to local habits and customs, a prohibition of all advertising directed at consumers in the form of advertisements in the press, on the radio and on television, the direct mailing of unsolicited material or the placing of posters on the public highway is liable to impede access to the market by products from other Member States more than it impedes access by domestic products, with which consumers are instantly more familiar.

So an advertising ban may lead to discrimination in fact against imported goods and if it does it is caught by Article 34 TFEU (and may stand only if justified).

The Court has in similar vein held that preventing a marketing method falls within the scope of Article 34 (and requires justification) where it 'affects products from other Member States more than it affects domestic products'.[8] This will normally be a matter for the national court to decide.

Litigation dealing with *restrictions on the use of products* has induced the Court once again to address the proper reach of Article 34 TFEU. Such measures are plainly within the scope of Article 34 TFEU if they are applied in a discriminatory manner, but absent discrimination they appear to restrict commercial freedom to the same degree whether use of domestically produced or imported products is involved. In *Åklagaren v Mickelsson and Roos* the Court was asked to consider the application of Article 34 TFEU to Swedish rules restricting the use of (inter alia) jet-skis on particular waterways.[9] Such a rule doubtless made the purchase of jet-skis in Sweden at least marginally less attractive than in a state where no such restrictions applied, but there was no evident difference in law or in fact in the rule's application to imported jet-skis as opposed to those made in Sweden. So, could Article 34 TFEU be relevant? The Court observed that:

> Even if the national regulations at issue do not have the aim or effect of treating goods coming from other Member States less favourably, which is for the national court to ascertain, the restriction which they impose on the use of a product in the territory of a Member State may, depending on its scope, have a considerable influence on the

[7] Case C-405/98 *Konsumentombudsmannen v Gourmet Intenational Products* [2001] ECR I-1795.

[8] Case C-441/04 *A-Punkt Schmuckhandels GmbH v Claudia Schmidt* [2006] ECR I-2093 para 23. This is probably also the best interpretation of Case C-108/09 *Ker-Optika bt*, Judgment of 2 December 2010, in connection with restrictions on sale over the internet, see in particular para 55, although the ruling is imprecise on which test is applied (illuminatingly so: see Caro de Sousa, 'Through Contact Lenses, Darkly' (2012) 37 *ELRev* 79) – and at para 48 commits the foul crime of claiming Art 34 contains a principle of mutual recognition, whereas it is fundamental that primary EU law insists only on a principle of non-absolute or conditional mutual recognition.

[9] Case C-142/05 *Åklagaren v Mickelsson and Roos* [2009] ECR I-4273.

> behaviour of consumers, which may, in turn, affect the access of that product to the market of that Member State.[10]

So, if the national measure has a *considerable* influence on the behaviour of consumers, it falls in principle within the scope of Article 34 TFEU (and requires justification). If the influence is not considerable, the measure escapes the scope of application of Article 34 TFEU. So the adjective *considerable* carries heavy constitutional weight. But how does one measure whether an influence is considerable or not?

The Court's cautious but imprecise insertion of the adjective *considerable* into its definition of the reach of Article 34 aims to capture the notion that just because national laws vary does not of itself mean there is (in short) 'an internal market problem'. The threshold at which divergence becomes a matter of concern for the EU is higher. But definitional precision remains elusive.[11] The consequence of the ruling is to require case-by-case analysis, and in practice an elusive task is placed on the shoulders of national judges who must assess whether an influence on consumer behaviour is 'considerable'.

The root of the problem does not lie principally in Article 34 TFEU; instead it lies principally in Article 26 TFEU. The Court is groping for something that the Treaty, and in particular Article 26 TFEU, simply does not provide: a precise and reliable means to determine when there is (in short) an internal market problem. At one extreme, it would be possible to review all national measures of regulation which exert some impact on the market; at the other extreme, a much narrower approach would confine review to physical or discriminatory obstacles to trade. The implications – for local autonomy, for the role of the EU's judicial and legislative institutions, for the workload of national courts – are profound, depending on which approach is preferred. The adjective *considerable* is designed exactly to signal that the Court has opted for a solution that is somewhere between these extremes: it rejects Article 34 as an instrument of general economic constitutional review, but it has instead fallen back on a test which is barren of precision and which is near enough *de minimis*. The internal market as a legal concept is not useful in any practical concrete sense here.

Insisting that Article 34 TFEU bites when a restriction on use exerts 'a considerable influence on the behaviour of consumers' is *a circumloquacious statement of the result, rather than a reason for arriving at it*. But it is understandable that the Court is forced to place such reliance on imprecise measures, because the Treaty itself fails to make decisive choices about the proper scope of economic freedom. In that sense, the Court's case law seems to me to amount to a *legitimate* choice among competing alternatives, and it is coherent in the sense that it is tied to one among several plausible interpretations of the proper scope

[10] Para 26.

[11] See eg P Wenneras and KB Moen, 'Selling Arrangements, Keeping Keck' (2010) 35 *ELRev* 397; G Davies, 'Understanding Market Access: Exploring the Economic Rationality of Different Conceptions of Free Movement Law' (2010) 11 *German Law Journal* 671; J Snell, 'The Notion of Market Access: A Concept or a Slogan?' (2010) 47 *CML Rev* 437.

of the Treaty in general and of the concept of the internal market in particular.

However, the Court needs to be careful not to deviate from its chosen course without explanation or, at least, recognition. Recently, in *Bonnarde*, the Court stated that Article 34 TFEU catches rules that 'may influence the behaviour of consumers and, consequently, affect the access of those [products] . . . to the market' of the regulating state (paragraph 30).[12] This formula drops the qualification that the influence on consumer behaviour must be *considerable*, and seems to throw the doors of Article 34 TFEU wide open. Even more odd is that this was in a decision that does not concern a restriction of use, but rather a classic instance of rule that imposed a protectionist 'dual burden' on imported goods, in the mainstream sense of *Cassis de Dijon*. *Bonnarde* is a decision of the Fifth Chamber and probably must be treated as a regrettably imprecisely written judgment, rather than as an attempt to rewrite the law on the free movement of goods. This is not the common law, but the Court of Justice has itself chosen to lay down important statements of principle in its case law, and it is therefore obliged to 'fit' its judgments within the pattern of previous decisions with much more care and attention to detail than is apparent in *Bonnarde*.

The Court's 'line-drawing' judgments are defensible as the best the Court can do with the difficult material provided by the Treaty. To that extent, they are apt to be treated as legitimate by national courts. But if the Court strays from its chosen path without explanation, it is imperilling that claim to legitimacy.

IV. A SERIOUS INCONVENIENCE

The trend of 'drawing lines' is readily visible in recent case law arising out of Article 21 TFEU. The precise terms used are different – the Court's test is directed at enquiry into whether a 'serious inconvenience' to the applicant is caused by the challenged national measures. But the thematic similarity with Article 34 TFEU is plain: the Court is drawing a line which, if crossed – that is, if there *is* a serious inconvenience – means that the national practice falls within the scope of Article 21 TFEU (and therefore requires justification) whereas, if the line is not crossed – if there is no inconvenience or if there is inconvenience but it is not serious – state autonomy is preserved. But what is meant by a 'serious inconvenience'? Case-by-case enquiry seems unavoidable: it is the familiar trick of the Court to load immense constitutional significance on to imprecise concepts.

The factual background to *Ilonka Sayn-Wittgenstein v Landeshauptmann von Wien* concerns an Austrian law of 1919 abolishing the nobility, which, inter alia, does away with titles, in contrast to Germany, which has a 1919 law which does away with privileges but allows parts of the noble title to be retained in the

[12] Case C-443/10 *Bonnarde*, Judgment of 6 October 2010, para 30.

surname.[13] Ilonka, having been adopted in Germany by Lothar Fürst von Sayn-Wittgenstein, was in Germany Ilonka Fürstin von Sayn-Wittgenstein. In Austria, she was to be registered more prosaically as Ilonka Sayn-Wittgenstein. This, she argued, would damage her economic interests as a cross-border castle seller. The matter could doubtless have been tackled under Article 56 TFEU as a restriction on the free movement of services but the national court referred questions pertaining to Article 21 TFEU. The Court found that serious inconvenience was caused to the applicant by the requirement to use a different name in Austria, so Austria had restricted the freedom envisaged by Article 21 TFEU. The matter then turned to whether the rules could be justified, on which point the Court was receptive to Austrian concerns, expressed at a constitutional level, to abolish titles in the service of equality of citizens before the law – a concern which the Court noted is also recognised under EU law.[14]

Runevič-Vardyn concerned a Lithuanian national who belonged to the Polish minority in Lithuania.[15] She had lived and worked in Poland, married a Pole and by the time of the litigation was living in Belgium. Her problem was that her Lithuanian birth certificate stated her name in its Lithuanian, not Polish, form; and the Lithuanian marriage certificate denied her Polish husband the necessary diacritical modification – specifically by not adding the slash across the letter 'l' used in Polish. The Lithuanian authorities refused her requests for modification. The Court observed that:

> According to the Court's case-law, in order to constitute a restriction on the freedoms recognised by Article 21 TFEU, the refusal to amend the joint surname of the applicants in the main proceedings under the national rules at issue must be liable to cause 'serious inconvenience' to those concerned at administrative, professional and private levels (see, to that effect, *Garcia Avello*, paragraph 36; *Grunkin and Paul*, paragraphs 23 to 28; and *Sayn-Wittgenstein*, paragraphs 67, 69 and 70).[16]

Accordingly, the Court decided this was a restriction within the meaning of Article 21 TFEU in so far as it caused her 'serious inconvenience'. Whether this was present was for the national court to decide, although the Court seemed receptive to the idea that refusal to change the marriage certificate would generate doubts about identity and the authenticity of the documents, and so potentially harm the exercise of the right of residence conferred by Article 21 TFEU.[17] The Lithuanian refusal to change the husband's name to include the diacritical marks seemed *not* to be a serious inconvenience, because such marks are commonly omitted anyway.[18] Then – as in *Sayn-Wittgenstein*, so too in *Runevič-Vardyn* – the Court proceeded to the possible justification of the national practices. It left the matter in the hands of the national court, while making some

[13] Case C-208/09 *Sayn-Wittgenstein*, Judgment of 22 December 2010.
[14] See especially Art 4(2) TEU.
[15] Case C-391/09 *Runevič-Vardyn*, Judgment of 12 May 2011.
[16] Para 76.
[17] Paras 77–78.
[18] Paras 81–82.

interesting observations about language as a 'constitutional asset',[19] referring to respect for language enshrined in the TEU and the Charter. That seems to support the Lithuanian case for treating the rules as justified. Against that, however, stand the right to privacy under the Charter and the European Convention on Human Rights (ECHR). The matter is left to the national court to find a 'fair balance', but the judgment contains a nudge that the Lithuanian rules are disproportionate and discriminatory.[20]

Whether an inconvenience is *serious* is crucial. If it is serious, the matter falls within the scope of Article 21 TFEU; if it is not serious, it is a matter of national autonomy. But how do we measure what is *serious*? It is a troublingly imprecise test which reflects the thematically familiar attempt to separate out national measures that escape the scope of application of EU free movement law from those that are sufficiently damaging to the objectives of the Treaty to require justification. The Court is once again forced to draw lines and pluck out new phrases. But the imprecision is rooted in the Treaty – specifically in Article 26 TFEU's inadequate definition of the 'internal market'.

V. THE SUBSTANCE OF RIGHTS

Early in 2011 in *Ruiz Zambrano* the Court drew a new line. It observed that Article 20 TFEU 'precludes national measures which have the effect of depriving citizens of the Union of the genuine enjoyment of the substance of the rights conferred by virtue of their status as citizens of the Union'.[21] So, if the national measure serves to deprive an individual of 'genuine enjoyment of the substance of the rights conferred by virtue of their status as citizens of the Union', it falls in principle within the scope of Article 20 TFEU. If the deprivation relates to the substance of other rights (or for that matter to the rights conferred by virtue of status as citizens of the Union, but not to the substance of those rights), the measure escapes the scope of application of Article 20 TFEU. But what is found in this special core – what is the *substance of rights* conferred by virtue of the status of citizen of the Union?

Ruiz Zambrano concerned a Colombian national in Belgium with dependent children who held Belgian nationality. The question was whether the Colombian acquired a right of residence in Belgium. Article 20 TFEU precludes national measures which have the effect of depriving citizens of the Union of the genuine enjoyment of the substance of the rights conferred by virtue of their status as citizens of the Union, and this was such a deprivation. A refusal to grant a right of residence to the Colombian would mean the children, who were citizens of the Union, would have to leave the territory of the Union – and as a result they

[19] Para 84.
[20] Paras 91–93.
[21] Case C-34/09 *Ruiz Zambrano*, Judgment of 8 March 2011, para 42.

would be unable to exercise the substance of the rights conferred on them by virtue of their status as citizens of the Union.

According to long-standing orthodoxy, the 'purely internal' situation escapes the scope of application of EU free movement law; a cross-border dimension is required. It is, admittedly, often easy to find that necessary cross-border element. In *Mary Carpenter*, the Court claimed to find a cross-border aspect – selling advertising in other Member States – even if it found it very easily and in circumstances where the cross-border element was incidental to the case.[22] In *Ruiz Zambrano*, the Court acknowledged that it had had pressed on it the absence of any cross-border element to the case and consequently the inapplicability of the free movement provisions,[23] but then it completely ignored the objection and calmly asserted the matter to fall within the scope of EU law. So, in understanding why EU law applied to an apparently internal situation, *Carpenter* had a fig leaf. *Ruiz Zambrano* does not have even that. It seems that measures which have the effect of depriving citizens of the Union of the genuine enjoyment of the substance of the rights conferred by virtue of their status as citizens of the Union are controlled under Article 20 TFEU, even if the matter appears to raise only issues internal to one Member State. This, then, is the line that the Court chooses to draw for the purposes of determining the intrusion of Article 20 TFEU into national autonomy. But it makes no attempt to explain what is the substance of the rights conferred, and its claim that the stated test derives from paragraph 42 of the 2010 ruling in *Rottmann*[24] does not convince. That paragraph of *Rottmann* is not written in such grand style at all, and in any event that ruling addresses a much narrower issue: loss of nationality suffered by a national of a Member State. So, in truth, *Ruiz Zambrano* strikes out in a new direction, offering a new test for determining when EU law applies to national measures. It is *a circumloquacious statement of the result, rather than a reason for arriving at it*.

One interpretation of *Ruiz Zambrano* was that the Court was minded to abandon the very notion of a 'purely internal' situation that escapes the scope of EU law, with consequent gross reduction in the scope of national autonomy. That this leap was *not* intended became clear two months later. *Shirley McCarthy* is much more cautious.[25] McCarthy was a dual Irish/ UK national but she was born and had always lived in the UK. She married a third-country national – a Jamaican – who had no leave to remain in the UK. The question was whether she was able to rely on EU law to protect him from deportation. Advocate General Kokott considered that the matter fell for determination (in Strasbourg or before a national court) in the light of the ECHR, not EU law. The Court instead cited *Ruiz Zambrano* and examined EU law, but it found that in this instance there was no deprivation of genuine enjoyment of the substance

22 Case C-60/00 *Carpenter* [2002] ECR I-6279.
23 Para 37.
24 Case C-135/08 *Rottmann* [2010] ECR I-1449.
25 Case C-434/09 *McCarthy*, Judgment of 5 May 2011.

of rights conferred by the status of Citizenship. 'By contrast' with *Ruiz Zambrano* the UK measure did not oblige her to leave the territory of the EU.[26]

Later, in 2011, the Court had its third opportunity to address the matter. In *Dereci*, the applicants were all third-country nationals who had been refused permission to live with family members who were EU citizens resident in and nationals of Austria.[27] The EU citizens concerned had never exercised their right to free movement. The Court repeated the test concocted in *Ruiz Zambrano*, then explained that there is a denial of the genuine enjoyment of the substance of the rights conferred by virtue of the status of Citizenship where the Union citizen in fact has to leave the territory of the Union as a result of the refusal to grant a right of residence to the family member. By contrast, where an individual simply wants to have third-country national family members live with him or her for economic reasons or in order to keep a family together in the territory of the Union, this is not enough to support the view that refusal would force the individual to leave the territory of the Union.

The law, in the light of this experimental trio of cases, holds that the protection envisaged by the status of Citizenship projects EU law into a situation which is apparently internal to one Member State – but only where otherwise the EU citizen will be forced to leave the EU entirely. This is doubtless how an individual seeking the protection of EU law should seek to frame such an argument in future. Primary EU law may apply even where there is no intra-EU cross-border movement – *provided* that there is a deprivation of the substance of rights founded on the status of Citizenship. That is where the line is drawn. This still leaves open awkward questions about when someone is really being 'forced' to leave Union territory, but – a deeper concern – the Court has left open just what the reasons underlying this specially protected status might be. The matter seems somehow loosely connected with the importance of Citizenship and the Court's approach could be plausibly be driven by the widened aims of the EU and deepened commitments to fundamental rights accepted under the Lisbon Treaty,[28] but in its case law, the Court evades any such statement of principle. Even if what is at stake here is more aggressive control of 'internal' national practices in the name of Citizenship, rather than the more restrained control in the name of the internal market covered elsewhere in this chapter, the thematic core of the structural enquiry remains the same as that pursued elsewhere in this chapter – there is a hard-to-fix dividing line between national practices that require justification under EU law and those that do not.

Dereci has gone some way to clarifying the location of the dividing line. There is a denial of the genuine enjoyment of the substance of the rights conferred by virtue of the status of Citizenship where the Union citizen in fact has to leave the territory of the Union as a result of the refusal to grant a right of residence. The Court has not, however, addressed deeper questions about just

[26] Para 50.
[27] Case C-256/11 *Dereci*, Judgment of 15 November 2011.
[28] See now Arts 2–3 TEU; and *cf* the Opinion of AG Sharpston in *Ruiz Zambrano*.

why the line should be drawn in this place. The thinness of the reasoning in *Ruiz Zambrano* in particular, and the subsequent caution of *McCarthy* and *Dereci*, suggests disagreement among the judges in Luxembourg. *Ruiz Zambrano* is a decision of the Grand Chamber, *McCarthy* of the Third Chamber, *Dereci* of the Grand Chamber; the Judge Rapporteur was Cunha Rodrigues in *Ruiz Zambrano* and Silva de Lapuerta in both *McCarthy* and *Dereci*; Advocates General were Sharpston, Kokott and Mengozzi, respectively. Consistency is unsurprisingly elusive. Hailbronner and Thym noted the opaque nature of the test newly introduced by *Ruiz Zambrano*, and observed that neither has the Court shown it to fit with existing case law nor has its future scope of application been made clear, and concluded that 'A Supreme Court should behave more responsibly'.[29] Probably it should. Among available explanations is that some Supreme Courts are able to produce dissenting judgments, so one may be able to track clearly where the fault lines lie between the judges. None of that is possible in Luxembourg.[30] The need to compromise on a single collegiate judgment may well be a reason why the Court is especially given to offering *a circumloquacious statement of the result, rather than a reason for arriving at it*: however bitterly divided the judges, a result has to be agreed, whereas reasons do not.

The 'considerable influence' test and the 'serious inconvenience' test are unavoidable attempts to set limits to Articles 34 and 21 TFEU's incursion into national autonomy respectively in the absence of any useful limiting wording provided by the Treaty itself. In *Ruiz Zambrano*, the Court chose to strike off in a new direction, creating a new type of protection under EU law available only to those deprived of 'the substance of rights founded on the status of Citizenship'. And the decision to base that protection on a deeper intrusion into national autonomy than applies in classic internal market cases is 'Citizenship-flavoured' but lacks clear explanation. Worse still, the Court took three bites of this cherry in 2011, and used slightly different teeth on each occasion. Coherence is absent: legal certainty imperilled, and it is particularly alarming that this should be so in cases involving vulnerable migrants. Under the perspective of this project,[31] this undermines the legitimacy of the Court's choices.

VI. THE SCOPE OF HARMONISATION

Defining EU free movement law finds a parallel in defining EU harmonisation law. Just as the EU reviews national measures but only where they are sufficiently

[29] K Hailbronner and D Thym, 'Annotation of Case C-34/09 *Ruiz Zambrano*' (2011) 48 *CML Rev* 1253, 1259.

[30] *cf* V Perju, 'Reason and Authority in the European Court of Justice' (2009) 49 *Virginia Journal of International Law* 307.

[31] And see also N Nic Shuibhne, '(Some of) the Kids Are All Right – Anotaton of *McCarthy* and *Dereci*' (2012) 49 *CML Rev* 349.

damaging to the functioning of the internal market, so too the EU may harmonise national laws but only where the differences are sufficiently damaging to the functioning of the internal market. As with Article 34 TFEU, so too Article 114 TFEU: simple diversity among national practices is not enough to justify EU intervention. But the Treaty helps little in pinning down precisely what that threshold shall involve, and so responsibility is delegated to the Court – and then, in practice, back to the EU legislative institutions.

In *Germany v Parliament and Council*, the famous first 'Tobacco Advertising' decision, the Court observed that in examining the lawfulness of a Directive adopted on the basis of what is now Article 114 TFEU, the Court 'is required to verify whether the distortion of competition which the measure purports to eliminate is appreciable'.[32] So, if the divergent national measures subject to harmonisation cause an *appreciable* distortion of competition, the matter falls in principle within the scope of Article 114 TFEU and legislative harmonisation by the EU is permitted. If the distortion of competition is not appreciable, the matter escapes the scope of application of Article 114 TFEU. The EU may not intervene to harmonise: the matter remains to be dealt with (in diverse ways) at national level.

The adjective *appreciable* carries heavy constitutional weight. There was no sufficient appreciable distortion in the Directive challenged in the first 'Tobacco Advertising' case and consequently it was annulled. The Court had drawn a line – the Directive did not cross it, and so was not within the scope of EU legislative competence. The structural familiarity to the rest of this chapter is plain: lines are drawn to separate the application of EU law and the autonomy of the Member States, but those lines are based on imprecise and unpredictable foundations.

The Court also accepts that Article 114 TFEU is adequate to support measures of 'preventive harmonisation' by the EU, but here too a line is drawn to determine when this is permitted, and this too is a line based on a notion that is hard to measure. In *Vodafone, O2 et al v Secretary of State* the Court explained that recourse to Article 114 is possible if the aim is to prevent the emergence of such obstacles to trade resulting from the divergent development of national laws, but the emergence of such obstacles must be likely and the measure in question must be designed to prevent them.[33] So if such emergence is not likely, the matter escapes the scope of application of Article 114 TFEU. The EU may not intervene to harmonise. The adjective *likely* carries heavy constitutional weight. But it is hard to measure.

Once again, the thematic point is that the Court is attempting to devise a legal formula that determines when diversity between national laws is of no concern to EU law and when instead such diversity has a sufficient impact on interstate trade patterns to require attention – to be at least *harmonisable*,

[32] Case C-376/98 *Germany v Parliament and Council* [2000] ECR I-8419, para 106.
[33] Case C-58/08 *Vodafone, O2 et al v Secretary of State*, Judgment of 8 June 2010, para 33.

albeit that it is a political decision whether in fact to proceed to harmonise it. Defining the scope of free movement law dictates the scope of control over national regulatory practice to be exercised by judges (at EU and at national level). Defining the scope of what is permitted in the name of harmonisation dictates the reach of legislative activity at EU level. This vertical shift in competence is constitutionally constrained. Legislative activity must comply with Article 5 TEU's principle of conferral, and the Court is responsible for ensuring such faithful compliance. But this constitutionally fundamental *principle* is far from satisfying in its *practical* application. The limits are written without precision – by the Court in these judgments but ultimately by the Treaty itself.

What on one level seems to promise a constitutionally proper standard of review, which wrests from majoritarianism practised by the political institutions and into judicial hands the ultimate source of authoritative ruling on the lawful scope of the Treaty mandate is, in truth, deceptive. The Court places enormous weight on slippery adjectives and adverbs in its attempt to define the limits of Article 114 TFEU in a more sophisticated manner than does the Treaty. The consequence is that a line of case law that began with the impression of judicial empowerment has been converted into legislative empowerment. It is easy for the legislature simply to copy-and-paste the Court's formula and very hard for such claims to be falsified. So, in practice, legislation is likely to be 'Court proofed', thanks to the ready adoption Court's own vague tests. And this is what has happened. The case law subsequent to the first 'Tobacco Advertising' case is (almost) entirely marked by judicial green lights for legislative harmonisation. The above-mentioned ruling in *Vodafone, O2 et al v Secretary of State* serves as a compelling example. An attack on the validity of the so-called 'Roaming Regulation', Regulation 717/2007, failed. The Regulation capped the wholesale and retail charges terrestrial mobile operators may charge for the provision of roaming services on public mobile networks for voice calls between Member States. It was based on Article 95 EC, now Article 114 TFEU. Advocate General Maduro's Opinion did *not* think the Court's criteria for valid 'preventive harmonisation' were satisfied in the case. But, by contrast, the Court held the measure valid. It declared that the Regulation had been adopted in response to the likelihood that national price control measures of divergent type would be adopted aiming to address the problem of the high level of retail charges for EU-wide roaming services. So this was treated as classic preventive harmonisation aimed at improving the conditions for the functioning of the internal market. The Court conspicuously reached its conclusions in *Vodafone* by reference only to the observations presented by the EU's own institutions and those found in the recitals attached to the measure. It drew on both the explanatory memorandum to the proposal and the impact assessment to substantiate the finding that there was a likelihood of divergent development of national laws. The recital stated there was pressure for Member States to take measures to address the problem of the high level of retail charges for roaming services, and the Court adds that this was moreover confirmed by the Commission at the hearing.[34] One would scarcely have expected otherwise! The Court did not stand outside the legislative choice that had been made; instead, it aligned itself uncritically with the institutions whose choices were being challenged by the applicants.

The Court, in striving to provide a more concrete shape to the limits of Article 114 TFEU than does the terms of the Treaty, has simply offered up an invitation to the legislature to enjoy the protection of its slipstream. The EU's legislature is able to exploit the broad and fuzzy contours of Article 114 TFEU to convert compliance with the principle of conferral into little more than a drafting exercise.[35]

In *Åklagaren v Mickelsson and Roos*[36] the Court's cautious but imprecise insertion of the adjective *considerable* into its definition of the reach of Article 34 has much in common with its use of words such as *appreciable* and *likely* in the case law fixing the reach of Article 114. In both instances, the aim is to capture the notion that just because national laws vary does not of itself mean there is (in short) 'an internal market problem' of a type that triggers EU law, whether Article 34 or Article 114. The threshold at which the existence of the national rule becomes a matter of concern to the EU is higher. The rule must have a *considerable* influence on consumer behaviour; the diversity must have an *appreciable* impact on competition. Only then is the vertical shift of competence activated. But definitional precision remains elusive, and consequently a case-by-case examination is required which delegates considerable power to the relevant institution – a national court in so far as Article 34 is at stake, the EU legislature where Article 114 is in question. The deep question asks what allocation of competence to the EU is required to ensure the effective functioning of the internal market foreseen by Articles 3(3) TEU and 26 TFEU? And the Treaty is deeply unhelpful. In this sense offering *a circumloquacious statement of the result, rather than a reason for arriving at it* is in part the choice forced on the Court by the absence of a fully articulated understanding of the nature of the internal market in the Treaty.

VII. QUESTIONS OF JUSTIFICATION

The functional imperative of creating an internal market logically produces a far-reaching – if ill-defined – set of legal rules. It brings with it pressure to allow a generous approach to the scope of justification too. How far national measures that restrict trade may be justified by reference to broader concerns than the purely economic reveals much about the complex phenomenon that is the 'internal market' – particularly that it is necessarily an exercise in more than

[34] Para 44.

[35] *cf* S Weatherill, 'The Limits of Legislative Harmonisation Ten Years After *Tobacco Advertising*: How the Court's Case Law Has Become a "Drafting Guide"' (2011) 12 *German Law Journal* 827.

[36] *Åklagaren v Mickelsson and Roos* (n 9 above).

setting aside trade restrictions because, as already foreseen by its status under the Treaties as a shared competence, it also involves paying due respect to national regulatory preferences which cannot be suppressed simply because of their trade-restrictive effect. That is plain from the Treaty, as evidenced by provisions such as Article 36 TFEU, which allow for derogations from the principle of free movement, but also provisions of wider application, such as Article 4(2) TEU, which has featured as a defence of constitutional identity recognised by EU law in some of the recent cases mentioned in this chapter.[37] Similar remarks may be directed at legislative harmonisation. Setting common rules is not simply a technical exercise: it requires that a choice be made about the appropriate EU level technique and intensity of regulation that shall prevail in the sector now taken (in whole or in part) out of the hands of diverse national regulators. This too is recognised in the Treaty in provisions directly associated with harmonisation, such as Article 114(3) TFEU but also in the several 'horizontal' clauses, such as Articles 11 and 12 TFEU.

Defining the scope of the Treaty provisions on the internal market is clearly a logically distinct issue from determining whether rules that fall within their scope are justified. And yet, the issues cannot be sensibly kept fully separate. The broader the scope of application, the more crucial the receptivity under EU law to justification, for once the matter is wrenched out of the autonomy of the national regulator, practices may be maintained only where EU law standards of justification are met. The more sceptical one is that the EU takes a sufficiently generous approach to justification, the more one strategically favours a narrow approach to the circumstances in which EU law applies in the first place. However, an enquiry into the case law on justification would stretch this chapter far beyond reasonable limits. The Court has, by way of general summary, conspicuously sought to buttress the legitimacy of its case law on justification by showing a receptivity to a broad range of possible justifications for trade barriers. This emerged from the landmark ruling in *Cassis de Dijon*[38] in the form of the justificatory 'mandatory requirements' and latterly the Court has readily allowed a wide range of interests to play a role in assessing whether a trade barrier is justified.[39] This carries with it the unavoidable implication that judges have to address some deeply awkward balancing of interests. In this sense, the judicial route to developing the internal market – the application of the free movement rules – shares with the legislative route – harmonisation – the need to confront some intensely political choices.

[37] eg *Ilonka Sayn-Wittgenstein* (n 13 above); *Runevič-Vardyn* (n 15 above). *cf* A Von Bogdandy and S Schill, 'Overcoming Absolute Primacy: Respect for National Identity under the Lisbon Treaty' (2011) 48 *CML Rev* 1417; S Rodin, 'National Identity and Market Freedoms after the Treaty of Lisbon' (2011) 7 *Croatian Yearbook of European Law & Policy* 11.

[38] *Rewe-Zentral* (n 6 above).

[39] PJ Oliver (ed), *Oliver on the Free Movement of Goods in the European Union* (Oxford, Hart Publishing, 2010) ch 8; SA de Vries, *Tensions within the Internal Market* (Groningen, Europa Law Publishing, 2006) ch 2.

The decisions that are most vulnerable to the accusation that the Court has strayed into areas it misunderstands and has therefore failed to adjudicate with proper contextual sensitivity are the December 2007 rulings of the Grand Chamber of the Court of Justice in *Viking Line* and *Laval*.[40] The main point of this chapter is to examine the *structure* of internal market law (and most of all its breadth and lack of precise limits or 'lines') rather than the merits of particular rulings, but at least one example of how sensitive the law of the internal market has become is worthwhile. *Viking Line*, stripped down to its core, involved the question whether EU free movement law protected a shipping firm wishing to reflag one of its vessels, the Rosella, from the Finnish flag to that of Estonia from collective action by labour unions aimed at deterring corporate migration. The potential losers were Finnish workers. The potential winners were corporate interests seeking lower costs and (in the short term) Estonian workers. In the longer term, the balancing of winners and losers invites assessment of the type of internal market that is being built: a freedom to trade; a freedom to act collectively to compete effectively against corporate power?[41] The unions were private parties, not public bodies, but the Court has long taken the view that such entities are subject to the Treaty rules governing the free movement of persons, including companies. It did not deviate from that approach in *Viking Line*. Nor did it find a way to exclude the collective action from the scope of the Treaty on the basis that the EU lacks *legislative* competence in regard to the right of association and the right to strike.[42] The rules of free movement apply even in areas where the EU's legislative reach is exhausted. Here too the Court was following its own orthodox approach. This left the Court to conclude that it was dealing with a restriction on cross-border economic activity. What mattered was whether the restrictive effects of the collective labour action were *justified*. And here the Court was breaking new ground. It had never before addressed the need to reconcile fundamental (but not absolute) rights in the context of labour disputes. And, as so often, it was forced to do so without any helpful map or priority list in the Treaty.

The Court accepted in principle that the right to take collective action to protect workers is a legitimate interest which justifies a restriction of economic freedoms guaranteed by the Treaty. It added that the Community, now Union, has 'not only an economic but also a social purpose'.[43] For those fearful of EU free

[40] Case C-438/05 *Viking Line* [2007] ECR I-10779; Case C-341/05 *Laval un Partneri* [2007] ECR I-11767. For critical comment, see eg L Azoulai, 'The Court of Justice and the Social Market Economy: The Emergence of an Ideal and the Conditions for its Realiszation' (2008) 45 *CML Rev* 1335; C Joerges and F Rödl, 'Informal Politics, Formalised Law and the "Social Deficit" of European Integration: Reflections after the Judgments of the ECJ in *Viking* and *Laval*' (2009) 15 *ELJ* 1; N Nic Shuibhne, 'Settling Dust? Reflections on the Judgments in *Viking* and *Laval*' (2010) 21 *European Business Law Review* 681; C Barnard, 'British Jobs for British Workers: The Lindsey Oil Refinery Dispute and the Future of Local Labour Clauses in an Integrated EU Market' (2009) 38 *Industrial Law Journal* 245.

[41] *Laval*, the second of these rulings, had many similarities and some differences.

[42] Now Art 153(5) TFEU.

[43] Para 79.

movement law's bite, this is the cheerful part of the judgment. But who actually wins? This was ultimately a matter for the national court before which the litigation had been initiated (though in fact *Viking Line* was settled out of court) but the Court of Justice in *Viking Line* explained that that court must ascertain whether the objectives pursued by means of the collective action concern the protection of workers; and that

> even if that action – aimed at protecting the jobs and conditions of employment of the members of that union liable to be adversely affected by the reflagging of the Rosella – could reasonably be considered to fall, at first sight, within the objective of protecting workers, such a view would no longer be tenable if it were established that the jobs or conditions of employment at issue were not jeopardised or under serious threat.[44]

If this test means that it must be checked *in the particular circumstances of this case*, whether the collective action is apt to achieve its stated ends of protecting workers' jobs and employment conditions, then the judgment is relatively narrow in its impact, although even here the required assessment of whether the action does not go beyond what is necessary to attain its objective is awkward and promises unpredictability. If, by contrast, the ruling means that *only* action aimed at protecting the jobs of union members is recognised as capable of being justified under EU law, then the Court has excluded the possibility of more long-term strategic action taken by unions and even the 'political strike' in so far as it impedes cross-border economic activity. That constitutes a dramatic incursion into the permitted scope of collective labour rights. In any event, the ambiguity of the Court's judgment is likely to place a deterrent effect on collective labour action. The Court has stumbled into the shaping of collective labour law and policy, an area in which it has little expertise and in which it has adopted a test which significantly favours corporate interests over worker protection. Disturbingly, the Court did not follow the model regularly preferred in its earlier case law pitting economic against social and political fundamental rights which arose outside the context of labour disputes.[45] Having taken an approach to the scope of application of EU law which is broad but in line with previous practice, it then at the stage of justification leaves wholly out of account any margin of appreciation apt to permit recognition of local circumstances. This seems inconsistent with previous practice and leaves the ruling vulnerable to the accusation that its intrusive nature strains the Court's legitimacy – both by curtailing the permitted scope of collective labour action in the EU and, the institutional consequence, by establishing obligations under an interpretation of the Treaty which has the effect of disabling the EU political process from choosing a different (re-regulatory) solution under secondary legislation.

[44] Para 81.

[45] Especially Case C-112/00 *Schmidberger v Austria* [2003] ECR I-5659; Case C-71/02 *Herbert Karner* [2004] ECR I-3025; Case C-36/02 *Omega Spielhallen* [2004] ECR I-9609.

VIII. IN CONCLUSION

According to Article 4(2)(a) TFEU, the internal market as a legal concept is built on a competence to open up markets and to regulate them, which is *shared* between the Union and the Member States. There are Member State laws and practices which are subject to judicial supervision (which does not necessarily entail that they be set aside) under EU free movement law and/or to (partial or total) replacement by legislative initiatives at EU level. Which route is preferred determines the shape of the internal market. The more aggressive the application of the free movement rules, the less space is allowed for national regulatory autonomy (the vertical dimension) and the role of legislative action at EU level is also reduced (the horizontal dimension). By contrast, a refusal to bring a matter within the scope of free movement law enhances national regulatory autonomy (vertical); and a broad scope to free movement law coupled to a generous approach to the availability of justification tends to shift responsibility to the EU legislative process (horizontal). Choice of model determines the balance between deregulation and re-regulation, the opportunities for inter-jurisdictional competition and ultimately the very nature of the internal market.

The Treaty is lacking in clear rules on the location of these dividing lines, which tends to delegate power to the Court to choose what shall be the nature of the internal market. I have criticised its carelessly written ruling in *Bonnarde*; I am unimpressed by the ungainly reel that staggers from *Ruiz Zambrano* to *Dereci* via *McCarthy*; and *Viking Line*, untypical of the Court's generally sensitive approach to the collision of economic rights and social and political rights, was ill-considered. More broadly, I think the Court would gain a lot more than it loses were it to permit dissenting judgments: they would surely be uncommon but would allow the quality of the reasoning in hard cases to be opened up to scrutiny and development rather than sealed down beneath the oppression of the single collegiate judgment. In general, however, I judge most of the trends in the case law as legitimate, in the sense that the Court is working with legal rules that leave open a host of vital questions, and most of its choices do not seem to me to strain the limits of judicial interpretation. The Court has to draw lines: it chooses to draw them in understandable places most of the time. Most of the Court's embrace of *a circumloquacious statement of the result, rather than a reason for arriving at it* is the result of the calculatedly imprecise concept of the internal market loaded into the Treaty.

4

The Legitimacy of Free Movement Case Law: Process and Substance

JUKKA SNELL

I. INTRODUCTION

FREE MOVEMENT LAW is hard for courts. On the other side of the Atlantic, the US Supreme Court has struggled mightily with the main free movement rule of the Constitution, the dormant Commerce Clause of Article I section 8. Among the current Justices, some think that the entire jurisprudence should just be abandoned,[1] while some have poured withering scorn on the convoluted case law.[2] Among even the most measured commentators, the law has sometimes been characterised as a series of ad hoc reactions to particular problems and lacking in principle.[3] Professor Thomas Reed Powell of Harvard, after a lifetime of study of the Commerce Clause, is reported to have prepared the following Restatement of it: 'Congress may regulate interstate commerce. The states may also regulate interstate commerce, but not too much.

[1] Justice Thomas in *Camps Newfound/Owatonna v Town of Harrison* 520 U.S. 564, 117 S Ct. 1590 (1997) (dissenting, joined by Justice Scalia and in part by the then Chief Justice Rehnquist). Contra most recently, B Friedman and DT Deacon, 'A Course Unbroken: The Constitutional Legitimacy of the Dormant Commerce Clause' (2011) 97 *Virginia Law Review* 1877.

[2] See Justice Scalia (concurring in the judgment) in *American Trucking Associations, Inc v Michigan Public Service Commission* 545 U.S. 429, 125 S Ct. 2419 (2005) who refers scathingly to 'various tests from our wardrobe of ever-changing negative Commerce Clause fashions'. See also Justice Thomas (concurring in the judgment) in *United Haulers Association, Inc v Oneida-Herkimer Solid Waste Management Authority* 550 U.S. 330, 127 S Ct. 1786 (2007) who writes that the 'negative Commerce Clause has no basis in the Constitution and has proved unworkable in practice . . . [A]pplication of the negative Commerce Clause turns solely on policy considerations, not on the Constitution'.

[3] LH Tribe, *American Constitutional Law, Vol 1* (New York, Foundation Press, 2000) writes at 1102: 'The Supreme Court's approach to Commerce Clause issues . . . often appears to turn more on *ad hoc* reactions to particular cases than on any consistent application of coherent principles'. See also Friedman and Deacon, n 1 above, who staunchly defend the constitutional legitimacy of the dormant Commerce Clause, while acknowledging at 1883 that there are 'questions . . . about the workability of the current approach and the byzantine case law to which it has given birth'.

How much is too much is beyond the scope of this restatement'.[4] A tongue-in-cheek restatement of EU free movement law might not look too dissimilar.

The present chapter investigates how the European Court of Justice (ECJ) has coped with the free movement provisions of the Treaties; has its case law been legitimate? The fundamental starting point of the analysis is simple. The European Court of Justice is both a court and a European institution. As a result, it needs to comply with two sets of standards: those required of judicial institutions and those required of EU institutions.[5] In other words, two questions need to be answered: has the Court behaved like a court should, and has the Court observed the limits that EU institutions should observe?[6] It will be argued that while many aspects of the Court's work in the field of free movement can be criticised, the final verdict should not be overly harsh, given the context.

II. COURT AS A JUDICIAL INSTITUTION

What are the standards that all Western judicial institutions should respect and why do they matter? It is contended that there are at least three minimum requirements.[7] First, any court, the European Court of Justice included, must employ the normal judicial methods. This includes using the correct sources of law, and ensuring that the rulings follow from them. To put it differently, the judgments must be decisions according to law.[8] Second, the case law must be consistent. Similar things must be decided in the same way. The rulings must not be arbitrary.[9] Third, the reasoning of the judgments must show that the two standards above have been adhered to.[10]

[4] Quoted in PA Freund, 'Review and Federalism' in E Cahn (ed), *Supreme Court and Supreme Law* (Bloomington, Indiana University Press, 1954) 96–97.

[5] The approach has some affinities with the analysis of G Conway, *The Limits of Legal Reasoning and the European Court of Justice* (Cambridge, Cambridge University Press, 2012) who focuses on rule of law and democracy.

[6] In the typology of RH Fallon, 'Legitimacy and the Constitution' (2005) 118 *Harvard Law Review* 1787, these questions pertain primarily to 'legal legitimacy'.

[7] A similar conception was put forward by Takis Tridimas in a conference on 'The Reach of Free Movement' at the University of Oslo (18 May 2011). See also the discussion of the characteristics of the rule of law in Conway, n 5 above, 114–15.

[8] See CL Black, *Decision According to Law* (New York, WW Norton & Company, 1981) in particular 19–26.

[9] This can be traced to the Kantian idea of universalisability. See also eg Conway, n 5 above, who refers at 115 to 'formal requirement . . . of the law being . . . applied equally', and from the social sciences perspective FW Scharpf, 'Perpetual Momentum: Directed and Unconstrained?' (2012) 19 *Journal of European Public Policy* 127, 129.

[10] See generally on the role of reasoning the comparative study of M Lasser, *Judicial Deliberations: A Comparative Analysis of Judicial Transparency and Legitimacy* (Oxford, Oxford University Press, 2004) which is critical of the ECJ's insufficiently discursive method of argumentation in particular at 356–59. Similarly JHH Weiler, 'Epilogue: The Judicial Après Nice' in G de Búrca and JHH Weiler (eds), *The European Court of Justice* (Oxford, Oxford University Press, 2001) calls at 225 for a less Cartesian style of reasoning.

Why is this important? In modern Western societies – and in the EU in particular – courts wield enormous power.[11] The basic starting point of our systems is that power must be kept in check.[12] Yet, at the same time, we want courts to be independent and able to protect even unpopular individuals and minorities, which makes it difficult to employ traditional democratic constraints – courts are supposed to be counter-majoritarian institutions.[13] One way to keep courts in check is to insist that they follow the law – play the law game of sources, consistency and reasoning.[14] This reduces the ability of judges to wield arbitrary power,[15] although, paradoxically, it may at the same time enhance their power in general by bolstering their standing among the public.[16] In other words, legitimacy may serve both as a constraint and source of power.[17]

How well does the Court's free movement case law comply with these three requirements? *First*, for the standard of normal judicial methods, including sources of law and so on, the assessment is not straightforward. Here, the problem is the inherent ambiguity of the whole internal market concept of Article 26 TFEU, which is explored in Stephen Weatherill's contribution to this volume. Almost any decisions could be justified on internal market grounds. As demonstrated by Miguel Poiares Maduro in *We the Court*,[18] at least three completely different models of internal market could be grounded on the Treaty. In other words, almost any ruling could potentially be derived from the notion of the internal market, given its vagueness.

However, there are some more detailed provisions of the Treaty that the Court has tended to conveniently ignore, or play rather fast and loose with.

[11] A Stone Sweet, *The Judicial Construction of Europe* (Oxford, Oxford University Press, 2004) writes at 1: 'Today, the ECJ has no rival as the most effective supranational judicial body in the history of the world, comparing favourably with the most powerful constitutional courts anywhere'. See also KJ Alter, *The European Court's Political Power: Selected Essays* (Oxford, Oxford University Press, 2009) in particular 92–108.

[12] A von Bogdandy and I Venzke, 'On the Democratic Legitimation of International Judicial Lawmaking' (2011) 12 *German Law Journal* 1341 write at 1342–43 in the context of international courts: 'History cautions that not too much confidence should be placed even in the benevolent and enlightened ruler'.

[13] See JH Ely, *Democracy and Distrust: A Theory of Judicial Review* (Cambridge, Mass, Harvard University Press, 1980).

[14] In the EU context, sufficient reasoning is also important to allow for a fruitful dialogue between the ECJ and national courts, which is one of the key elements of the European system. See eg A Torres Pérez, *Conflicts of Rights in the European Union: A Theory of Supranational Adjudication* (Oxford, Oxford University Press, 2009).

[15] It also safeguards democracy, as judges have to follow the will of the legislature, and increases predictability, thus reducing transaction costs.

[16] See eg A-M Burley and W Mattli, 'Europe before the Court: A Political Theory of Legal Integration' (1993) 47 *International Organization* 41 who refer (at 72–73) to law as a 'mask and shield'. See in the US context Fallon, n 6 above, who writes at 1840–41: 'As the [US Supreme] Court recognized, however, its sociological legitimacy depends on its adherence or apparent adherence to legal norms. If the Court did not base its decisions on legal principles, the public would lose respect for it'.

[17] BMJ Szewczyk, 'European Citizenship and National Democracy: Contemporary Sources of Legitimacy of the European Union' (2011) 17 *Colum J Eur L* 151, 163.

[18] M Poiares Maduro, *We The Court: The European Court of Justice and the European Economic Constitution* (Oxford, Hart Publishing, 1998).

Here, I will use the example of Article 57 TFEU on services. This provision starts by saying that services are only services within the meaning of the Treaty when they are normally provided for remuneration. Yet, the Court has found, in cases such as *Smits-Peerbooms* and *Watts*, that medical services in the context of a benefits-in-kind or an NHS system fall within the Treaty.[19] Article 57 TFEU then continues to provide that things are 'services' only in so far as they are not governed by the provisions relating to freedom of movement of goods, capital and persons. Yet, in *Fidium Finanz*, the Court found that a German law that restricted movement of both financial services and capital from Switzerland was only covered by the rules on services, which do not apply to extra-EU movements, unlike Article 63 TFEU on the free movement of capital.[20] Finally, the last paragraph of Article 57 TFEU gives a service provider the right to temporarily pursue his activity in the host state under the same conditions as the nationals of that state – a right to national treatment. Yet, the Court has made it clear in cases such as *Säger* that the service providers can rely on a much broader right of mutual recognition,[21] not only on national treatment.

Anyone coming anew to the case law, armed only with the text of the Treaty, would be likely to raise an eyebrow at these judgments and ask: how did the Court justify this? This, of course, brings us to the *third* standard – the need to employ reasoning that shows how the Court's rulings follow from the sources of law, the Treaty. When it comes to the health care cases, there are some difficulties in this respect. In *Smits-Peerbooms*, an argument was made, in the context of the Dutch benefits-in-kind system, that there was no remuneration and therefore no services: although sickness funds paid the hospitals, the payments were at a flat rate and not related to the cost of the treatment that had been provided free-of-charge to the patient. In other words, in many instances the payment was well below what it cost to deliver the service. In the view of Advocate General Ruiz-Jarabo Colomer, this excluded the application of the free movement of services. The Court disagreed, simply asserting that

> [i]n the present cases, the payments made by the sickness insurance funds . . . albeit set at a flat rate, are indeed the consideration for the hospital services and unquestionably represent remuneration for the hospital which receives them and which is engaged in an activity of an economic character.[22]

There was no attempt to explain how a payment that bears no relation to the cost of a service represents 'consideration' for the service.[23] In *Watts*, when it

[19] Case C-157/99 *Smits and Peerbooms* [2001] ECR I-5473 and Case C-372/04 *Watts* [2006] ECR I-4325.

[20] Case C-452/04 *Fidium Finanz* [2006] ECR I-9521.

[21] Case C-76/90 *Säger* [1991] ECR I-4221.

[22] n 19 above, para 58. Contrast AG Saggio in Case C-368/98 *Vanbraekel* [2001] ECR I-5363, para 21.

[23] cp the view of the Commission in Case C-76/05 *Schwarz and Gootjes-Schwarz* [2007] ECR I-6849, para 28, where it argued in the case of educational services that: 'It is clear from [previous judgments in the field of education] that the essential characteristic of teaching services provided for remuneration is the payment, by the pupil or another person, of fees corresponding more or less to the economic cost of the teaching'.

came to the NHS system, the reasoning of the Court relied heavily on the fact that the claimant, Mrs Watts, had on the facts travelled to France to be treated and had paid for the treatment herself. Yet, the Treaty talks about the service being '*normally*' provided for remuneration. Here, the normal situation would seem to be one of free treatment, but the Court focused on the 'abnormal' without explaining why.

In *Fidium Finanz*, the Court again ruled contrary to the Opinion of the Advocate General, who had thought that the Swiss company providing loans over the internet to customers in Germany could rely on free movement of capital, which alone among the freedoms has an *erga omnes* effect and applies to movements of capital between EU Member States and third countries. The reasoning is again laconic, with the Court cryptically stating that

> [a]lthough in the definition of the notion of 'services' laid down in the first paragraph of Article [57 TFEU] it is specified that the services 'are not governed by the provisions relating to freedom of movement for goods, capital and persons', that relates to the definition of that notion and does not establish any order of priority between the freedom to provide services and the other fundamental freedoms.[24]

The reasoning continued to find that the German rules 'affect primarily the freedom to provide services' despite the fact that this freedom was manifestly inapplicable, given that the loans originated from Switzerland, and decided it was 'not necessary' to consider the free movement of capital, despite the fact that this freedom was the only one that could have come into play at all.[25] A significant plank in the reasoning was that the purpose of the relevant German rules was to regulate financial services; yet, in other free movement case law the Court tends to ignore the purpose of national rules and focus on effects.[26]

Finally, it is of course well known that mutual recognition is a part of the law of free movement of services, even though the European Parliament decided it was politically unacceptable to refer to it,[27] let alone to the country of origin principle, in the Services Directive.[28] However, the Court has never properly explained where the notion is derived from, given that Article 57(3) TFEU only contemplates national treatment.[29] The attempt in *Säger* to rely on the general prohibition of restrictions in Article 56 TFEU is vulnerable to the criticism that Article 57(3) TFEU is *lex specialis* and should therefore have priority.[30]

[24] n 20 above, para 32.

[25] ibid, para 49.

[26] For criticism, see eg S Hindelang, *The Free Movement of Capital and Foreign Direct Investment: The Scope of Protection in EU Law* (Oxford, Oxford University Press, 2009) 96–101.

[27] K Nicolaïdis and SK Schmidt, 'Mutual Recognition "on Trial": The Long Road to Services Liberalization' (2007) 14 *Journal of European Public Policy* 717, 729.

[28] Directive (EC) 2006/123 of the European Parliament and of the Council on services in the internal market [2006] OJ L376/36.

[29] See on the justification of mutual recognition in the field of services, J Snell, 'Free Movement of Services and the Services Directive: The Legitimacy of the Case Law' in J van de Gronden (ed), *The EU and WTO Law on Services* (Alphen aan den Rijn, Kluwer Law International, 2009).

[30] Conway, n 5 above, 153 criticises the Court more generally for failing to take heed of the *lex specialis* maxim.

None of the above is meant as a criticism of the results of the rulings. There may have been very good reasons for them, although they have never been put forward by the Court. The inclusion of health care within the remit of free movement of services has allowed integration to move forward in this important sector.[31] The move away from the parallel application of the free movement of capital and the other freedoms witnessed for the first time in *Fidium Finanz* responded to Member State concerns relating to the potential erosion of their tax powers, given that free movement of capital can be used to challenge national tax rules in the context of capital movements between the EU and third countries.[32] Finally, effective mutual recognition is generally considered a critical component of a well functioning internal market.[33] However, it seems that the Court has been quite willing to play fast and loose with the actual wording of the Treaty, without properly explaining what justifies the departures from the text. The reasons for ignoring some of the rules of the Treaty remain unarticulated.

The *second* standard that was posited earlier is one of consistency. Similar cases have to be decided in the same way. There must be no arbitrary decisions. If there are rulings that do look inconsistent, the reasoning must convincingly distinguish the situations. How does the free movement law fare in this respect? Three examples will be considered here; many more could be offered.[34]

The first example concerns the free movement of goods. As is well known, in *Commission v Italy* (trailers) and *Mickelsson and Roos*, the Court decided to employ a market access approach to use restrictions, and not apply *Keck* by analogy.[35] Consequently, a use restriction is caught by Article 34 TFEU if it has 'considerable influence on the behaviour of consumers'[36] as a result of which

[31] Resulting most recently in Directive (EC) 2011/24 of the European Parliament and of the Council on the application of patients' rights in cross-border healthcare [2011] OJ L88/45. For a critical view, see C Newdick, 'Citizenship, Free Movement and Health Care: Cementing Individual Rights by Corroding Social Solidarity' (2006) 43 *CML Rev* 1645, who argues that the case law may corrode the social solidarity essential to any fair public health system.

[32] See generally J Snell, 'Free Movement of Capital: Evolution as a Non-Linear Process' in P Craig and G de Búrca (eds), *The Evolution of EU Law* (Oxford, Oxford University Press, 2011).

[33] See eg J Pelkmans, 'Mutual Recognition in Goods and Services: An Economic Perspective' in F Kostoris Padoa Schioppa (ed), *The Principle of Mutual Recognition in the European Integration Process* (Basingstoke, Palgrave Macmillan, 2005).

[34] The Court sometimes investigates overriding requirements even when the national measure is discriminatory, but sometimes is only prepared to consider Treaty derogations; cp Case C-531/07 *LIBRO* [2009] ECR I-3717 with Case C-341/05 *Laval un Partneri* [2007] ECR I-11767. The Court has deemed most freedoms horizontally applicable, but rules this out in the case of goods; cp Case C-281/98 *Angonese* [2000] ECR I-4139 with Case 311/85 *Vlaamse Reisbureaus* [1987] ECR 3801. The Court is not prepared to countenance economic justifications, such as the avoidance of the erosion of tax base, but accepts the aim of safeguarding the financial balance of social security systems; cp Case C-168/01 *Bosal Holding* [2003] ECR I-9409 with Case C-158/96 *Kohll v Union des Caisses de Maladie* [1998] ECR I-1931.

[35] Case C-110/05 *Commission v Italy* [2009] ECR I-519; Case C-142/05 *Åklagaren v Mickelsson and Roos* [2009] ECR I-4273; and Joined Cases C-267/91 and C-268/91 *Keck and Mithouard* [1993] ECR I-6097. See generally, eg J Snell, 'The Notion of Market Access: A Concept or a Slogan?' (2010) 47 *CML Rev* 437.

[36] *Mickelsson and Roos*, n 35 above, para 26. See similarly the reference to 'substantial effect on the transit of goods' in Case C-28/09 *Commission v Austria* [2011] ECR I-0000, para 116.

market access is hindered. In other words, if enough consumers stop buying a product, there is a restriction. By contrast, in *Keck* in the context of rules concerning selling arrangements the Court had decided that a mere reduction in the volume of sales is not enough to trigger Article 34 TFEU,[37] and that non-discriminatory rules concerning selling arrangements do not amount to restrictions, because they neither prevent nor impose an unequal impact on market access. Consequently, as the law now stands, a use restriction is contrary to free movement of goods if it affects the volume of sales enough to hinder market access, while rules concerning selling arrangements only infringe in the event of discrimination or the prevention of market access.[38] Unfortunately, there is no reasoning to explain why these two categories of national rules ought to be treated differently, contrary to the view of Advocate General Kokott, who argued in *Mickelsson and Roos* that arrangements for use and selling arrangements are comparable in their nature and effects and should be dealt with in the same way.[39]

The second example concerns the difference in the treatment of regulatory and fiscal barriers to free movement. Here, the same Treaty provisions have been given fundamentally different readings, depending on the type of the national rule under consideration. As regards regulatory barriers, a classic way of infringing the Treaty is double regulation. Ever since *Cassis*,[40] and even earlier in the case of services,[41] this has been one of the prime targets of free movement case law.[42] By contrast, the Court has ruled that double taxation does not infringe free movement law.[43] In *Kerckhaert*, the Court decided that the imposition of a Belgian tax on dividends already taxed in France was not a restriction at all, but simply results 'from the exercise in parallel by two Member States of their fiscal sovereignty'.[44] The Court explained that this was, inter alia, due to Article 293 EC (repealed at Lisbon) envisaging conventions preventing double taxation, in the absence of which Community law did 'not lay down any general criteria for the attribution of areas of competence between the Member States in relation to the elimination of double taxation within the Community'.[45] The problem with this reasoning is that, in the field of regulatory barriers, the Court has been ready to attribute regulatory competences without any explicit Treaty

[37] *Keck*, n 35 above, para 13.

[38] For criticism, see eg S Enchelmaier, '*Moped Trailers, Mickelsson and Roos, Gysbrechts*: The ECJ's Case Law on Goods Keeps on Moving' (2010) 29 *YEL* 190.

[39] *Mickelsson and Roos*, n 35 above, paras 42–56 of the Opinion of the AG.

[40] Case 120/78 *Rewe-Zentral v Bundesmonopolverwaltung für Branntwein* [1979] ECR 649.

[41] Joined Cases 110/78 and 111/78 *Van Wesemael* [1979] ECR 35.

[42] For discussion of the legal development of principle, see eg C Barnard, *The Substantive Law of the EU: The Four Freedoms* (Oxford, Oxford University Press, 2010) 91–96.

[43] See generally eg J Snell, 'Non-discriminatory Tax Obstacles in Community Law' (2007) 56 *ICLQ* 339, 358–66.

[44] Case C-513/04 *Kerckhaert and Morres* [2006] ECR I-10967, para 20.

[45] ibid, para 22.

support,[46] and has rejected all arguments based on the lack of conventions envisaged in Article 293 EC, for example in the case of *Überseering*.[47]

The final example relates to the export of goods. Even after the recent ruling in *Gysbrechts*,[48] national rules concerning the export of products only violate Article 35 TFEU if they discriminate in law or in fact.[49] Yet, outside the selling arrangements exception, national rules can be classified as import restrictions even in the absence of discrimination, and the other freedoms of persons, services and capital do not rely on discrimination in the case of exports.[50] Again, there is no explanation in the reasoning. Further, in many cases, the same national rule can be challenged equally well under both Articles 34 and 35 TFEU. If a national rule prohibits the use of horse meat in the manufacture of sausages, should it be deemed a use restriction of horse meat, which infringes Article 34 TFEU if its influence is considerable, or a restriction on the export of sausages, which only violates Article 35 TFEU in the event of discrimination?[51]

The examples above suggest that the Court has a problem with consistency, and its reasoning fails to explain the different approaches taken; in reality, it does not even try to distinguish the cases. It seems that the Court actually has two different visions of the internal market:[52] one insists on the abolition of national rules with a considerable impact on the market, unless a proportionate justification can save a particular measure; the other merely requires Member States to refrain from discrimination. No matter how ambiguous the concept of internal market is, it surely cannot mean two different things at the same time.[53]

[46] eg, in the field of goods the competence to regulate product characteristics is held by the home state, while selling arrangements are left for the host state. See N Bernard, 'La libre circulation des merchandises, des personnes et des services dans la Traité CE sous l'angle de la compétence' (1998) 34 *Cahiers de Droit Européen* 11, 33–35 and J Snell and M Andenas, 'Exploring the Outer Limits: Restrictions on the Free Movement of Goods and Services' (1999) 10 *European Business Law Review* 252, 264–67.

[47] Case C-208/00 *Überseering* [2002] ECR I-9919.

[48] Case C-205/07 *Gysbrechts and Santurel* [2008] ECR I-9947.

[49] PJ Oliver (ed), *Oliver on Free Movement of Goods in the European Union* (Oxford, Hart Publishing, 2010) 140.

[50] See eg Case C-384/93 *Alpine Investments* [1995] ECR I-1141.

[51] Case 15/79 *Groenveld* [1979] ECR 3409.

[52] A Saydé, 'One Law, Two Competitions: An Enquiry into the Contradictions of Free Movement Law' (2010–11) 13 *CYELS* 365 argues that contradictions of free movement law are caused by adherence to two conflicting paradigms of economic integration: regulatory neutrality paradigm and regulatory competition paradigm.

[53] The academic community may have to bear a part of the blame. The theoretical background of EU free movement law has been insufficiently explored, although see Poiares Maduro, n 18 above, for a prominent counter-example. This can be contrasted with the US position, where the theoretical underpinnings of the dormant commerce clause are contested more openly. Contrast eg the process based approach in Tribe, n 3 above, 1049–59, with the anti-protectionism approach in DH Regan, 'The Supreme Court and State Protectionism: Making Sense of the Dormant Commerce Clause' (1986) 84 *Michigan Law Review* 1091.

Of course, when the Court is criticised, the constraint of unanimous rulings on the quality of the Court's reasoning is an important factor to bear in mind.[54] In the English context, Lord Reid remarked in the early 1970s:

> Until recently there could only be one judgment in the Privy Council . . . If you compare the quality of Privy Council judgments with speeches in the House of Lords for a long time back I think you will agree that from the point of view of developing the law Privy Council judgments have been much inferior. They are perfectly adequate to decide the particular case but not often of wider importance. Yet the same Law Lords have sat and they have taken just as much trouble. The reason is that a single judgment must get the agreement of at least all in the majority so it tends to be no more than the highest common factor in their views.[55]

In other words, the requirement of a single judgment has in practice proven detrimental to the quality of reasoning even when it comes to judges steeped in the tradition and the discursive judicial style of the common law. Nevertheless, it is difficult to avoid a verdict: 'could do better' in the case of the European Court.[56] Free movement law has been at the heart of the integration project and the case law since the beginning, and the Court surely has had an opportunity to develop expertise, set out clearer reasons for its approach and impose coherence on the field. Far too many unexplained anomalies and inconsistencies remain.[57] In the words of Eleanor Spaventa: 'When the [free movement] cases are closely scrutinized one might be excused for feeling a slight desperation as to the chaotic picture arising from the Court's jurisprudence'.[58]

III. THE COURT AS AN EU INSTITUTION

The European Court of Justice is not just any judicial body; it is an institution of the European Union, and as such is subject to the principle of conferral, the

[54] The anonymity of judges provides an important safeguard for their independence; otherwise a Member State could threaten its judge with non-reappointment in the case of an unfavourable ruling. Cp the non-renewable term of office of eight years for members of the Executive Board of the European Central Bank, set out in Protocol on the Statute of the European System of Central Banks and of the European Central Bank [2008] OJ C115/230, Art 11(2). But see V Perju, 'Reason and Authority in the European Court of Justice' (2009) 49 *Virginia Journal of International Law* 307, 347–51.

[55] Lord Reid, 'The Judge as a Lawmaker' (1972–73) 12 *Journal of the Society of Public Teachers of Law* 22, 29.

[56] Various methods of improving the reasoning even in the context of a single collegiate judgment are discussed in A Arnull, *The European Union and its Court of Justice*, 2nd edn (Oxford, Oxford University Press, 2006) 10–14 and E Sharpston, 'Transparency and Clear Legal Language in the European Union: Ambiguous Legislative Texts, Laconic Pronouncements and the Credibility of the Judicial System' (2009–10) 12 *CYELS* 409, 421–22.

[57] LW Gormley, 'Free Movement of Goods and their Use – What is the Use of It?' (2010) 33 *Fordham Intl LJ* 1589 argues at 1626 that 'the ECJ is not thinking in terms of grand theory, but is actually simply deciding, on a case-by-case basis, the reasonableness of national measures'.

[58] E Spaventa, 'The Outer Limit of the Treaty Free Movement Provisions: Some Reflections on the Significance of *Keck*, Remoteness and *Deliège*' in C Barnard and O Odudu (eds), *The Outer Limits of European Union Law* (Oxford, Hart Publishing, 2009) 270.

requirement to respect the national identities of Member States and so on. Does this impose substantive limits on the Court's case law?[59] Are there interpretations of the free movement provisions that are not legitimate due to the structure, objectives and general principles of the EU legal system,[60] despite the fact that they might fall within the textual ambit of the relevant Treaty Article? The difficulty is that while it can be readily agreed that no EU institution may legitimately push integration beyond its proper limits,[61] it is not easy to establish where exactly those limits might lie.

The German Constitutional Court in its Lisbon judgment sought to set out its views of what the democratic principles of the German Constitution allow the Union to do:

> European unification on the basis of a treaty union of sovereign states may, however, not be achieved in such a way that not sufficient space is left to the Member States for the political formation of the economic, cultural and social living conditions . . . Particularly sensitive for the ability of a constitutional state to democratically shape itself are decisions on substantive and formal criminal law (1), on the disposition of the monopoly on the use of force by the police within the state and by the military towards the exterior (2), fundamental fiscal decisions on public revenue and public expenditure, the latter being particularly motivated, inter alia, by social policy considerations (3), decisions on the shaping of living conditions in a social state (4) and decisions of particular cultural importance, for example on family law, the school and education system and on dealing with religious communities (5).[62]

The problem with this is that there is no reasoning explaining why it is these areas that need protection from excessive integration, and not others. This renders the listing of sensitive areas unconvincing from the legal perspective,[63] and in any event, the decision only concerns the requirements imposed by the constitution of one Member State, although the judgment, of course, is of political significance and its general anxiety about ensuring sufficient state autonomy is widely shared.

It is generally agreed that one of the biggest questions for the legitimacy of free movement law concerns the very wide notion of restriction that the Court has adopted, and which it has been grappling with for a long time. As is well known, the broader the notion, the more power flows vertically from Member States to the EU and horizontally from legislatures to courts. In the words of Judge Joliet, one of the judges deciding *Keck*[64] where the Court sought to deal with the issue:

[59] See also Conway, n 5 above, who discusses the substantive limits of integration, eg at 274.

[60] Cp the notion of 'functional aspects of legitimacy' in MA Loth, 'Courts in a Quest for Legitimacy: A Comparative Approach' in N Huls, M Adams and J Bomhoff (eds), *The Legitimacy of Highest Courts' Rulings: Judicial Deliberations and Beyond* (The Hague, TMC Asser Press, 2009).

[61] In any case, it can be argued that the desired breadth and depth of integration are political issues, so that the Court should proceed with caution. See Conway, n 5 above, eg at 245–46.

[62] BVerfG, 2 BvE 2/08 of 30.6.2009, paras 249 and 252.

[63] See D Halberstam and C Möllers, 'The German Constitutional Court says "Ja zu Deutschland!"' (2009) 10 *German Law Journal* 1241, 1249–51.

[64] n 35 above.

> The extension of the *Cassis de Dijon* principle beyond regulations relating to product characteristics had led the Court to review a large variety of national laws having little or nothing to do with importation, and to make purely political judgments about them . . . Could we judges by ourselves claim to possess greater wisdom and intelligence than all the governments and the national parliaments of the Community's Member States?[65]

In other words, the legitimacy of the case law was questionable. The present contribution will not focus on this issue. It is covered well in Stephen Weatherill's chapter (chapter 3), and I have expressed my views at length elsewhere.[66] Also, the concept of restriction may not always matter for the final result of a case, due to the doctrine of justifications and proportionality. Instead, my focus will be on two scenarios where the issue of legitimacy and the proper limits of integration have arisen in a particularly acute form in recent years; namely, cases that challenge national economic models[67] and cases that question national laws in the fields that the Treaty leaves for the Member States.[68]

When considering the *first* scenario, the cases that question national economic models, it is important to note that the notion of 'internal market' is deeply ambiguous; it lacks a precise meaning.[69] As a result, it can be argued that the Treaty does not contain a mandate for the Court to choose one particular economic model over another in the name of the internal market.[70] An attempt to do so would be illegitimate for reasons of democracy, which, according to Article 2 TEU, is a value the Union is founded on, and which undoubtedly forms

[65] R Joliet, 'The Free Circulation of Goods: The *Keck and Mithouard* Decision and the New Directions in the Case Law' (1995) 1 *Colum J Eur L* 436, 445.

[66] See J Snell, 'Who's Got the Power? Free Movement and Allocation of Competences in EC Law' (2003) 22 *YEL* 323; J Snell, 'And Then There Were Two: Products and Citizens in Community Law' in T Tridimas and P Nebbia (eds), *European Union Law for the Twenty-First Century: Vol II* (Oxford, Hart Publishing, 2004) and Snell, 'The Notion of Market Access', n 35 above.

[67] See generally J Snell, 'Varieties of Capitalism and the Limits of European Economic Integration' (2010–11) 13 *CYELS* 415.

[68] L Azoulai, 'The Court of Justice and the Social Market Economy: The Emergence of an Ideal and the Conditions for its Realization' (2008) 45 *CML Rev* 1335 writes at 1341 that the 'penetration of Community law in all the areas of competence of the Member States is perhaps the most important phenomenon in Community case law in the last ten years'.

[69] See ch 3 this volume.

[70] Admittedly following the Lisbon Treaty there is now a reference to a 'highly competitive social market economy' in Art 3(3) TEU, but just like with 'internal market' its precise meaning is not spelled out. 'Social market economy' was not defined by the European Convention Working Group on Social Europe, which proposed its inclusion in the Constitutional Treaty in CONV 516/1/03 Rev 1 at 10, from where it made its way into the Lisbon Treaty. The Working Group simply thought that the notion would underline the link between economic and social development, and the efforts made to ensure greater coherence between economic and social policies, but noted the need to respect a Europe of diverse ways of doing things. If 'social market economy' is to be understood as an expression of a historical German-style mix of welfare and economic performance, it seems that the Union lacks the necessary competences to put the concept into effect. Its relationship with other notions, such as the principle of an open market economy with free competition expressed in Article 119 TFEU, remains unclear. The best reading of the Treaty is that it avoids imposing a specific detailed economic model on its Member States.

a part of Member State national identities in the meaning of Article 4(2) TEU.[71] Yet, a number of recent, often notorious, free movement cases have questioned important features of national production systems – the basic economic models of Member States.

In this context, it is worth noting how much more controversial the free movement case law has become in recent years.[72] As long as the focus was essentially on the free movement of goods, national economic models were only challenged indirectly, as a result of the increased competition on product markets that the free movement entails. In other words, when products move freely, companies and national systems need to ensure that they stay competitive, but each of them is free to do so in its own way. Today, the free movement rulings may have a much more direct effect on national economic models.[73] They influence labour relations, as exemplified by rulings in *Viking* and *Laval*.[74] They regulate corporations and their governance, as seen in *Centros* and *Volkswagen*.[75] Such decisions are going to be much more sensitive, and their impact potentially more far reaching, than those dealing with goods.

Why is this? Modern theories of capitalism tend to identify different varieties,[76] in particular distinguishing liberal market economies, such as the UK, and coordinated market economies, such as Germany. Both varieties are seen as equally valid ways of organising production. The special quality – and strength – of coordinated market economies lies in their ability to rely on institutions such as trade unions, business associations and regulatory regimes that increase predictability and deliberation, and create common expectations and informal understandings. Key features are capital markets that are relatively patient and allow company management to adopt a longer time horizon, company structures that ensure consensual decision making and employee engagement, and industrial relations systems that equalise wages and promote job security. These features provide coordinated market economies with comparative institutional advantages, in particular allowing them to perform strongly in sectors where incremental innovation is critical for success. Put simply, the security of employment that flows from the coordination mechanisms allows workers to invest in highly specific skills that are critical in sectors where the key

[71] A von Bogdandy and S Schill, 'Overcoming Absolute Primacy: Respect for National Identity under the Lisbon Treaty' (2011) 48 *CML Rev* 1417, 1435–40.

[72] eg, rulings on workers' rights played a significant role in the Irish debates on the Lisbon Treaty; see Houses of the Oireachtas, Joint Committee on European Affairs, 'Seventh Report: The Lisbon Treaty and Workers' Rights' (September 2009) 11–12.

[73] See M Höpner and A Schäfer, 'A New Phase of European Integration: Organised Capitalisms in Post-Ricardian Europe' (2010) 33 *West European Politics* 344.

[74] Case C-438/05 *International Transport Workers' Federation and Finnish Seamen's* Union [2007] ECR I-10779 and *Laval*, n 34 above.

[75] Case C-212/97 *Centros* [1999] ECR I-1459 and Case C-112/05 *Commission v Germany* [2007] ECR I-8995.

[76] Many of the key texts have been helpfully collected in B Hancké (ed), *Debating Varieties of Capitalism* (Oxford, Oxford University Press, 2009).

competitive advantage is a workforce that autonomously engages in the continuous improvement of products.[77]

There is potential for insensitive case law espousing liberal market principles to disrupt and destabilise the coordination mechanisms that certain national economic models rely on.[78] Decisions that undermine trade unions or allow companies to opt out of national regimes might inadvertently interfere with the key features of a given variety of capitalism. I do not think this has happened yet, at least to any massive degree.[79] However, the risks are there, in particular as the different elements of national production systems are said to be complementary and interconnected,[80] so that disturbing one feature may have significant and unexpected knock-on effects elsewhere in the system.

From the perspective of democracy, it would not be acceptable for the EU to impose a liberal market regime on all its Member States.[81] Any attempt by the Court to do so without a clear and explicit mandate from the Treaties would be particularly illegitimate. The nature of a given national production system has implications for income distribution. It is usually thought that coordinated market economies have a more equal distribution than liberal ones, inter alia, due to generous welfare systems acting as insurance against the risk of a loss of a job for highly specialised workers, while in liberal systems low benefits further contribute to the flexible labour markets that count among their main strengths.[82] According to democratic theory, decisions likely to have profound implications for income distribution can only be taken within a *demos* following a process with input legitimacy.[83] Further, decisions that affect matters such as workers' rights are highly salient and cannot legitimately be delegated away from democratic contestation.[84] In the words of the German Constitutional Court, there could be a danger that 'not sufficient space is left to the Member States for the political formation of the economic, cultural and social living conditions'.[85]

[77] For the seminal exposition of the key arguments, see P Hall and D Soskice, 'An Introduction to Varieties of Capitalism' in P Hall and D Soskice (eds), *Varieties of Capitalism: The Institutional Foundations of Comparative Advantage* (Oxford, Oxford University Press, 2001).

[78] See FW Scharpf, 'The Asymmetry of European Integration, or Why the EU Cannot be a "Social Market Economy"' (2010) 8 *Socio-Economic Review* 211.

[79] M Blauberger, 'With Luxembourg in Mind . . . The Remaking of National Policies in the Face of ECJ Jurisprudence' (2012) 19 *Journal of European Pubic Policy* 109 argues, based on a number of case studies concerning judgments on workers' rights, that Member States have at their disposal various strategies that allow them to preserve significant parts of their original legislation even in the event of adverse rulings by the ECJ.

[80] Hall and Soskice, n 77 above, 17–21.

[81] See generally J Snell, '"European Constitutional Settlement", An Ever Closer Union, and the Treaty of Lisbon: Democracy or Relevance?' (2008) 33 *ELRev* 619.

[82] See M Estervez-Abe, T Iversen and D Soskice, 'Social Protection and the Formation of Skills: A Reinterpretation of the Welfare State' in P Hall and D Soskice (eds), *Varieties of Capitalism: The Institutional Foundations of Comparative Advantage* (Oxford, Oxford University Press, 2001) for a study of the link between national economic models and different types of equality.

[83] See eg G Majone, 'Europe's "Democratic Deficit": The Question of Standards' (1998) 4 *ELJ* 5.

[84] See eg A Moravcsik, 'In Defence of the "Democratic Deficit": Reassessing Legitimacy in the European Union' (2002) 40 *Journal of Common Market Studies* 603.

[85] n 62 above.

The Court's case law has the potential to cause disruption when it touches on key areas in the name of the right of establishment or the free movement of capital or services.[86] Fortunately, the structure of the jurisprudence makes it possible to avoid this, provided the Court is sensitive to the existence and needs of the different varieties of capitalism. In practice, free movement cases are won or lost on the principle of proportionality, which is well suited for context-sensitive decision-making. In Article 267 TFEU proceedings, the Court is only competent to interpret EU law, while the final judgment on its application rests in the hands of the referring national court,[87] which is unlikely to wish to destabilise the national economic model. As long as care is taken and liberal solutions are not automatically preferred in all cases, it seems unlikely that the free movement case law will ride roughshod over this potential substantive limit to integration.[88]

In any event, the Lisbon Treaty has sent the Court a number of signals that tell it to proceed with caution. The objective of social market economy has been written into the Treaty, the notion of undistorted competition has been banished to a protocol, the Charter of Fundamental Rights with its social rights has been rendered binding and Article 9 TFEU now provides that requirements linked to the promotion of a high level of employment and the guarantee of adequate social protection are to be taken into account in the definition and implementation of all Union polices. The Commission[89] and some of the Advocates General have already taken notice.[90]

The *second* scenario that may require consideration concerns cases that question national laws in the fields that the Treaty primarily leaves for the Member States. The EU is only supposed to have limited powers in areas such as health care and education.[91] This has been stressed in the Lisbon Treaty, which in

[86] See C Gerner-Beuerle, 'Shareholders between the Market and the State: The VW Law and Other Interventions in the Market Economy' (2012) 49 *CML Rev* 97 for an argument that the case law on free movement of capital should not seek to set a single model of corporate governance for the EU.

[87] The role of national courts is emphasised in G Davies, 'Activism Relocated. The Self-Restraint of the European Court of Justice in its National Context' (2012) 19 *Journal of European Public Policy* 76. See generally on the distinction between application and interpretation, eg, the contribution by K Lenaerts, ch 1 this volume and also J Snell, 'European Courts and Intellectual Property: A Tale of Hercules, Zeus and Cyclops' (2004) 29 *ELRev* 178.

[88] For an optimistic assessment of the role of the ECJ from a social science perspective, see J Caporaso and S Tarrow, 'Polanyi in Brussels: Supranational Institutions and the Transnational Embedding of Markets' (2009) 63 *International Organization* 593, but see M Höpner and A Schäfer, 'Embeddedness and Regional Integration: Waiting for Polanyi in a Hayekian Setting' (2012) 66 *International Organization* 429.

[89] Commission Communication, 'Towards a Single Market Act for a highly competitive social market economy: 50 proposals for improving our work, business and exchanges with one another' COM (2010) 608 states at 23 that the Lisbon Treaty requires it to 'adopt a more all-embracing view of the single market', and in Commission Communication, 'Single Market Act: Twelve levers to boost growth and strengthen confidence' COM (2011) 206/4 it emphasises the importance of the social dimension, eg at 5 and 16–17, citing Art 9 TFEU and the Charter of Fundamental Rights.

[90] See AG Cruz Villalón in Case C-515/08 *Santos Palhota* [2010] ECR I-9133, in particular para 53.

[91] See Arts 6, 165 and 168 TFEU.

Article 1 TEU emphasises Member States as the original source of competences, in Article 4(1) TEU issues a reminder that they hold residual powers, and in Articles 2–6 TFEU seeks to establish a clearer categorisation of EU competences. Yet, the areas of primary Member State responsibility are not immune to free movement law.[92] Any attempt to rely on the limited powers of the Union is routinely met with the formula that while the relevant area is indeed within Member State competence, that competence has to be exercised in a manner that complies with EU law.[93] The result is that national measures are struck down from time to time and the EU is empowered to regulate using its Article 114 TFEU internal market power.[94] As a consequence, the competence limitations written into the Treaty, and the notion of limited powers more generally, lose some of their force.

The ultimate problem for the Court is that markets touch almost everything. Although issues such as direct taxation are primarily a matter for the Member States, this does not render a discriminatory tax rule any less harmful for the internal market. It seems impossible to object to the Court's basic finding that what really counts is whether there is a restriction, not what area of law the restriction arises from. However, it can be argued that more regard could be given to the division of competences envisaged in the Treaty. In particular, the notion of restriction could be interpreted in a more limited fashion or a softer version of proportionality test could be applied in those areas where the primary responsibility has been left to the Member States, so that EU law does not unduly hinder them in the performance of their tasks, which often involve complex evaluations and value judgements and carry political responsibilities. In the context of the review of EU measures, such arguments have carried weight,[95] and the Court in many instances has been loath to second-guess a decision of an EU institution in the absence of a manifest failure to comply with the limits of its discretion.[96] In other words, if concerns that can ultimately be traced back to the horizontal division of powers between the various EU institutions have led the Court to show deference to the other EU institutions when they are carrying out their tasks, should not the vertical division of powers between the EU and

[92] In this context, K Lenaerts, 'Federalism and the Rule of Law: Perspectives from the European Court of Justice' (2010) 33 *Fordham Intl LJ* 1338 writes at 1344 that from 'a federal perspective, a broad link with EU law would significantly restrict the exercise of competences pertaining to the Member States . . . The case law relating to free movement and EU citizenship indicates that the ECJ has opted for a rather broad interpretation of the required EU link'.

[93] See eg *Kohll*, n 34 above, para 19.

[94] See eg the Directive on Patients' Rights, n 31 above. The ruling in Case C-376/98 *Germany v Parliament and Council* [2000] ECR I-8419 established that the EU legislature can rely on Art 114 TFEU to deal with obstacles and appreciable distortions of competition even if public health concerns play a decisive role in guiding the legislative choices. For a sustained critique, see A Somek, *Individualism: An Essay on the Authority of the European Union* (Oxford, Oxford University Press, 2008).

[95] See generally eg P Craig and G de Búrca (eds), *EU Law: Text, Cases, and Materials* (Oxford, Oxford University Press, 2011) 551–53.

[96] See A Fritzsche, 'Discretion, Scope of Judicial Review and Institutional Balance in European Law' (2010) 47 *CML Rev* 361.

its Member States have the same effect when the Court is questioning decisions of Member States in the areas of their primary responsibility? Such an approach could also alleviate some of the concerns about competence creep under Article 114 TFEU.[97] A curtailed notion of restriction would limit the scope of positive harmonisation, while a softer proportionality test would reduce the need for EU legislative intervention by leaving Member States with more freedom to regulate matters.

It can be argued that the Court, at times, has already crafted special regimes for matters that are primarily for Member States, in line with the argument above. For example, in direct taxation cases, discrimination rather than the normal deterrence standard is applied.[98] In health service cases, the Court has accepted an economic justification, the need to safeguard the financial balance of national systems, while economic aims are rejected elsewhere.[99] Similarly, in education cases decided under the principle of non-discrimination, the Court's strict attitude in *Commission v Austria*[100] was softened in *Bressol*,[101] perhaps in '[response] to adverse Member State reactions'.[102] Unfortunately, the Court has proceeded on an ad hoc basis and has failed to adopt a principled, consistent stance that applies across the board and has missed the opportunity to spell out the basis of its approach in its reasoning.

IV. CONCLUSION

The present chapter has analysed free movement law and its legitimacy first from the perspective of the Court as a judicial institution and then from the perspective of the Court as a European institution. It has been pointed out that the legitimacy of the case law has been weakened by insufficiently reasoned judgments[103] that at the very least leave the Court open to charges that it is ignoring the text of the Treaties and acting inconsistently. It has also been argued that the Court needs to ensure that it does not interfere excessively with

[97] Laeken Declaration on the Future of the European Union identified Arts 114 and 352 TFEU as provisions of particular concern. The latter was amended at Lisbon, the former was not. For discussion, see D Wyatt, 'Community Competence to Regulate the Internal Market' in M Dougan and S Currie (eds), *50 Years of the European Treaties: Looking Back and Thinking Forward* (Oxford, Hart Publishing, 2009).

[98] See eg K Banks, 'The Application of the Fundamental Freedoms to Member State Tax Measures: Guarding Against Protectionism or Second-guessing National Policy Choices?' (2008) 33 *ELRev* 482, and also Lenaerts, n 92 above, 1361–67.

[99] See J Snell, 'Economic Aims as Justification for Restrictions on Free Movement' in A Schrauwen (ed), *Rule of Reason: Rethinking another Classic of EC Legal Doctrine* (Groningen, Europa Law Publishing, 2005).

[100] Case C-147/03 *Commission v Austria* [2005] ECR I-5969.

[101] Case C-73/08 *Bressol* [2010] ECR I-2735, discussed in detail by Koen Lenaerts in ch 1.

[102] Craig and de Búrca, n 95 above, 841.

[103] For a general acknowledgment from within the Court, see Sharpston, n 56 above, who talks eg at 415 and 422 of the importance of clear legal language and coherence for the 'credibility' and 'authority' of the Court.

national economic models and in areas that the Treaties allocate to Member States.

However, in the end, the wider institutional context of the EU and free movement law should not be forgotten.[104] First, if a legislature disagrees with a ruling of a court, it is always free to change the law. However, free movement law, despite its character as substantive law, is constitutional law. This means that, typically, the only way to amend a ruling is to amend the Treaty, and unanimity among Member States, coupled with successful national ratifications, is needed for such legislative overrule. In the last 25 years or so, this has not been impossible, at least in theory, due to the ongoing Treaty revision process: indeed, the rules on the free movement of capital have been subject to significant amendment. However, it may well be that the Lisbon Treaty will prove the last general revision of the Treaties for some time, and future amendments will be targeted at specific issues such as eurozone governance.[105] This will offer temptations for and impose a heavy responsibility on the Court.[106] Its word is likely to be final. There will not be a legislative overrule.[107]

Second, in general, the Court is unlikely to be greatly constrained by European public opinion[108] since, in the main, there is none.[109] An EU-wide public discourse is lacking. Instead, we find a series of national discourses and opinions. As a result, the Court usually does not have to fear any broad, generalised backlash from an outraged European public.[110] Typically, any judgment will only be of salience for the public of one country, although the presence of organised European interest groups may on occasion mobilise a broader consciousness,[111]

[104] See also D Halberstam, 'The Bride of Messina: Constitutionalism and Democracy in Europe' (2005) 30 *ELRev* 775, 779–82.

[105] See eg Treaty on Stability, Coordination and Governance in the Economic and Monetary Union.

[106] See A von Bogdandy and I Venzke, 'Beyond Dispute: International Judicial Institutions as Lawmakers' (2011) 12 *German Law Journal* 979, who at 993–96 discuss the problem that while in a domestic context judicial law-making is embedded in a responsive political system, this is not the case at the international level.

[107] It should be remembered that EU legislation such as directives and regulations need to comply with the Treaty. For a recent overview, see K Engsig Sørensen, 'Reconciling Secondary Legislation and the Treaty Rights of Free Movement' (2011) 36 *ELRev* 339.

[108] cp N Baeten, 'Judging the European Court of Justice: The Jurisprudence of Aharon Barak through a European Lens' (2011) 18 *Colum J Eur L* 135, 149–54, who gives 'social consensus' a strong role.

[109] D Grimm, 'Does Europe Need a Constitution?' (1995) 1 *ELJ* 282, 292–97. More recently, see eg J Neyer, 'Justice, Not Democracy: Legitimacy in the European Union' (2010) 48 *Journal of Common Market Studies* 903, 906.

[110] Although courts are supposed to be counter-majoritarian and able to defy the popular will in individual rulings, they are not isolated from the rest of the society. Fallon, n 6 above, writes in the US context at 1833: 'Justices who defy aroused public opinion risk, and know that they risk, provoking a political backlash that ultimately could cause their doctrinal handiwork to collapse. Possibly as a result of the [US Supreme] Court's concern for its sociological legitimacy, it has seldom remained dramatically at odds with aroused public opinion for extended periods' (fns omitted).

[111] This has happened in the context of rulings relating to labour law. See the discussion above at n 72.

and in any event public opinion generally 'provides a solid base of "diffuse support" for the Court'.[112]

Third, national courts play a critical role in the EU system. They serve as a force for additional legitimacy by delivering the final verdict in preliminary reference cases, and often by applying the principle of proportionality to the facts.[113] However, they are also the key interlocutors that the European Court really must convince with the quality of its rulings.[114] In a way, their role may at least partially compensate for the weakness of European public opinion. Without the cooperation of national courts, the free movement law would become a dead letter. Furthermore, they are supposed to act as courts of the European Union, deciding cases on their own when a reference is not warranted. This imposes important requirements for the jurisprudence of the European Court. Rulings that are not logical, consistent or properly explained, or that simply fail to convince national judges, are liable to be misunderstood or sidelined by national courts resulting in erroneous application of EU law and lack of uniformity. In this context, studies on the application of free movement of goods in national courts are instructive. When national judges were faced with expansive case law they did not find convincing, they simply failed to follow the lead of the European Court of Justice.[115] In other words, a critical challenge for the European Court of Justice is to ensure that its decisions are sufficiently consistent, clear, well-explained and convincing that they can and will be correctly followed and put into effect by national courts everywhere in the Union. If not, the whole objective of ensuring the effectiveness and uniform application of EU law will be compromised.[116]

Finally, it should be asked whether there is an alternative to the Court. The last time the EU legislature tried to grapple with free movement in a truly major way, it produced the Services Directive.[117] This directive will not win prizes for elegance or coherence. Furthermore, it ultimately failed to settle many of the major questions, leaving the really hard free movement issues, once again, for the Court to sort out. For all its flaws, it looks like the Court may be the least bad option.

[112] RD Kelemen, 'The Political Foundations of Judicial Independence in the European Union' (2012) 19 *Journal of European Public Policy* 43, 44.

[113] See generally D Sarmiento, 'The Silent Lamb and the Deaf Wolves' in M Avbelj and J Komárek (eds), *Constitutional Pluralism in the European Union and Beyond* (Oxford, Hart Publishing, 2012).

[114] JHH Weiler, 'Rewriting *Van Gend and Loos:* Towards a Normative Theory of ECJ Hermeneutics' in O Wiklund (ed), *Judicial Discretion in European Perspective* (The Hague, Kluwer Law International, 2003) argues at 150 that the national courts' acceptance of the case law of the ECJ is driven in large degree by their sense of hermeneutic propriety.

[115] See M Jarvis, *The Application of EC Law by National Courts: The Free Movement of Goods* (Oxford, Oxford University Press, 1998) eg at 432–33. See also Stone Sweet, n 11 above, 140.

[116] The Court has always seen legal uniformity as a core part of its task; see eg Case 66/80 *ICI* [1981] ECR 1191, para 11.

[117] n 28 above. For a critical analysis, see eg J Snell, 'Freedom to Provide Services in the Case Law and in the Services Directive: Problems, Solutions and Institutions' in UB Neergaard, R Nielsen and LM Roseberry (eds), *The Services Directive – Consequences for the Welfare State and the European Social Model* (Copenhagen, DJØF Publishing, 2008).

5

The Bubble that Burst: Exploring the Legitimacy of the Case Law on the Free Movement of Union Citizens

MICHAEL DOUGAN*

I. INTRODUCTION

THIS CHAPTER EXAMINES issues surrounding the legitimacy of the European Court of Justice through the lens of the case law concerning the free movement of Union citizens. In this field, issues of judicial legitimacy are usually explored by reference to allegations of judicial activism; more specifically, claims that the Court has embarked upon an unwarranted programme of social engineering that elevates judicial policy choices above those of the competent (national and Union) political actors. We begin with some preliminary remarks about the inevitably selective and subjective nature of allegations of judicial activism within the Union legal order, where there is neither a clear constitutional definition of, nor a common political and intellectual consensus on, the proper functions and limits of judicial power. Against that background, we will consider the core criticisms of unilateral judicial policy-making, especially in the sensitive field of welfare rights and responsibilities, levelled against the Court's case law as it developed in the decade following the *Sala* ruling in 1998.[1] However, consideration of the more recent case law, which especially since 2008 has suggested a shaking of judicial confidence about the previously stable trajectory of Union citizenship, should prompt us to re-evaluate that jurisprudence. Indeed, a longer-term and broader perspective suggests that the Court's relationship to the other Union institutions has been one of continuous dialogue about how best to construct a meaningful yet balanced legal framework for Union citizenship, while at the same time remaining sensitive to the often tumultuous political environment which has prevailed, almost

* I am very grateful to participants at the Antwerp conference – and especially to Daniel Thym – for their valuable comments and suggestions.

[1] Case C-85/96 *María Martínez Sala* [1998] ECR I-2691.

unbroken, since the constitutional reform process initiated by the European Council at Nice and Laeken.[2]

II. SOME PRELIMINARY REMARKS ON 'JUDICIAL ACTIVISM'

Allegations of judicial activism against the ECJ are hardly anything new. Time and again, the Court has stood accused of (and been defended against) the charge of overstepping its proper judicial function, in particular, by advancing its own pro-integrationist political agenda.[3] Such allegations were once common currency in debates (for example) about the Court's case law on the principles of direct effect and supremacy,[4] its recognition of fundamental rights as general principles of Union law[5] and the jurisprudence on effective judicial protection as regards remedies and procedural rules before the national courts[6] – all doctrines which, even if they are still controversial for other reasons, have nevertheless since been accepted as core, indeed essential, tenets of the Union's constitutional order.

Yet, the charges of judicial activism persist, sounding the same tone of 'integrationist bias', though now more likely to be framed in terms of distorting the federal balance between Union and Member State competences.[7] Thus, in some recent rulings, the Court is accused of endorsing an interpretation of the Treaties that fails to offer any meaningful constraint upon the Union institutions' expansionist conception of their own regulatory competences: consider, for example, the Environmental Crimes decision which (pre-Lisbon) recognised a derived competence to harmonise various aspects of national criminal law under the Community's First Pillar rather than the Union's Third Pillar powers.[8]

[2] Nice European Council Presidency Conclusions of 8 December 2000; Laeken European Council Presidency Conclusions of 14 December 2001.

[3] eg H Rasmussen, *On Law and Policy in the European Court of Justice. A Comparative Study in Judicial Policy-Making* (Dordrecht, Martinus Nijhoff Publishers, 1986); M Cappelletti, 'Is the European Court of Justice "Running Wild"?' (1987) 12 *ELRev* 3. Also eg TC Hartley, 'The European Court, Judicial Objectivity and the Constitution of the European Union' (1996) 112 *LQR* 95; A Arnull, 'The European Court and Judicial Objectivity: A Reply to Professor Hartley' (1996) *112 LQR* 411.

[4] See further, eg P Craig, 'Once Upon a Time in the West: Direct Effect and the Federalization of EEC Law' (1992) 12 *OJLS* 453.

[5] See further, eg J Coppel and A O'Neill, 'The European Court of Justice: Taking Rights Seriously?' (1992) 29 *CML Rev* 669; J Weiler and N Lockhart, '"Taking Rights Seriously" Seriously: The European Court and its Fundamental Rights Jurisprudence' (1995) 32 *CML Rev* 51, 579.

[6] See further, eg A Biondi, 'The European Court of Justice and Certain National Procedural Limitations: Not Such a Tough Relationship' (1999) 36 *CML Rev* 1271.

[7] The following analysis draws upon certain ideas presented in greater detail in M Dougan, 'Judicial Activism or Constitutional Interaction? Policymaking by the ECJ in the Field of Union Citizenship' in H-W Micklitz and B de Witte (eds), *The European Court of Justice and the Autonomy of the Member States* (Cambridge, Intersentia, 2012).

[8] Case C-176/03 *Commission v Council* [2005] ECR I-7879. Also: Case C-440/05 *Commission v Council* [2007] ECR I-9097. See now Art 83(2) TFEU. See further, eg E Herlin-Karnell, '*Commission v Council:* Some Reflections on Criminal Law in the First Pillar' (2007) 13 *European Public Law* 69; A Dawes and O Lynskey, 'The Ever-Longer Arm of EC Law: The Extension of Community Competence into the Field of Criminal Law' (2008) 45 *CML Rev* 131.

In other recent cases, the Court is alleged rather to have pursued its own aggressive construction of Union law, to the cost of sensitive national policy choices: consider, for example, the decision in *Commission v Austria*, forcefully reaffirming the principle of equal treatment on grounds of nationality as regards access to university, despite grave domestic concerns about the (allegedly) exceptional scale and detrimental effects of cross-border educational mobility.[9]

Indeed, a whole series of rulings in recent years – such as *Geraerts-Smits and Peerbooms*,[10] *Carpenter*,[11] *Mangold*,[12] *Viking Line* and *Laval un Partneri*,[13] *Metock*[14] and *Soysal*[15] – have provided fuel for a contemporary critique of judicial activism based on the nonetheless familiar argument that the ECJ improperly substitutes itself as legislature in place of the competent (national and/or Union) political institutions. The Court, so it goes, is too willing to deliver judgments that are not explicable primarily by hermeneutic techniques, but are the product of subjective preferences as regards deeply contested economic and/or social questions. Furthermore, the Court often appears too ready to frame such policy judgments in terms of the primary Treaty provisions, or the general principles of Union law, in a manner that effectively reduces the capacity of the Member States acting in the exercise of their individual regulatory autonomy, the Council and/or European Parliament performing their legislative functions,

[9] Case C-147/03 *Commission v Austria* [2005] ECR I-5969. cp Case C-73/08 *Bressol and Chaverot* [2010] ECR I-2735. See further, eg D Damjanovic, '"Reserved Areas" of the Member States and the ECJ: The Case of Higher Education' in H-W Micklitz and B de Witte (eds), *The European Court of Justice and the Autonomy of the Member States* (Cambridge, Intersentia, 2012).

[10] Case C-157/99 *Smits and Peerbooms* [2001] ECR I-5473. cp Case C-385/99 *Müller-Fauré and van Riet* [2003] ECR I-4509; Case C-372/04 *Watts* [2006] ECR I-4325. See further, eg J Montgomery, 'Impact of European Union Law on English Healthcare Law' in M Dougan and E Spaventa (eds), *Social Welfare and EU Law* (Oxford, Hart Publishing, 2005); C Newdick, 'Citizenship, Free Movement and Health Care: Cementing Individual Rights by Corroding Social Solidarity' (2006) 43 *CML Rev* 1645.

[11] Case C-60/00 *Carpenter* [2002] ECR I-6279. See further, eg Editorial 'Freedoms Unlimited? Reflections on *Mary Carpenter v Secretary of State*' (2003) 40 *CML Rev* 537; E Spaventa, 'From *Gebhard* to *Carpenter*: Towards a (Non-)Economic European Constitution' (2004) 41 *CML Rev* 743.

[12] Case C-144/04 *Mangold* [2005] ECR I-9981. cp Case C-427/06 *Barstch* [2008] ECR I-7245; Case C-555/07 *Kücükdeveci* [2010] ECR I-365. See further, eg E Muir, 'Enhancing the Effects of Community Law on National Employment Policies: The *Mangold* Case' (2006) 31 *ELRev* 879; A Dashwood, 'From *Van Duyn* to *Mangold* via *Marshall*: Reducing Direct Effect to Absurdity?' (2006–07) 9 *CYELS* 81.

[13] Case C-438/05 *Viking Line* [2007] ECR I-10779; Case C-341/05 *Laval un Partneri* [2007] ECR I-11767. Further, eg P Syrpis and T Novitz, 'Economic and Social Rights in Conflict: Political and Judicial Approaches to their Reconciliation' (2008) 33 *ELRev* 411; L Azoulai, 'The Court of Justice and the Social Market Economy: The Emergence of an Ideal and the Conditions for its Realization' (2008) 45 *CML Rev* 1335.

[14] Case C-127/08 *Metock* [2008] ECR I-6241. cp Case C-551/07 *Sahin* [2008] ECR I-10453; Case C-578/08 *Chakroun* [2010] ECR I-1839. See further, eg S Currie, 'Accelerated Justice or a Step Too Far? Residence Rights of Non-EU Family Members and the Court's Ruling in *Metock*' (2009) 34 *ELRev* 310; C Costello, '*Metock*: Free Movement and 'Normal Family Life' in the Union' (2009) 46 *CML Rev* 587.

[15] Case C-228/06 *Soysal* [2009] ECR I-1031. See further, eg N Tezcan/Idriz, 'Free Movement of Persons between Turkey and the EU: To Move or Not to Move? The Response of the Judiciary' (2009) 46 *CML Rev* 1621.

or even the Member States exercising constitutional power as 'masters of the Treaties', to negotiate and adopt a different policy choice.

Against such criticisms, it is important to recall two obvious points. First, any critique of judicial activism is usually built up from a highly selective crop of rulings: as Schmitz has observed, alleged difficulties with the case law invariably concern only a relatively small proportion of the Court's overall output; for its part, each awkward case is usually capable of being explained and defended in its own particular context.[16] Indeed, for every example of 'judicial activism', one can usually point to a converse instance of 'judicial restraint': the ruling in *UPA*, after all, is as much a product of Luxembourg as the decisions in *Peerbooms* or *Mangold*.[17] Moreover, to draw attention to the various problems implied by certain rulings is not necessarily to subscribe to conspiracy theories about the ECJ's hidden federalist agendas or self-aggrandising motivations. Difficulties are just as likely to arise from poorly articulated (and sometimes simply poor) judicial reasoning, or only an incomplete appreciation of the full consequences of a given line of argumentation, each such weakness being partly attributable to underlying considerations relating to the logistical functioning of the institution itself.[18]

Second, any allegation of judicial activism against the Union courts merely begs difficult questions about how one can possibly define what to consider 'activist' within a highly idiosyncratic constitutional order. For present purposes, it should suffice to distil only a few relevant observations from the extensive literature exploring the nature and limits of the ECJ's position *qua* 'supreme court' for the Union.[19] It is generally accepted that the Treaties enshrine no particular model for the exercise of higher judicial powers: there is neither a clear mandate for, nor express prohibition against, the Court accruing to itself the power to participate actively in, and indeed to pronounce definitively on, matters of substantive economic and social policy based on the Union's primary law (in a manner akin to that often attributed to, say, the US Supreme Court); or, for that matter, the Court acting merely as executor of the legislature's binding

[16] T Schmitz, 'On the Limits of Obedience to the European Courts', and other comments, presented at the conference 'The Principle of Accountability in the EU: The European Parliament, National Parliaments and the European Court of Justice' (University of Gothenburg, 26 February 2009).

[17] Case C-50/00 *Unión de Pequeños Agricultores* [2002] ECR I-6677.

[18] See further, eg T Tridimas, 'The Court of Justice and Judicial Activism' (1996) 21 *ELRev* 199. For critical analysis of the ECJ's legal reasoning, consider J Bengoetxea, N MacCormick and LM Soriano, 'Integration and Integrity in the Legal Reasoning of the European Court of Justice' in G de Búrca and JHH Weiler (eds), *The European Court of Justice* (Oxford, Oxford University Press, 2001); J Bengoetxea, 'Legal Reasoning and the Hermeneutic Turn in the Law: Remarks on the European Court of Justice' in U Neergaard, R Nielsen and L Roseberry (eds), *The Role of Courts in Developing a European Social Model: Theoretical and Methodological Perspectives* (Copenhagen, DJØF Publishing, 2010).

[19] See further, eg AM Slaughter, A Stone Sweet and JHH Weiler (eds), *The European Court and National Courts: Doctrine and Jurisprudence* (Oxford, Hart Publishing, 1998); G de Búrca and J Weiler (eds), *The European Court of Justice* (Oxford, Oxford University Press, 2001); A Arnull, *The European Union and its Court of Justice*, 2nd edn (Oxford, Oxford University Press, 2006); K Alter, *The European Court's Political Power: Selected Essays* (Oxford, Oxford University Press, 2009).

will, lacking the competence or authority to pass final judgment upon contested policy issues, and averse to treating its own preferences in economic and social matters as the expression of inalienable constitutional values (a position often adopted, say, by the UK Supreme Court).

The existence of such fundamental open questions implies that any accusation of judicial activism against the Court rests upon certain unproven and ultimately unproveable assumptions about the proper nature of the Union's judicial function – and serves to underline the essentially selective and subjective nature of the judicial activism debate. Any given ruling addressing some controversial policy issue might well be isolated under a critical spotlight and convincingly portrayed as an instance of unilateralist judicial policymaking at the expense of the rightful prerogatives of the competent (national and/or Union) political institutions. But when exactly the same ruling is viewed from a longer term perspective and located within its broader legal context – one which acknowledges that the Union's current constitutional framework indeed offers a wide margin of discretion to the ECJ to determine for itself the terms of its interaction with the relevant (national and/or Union) political institutions – a very different impression can emerge. In negotiating the relationship between its own interpretation of the primary Treaty provisions and/or the general principles of Union law (on the one hand) and the existence of regulatory discretion conferred by or recognised under the Treaties (on the other hand), the Court is clearly capable of engaging in more multilateral and constructive processes of 'constitutional dialogue' whereby judicial preferences respond to, stimulate and reshape legislative action.[20]

In that regard, many authors in various contexts have identified and discussed potential patterns of interaction between the judicial and political institutions in the development of Union law. Sometimes the Court appears to take an assertive lead in policymaking when the political authorities languish in a state of legislative sclerosis, and conversely to slip back into the shadows when the other Union institutions assume a more active and effective responsibility for addressing the relevant policy problem.[21] Other commentators have suggested that the Court can be highly sensitive to the broader political context of judicial policymaking, especially as concerns the general direction and public reception of the European integration process – even if such diffuse perceptions and reactions are things more sensed than proven. Readers will no doubt recall academic discussion about the potential impact of the ratification problems surrounding the Maastricht Treaty upon the Court's short-term confidence in the case law on the free movement of goods,[22] and effective judicial protection.[23]

[20] cp K Lenaerts, 'Some Thoughts about the Interaction Between Judges and Politicians in the European Community' (1992) 12 *YEL* 1.

[21] See the influential analyses by J Weiler, 'The Dual Character of Supranationalism' (1981) 1 *YEL* 267 and 'The Transformation of Europe' (1991) 100 *Yale Law Journal* 2403.

[22] Further, eg N Reich, 'The 'November Revolution' of the European Court of Justice: *Keck*, *Meng* and *Audi* Revisited' (1994) 31 *CML Rev* 459.

[23] Further, eg A Ward, 'Effective Sanctions in EC Law: A Moving Boundary in the Division of Competence' (1995) 1 *ELJ* 205.

Perhaps most interesting are those areas of Union law where the relationship between judicial and political institutions has resembled a direct conversation about how best to address a given regulatory dilemma. Consider, for example, the difficult problems once raised by the application of Regulation 1408/71 to so-called 'hybrid benefits'.[24] The Court in rulings such as *Newton* openly recognised that the Treaty's objective of eliminating obstacles to free movement resulting from the operation of the national social security systems needed to be balanced against the changing nature and fragile equilibrium of domestic welfare provision, while also explicitly acknowledging that any judicial policy choice in that regard should be made only in default of a legislative solution which (once adopted) would necessarily take priority over the previous case law.[25] True enough: once Regulation 1408/71 was amended so as to introduce a new regime on 'special non-contributory benefits',[26] the Court in cases such as *Snares* found that the Union legislature was perfectly entitled to pursue a different solution to the problem of 'hybrid benefits' from that previously advocated by the judges.[27] What could have been portrayed as an instance of improper judicial activism actually emerges as a positive engagement between judicial and political power, so as to articulate a common understanding of the relevant policy problem and work towards an effective solution.[28]

Those tensions in our interpretation of the Court's case law will now be explored in greater detail with specific reference to the jurisprudence on Union citizenship. In particular, it will be argued that that case law, as it developed in the ten years following the groundbreaking ruling in *Sala* in 1998,[29] attracted a considerable academic criticism: the Court was accused of embarking upon a unilateral process of transforming Union citizenship, particularly in the sphere of welfare provision, often to the cost of the political autonomy of the Member States and the regulatory discretion of the Union legislature. However, much of the more recent case law suggests that the Court's confidence has been shaken and its vision for Union citizenship rendered more complex. Further reflection might lead one to accept that, viewed in its longer term and broader perspective, the case law on Union citizenship is less the product of judicial unilateralism than of an ongoing process of constitutional dialogue between the ECJ and

[24] Last consolidated text published at [1997] OJ L28/1. See further, eg A-P van der Mei, 'Regulation 1408/71 and Coordination of Special Non-Contributory Benefits' (2002) 27 *ELRev* 551.

[25] Case C-356/89 *Newton* [1991] ECR I-3017. cp Case 24/74 *Biason* [1974] ECR 999; Case 139/82 *Piscitello* [1983] *ECR* 1427.

[26] See Art 4(2a) Regulation 1408/71 (subsequently changed to 'special non-contributory cash benefits' by Regulation 647/2005 [2005] OJ L117/1). See now Arts 3(3) and 70 Regulation 883/2004 [2004] OJ L200/1.

[27] Case C-20/96 *Snares* [1997] ECR I-6057. cp Case C-297/96 *Partridge* [1998] ECR I-3467; Case C-154/05 *Kersbergen-Lap* [2006] ECR I-6249.

[28] However, note the impact of Case C-287/05 *Hendrix* [2007] ECR I-6909 (see further the discussion below concerning Union citizenship and its impact upon the social security coordination regime).

[29] *Sala*, above n 1.

the competent political authorities on the true constitutional significance and precise legal content of EU free movement rights.

III. A CRITICAL READING OF THE CITIZENSHIP CASE LAW FROM 1998–2008

In the ten years following the ruling in *Sala*,[30] the Court – at first slowly and with hesitation, then particularly after the rulings in *Grzelczyk* and *Baumbast*,[31] more quickly and with increasing confidence – developed a clear, distinctive and consistent vision for Union citizenship, especially as regards the free movement rights referred to in Article 21 TFEU, based on its conviction that Union citizenship is destined to be the fundamental status of Member State nationals.[32] Rich and insightful accounts of that case law abound.[33] We shall content ourselves with identifying some of the key elements of the critical reception accorded to the Court's interpretation of Union citizenship, with specific reference to those concerned about an apparent tendency towards unilateral policymaking at the expense of the competent political authorities.[34]

To begin with, the Court's willingness to apply the Union citizen's rights of residency, equal treatment and freedom from 'barriers to movement' with almost mechanical logic, to any and every national rule which actually or potentially crosses the individual migrant's path, has resulted in the creation out of the primary Treaty provisions of a remarkable series of second-order rights.[35]

[30] ibid.

[31] Case C-184/99 *Grzelczyk* [2001] ECR I-6193; Case C-413/99 *Baumbast* [2002] ECR I-7091.

[32] *Grzelczyk*, above n 31, para 31. Repeated in many other cases since, eg Case C-224/98 *D'Hoop* [2002] ECR I-6191, para 28; Case C-148/02 *Garcia Avello* [2003] ECR I-11613, para 22; Case C-224/02 *Pusa* [2004] ECR I-5763, para 16; Cases C-482 and C-493/01 *Orfanopoulos* [2004] ECR I-5257, para 65; Case C-403/03 *Schempp* [2005] ECR I-6421, para 15; Case C-520/04 *Turpeinen* [2006] ECR I-10685, para 18; Case C-50/06 *Commission v Netherlands* [2007] ECR I-4383, para 32.

[33] See further, eg C Jacqueson, 'Union Citizenship and the Court of Justice: Something New Under the Sun? Towards Social Citizenship' (2002) 27 *ELRev* 260; A-P van der Mei, *Free Movement of Persons within the European Community: Cross-Border Access to Public Benefits* (Oxford, Hart Publishing, 2003); E Spaventa, *Free Movement of Persons in the European Union* (The Hague, Kluwer Law International, 2007); H Verschueren, 'European (Internal) Migration Law as an Instrument for Defining the Boundaries of National Solidarity Systems' (2007) 9 *European Journal of Migration and Law* 307; S Giubboni, 'Free Movement of Persons and European Solidarity' (2007) 13 *ELJ* 360; A Somek, 'Solidarity Decomposed: Being and Time in European Citizenship' (2007) 32 *ELRev* 787; A Iliopoulou, *Libre circulation et non-discrimination, éléments du statut de citoyen de l'Union européenne* (Brussels, Bruylant, 2007).

[34] The following analysis draws upon certain ideas presented in greater detail in M Dougan, 'The Spatial Restructuring of National Welfare States within the European Union: The Contribution of Union Citizenship and the Relevance of the Treaty of Lisbon' in U Neergaard, R Nielsen and L Roseberry (eds), *Integrating Welfare Functions into EU Law: From Rome to Lisbon* (Copenhagen, DJØF Publishing, 2009).

[35] On the expanded personal and material scope of Union law in the light of Union citizenship, eg A Epiney, 'The Scope of Article 12 EC: Some Remarks on the Influence of European Citizenship' (2007) 13 *ELJ* 611; E Spaventa, 'Seeing the Wood despite the Trees? On the Scope of Union Citizenship and its Constitutional Effects' (2008) 45 *CML Rev* 13; Y Borgmann-Prebil, 'The Rule of Reason in European Citizenship' (2008) 14 *ELJ* 328.

Those derived rights cover fields as diverse as the language in which criminal proceedings are conducted,[36] the individual's freedom of choice over his or her surname[37] and the collection and retention of personal data for security purposes.[38] Most importantly, perhaps, the Court's second-order rights extend to the provision of welfare support by the host or home society for the benefit of economically inactive Union citizens who are not or may not be entirely capable of supporting themselves and their families.[39]

The content of those second-order rights appears to have been determined in large part by policy choices made by the Court itself. In the case of welfare provision, such policy choices are orientated around the assumption that the creation of Union citizenship by the Maastricht Treaty implied a willingness on the part of the Member States and their populations to accept a degree of mutual cross-border social solidarity. In particular, as regards relations between an economically inactive migrant and his or her host state, the inevitable compromise between (on the one hand) the desire to offer meaningful benefits to Union citizens regardless of their economic or financial status and (on the other hand) the need to respect the Member State's limited willingness to pay for the upkeep of foreign nationals who might otherwise present an unreasonable burden on its public finances, has gradually manifested itself in the task of identifying a 'real link' between migrant and host society.[40] The closer the bond between the individual claimant and the Member State, the more secure will be the claimant's right to reside within the territory, free from the fear of expulsion on economic or financial grounds;[41] and the more extensive his or her right to equal treatment within the host society, as regards welfare and other social benefits.[42]

A similar approach emerged as regards relations between a migrant Union citizen and his or her home state.[43] The tension between (on the one hand) the desire not to hinder the movement of Union citizens who may be dependent upon some form of public support and (on the other hand) the political, financial and practical constraints that favour respect for the territorially bounded

36 eg Case C-274/96 *Bickel and Franz* [1998] ECR I-7637.

37 eg *Garcia Avello*, above n 32.

38 eg Case C-524/06 *Huber* [2008] ECR I-9705.

39 *Sala*, above n 1; *Grzelczyk*, above n 31; *Baumbast*, above n 31.

40 The concept was first employed by the ECJ in *D'Hoop*, above n 32. Its potential relevance is not restricted to migrant welfare rights, or even Union citizenship: consider, eg the rulings in Case C-145/04 *Spain v United Kingdom* [2006] ECR I-7917 on voting rights to the European Parliament for certain TCNs and Case C-66/08 *Kozłowski* [2008] ECR I-6041 on grounds for non-execution of a European Arrest Warrant.

41 eg *Grzelczyk*, above n 31; *Baumbast*, above n 31; Case C-456/02 *Trojani* [2004] ECR I-7573.

42 eg *Sala*, above n 1; *Grzelczyk*, above n 31; *D'Hoop*, above n 32; Case C-138/02 *Collins* [2004] ECR I-2703; Case C-209/03 *Bidar* [2005] ECR I-2119; Case C-258/04 *Ioannidis* [2005] ECR I-8275. Indeed, the Court considered that only migrants already either in possession of a residence permit, or able to demonstrate a certain period of residence, could be considered in a comparable position to established residents and thus entitled to equal treatment within the host state at all: see, eg *Trojani*, above n 41.

43 Either in tandem with (as in Cases C-502/01 and C-31/02 *Gaumain-Cerri* [2004] ECR I-6483) or even in contradiction to (in rulings such as *Hendrix*, above n 28) the coordination rules contained in Regulation 1408/71 and Regulation 883/2004: see further below.

nature particularly of non-contributory welfare provision, has also been resolved through resort to a 'real link' principle.[44] In this context, the stronger the relationship between a given welfare benefit and the domestic system of social solidarity, the weaker the force of the argument for severing the cord connecting payment of benefits to residence within the national territory.[45] In addition, however, the Court will examine the degree to which the individual claimant may assert membership of his or her home state's welfare community, even after having left the national territory, on the basis of past or present links other than continuing residence alone, which are nevertheless sufficient to warrant a right of access to the relevant benefits.[46]

Such judicial choices about the existence and extent of the migrant's second-order rights are then substituted quite readily for the views of the relevant Member State; and in some cases, even in place of the wishes expressed by the Union legislature itself. Against the Member State, the Court's chief weapon is the proportionality test. Even where it is legitimate in principle for the (host or home) authorities to expect a 'real link' between a given claimant and the relevant welfare community, evidence to support that 'real link' cannot be gathered exclusively on the basis of generalised criteria (such as past or continuing residency). The Member State must also give due consideration to the 'personal circumstances' of each individual claimant, even if this implies taking into account factors or circumstances not recognised as relevant or compelling under the applicable domestic legislation.[47] Against the Union legislature, the Court has relied upon the idea that secondary legislation which itself purports to restrict the migrant's opportunities for free movement is nevertheless amenable to a form of 'indirect judicial review' intended to guarantee that it does not unduly prejudice the existence or exercise of the Union citizen's rights; ie, whereby Member States are obliged to apply Union legislation which appears to limit the rights of Union citizens in accordance with the general principles of Union law, so that the relevant Union rules may not be enforced against an individual where that would exceed what is necessary to protect the Member State's legitimate interests.[48]

[44] See further, eg M Dougan, 'Expanding the Frontiers of Union Citizenship by Dismantling the Territorial Boundaries of the National Welfare States?' in C Barnard and O Odudu (eds), *The Outer Limits of European Union Law* (Oxford, Hart Publishing, 2009). Note also the importance attached to monitoring non-resident benefit recipients, eg Case C-406/04 *De Cuyper* [2006] ECR I-6947; Case C-221/07 *Zablocka-Weyhermüller* [2008] ECR I-9029.

[45] Consider, eg Case 313/86 *Lenoir* [1988] ECR 5391; Case C-43/99 *Leclere* [2001] ECR I-4265; Cases C-396/05, C-419/05 and C-450/05 *Habelt* [2007] ECR I-11895; Case C-228/07 *Petersen* [2008] ECR I-6989.

[46] Consider, eg Case C-192/05 *Tas-Hagen* [2006] ECR I-10451; *Hendrix*, above n 28; Cases C-11–12/06 *Morgan and Bucher* [2007] ECR I-9161; Case C-499/06 *Nerkowska* [2008] ECR I-3993.

[47] Consider the rulings in *D'Hoop*, above n 32; *Collins*, above n 42; *Bidar*, above n 42; *Ioannidis*, above n 42; *Hendrix*, above n 28; *Morgan and Bucher*, above n 46; *Nerkowska*, above n 46. See further, eg Spaventa, 'Seeing the Wood Despite the Trees?' above n 35.

[48] In particular: *Grzelczyk*, above n 31; *Baumbast*, above n 31. Consider also the rulings in *De Cuyper*, above n 44; *Hendrix*, above n 28; *Petersen*, above n 45. See further, eg M Dougan, 'The Constitutional Dimension to the Case Law on Union Citizenship (2006) 31 *ELRev* 613.

Moreover, the nature of the migrant Union citizen's second-order rights seems to be shaped by a structure and style of judicial reasoning which treats 'free movement' as an overriding (Union) policy goal at the expense of other legitimate manifestations of the (national) public interest. Despite Marshall's influential categorisation of social rights alongside more traditional civil and political rights in the triptych of modern citizenship,[49] other scholars have argued that social – and especially welfare rights – are marked by an important difference: they are fundamentally about the redistribution of income between social groups, and imply a claim on resources and legitimisation of the redistributive role of the state.[50] Questions about entitlement to welfare engage not only the individual's personal expectation of social support, but also the relevant society's choices about the allocation of its available resources, which in turn reflect collective moral judgements concerning the nature of its social solidarity: what risks to protect against, what levels of support to offer and which individuals fall within the catchment area of collective responsibility.[51] Yet, it is arguable that the Court's approach risks neglecting that crucial collective dimension to social solidarity.[52]

In that regard, one might begin with the observation that it has become so easy to trigger the application of the provisions on Union citizenship that the mere existence of a prima facie infringement of the Treaty has surely lost its ability to tell us anything meaningful about the balance of policy interests at stake in any given dispute. In other words, breaching the Treaty has become so commonplace that the relevant national rules should not per se be treated with antagonism, as if it can thenceforth be taken for granted that they have offended against some higher public interest.[53] That would be to elevate the simple principle of movement – and incidentally, all of the second-order rights derived from that movement, such as individual rights to welfare support from the host or home state – above all other manifestations of the general good. Yet that often appears to be exactly the nature and outcome of judicial reasoning in free movement cases: having triggered the application of the Treaty on the basis of

[49] TH Marshall, *Citizenship and Social Class* (Cambridge, Cambridge University Press, 1949; reprinted London, Pluto Press, 1991).

[50] M Kleinman, *A European Welfare State?* (Basingstoke, Palgrave Macmillan, 2002) 194–95.

[51] For a detailed analysis of the theoretical nature of social solidarity, including the relationship between individual and collective interests, see S Stjernø, *Solidarity in Europe: The History of an Idea* (Cambridge, Cambridge University Press, 2005).

[52] Similar allegations have been raised against the 'individualistic' approach to social and welfare rights in the EU's Charter of Fundamental Rights: see, eg M Berezin and M Schain (eds), *Europe Without Borders: Remapping Territory, Citizenship and Identity in a Transnational Age* (Baltimore, John Hopkins University Press, 2003). See further, eg J Tooze, 'Social Security and Social Assistance' in T Hervey and J Kenner (eds), *Economic and Social Rights Under the EU Charter of Fundamental Rights* (Oxford, Hart Publishing, 2003); D Damjanovic and B de Witte, 'Welfare Integration through EU Law: The Overall Picture in the Light of the Lisbon Treaty' in U Neergaard, R Nielsen and L Roseberry (eds), *Integrating Welfare Functions into EU Law: From Rome to Lisbon* (Copenhagen, DJØF Publishing, 2009).

[53] See, in a similar sense, N Nic Shuibhne, Annotation of *Schwarz, Commission v Germany* and *Morgan and Bucher*' (2008) 45 *CML Rev* 771.

an individual right connected to movement, the onus then falls upon the Member State to explain and defend its disputed national rules, in accordance with the constraints imposed by the principle of proportionality and other general principles of Union law. The very structure of legal argumentation before the Court of Justice therefore emphasises from the outset the importance of the individual and endorses his or her claim of entitlement to welfare support, whereas the collective aspects of social solidarity are put on the defensive and thereby at an inherent disadvantage.[54]

That inherent disadvantage is aggravated by certain other features of adjudication before the Court of Justice. On one side, the Court does not allow the process of triggering the Treaty (for example, on the basis of unequal treatment by the host state or a barrier to movement by the home state) to be complicated by the need for the individual to demonstrate empirically that his or her movement has actually been deterred or impeded in any meaningful way. The Court relies on intuitive – sometimes even counter-intuitive – assessments which attribute the average citizen with both penetrating foresight and inordinate sensitivity, such that almost any inequality of treatment for migrants acts as a deterrent to their apparently boundless expectation of unimpeded mobility.[55] On the other side, the Court often insists that Member States fearful of the consequences that rights to free movement and/or equal treatment for individual Union citizens might inflict upon national policy choices, even those recognised as valid imperative requirements capable in principle of justifying an infringement of the Treaty, must nevertheless produce firm evidence to substantiate those fears.[56] In several cases, Member States have failed to defend their national policy choices simply because they were unable to present to the Court fully documented empirical analyses to substantiate their concerns.[57] In the battle between competing suppositions, it seems that those favouring the individual will often trump those designed to protect the public interest, so that the nature as well as the burden of proof in free movement cases conspires against the collective aspects of social solidarity.

The case law on Union citizenship also illustrates how the process of judicial policymaking through the medium of the primary Treaty provisions often stands at odds with the system of variegated Union competences which underpinned the old TEU and EC Treaties (and are now expressly enshrined in the post-Lisbon TEU and TFEU). In fields such as health, education and social security, the Treaties confer upon the Union legislature only limited powers to

[54] See further, eg M Dougan and E Spaventa, 'Wish You Weren't Here . . . New Models of Social Solidarity in the European Union' in M Dougan and E Spaventa (eds), *Social Welfare and EU Law* (Oxford, Hart Publishing, 2005).

[55] For a vivid example, consider Case C-212/06 *Government of the French Community and Walloon Government v Flemish Government* [2008] ECR I-1683.

[56] Though not in every dispute: consider, eg *Peerbooms*, above n 10; *Morgan and Bucher*, above n 46.

[57] Consider, eg *Müller-Fauré*, above n 10; *Commission v Austria*, above n 9; Case C-269/07 *Commission v Germany* [2009] ECR I-7811.

intervene in the national legal systems, strictly circumscribed by the terms of the applicable legal bases (which, in most cases, expressly rule out the possibility of harmonising domestic law).[58] Yet, the Member State's duty to respect the obligations imposed directly under the Treaty, as interpreted by the ECJ in its free movement case law, manages to exert an increasingly profound influence on the exercise of domestic prerogatives concerning the organisation and functioning of their healthcare, education and social protection systems.

It is true that the Court's case law pursues an admirable logic when it refuses to exclude per se such matters as health, education and social security from the impact of the primary Treaty provisions.[59] But logic can provide Union law with only so much legitimacy. After all, the social, economic, political and cultural sensitivities of interfering with national rules on health, educational or welfare policy are similar regardless of whether that interference emanates from the Union legislature or the judiciary. Indeed, it is arguable that judicial intervention – precisely because it lacks a clear mandate, bypasses deliberation by democratic institutions, and (especially in cases concerning the interpretation of primary Treaty provisions) is difficult to amend or reverse – raises even greater legitimacy problems in fields of marginal Union responsibility than action by the accountable political institutions.

This incongruous disjunction between the willingness of the Court to rely upon the primary Treaty provisions as a means of interfering in all manner of domestic policy choices, and the apparent inability of the Union's political institutions to take the initiative in exercising any binding influence of their own over exactly the same range of issues, can give rise to further difficulties. In some situations, such disjunction may actually have the incidental effect of expanding the Union's regulatory powers beyond the limits intended by the Treaties, as matters previously considered to be of purely complementary competence become amenable to harmonisation pursuant to the Union's free movement legal bases.[60] In other situations, where recourse to such legal bases is either not possible or simply not likely, the result of the Court's policymaking under the primary Treaty provisions may be to privilege the assertion of judicial

[58] On health: ex Art 152 EC (now Art 168 TFEU). On education: ex Arts 149–50 EC (now Arts 165–66 TFEU). On social security: ex Arts 18 and 137 EC (now Arts 21 and 153 TFEU – the former provision extending the Union institutions' competence over social security/social protection for migrant Union citizens).

[59] See eg *Watts*, above n 10, para 92 (as regards health care); Case C-76/05 *Schwarz and Gootjes-Schwarz* [2007] ECR I-6849, para 70 (as regards education); *Nerkowska*, above n 46, paras 23–24 (as regards welfare benefits).

[60] Consider Directive 2011/24 on the application of patients' rights in cross-border health care [2011] L88/45 (based on Art 114 TFEU). Further, eg W Sauter, 'The Proposed Patients' Rights Directive and the Reform of (Cross-Border) Healthcare in the European Union' (2009) 36 *Legal Issues of Economic Integration* 109; S de la Rosa, 'The Directive on Cross-Border Healthcare or the Art of Codifying Complex Case law' (2012) 49 *CML Rev* 15. See also: D Wyatt, 'Community Competence to Regulate Medical Services' in M Dougan and E Spaventa (eds), *Social Welfare and EU Law* (Oxford, Hart Publishing, 2005); G Davies, 'The Community's Internal Market-Based Competence to Regulate Healthcare: Scope, Strategies and Consequences' (2007) 14 *Maastricht Journal of European and Comparative Law* 215.

authority over the exercise of political power: the Court is free to express certain regulatory choices, but the other Union institutions are simply unable to respond with (different) policy preferences of their own.[61]

To a degree, such a phenomenon is hardly new to the Union legal order. Indeed, the early spillover effects of the primary Treaty provisions were often the subject of favourable academic comment: the judicial nurturing of embryonic policies towards (say) the protection of the environment, workers or consumers took place under the auspices of the free movement provisions, and was accompanied by the articulation of common social policy values by the political institutions in the exercise of their market-building competences, well before the introduction into the Treaties of any explicit regulatory powers in such fields.[62] But the relevant legal and political circumstances have since changed enormously. Legally, there are few policy fields left where the Treaties do not define explicitly the nature and limits of Union competences – and such definitions are phrased in more variegated and more precise terms than in earlier versions of the Treaties – making the process of spillover more complex and contested than in the past.[63] Politically, the state of benign neglect from which the Court surely benefited in the pre-Maastricht era has given way to a closer and more critical scrutiny of the impact of judicial law-making on Member State competences and inter-institutional relations.[64] Similarly, as disputes such as *Tobacco Advertising* and *Environmental Crimes* show, the ability of the Union institutions to persuade the Court to endorse a broad construction of their existing competences now gives rise to acute concerns as regards the principle of attributed powers.[65]

In short: the case law on Union citizenship in the decade following *Sala* provided the basis for an extensive body of academic criticism focusing on allegations that the Court had (1) embarked upon a process of social engineering through the top-down manufacture of novel welfare rights and obligations; (2) embedded its own policy preferences into the primary Treaty provisions in a manner that appreciably constricts the room for choosing to adopt a different policy choice, certainly of the Member States acting individually, and to some

[61] Consider, eg the limitations on internal market competence imposed under Art 114(2) TFEU.

[62] Further, eg D Chalmers, 'The Single Market: From Prima Donna to Journeyman' in J Shaw and G More (eds), *New Legal Dynamics of European Union* (Oxford, Clarendon Press, 1995); P Craig, 'The Evolution of the Single Market' in C Barnard and J Scott (eds), *The Law of the Single European Market: Unpacking the Premises* (Oxford, Hart Publishing, 2002).

[63] See eg A von Bogdandy and J Bast, 'The Federal Order of Competences' in A von Bogdandy and J Bast (eds), *Principles of European Constitutional Law*, 2nd edn (Oxford, Hart Publishing, 2009). Further: R Schütze, *From Dual to Cooperative Federalism: The Changing Structure of European Law* (Oxford, Oxford University Press, 2009).

[64] Further, eg J Weiler, 'Journey to an Unknown Destination: A Retrospective and Prospective of the European Court of Justice in the Arena of Political Integration' (1993) 31 *Journal of Common Market Studies* 417.

[65] Case C-376/98 *Germany v Parliament and Council* [2000] ECR I-8419 and *Commission v Council*, above n 8 (respectively). See further, eg S Weatherill, 'Competence and Legitimacy' in C Barnard and O Odudu (eds), *The Outer Limits of European Union Law* (Oxford, Hart Publishing, 2009).

extent also of the Council and European Parliament in the exercise of the regulatory competences conferred upon them by the Treaties; (3) tended to elevate free movement within the EU over all other manifestations of the general interest, in particular, by privileging individual welfare rights and expectations over the collective interests and priorities normally inherent in concepts of social solidarity; and (4) risked aggravating such a state of 'constitutional asymmetry' by the way in which the political institutions, even if minded to do so, might be hamstrung by their limited regulatory competences and thus unable to substitute a different assessment of how to balance the competing public goals.[66]

IV. DEVELOPMENTS IN THE CITIZENSHIP CASE LAW SINCE 2008

Since 2008, however, the Court's previously clear and consistent case law on the free movement rights associated with Union citizenship has undergone a strikingly sudden change, becoming more confused and more unpredictable, which might well suggest a new mood of uncertainty about the appropriate direction of judicial policymaking and its constitutional relationship to the Union's political institutions. Such developments have concerned, in particular, both the technique of 'indirect judicial review' over regulatory choices of the Union legislature which restrict the rights enjoyed by Union citizens, and the obligation incumbent upon the Member States to undertake a 'personal circumstances' assessment in order to comply with the proportionality principle.

Dealing first with indirect judicial review, rulings such as *Förster* and *Vatsouras* have explored the Court's attitude towards the restrictive provisions now contained in Directive 2004/38,[67] which derogate from the general right of Union citizens to equal treatment on grounds of nationality, by providing that the Member State is not obliged to offer maintenance assistance to migrant students unless and until they qualify as permanent residents after living in the host territory for five years, or to provide social assistance to migrant work seekers throughout the period when they reside in the host state prior to becoming engaged in gainful employment.[68]

Thus, in *Förster*, the Court distinguished its previous ruling in *Bidar*,[69] so as to approve of Dutch rules which required five years' residence within the Netherlands before migrant students could qualify for the grant of maintenance assistance – a test which undoubtedly had the effect of restricting state support

[66] cp F Scharpf, 'The European Social Model: Coping With the Challenges of Diversity' (2002) 40 *Journal of Common Market Studies* 645.

[67] Case C-158/07 *Förster* [2008] ECR I-8507; Joined Cases C-22/08 and C-23/08 *Vatsouras* [2009] ECR I-4585.

[68] See Art 24(2) Directive 2004/38 [2004] OJ L158/77.

[69] *Bidar*, above n 42. See further, eg M Dougan, 'Fees, Grants, Loans and Dole Cheques: Who Covers the Costs of Migrant Education within the EU?' (2005) 42 *CML Rev* 943; C Barnard, 'Annotation of *Bidar*' (2005) 42 *CML Rev* 1465; O Golynker, 'Student Loans: The European Concept of Social Justice According to *Bidar*' (2006) 31 *ELRev* 390.

for individuals who could nevertheless demonstrate a certain degree of integration into the host society by other means. In so holding, the Court in *Förster* seemed to backtrack from the technique of indirect judicial review previously cultivated in its case law on Union citizenship: the clear signal sent by the ruling was that national rules on access to student financial assistance, adopted in compliance with the five-year test for maintenance assistance contained in Directive 2004/38, would be treated as enforceable per se.[70] By contrast, *Vatsouras* dealt with the right of migrant work seekers to access social benefits under Union law. In this context, there was a confusing divergence between the Court's ruling in *Collins* (which suggested that claimants with a real link to the host state's labour market should be entitled to claim unemployment assistance);[71] and the Union legislature's subsequent regulatory choice to deny any right to equal treatment for migrant work seekers as regards social assistance within the host territory. The Court in *Vatsouras* resolved that tension by finding that the reference to 'social assistance' in Directive 2004/38 does not include benefits which are intended to facilitate access to the national labour market; on that basis, the veracity of the ruling in *Collins* was not affected by the adoption of the new Directive, while the validity of the new Directive is not called into question by upholding the ruling in *Collins*.[72]

If (on the one hand) the Court in *Vatsouras* had followed *Förster* and denied that the disputed national rules were in breach of Union law, we would at least have had a clear signal that the technique of indirect judicial review was in full-scale retreat. If (on the other hand) the Court in *Vatsouras* had simply applied its established case law and insisted on the proportionate application of Directive 2004/38, we could have assumed that the case law on Union citizenship was still generally on the march – with the possible exception of the rights enjoyed by migrant students vis-a-vis their host state, where *Förster* suggested an appreciable but specific and limited change in the Court's approach.[73] Instead, the rulings

[70] See further, eg O Golynker, 'Annotation of *Förster*' (2009) 46 *CML Rev* 2021; S O'Leary, 'Equal Treatment and EU Citizens: A New Chapter on Cross-Border Educational Mobility and Access to Student Financial Assistance' (2009) 34 *ELRev* 612; S de la Rosa, 'La Citoyenneté Européenne à la Mesure des Intérêts Nationaux: A Propos de l'arrêt *Förster*' [2009] *Cahiers de Droit Européen* 549; C Marzo, 'La Définition d'une Nouvelle Méthode de Jugement Attachée à la Citoyenneté Européenne: Réflexions Autour de l'arrêt *Förster*' (2009) 45 *RTD eur* 439.

[71] *Collins*, above n 42. See also *Ioannidis*, above n 42. See further, eg J Meulman and H de Waele, 'Funding the Life of Brian: Jobseekers, Welfare Shopping and the Frontiers of European Citizenship' (2004) 31 *Legal Issues of Economic Integration* 275; H Oosterom-Staples, 'Annotation of *Collins*' (2005) 42 *CML Rev* 205; See further, eg M Dougan, 'The Court Helps Those Who Help Themselves . . . The Legal Status of Migrant Workseekers Under Community Law in the Light of the *Collins* Judgment' [2005] *European Journal of Social Security* 7; O Golynker, 'Jobseekers' Rights in the European Union: Challenges of Changing the Paradigm of Social Solidarity' (2005) 30 *ELRev* 111.

[72] See further, eg E Fahey, 'Interpretive Legitimacy and the Distinction Between "Social Assistance" and "Workseekers Allowance"' (2009) 34 *ELRev* 933; D Damjanovic, 'Annotation of *Vatsouras*' (2010) 47 *CML Rev* 847.

[73] And possible a shift of emphasis from the financial responsibilities of the host state to those of the home state: cp *Morgan and Bucher*, above n 46. See further, eg M Dougan, 'Cross-border Educational Mobility and the Exportation of Student Financial Assistance' (2008) 33 *ELRev* 723.

in *Förster* and *Vatsouras* together suggest a degree of judicial hesitation about the proper interaction between the primary rights associated with Union citizenship and Union secondary legislation adopted to regulate the rights to residency and equal treatment.[74]

Turning secondly to the requirement for Member States to undertake a personal circumstances assessment of each individual migrant Union citizen, before refusing access to any given social benefit, the post-2008 case law has (if anything) proved even more confusing and incoherent. The *Förster* ruling again provides a useful reference point. It is particularly striking that the Court in that case made no effort whatsoever to require the Dutch authorities to examine the claimant's personal circumstances, with a view to establishing whether her 'real link' to Dutch society could be verified by reference to factors other than the generalised requirement of five years' lawful residency within the national territory. Yet if her personal circumstances had indeed been taken into account, the claimant would surely have had a strong case for arguing that the blanket application of the disputed Dutch rule was entirely disproportionate in her case, since she had apparently become fully integrated into Dutch society at an educational, professional and personal level.[75] Did *Förster* therefore indicate that the Court had begun to retreat back, not just from the principle of indirect judicial review over Union secondary legislation, but also from an interventionist approach to the justification of national rules hindering the free movement or equal treatment rights of migrant Union citizens, based on the personal circumstances assessment? If so, that would seem to vindicate O'Brien's argument that the Court's understanding of Union citizenship is more concerned with guaranteeing procedural fairness than with promoting any particular substantive vision of transnational solidarity – rendering academic concerns about intrusive judicial policymaking at the expense of vital Member State competences premature if not altogether exaggerated.[76]

Again, however, the judicial will might seem determined to remain inscrutable. After all, if *Förster* really marked the Court's abandonment of its personal circumstances approach to Union citizenship, it would have amounted to a remarkably sudden as well as silent *volte face*. Consider, for example, the rulings in *Nerkowska* and *Grunkin and Paul* (both delivered shortly before the

[74] Consider also various recent rulings concerning the interaction between the primary Treaty provisions and the secondary legislation on social security coordination. In particular: contrast *Hendrix*, above n 28; with Case C-537/09 *Bartlett*, Judgment of 5 May 2011. Also: contrast Case C-208/07 *von Chamier-Glisczinski* [2009] ECR I-6095; with Case C-3/08 *Leyman* [2009] ECR I-9085. Consider also Case C-345/09 *van Delft*, Judgment of 14 October 2010.

[75] cp Opinion of AG Mazák in *Förster*, above n 67, paras 128–33.

[76] C O'Brien, 'Real links, Abstract Rights and False Alarms: The Relationship between the ECJ's "Real Link" Case Law and National Solidarity' (2008) 33 *ELRev* 643. cp criticism of the vague and flexible nature of the 'real link' concept by S O'Leary, 'Solidarity and Citizenship Rights in the Charter of Fundamental Rights of the European Union' in G de Búrca (ed), *EU Law and the Welfare State* (Oxford, Oxford University Press, 2005); S Besson and A Utzinger, 'Future Challenges of European Citizenship: Facing a Wide-Open Pandora's Box' (2007) 13 *ELJ* 573.

judgment in *Förster*).[77] In the former case, Polish rules under which the payment of civilian war benefits was limited to resident nationals were found to breach the Union citizen's right to free movement, and could not be objectively justified where an overall assessment of the claimant's personal circumstances indicated that, despite being non-resident, he or she could nevertheless demonstrate a certain degree of connection to the relevant society. In the latter case, Article 21 TFEU was held to preclude the German authorities from refusing to recognise an own national's surname as it had been determined and registered in another Member State, where the claimant had actually been born and since resided; however legitimate the Member State's objectives in regulating the use of surnames by its own nationals, those objectives were outweighed by considerations relating to the specific situation of this particular claimant.

Nor has the situation become much clearer since the ruling in *Förster*. On the one hand, the Court in some cases has indeed endorsed the use by Member States of entirely generalised criteria by which to restrict the free movement rights of migrant Union citizens, appearing to accept that such blanket rules protect the public interest in a proportionate manner, without imposing any additional obligation to undertake specific consideration also of the individual circumstances of any given claimant. Consider, for example, the judgment in *Wolzenburg*,[78] which concerned the principle of equal treatment as regards, not the provision of welfare support to migrant Union citizens, but rather national implementation of the European Arrest Warrant Framework Decision.[79] In particular, Dutch rules providing for the non-execution of a European Arrest Warrant in the case of migrant Union citizens, with a view to the enforcement of a custodial sentence, only if they had been lawfully resident within the national territory for a continuous period of five years, were not considered incompatible with Article 18 TFEU: such a blanket requirement was judged both appropriate and necessary to its objective of reserving the possibility of non-execution to persons who could demonstrate a certain degree of integration into the host society.[80] Consider also the dispute in *Sayn-Wittgenstein*, where the Court upheld the proportionality of an Austrian decision refusing to recognise a title of nobility assumed by an own national (even though that title was lawfully acquired under German law) on the basis of public policy concerns about constitutional equality between Austrian citizens.[81] Within the context of that proportionality assessment, there was no engagement with (let alone allowance for) the personal circumstances of the particular claimant: for example, the fact that the Austrian authorities had already registered her German title for

[77] *Nerkowska*, above n 46; Case C-353/06 *Grunkin and Paul* [2008] ECR I-7639.

[78] Case C-123/08 *Wolzenburg* [2009] ECR I-9621. See further, eg C Janssens, 'Annotation of *Wolzenburg*' (2010) 47 *CML Rev* 831.

[79] Framework Decision 2002/584 [2002] OJ L190/1.

[80] It is worth noting that the ECJ in *Wolzenburg* referred explicitly to both the ruling in *Förster* and the period laid down in Directive 2004/38 for acquisition of the right to permanent residence.

[81] Case C-208/09 *Sayn-Wittgenstein*, Judgment of 22 December 2010.

a period of around 15 years and on that basis had issued or renewed various personal identity documents.[82]

On the other hand, more light-touch rulings such as *Förster* and *Wolzenburg* live cheek-by-jowl with decisions where the Court still insists that Member States undertake an assessment of each individual Union citizen's personal circumstances before restricting the exercise of his or her fundamental Treaty freedoms.[83] For example, in *Gottwald*, Austrian rules restricting free travel on toll roads to disabled persons ordinarily resident in the national territory were judged compatible with Article 18 TFEU, taking into account the flexible manner in which the national authorities were prepared to recognise other factors (such as regular travel by a non-resident to the territory for professional or personal reasons) capable of demonstrating a certain degree of integration between the claimant and the host society.[84] Similarly, in *Rottmann*, German rules providing for the withdrawal of nationality acquired by naturalisation, on the grounds that the claimant had perpetrated a deception, and thus leading to the loss also of Union citizenship and its associated rights, fell within the scope of Union law and had to be objectively justified. For those purposes, the principle of proportionality required the competent national court to have regard to all relevant circumstances, including any adverse consequences for the claimant and his or her family, the gravity of the deception offence, the time elapsed since naturalisation and the possibilities for recovering the claimant's original nationality.[85]

Viewed as a whole, therefore, the post-2008 case law suggests not only the potential emergence of a significant differentiation in the quality of the rights enjoyed by various categories of Union citizens, but also an unhelpful fragmentation in the range of legal tools by which the Court reasons through the impact of Union citizenship upon both individual national policy choices and the complex political bargains struck by the other Union institutions.[86]

A similarly confused picture emerges from other recent developments in the Court's case law, which concern neither the technique of 'indirect judicial review' nor the 'personal circumstances' test, but rather the newly-discovered powers to scrutinise national rules which deprive Union citizens of the genuine enjoyment of the substance of a right conferred by virtue of their status as

[82] Consider also Case C-391/09 *Runevič-Vardyn*, Judgment of 12 May 2011. And furthermore: *Bartlett*, above n 74; especially contrasted with *Hendrix*, above n 28.

[83] For a particularly striking recent example, see Case C-503/09 *Stewart*, Judgment of 21 July 2011. Note also the particular circumstances (even if they were not entirely personalised) taken into account by the ECJ in Case C-544/07 *Rüffler* [2009] ECR I-3389.

[84] Case C-103/08 *Gottwald* [2009] ECR I-9117.

[85] Case C-135/08 *Rottmann* [2010] ECR I-1449. See further, eg T Konstadinides, 'La Fraternité Européenne? The Extent of National Competence to Condition the Acquisition and Loss of Nationality from the Perspective of EU Citizenship' (2010) 35 *ELRev* 401; D Kochenov, Annotation of *Rottmann*' (2010) 47 *CML Rev* 1831.

[86] cp E Spaventa, 'The Constitutional Impact of Union Citizenship' in U Neergaard, R Nielsen and L Roseberry (eds), *The Role of Courts in Developing a European Social Model: Theoretical and Methodological Perspectives* (Copenhagen, DJØF Publishing, 2010).

Union citizens.[87] Rulings such as *Zambrano*, *McCarthy* and *Dereci* have already attracted considerable critical scrutiny in the literature.[88] For present purposes, suffice to observe that the judgment in *Zambrano* laid down the 'deprivation of genuine enjoyment' test in apparently broad terms – in the case itself, operating so as to override Belgium's refusal to grant a right of residence and a right to work in favour of the third-country national carer of minor Union citizens, within their Member State of nationality and absent any actual or potential intra-Union cross-border element, based on the assumption that those minor citizens might otherwise be forced to leave the Union territory altogether.

However, the Court in *McCarthy* refused to recognise that an equivalent 'deprivation of genuine enjoyment' arose from the UK's refusal to recognise a right of residence for the third-country national spouse of a dual British–Irish national who had always resided within the UK. The reasoning used to achieve that outcome seems rather unconvincing: the Court argued that McCarthy was not deprived of the genuine enjoyment of her rights as a Union citizen because the family could choose to go and live elsewhere within the Union; yet one might rightly query why the same choice was not (in principle) open also to the Zambrano family, who could have chosen to move to a Member State other than Belgium and there exercised their Union right to family reunification under Directive 2004/38. Nevertheless, the Court in *Dereci* affirmed that the 'deprivation of genuine enjoyment' test refers to a specific and indeed exceptional category of situations, ie, those in which the effect of the disputed national measure would be to force a Union citizen to leave the territory not only of his or her own Member State, but of the entire Union. Of course, that restrictive approach to the 'deprivation of genuine enjoyment' test will not stop scholars from speculating about its potential for future development along new directions.[89] But for us, the point remains that the Court's case law concerning this new dimension to the status of Union citizenship suggests a similar ebbing-and-flowing of judicial confidence as we identified in rulings such as *Förster*, *Vatsouras*, *Wolzenburg* and *Rottmann*.

V. A MORE CONSTRUCTIVE READING OF THE CITIZENSHIP CASE LAW?

From a purely doctrinal viewpoint, the most recent case law on Union citizenship therefore appears increasingly confusing and unpredictable. It does nevertheless serve the valuable function of reminding us to keep allegations of judicial activism within their proper perspective and context. In particular, a (necessarily

[87] *cf Rottmann*, above n 85.

[88] Case C-34/09 *Zambrano*, Judgment of 8 March 2011; Case C-434/09 *McCarthy*, Judgment of 5 May 2011; Case C-256/11 *Dereci*, Judgment of 15 November 2011. See eg K Hailbronner and D Thym, 'Annotation of Case 34/09 *Ruiz Zambrano*' (2011) 48 *CML Rev* 1253; N Nic Shuibhne, '(Some of) the Kids Are All Right – Annotation of *McCarthy* and *Dereci*' (2012) 49 *CML Rev* 349.

[89] eg A von Bogdandy et al, 'Reverse Solange – Protecting the Essence of Fundamental Rights against EU Member States' (2012) 49 *CML Rev* 489.

brief) retrospective on the Court's jurisprudence suggests that the judicial transformation of Union citizenship has in fact taken place within a long-term process of constitutional dialogue and may well have been decisively influenced by the evolving political environment of European integration.

To begin with, it is worth recalling that the Court's expansive definition of 'worker' for the purposes of Article 45 TFEU,[90] and its equally generous interpretation of the social benefits attached to the status of economically active migrant,[91] meant that, by the 1980s, the right to free movement had already drifted away from its original and purely functional relationship to the construction of an Internal Market. Insofar as the Court's case law helped pave the way towards a more socially oriented conception of free movement, one could argue that it was perfectly in tune with the political leanings of the time. Since the early 1970s, and increasingly throughout the period building up to and following the Single European Act, the (then) Community institutions, as well as the European Council, had been encouraging a more balanced orientation in the EEC's activities and priorities so that economic integration and growth were not pursued to the total neglect of social protection and inclusion.[92] The political institutions also picked up where the Court's case law under Article 45 TFEU had necessarily left off: the legislature enacted the three Residency Directives in 1990–93, extending rights beyond the economically active also for the benefit of the financially independent;[93] for their part, the Member States in their capacity as 'masters of the Treaties' created Union citizenship, and its associated right to free movement, under the Maastricht Treaty.[94]

Even if there is a general sense that the Member States did not intend any substantive changes to result from the introduction of Article 21 TFEU, they could hardly have been surprised if the ECJ felt entitled to infuse that provision with new meaning for itself.[95] The real question was how far the Court would go in interpreting the new provisions on Union citizenship and thus in extend-

[90] eg Case 53/81 *Levin* [1982] ECR 1035; Case 139/85 *Kempf* [1986] ECR 1741; Case C-357/89 *Raulin* [1992] ECR I-1027.

[91] eg Case 32/75 *Fiorini v SNCF* [1975] ECR 1085; Case 65/81 *Reina* [1982] ECR I-33; Case C-111/91 *Commission v Luxembourg* [1993] ECR I-817; Case C-237/94 *O'Flynn* [1996] ECR I-2617.

[92] See further, eg M Dougan, 'Free Movement: The Workseeker as Citizen' (2001) 4 *CYELS* 9. Note in particular: Declaration by the Heads of Government of the Member States meeting at Paris on 19–20 October 1972 (EC Bull 10-1972); Reports from the *ad hoc* Committee on 'A People's Europe' (EC Bull Supp 7/85).

[93] Directive 90/364 [1990] OJ L180/26; Directive 90/365 [1990] OJ L180/28; Directive 93/96 [1993] OJ L317/59.

[94] For early analyses of Union citizenship after its introduction by the Maastricht Treaty, eg C Closa, 'The Concept of Citizenship in the Treaty on European Union' (1992) 29 *CML Rev* 1137; R Kovar and D Simon, 'La Citoyenneté Européenne' [1993] *Cahiers de Droit Européen* 285; S Hall, *Nationality, Migration Rights and Citizenship of the Union* (Dordrecht, Martinus Nijhoff, 1995); S O'Leary, *The Evolving Concept of Community Citizenship: From the Free Movement of Persons to Union Citizenship* (The Hague, Kluwer Law International, 1996).

[95] cp N Nic Shuibhne, 'The Outer Limits of EU Citizenship: Displacing Economic Free Movement Rights?' in C Barnard and O Odudu (eds), *The Outer Limits of European Union Law* (Oxford, Hart Publishing, 2009).

ing rights to residency, equal treatment and (more generally) freedom from 'barriers to movement' beyond the existing categories of economically active persons under the primary Treaty provisions on workers and self-employed persons, and financially independent persons under the three Residency Directives. We have seen the Court's basic response in rulings such as *Sala*, *Grzelczyk* and *Baumbast*; then the flood of case law which followed and elaborated on them.[96] Adventurous and creative though those decisions undoubtedly were, it is worth making two observations.

In the first place, the underlying parameters for the Court's interpretation of Union citizenship continued to be provided by the provisions of the three Residency Directives as previously enacted by the legislature, and the qualified right to free movement under the Treaty as agreed upon by the Member States: ideas such as sufficient resources, comprehensive medical insurance and unreasonable burdens on the public finances still furnished the legal foundations upon which concepts such as real links, personal circumstances and indirect judicial review were then built by the Court (even if it became more difficult to see them, or at least easier to forget them, as the case law developed in more interesting ways). In the second place, it is tempting to speculate about the timing of the Court's rulings – particularly the long delay in delivering the *Sala* decision, followed by another significant gap before Union citizenship really took flight in *Grzelczyk* and *Baumbast*. Is it mere coincidence that the latter judgments were delivered in the early and essentially optimistic stages of the constitutional reform process begun in Nice and developed at Laeken?[97] Or did those decisions seem to the Court a timely and distinctive judicial contribution to the process of 'bringing Europe closer to its citizens', in the midst of a major review of the Union's constitutional basis and constructive re-evaluation of its policy activities?

The latter hypothesis could go some way to explaining the Court's confident assertion in *Grzelczyk* that Union citizenship is destined to become the fundamental status of Member State nationals.[98] Indeed, without taking into account that broader political context, the normative basis for such an assertion would otherwise appear weak, and the allegation of activist and ambitious judicial policymaking all the more plausible to sustain. Certainly, the substantive legal content of the case law as it developed after *Grzelczyk* and *Baumbast* – and particularly the technique of indirect judicial review – attracted criticism on the grounds that the Court seemed to be usurping the role of the accountable political institutions, and extending rights to Union citizens beyond (and indeed despite) the clear limits negotiated and agreed by the Union legislature.[99] Yet it

[96] *Sala*, above n 1; *Grzelczyk*, above n 31; *Baumbast*, above n 31.

[97] Nice European Council Presidency Conclusions of 8 December 2000; Laeken European Council Presidency Conclusions of 14 December 2001. *Grzelczyk* was delivered between the Nice and Laeken European Council meetings; *Baumbast* was decided during the deliberations of the Convention of the Future of Europe.

[98] *Grzelczyk*, above n 31, para 31.

[99] In particular K Hailbronner, 'Union Citizenship and Access to Social Benefits' (2005) 42 *CML Rev* 1245.

is striking how much of the Court's case law was to be effectively codified by the Council and European Parliament when they adopted Directive 2004/38: not only the key idea in *Grzelczyk* and *Baumbast* that recourse to social assistance should not justify automatic expulsion from the host state,[100] but also the emphasis on identifying a 'real link' between claimant and host society, not least in the introduction of the right to permanent residency.[101] Much of what we once thought of as the Court's swaggering approach to cross-border social solidarity was thus effectively endorsed by the other Union institutions.[102]

It is true that not every aspect of the Court's case law on Union citizenship was adopted as its own by the Union legislature. Within Directive 2004/38 itself, as we have seen, the derogations from the principle of equal treatment in respect of students and work seekers seemed directly to contradict the rulings in *Bidar* and *Collins*.[103] Beyond that, the technique of indirect judicial review, and the requirement to assess each individual's personal circumstances, implied that application of the primary Treaty provisions on Union citizenship could wreak havoc with a whole range of Union secondary legislation capable of adversely affecting free movement rights. That was true not least as regards the social security coordination regime contained in Regulation 1408/71 (and now Regulation 883/2004),[104] which appeared positively to restrict or preclude the exportation of certain benefits (such as unemployment benefits and special non-contributory [cash] benefits) by non-resident claimants, and thus create barriers to movement from their home state by migrant Union citizens.[105]

If the Court had really been bent on a campaign of unilateral policymaking to enforce its own will regardless of – and if necessary despite – the preferences of the Union legislature, as expressed in measures such as Directive 2004/38 and Regulation 1408/71 or 883/2004, then the clear and consistent case law developed between 1998 and 2008 could have provided it with the legal tools (indirect judicial review and personal circumstances assessment) to do so. To have stood by the assertion that Union citizenship is destined to be the fundamental status of Member States nationals would also have continued to furnish a respectable constitutional basis for elevating the relevant primary Treaty provisions to a special place within the Union's hierarchy of norms – justifying the Court's

[100] Art 14(3) Directive 2004/38.

[101] Chapter IV Directive 2004/38. Note also the limited entitlement to equal treatment associated with the right to three months' residency; arguably reflected in the ECJ's ruling in *Trojani*, above n 41 as regards the equal treatment rights of short-term economically inactive migrants.

[102] See further, eg Dougan, 'The Constitutional Dimension to the Case Law on Union Citizenship', above n 48.

[103] *Bidar*, above n 42; *Collins*, above n 42.

[104] Regulation 1408/71, last consolidated text published at [1997] OJ L28/1; Regulation 883/2004 [2004] OJ L200/1.

[105] On the latter concept, as applied to Union citizenship, eg *D'Hoop*, above n 32; Case C-364/01 *Barbier* [2003] ECR I-15013; *Pusa*, above n 32; Case C-345/05 *Commission v Portugal* [2006] ECR I-10633; Case *Turpeinen*, above n 32; Case C-522/04 *Commission v Belgium* [2007] ECR I-5701; *Schwarz and Gootjes-Schwarz*, above n 59; Case C-318/05 *Commission v Germany* [2007] ECR I-6957; Case C-152/05 *Commission v Germany* [2008] ECR I-39. *cf* Case C-386/02 *Baldinger* [2004] ECR I-8411; *Schempp*, above n 32.

more rigorous examination of the impact of political choices by the national/Union authorities upon the exercise of the individual's fundamental freedoms.[106] However, the Court has not proven so intransigent. Instead, the case law since 2008 can be seen as a new phase in an already well-established process of constitutional dialogue between judges and legislators, and also as a reflection of the changed political climate surrounding European integration since the negative French, Dutch and Irish referenda on constitutional reform.

In terms of constitutional dialogue, the case law since 2008 seems to reveal the Court struggling to reconcile its previous jurisprudence on indirect judicial review over Union secondary legislation, and on assessing the personal circumstances of individual claimants, with the fact that the Union legislature has since positively intervened in the legal framework governing the free movement rights of Union citizens. As regards Directive 2004/38 especially, rulings such as *Förster* and *Vatsouras* suggest that the Court remains unsure as to how to smooth out the rough dovetails between Article 24(2) and its own case law on migrant students and work seekers. The picture is similarly messy as regards Regulation 1408/71 (and now Regulation 883/2004), where the parallel application of the primary Treaty provisions and the secondary coordination regime has also become standard practice.[107] On the one hand, the Court repeatedly invoked the legal tools developed in the context of Union citizenship so as to extend the right to exportation to persons and benefits deliberately excluded by the Union legislature from its coordination regime.[108] Furthermore, the Court in cases such as *Hendrix* was clearly willing to employ the primary Treaty provisions as a means of distorting the allocation of financial responsibilities intended by the Union legislature in respect of certain benefits (*in casu*, special non-contributory [cash] benefits) clearly included within and directly regulated by the coordination system.[109] On the other hand, rulings such as *Petersen* have hinted that, although parallel application of the Treaty and Regulation 1408/71 or 883/2004 will remain possible, and in particularly compelling circumstances may well result in divergent approaches, Member States whose social security legislation complies with the obligations imposed by the Union legislature will not be subject to a significantly more probing analysis by the Court on the basis of the Union citizenship provisions.[110] Indeed, in *Bartlett*, the Court completely refrained from assessing Union law's own restrictions on the exportability of

[106] In particular Dougan, 'The Constitutional Dimension to the Case Law on Union Citizenship', above n 48.

[107] eg *Gaumain-Cerri*, above n 43; *von Chamier-Glisczinski*, above n 74; *Stewart*, above n 83; *van Delft*, above n 74.

[108] *Tas-Hagen*, above n 46; Case C-213/05 *Geven* [2007] ECR I-6347; Case C-212/05 *Hartmann* [2007] ECR I-6303; *Morgan and Bucher*, above n 46; *Nerkowska*, above n 46; *Zablocka-Weyhermüller*, above n 44; Case C-379/09 *Casteels*, Judgment of 10 March 2011. Note the expanded list of excluded benefits now contained in Art 3(5) Regulation 883/2004 as amended by Regulation 988/2009 [2009] OJ L284/43.

[109] *Hendrix*, above n 28.

[110] *Petersen*, above n 45. cp *De Cuyper*, above n 44. Consider also: *von Chamier-Glisczinski*, above n 74; but note *Leyman*, above n 74; and *van Delft*, above n 74.

special non-contributory cash benefits by reference to the free movement demands which might be imposed by the hierarchically superior primary Treaty provisions.[111]

That sense of confusion and contradiction is reinforced when one turns to consider the broader political context of the Court's case law since 2008. While the Union's generous approach to free movement by the economically active had always enjoyed an express mandate in the Treaty, benefited from a reasonably clear teleology to guide its development and been furnished with the hard legal tools required to achieve its goals,[112] it must be admitted that the Court's bold conception of free movement by economically inactive Union citizens could call upon only an ambiguous mandate under the Treaty and lacked any distinct teleology to direct its interpretation, while the legal armoury potentially available to the Union institutions was more limited in scope and strength. The Court's fragile normative basis for proceeding, regardless – the idea that Union citizenship *really is* destined to be the fundamental status of all Member States nationals – therefore exposed a weak flank in the case law as the constitutional reform process began to unravel and its once grand ambitions implode.[113]

It might be an interesting game to speculate about whether the smooth ratification and entry into force of the original Constitutional Treaty, as proposed by the Convention on the Future of Europe and adopted by the IGC in 2004, would have vindicated the Court's trailblazing vision of Union citizenship and emboldened the judges to push further their particular conception of supranational welfare solidarity.[114] But as events turned out, the crisis triggered by the negative referenda in France and the Netherlands in 2005, together with the fresh jolts from the Irish 'no' vote in 2008, perhaps left dangerously exposed the main problems – allegations of social engineering and judicial activism – associated with the Court's case law on the welfare rights of Union citizens. Had the Court's adventurous interpretative approach to Article 21 TFEU in fact been ahead of its time? Should the Court now retreat back towards a more restrained interpretation of Union citizenship, in which there was greater judicial deference towards political choices about how best to allocate a given society's available welfare resources? Recent rulings – from *Förster*, *Vatsouras*, *Wolzenburg* and *Rottmann* to *Zambrano*, *McCarthy* and *Dereci* – might suggest that the ECJ's vision has indeed become more complex, reflecting the

[111] *Bartlett*, above n 74.

[112] But note the argument that, in certain cases involving migrant workers (eg *Geven*, above n 108; *Hartmann*, above n 108), the 'real link' as developed in the context of economically inactive citizens has actually triggered a contraction in the rights also of economically active individuals: see S Currie, 'The Transformation of Union Citizenship' in M Dougan and S Currie (eds), *50 Years of the European Treaties: Looking Back and Thinking Forward* (Oxford, Hart Publishing, 2009); S O'Leary, 'Developing an Ever Closer Union between the Peoples of Europe? A Reappraisal of the Case Law of the Court of Justice on the Free Movement of Persons and EU Citizenship' (2008) 27 *YEL* 167.

[113] See further, eg M Dougan, 'The Treaty of Lisbon 2007: Winning Minds, Not Hearts' (2008) 45 *CML Rev* 617.

[114] [2003] OJ C169 (draft Constitutional Treaty); [2004] OJ C310 (final Constitutional Treaty).

political and social uncertainties of what it actually means to be a Union citizen, and of what the 'fundamental destiny' of Union citizenship itself might be, in a world where the optimism expressed at Laeken appears to have borne (at best) only limited success.[115]

Moreover, thanks to the eurozone debt crisis, the political context in which the Court is expected to develop its vision of Union citizenship has surely become even more fraught and complex than before. The eurozone debt crisis has already proved to be a rich testing ground for reflections about European togetherness: from those who argue that the rush to xenophobic stereotyping in mass discourse, or legally dubious protectionism in public policymaking, has revealed the shallow and fragile character of our commitment to the sharing of a collective fate; to those who see the crisis as a moment of opportunity through which to forge more meaningful popular and psychological (as well as merely legal or political) ties between the eurozone nations. An important part of those reflections must surely concern the dangers facing the cohesion of the Union as a whole – not least the threat of the Union breaking down into a 'two-speed Europe'. Of course, flexible integration is far from being a new phenomenon under EU law: EMU demonstrated that from its very outset, even besides other large scale manifestations of 'variable geometry' in fields such as the AFSJ.[116] Yet, many sense that the eurozone crisis has set us on the trajectory towards an altogether more significant division between 'fast lane' versus 'slow lane' Member States: it seems inevitable that new layers of substantive rules and decision-making structures, designed to bind the single currency states ever closer together, will to some degree create a relative distancing of the other Member States;[117] meanwhile, the 2012 Treaty on Stability, Coordination and Governance also signals an important division between the 25 Member States which signed the new international agreement and the two countries (the UK and the Czech Republic) that chose to stand aside.[118] Such flexibility (at best) or fragmentation (at worst) implies difficult questions also for Union citizenship: how far will/can/should legal concepts about cross-border solidarity, which have hitherto been linked to the unitary status of Union citizenship, manage to map onto the

[115] Other recent rulings deemed particularly controversial could also be located within the broader trajectory of the constitutional reform process, ie, as examples of the Court anticipating certain reforms confident that they reflected the clear political will of the Member States (overlooking for present purposes whether such anticipation could be justified having regard to the ratification problems surrounding the Constitutional Treaty after the French and Dutch referenda). Consider case law on the legal value of the Charter of Fundamental Rights, eg Case C-540/03 *Parliament v Council* [2006] ECR I-5769. Consider also case law gradually breaking down the barrier between the old First and Third Pillars, eg Case C-105/03, *Pupino*, [2005] ECR I-5285 and Case C-176/03 *Commission v Council*, above n 8.

[116] See further, eg F Tuytschaever, *Differentiation in European Union Law* (Oxford, Hart Publishing, 1999); G de Búrca and J Scott (eds), *Constitutional Change in the EU: From Uniformity to Flexibility?* (Oxford, Hart Publishing, 2000); B de Witte, D Hanf and E Vos (eds), *The Many Faces of Differentiation in EU Law* (Cambridge, Intersentia, 2001).

[117] *cf* M Ruffert, 'The European Debt Crisis and European Union Law' (2011) 48 *CML Rev* 1777.

[118] *cf* Editorial:, 'Some Thoughts Concerning the Draft Treaty on a Reinforced Economic Union' (2012) 49 *CML Rev* 1.

emerging reality of strongly differentiated levels of economic and political integration between groupings of Member States within one and the same Union?[119]

In any event, if our analysis is correct, it suggests that focusing our critical attention on traditional constitutional concerns about judicial activism risks not only exaggerating a problem which is perhaps less worrying than is often portrayed, but also distracting attention away from more pressing questions, about what substantive policies are actually being developed by the judges and therefore the *quality* of the rights being created under Union law. Take one example: the emergence of the 'real link' as a central organising concept in how Union law constructs relations between migrant citizens and their home/host societies.[120] One of the most interesting facets of this phenomenon is the way in which Union law increasingly treats certain 'links' as indeed being 'real', while other 'links' are devalued as being either subjective or irrelevant. Yet, the choices thus made by Union law do not necessarily tally with the bonds and relationships that individuals themselves most value, in terms of their self-identification as migrant Union citizens – creating a revealing disjunction between the Union's own understanding of Union citizenship (on the one hand) and the individual's personal expectations and experiences of being a European migrant (on the other hand).

The ruling in *McCarthy* illustrates the problem very well.[121] The case law created by Ireland's citizenship laws tends to elicit a particular line of enquiry among the wider scholarship: what happens when someone (whether the national of another Member State, or a third-country national) takes advantage of Ireland's relatively generous citizenship rules in an instrumental fashion so as to 'manufacture' potentially useful Union law rights?[122] But that fails to do justice to a much more interesting and important problem: the fact that among the primary beneficiaries of Ireland's citizenship rules are the substantial number of individuals among the Northern Irish population (usually Catholics/nationalists) who chose (for complex historical and cultural reasons) to adopt citizenship of the Irish Republic (despite their also being UK nationals). The effect of the Court's ruling in *McCarthy* is to deny any recognition of that phenomenon under EU free movement law: the individual's political and cultural self-identification as the citizen of another Member State, expressed in the formal adoption of the latter's nationality, seems to matter less to the Court than does the objective fact of cross-border movement (even though the latter would, for many such individuals, be an altogether artificial or even unattainable legal construct).

Of course, one can understand why the Union should feel wary when dealing with minorities that benefit systematically from generous dual nationality

[119] For an early analysis highlighting the potential future challenges: J Shaw, 'The Treaty of Amsterdam: Challenges of Flexibility and Legitimacy' (1998) 4 *ELJ* 63.

[120] See the discussion above.

[121] *McCarthy*, above n 88.

[122] One thinks here also of rulings such as *Collins*, above n 42 and Case C-200/02 *Zhu and Chen* [2004] ECR I-9925.

regimes spanning the territories of two or more Member States: it might imply the Union assuming a wholesale responsibility for the legal protection of entire populations in a manner reminiscent of a League of Nations protectorate. But such political realism does not detract from the fact that the spatial identities which individuals evolve for themselves through their lived experience as migrant Union citizens do not necessarily marry well with the assumed identities which become embedded and rewarded (or penalised) in the structures of Union law.[123] And returning to the point: that is exactly the type of avenue for further research that leaves behind traditional concerns about the Court's alleged policy activism.

VI. CONCLUDING REMARKS

Debates about judicial activism are always contingent upon unresolved questions concerning the proper nature of the judicial function within the Union legal order, and often depend upon a highly selective analysis of a small number of rulings, sometimes taken inappropriately out of their broader legal and political contexts, in a way that fails to offer a balanced and rounded portrait of the Court's vital contribution to the development of Union law. The case law on Union citizenship is no exception. On the one hand, that case law can indeed be portrayed as a case study in unilateral judicial policymaking, wherein the ECJ has spontaneously initiated an audacious process of social engineering, to the detriment of the political preferences of the Member States, as well as the regulatory prerogatives of the Union legislature itself. On the other hand, however, exactly the same jurisprudence can instead be interpreted as a more long-term, and more interactive, process of constitutional dialogue. In discharging the entirely proper but inherently difficult task of defining the relationship between its own interpretation of the primary Treaty provisions and/or the general principles of Union law (on the one hand) and the exercise of political discretion conferred by or recognised under the Treaties (on the other hand), the Court in its case law on free movement and Union citizenship has both prompted and accommodated the exercise of Union legislative power – in effect, a two-way dialogue between judges and politicians about how best to balance the construction of a meaningful form of Union citizenship, against the need to respect the social competences and financial concerns of the Member States – while at the same time remaining sensitive to significant changes in the broader landscape of European integration.

It would be foolhardy to predict the future direction of the case law on Union citizenship. But the constellation of a Union legislature which has taken a more proactive interest in regulating the free movement and welfare rights of Union citizens, together with a public discourse which seems (at least) as sceptical as it

[123] *cf* M Dougan, 'What are we to make of the Citizens' Initiative?' (2011) 48 *CML Rev* 1807.

has ever been about the ends and means of the integration process, might lead us to expect two trends to become more pronounced in the Court's approach to free movement. First, the parallel application of primary law and secondary legislation will continue, but the technique of indirect judicial review might become more muted, so that scrutiny under the Treaty itself is more closely tied to the regulatory preferences expressed by the other Union institutions.[124] Second, the Court's approach to the principle of proportionality may well prove more accommodating of national choices in particularly sensitive policy fields, particularly those characterised by only complementary Union competence,[125] so that condemnation is reserved primarily for those rules which can be considered unfairly arbitrary or intolerably inconsistent.[126] Overall, one senses that the opportunity to effect a more profound transformation in relations between State, Union and Citizen either was squandered in the period after Laeken by the inept political salesmanship of the Member States and Union institutions alike; or that such an opportunity never really existed in the first place because it actually fell so far out of tune with the deeply-held wishes of the general European population.[127] The joint efforts of the Court and the legislature may well have delivered appreciable improvements in the rights enjoyed by certain categories of migrant, but perhaps we must now content ourselves with a period of consolidation and reflection,[128] awaiting the next 'constitutional moment' before we can or should expect significant further advances in the legal construction of free movement and welfare rights for Union citizens.[129]

[124] cp C Timmermans, '*Martínez Sala* and *Baumbast* Revisited' in M Maduro and L Azoulai (eds), *The Past and Future of EU Law* (Oxford, Hart Publishing, 2010).

[125] For a similar view, see F Jacobs, 'Citizenship of the European Union: A Legal Analysis' (2007) 13 *ELJ* 591; M Cousins, 'Citizenship, Residence and Social Security' (2007) 32 *ELRev* 386.

[126] cp the gambling case law under Art 56 TFEU. On the one hand, eg Case C-275/92 *Schindler* [1994] ECR I-1039; Case C-124/97 *Läärä* (*Cotswold Microsystems)* [1999] ECR I-6067; Case C-42/07 *Liga Portuguesa de Futebol Profissional* [2009] ECR I-7633. On the other hand, eg Case C-67/98 *Zenatti* [1999] ECR I-7289; Case C-243/01 *Gambelli* [2003] ECR I-13031; Joined Cases C-338/04, C-359/04 and C-360/04 *Placanica and Others* [2007] ECR I-1891. See further, eg S Van den Bogaert and A Cuyvers, '"Money for Nothing": The Case Law of the EU Court of Justice on the Regulation of Gambling' (2011) 48 *CML Rev* 1175. More generally, eg G Mathisen, 'Consistency and Coherence as Conditions for Justification of Member State Measures Restricting Free Movement' (2010) 47 *CML Rev* 1021.

[127] cp Besson and Utzinger, above n 76; P Magnette, 'How Can One be European? Reflections on the Pillars of European Civic Identity' (2007) 13 *ELJ* 664.

[128] A sentiment echoing that of Spaventa, 'The Constitutional Impact of Union Citizenship', above n 86; and also of N Nic Shuibhne, 'The Resilience of EU Market Citizenship' (2010) 47 *CML Rev* 1597.

[129] Though prospects for enhancing the political participation of Union citizens in the exercise of public power by the Union institutions might seem more fruitful: consider, in particular, Art 11(4) TEU and Art 24 TFEU together with Regulation 211/2011 on the citizens' initiative [2011] OJ L65/1. For discussion, eg Dougan, 'What are we to make of the Citizens' Initiative?', above n 123; J Mendes, 'Participation and the Role of Law After Lisbon: A Legal View on Article 11 TEU' (2011) 48 *CML Rev* 1849. More generally: J Shaw, *The Transformation of Union Citizenship: Electoral Rights and the Restructuring of Political Space* (Cambridge, Cambridge University Press, 2007); J Shaw, 'Citizenship: Contrasting Dynamics at the Interface of Integration and Constitutionalism' in P Craig and G de Búrca (eds), *The Evolution of EU Law* (Oxford, Oxford University Press, 2011).

6

Towards 'Real' Citizenship? The Judicial Construction of Union Citizenship and its Limits

DANIEL THYM

THERE IS NOTHING new in describing the process of European integration as judge-made constitutionalisation. Citizens of the Member States have benefited, for decades, from judicial innovations such as direct effect and the generous interpretation of the fundamental freedoms.[1] It did therefore not come as a great surprise when the European Court of Justice (ECJ) started exploring the legal potential of Union citizenship. It would have been naïve of the drafters of the Maastricht Treaty to assume that the introduction of the new status would permanently remain an empty normative shell.[2] At the same time, the imprecision of the Treaty provisions made it inevitable that the judicial expansion of Union citizenship would be criticised. This contribution considers the countervailing forces restraining the Court's citizenship cases – both in the conventional discussion about social benefits and the more recent debate about third-country national family members, who arguably constitute the new 'frontier' of Union citizenship.

During the past 15 years, the controversy focused on social benefits for economically inactive Union citizens on the basis of landmark rulings such as *Martínez Sala*, *Grzelczyk* and *Förster*. Although the evolution of the case law was controversial and at times spectacular, we may, with the wisdom of hindsight, identify its limited conceptual implications. Wider constitutional repercussions are less pronounced than the dogmatic controversy surrounding the judgments suggests, as discussed in section I of this chapter. When it comes to the new frontier of Union citizenship, at present the outcome is less clear.

[1] Read the classic account by J Weiler, 'The Transformation of Europe' (1990/91) 100 *Yale Law Journal* 2403, 2410–83.

[2] See J Shaw, 'Citizenship of the Union: Towards a Post-National Membership?' in *Collected Courses of the Academy of European Law* vol VI-1 (The Hague, Kluwer Law International, 1998) 237, 278–96 and C Tomuschat, 'Staatsbürgerschaft – Unionsbürgerschaft – Weltbürgerschaft' in J Drexl et al (eds), *Europäische Demokratie* (Baden-Baden, Nomos, 1999) 73, 75.

These recent controversies will be considered in section II, and concern a line of judgments regarding third-country national family members and corresponding challenges for the vertical and horizontal balance of power. The judicial choices will define the Court's vision of 'real' Union citizenship beyond the market paradigm, as shown in section III.

Within the overall framework of this book, the current chapter considers the ECJ's citizenship case law. Instead of focusing on legitimacy of the judgments in hermeneutic–dogmatic terms, this contribution concentrates on constitutional and conceptual implications, which are raised by the case law. Two research questions are crucial for assessing constitutional legitimacy: the impact upon and the acceptance of ECJ case law by both the EU legislator and the Member States.[3] Whereas horizontal interaction with parliamentary law-making presents the classic test for judicial review, the vertical relationship with the Member States (and their constitutional courts) has always been a vocal challenge for the ECJ.[4] When considering constitutional implications for the horizontal and vertical balance of powers, the quality and responsiveness of the Court's legal argument constitute supportive qualities in themselves, as they facilitate the acceptance of judgments and thereby contribute to their legitimacy.[5]

I. CLASSIC DISPUTES REVISITED: ACCESS TO SOCIAL BENEFITS

As a preliminary remark, it may be helpful to remember the early years of the debate about innovative citizenship judgments: the widespread confusion after *Martínez Sala* or the consternation caused by *Grzelczyk* and the respite when cases such as *Baumbast* or *Collins* gradually established a coherent dogmatic framework.[6] One may have loved or have hated these judgments for different reasons, but a feeling of amazement was tangible in the late 1990s and early 2000s. Early citizenship cases were ground-breaking[7] and met stiff resistance.[8] These early years of citizenship case law were the high tide from which the Court retreated only gradually. Michal Dougan is right to identify the *Förster* judgment as the moment when the ECJ bowed to opposing forces and accepted the limits of judicial innovation.[9]

[3] *cf* Lenaerts, ch1, section I in this volume.

[4] See the argument by M Rosenfeld, 'Comparing Constitutional Review by the European Court of Justice and the US Supreme Court' (2006) 4 *International Journal of Constitutional Law* 618.

[5] See A von Bogdandy and I Venzke, 'On the Democratic Legitimation of International Judicial Lawmaking' (2011) 12 *German Law Journal* 1341, 1344–51.

[6] For a recent overview of prominent cases, see F Wollenschläger, 'A New Fundamental Freedom beyond Market Integration' (2011) 17 *ELJ* 1, 14–29.

[7] *cf* the first comments by C Tomuschat, 'Case C-86/96 *María Martínez Sala v Freistaat Bayern*' (2000) 37 *CML Rev* 449 (note).

[8] The most prominent criticism was voiced by K Hailbronner, 'Union Citizenship and Access to Social Benefits' (2005) 42 *CML Rev* 1245.

[9] See ch 5, sections III and IV by Michael Dougan in this volume.

During the past 5 years, the ECJ has balanced its relationship both horizontally with the EU legislator (A) and vertically with Member States (B), albeit at the price of persisting uncertainties about the scope and limits of citizenship rights (C). It is a formidable challenge to identify overarching themes of such complex and sometimes contradictory case law. Yet Michael Dougan presents all core arguments in a balanced and nuanced way in relation to both dogmatic detail and constitutional superstructure.[10] There are no arguments I fundamentally disagree with. I therefore approach his theses from a different angle in this first section, by illustrating that long-term implications of the dispute over social benefits are, from today's viewpoint, less revolutionary than initial analyses suggested. I suggest shifting our attention to Union citizenship's new frontier instead, which will be presented later in this chapter.

A Dialogue with the Union Legislator

When it comes to the legislator, Michael Dougan asserts that the ECJ engaged in a 'dialogue' with the Union legislator, which convinced the Court to indirectly confirm the compatibility of Citizenship Directive 2004/38/EC with primary law, as far as the five-year time limit for access to study grants (*Förster*) and the exclusion of job-seekers from basic social benefits (*Vatsouras*) is concerned.[11] This outcome was certainly no foregone conclusion in the light of earlier judgments, and it confirms the view shared by many observers that the Court backtracked from a more expansive reading of Union citizenship in order to avert open confrontation with the legislator.[12] While I agree with the essence of this argument, I am less optimistic about the overall potential for inter-institutional dialogue. If 'dialogue' means a conversation among equals, we should be careful not to overstate the influence of the legislator for two reasons.

i Extended Interpretative Autonomy

Social science helps us to identify the extended interpretative autonomy of the ECJ. Considering the citizenship case law against the background of the principal–agent theory illustrates the relative weakness of the legislator in comparison to the Court. Generally speaking, the legislator may restrain judicial autonomy by means of ex ante control, by drafting new rules which the Court is bound to

[10] See, again, Dougan, ch 5 in this volume.

[11] See the two express exceptions from equal treatment in Art 24(2) Directive 2004/38/EC [2004] OJ L158/77 and Dougan, ch 5, section V in this volume.

[12] Similarly, M Ross, 'The Struggle for EU Citizenship' in A Arnull, C Barnard, M Dougan and E Spaventa (eds), *A Constitutional Order of States? Essays in EU Law in Honour of Alan Dashwood* (Oxford, Hart Publishing, 2011) 283, 289–93 and S Stewen, *Die Entwicklung des allgemeinen Freizügigkeitsrechts der Unionsbürger und seiner sozialen Begleitrechte* (Tübingen, Mohr Siebeck, 2011) ch 3.

interpret, or by means of ex post control by reacting to Court cases with legislative amendments.[13] Both control channels are however hampered by structural difficulties when it comes to the interaction between the Union legislator and the ECJ (leaving aside the uncertain degree of constitutional constraints, for the moment).[14] During the legislative process, and in reaction to ECJ judgments, the Union legislator holds little sway.

First, ex ante control is complicated by open-ended compromise formulae, which often characterise EU legislation as a result of internal disputes between the Member States in the Council or inter-institutional discussions between the Council, the Commission and Parliament. Abstract terminology and formulaic compromises reflect the tradition of diplomatic negotiations and almost necessarily leave much interpretative leeway to the Court.[15] The Citizenship Directive, with its internal discrepancies and vague formulae, amply illustrates this point. Expressions such as 'unreasonable burden on the social assistance system'[16] are no clear indication of the legislator's will.[17] The exceptions from equal treatment in Article 24(2) are among the few examples where the legislator drew a red line, to which the Court paid due respect in *Förster* and *Vatsouras*.[18] In other situations, ex ante control is much more limited.

Second, ex post control by means of legislative amendment is thwarted by procedural hurdles. Any revision of secondary law is notoriously difficult. Not only does the Commission hold the monopoly of initiative, but moreover, Member States may be affected asymmetrically by different rulings. What matters to A may not convince B to support a legislative amendment, and vice versa.[19] Even if the Court wanted to pay due regard to political considerations, the necessary balance is difficult to strike, since the judges may be confronted with 28 different political sensitivities and 28 national communicative discourses.[20] That is not to say that the Court should bow to populist pressure,[21] but it describes structural reasons why the Court holds an extended interpretative leeway in practice.

[13] See A Stone Sweet, 'The European Court of Justice' in P Craig and G de Búrca (eds), *The Evolution of EU Law* (Oxford, Oxford University Press, 2011) 121, 126–28.

[14] See below, I.C.

[15] Similarly with regard to drafting deficits, see E Sharpston, 'Transparency and Clear Legal Language in the European Union' (2009–10) 12 *CYELS* 409, 411–12.

[16] Art 14(1) Directive 2004/38.

[17] For a more extensive survey of ambiguities and discrepancies in the formulation of the directive, see Hailbronner (n 8) 1258–64.

[18] See, again, Dougan ch 5, section V in this volume.

[19] As the futile attempt by some Member States to correct the implications of the *Metock* judgment, which is in most parts based on an interpretation the Citizenship Directive (not primary law), amply illustrates; the (small) Member States concerned did not have the political leverage to convince the Commission to table a proposal.

[20] For an overtly critical assessment, see FW Scharpf, 'Legitimacy in the Multilevel European Polity' (2009) 1 *European Political Science Review* 173, 188–98.

[21] *cf* on citizenship and immigration, Editorial Comments: 'The Court of Justice in the Limelight – Again' (2008) 45 *CML Rev* 1571, 1576–77.

ii Continuity as a Dogmatic Assumption

In recent citizenship judgments, the Court presents a new dogmatic argument. When the judges in Luxembourg are confronted with changes to EU legislation which may have repercussions on earlier case law interpreting legislative instruments that have been amended or complemented, it opts for continuity. To my knowledge, the argument appeared first in *Metock* when the Court departed from its earlier assumption that secondary law does not regulate the first entry of third-country national family members into EU territory. Uncertainties about how to interpret the Citizenship Directive are brushed aside with a simple teleological argument: Since the directive aims at strengthening the rights of Union citizens, they 'cannot derive less rights from that directive than from the instruments of secondary legislation which it amends or repeals'.[22]

In a similar vein, the Court argued in *Teixeira* and *Ibrahim* that some ambiguous formulation in the Citizenship Directive cannot be interpreted so as to change the former rules of Regulation 1612/68 on income requirements for children of migrant workers after the sponsor has left the country.[23] Again, the Court opts for continuity. It should be noted that the ECJ's conclusion can be defended in both cases.[24] What is problematic, however, is the more principled judicial assumption that new legal instruments should be interpreted in line with earlier judgments, since it can – in the eyes of the Court – not be assumed that the legislator wanted to deviate from earlier case law when amending citizenship legislation.[25] If the legislature had this intention, it must say so explicitly – a requirement which will rarely be fulfilled.[26] This dogmatic conservatism shown by the Court restrains the impact of legislative amendments. As a result, the Court's interpretation of the directive is effectively set in stone. The Court may have yielded to the legislator in *Förster* and *Vatsouras*, but it has the upper hand for structural reasons in regular circumstances.

B Federal Balance of Power

In comparison with the Union legislator, the Member States are in a weaker position when it comes to citizenship cases. From a practical perspective, the option

[22] Case C-127/08 *Metock* [2008] ECR I-6241, para 59.

[23] See Case C-480/08 *Teixeira* [2010] ECR I-1107, paras 54–61 and Case C-310/08 *Ibrahim* [2010] ECR I-1065, para 49.

[24] On different arguments supporting the Court's stance, see P Starup and M Elsmore, 'Taking a Logical or Giant Step Forward?' (2010) 35 *ELRev* 571, 574–76.

[25] The teleological reference to the legislative intention to 'strengthen' the rights of EU citizens is certainly valid, but does not mandatorily support such a principled conclusion.

[26] The ECJ stops short of establishing a primary law, standstill obligations mirroring the interpretation of Art 41 of the Additional Protocol to the EEC-Turkey Association Agreement and Art 13 of the Association Council Decision No 1/80 in Joined Cases C-300/09 and C-301/09 *Toprak* [2010] ECR I-12845, paras 51–57, which prevents Union and national legislators from downgrading the position of Turkish nationals.

of changing primary law and forcing their opinion upon the ECJ is as implausible as the theoretical possibility of withdrawing from the Union.[27] When the Court interprets primary law, it is not simply the agent of the 'Masters of the Treaty', but it benefits from an extended autonomy as a trustee, mirroring the position of national constitutional courts.[28] It is therefore of crucial importance for the federal balance of power that the Court treats the Member States with suspicion in day-to-day management of citizenship cases, while preserving their autonomy in economic and social policy. Both considerations illustrate the limits of the social benefits case law: the Court mandates equal treatment but does not force the Member States to harmonise their economic or social model.

i Control Density with Regard to Justification

Michael Dougan rightly reminds us that the Court has traditionally approached the Member States with suspicion in citizenship cases. Luxembourg is rather generous in finding a restriction to free movement which triggers the application of citizenship rules, while the Member States are subject to a strict burden of proof when it comes to justification. I support his proposal that the Court should grant the Member States more leeway in such circumstances, especially in areas where the Union holds no legislative competences.[29] It may in so far replicate its case law on the internal market, where the Court has recently shown more flexibility.[30] Indeed, the *Sayn-Wittgenstein* and *Runeviĕ Vardyn and Wardyn* rulings may indicate that the ECJ is becoming more flexible in citizenship cases, analysing the restricting effects of national measures more carefully and leaving the Member States discretion in proportionality assessments, especially in culturally or politically sensitive policy fields that relate back to principled considerations of national constitutional identity.[31]

Moreover, there may be more wisdom in the Court's handling of public policy considerations than the initial analysis suggests. Lawyers specialising in EU law know the standard justification formula that equal treatment is not meant '[to] become an unreasonable burden which could have consequences for the overall level of assistance which may be granted by that State'.[32] It is true that the Court has traditionally handled the criterion strictly, but it might have sec-

[27] The implausibility of withdrawal from (most) international agreements is one reason why the legitimacy of international courts requires closer scrutiny, *cf* A von Bogdandy and I Venzke, 'Beyond Dispute: International Judicial Institutions as Lawmakers' (2011) 12 *German Law Journal* 979, 995.

[28] See Stone Sweet (n 13) 126–28.

[29] See Dougan, ch 5, section III in this volume.

[30] See the chapter by Jukka Snell in this volume.

[31] For a careful reading of 'restrictions' see Case C-391/09 *Runevič-Vardyn and Wardyn* [2011] ECR I-3787, paras 66–82; for the role of Art 4(2) TEU in justification, see ibid, para 86 and Case C-208/09 *Sayn-Wittgenstein* [2010] ECR I-13693, para 92.

[32] Case C-209/03 *Bidar* [2005] ECR I-2119, para 56; the 'unreasonable burden' formula, which Art 14(1) Directive 2004/38 takes up, was first used in Case C-184/9 *Grzelczyk* [2001] ECR I-6193, para 44 without specifying the *telos* of protecting the overall level of assistance (it should be noted that loss of financial income is no justification per se and can be considered only where it results in loss of public services in general); *cf* Case C-76/05 *Schwarz and Gootjes-Schwarz* [2007] ECR I-6849, paras 77–78.

ond thoughts. In its 2010 *Bressol and Chaverot* judgment on access to Wallonian universities for medical and para-medical studies, the Court was generous enough to leave the ultimate assessment of whether full equal treatment would undermine the Wallonian medical system to the national court[33] (albeit after laying down a detailed programme showing how the referring court should handle proportionality).[34] These considerations hint at the more general point that the Court does not dictate a specific social or economic model.

ii Respect for National Economic or Social Models

We should be careful not to overstate the impact of equal treatment requirements on national economic or social policies. Their limited impact on policy choices arguably constitutes the core reason why the controversy over access to social benefits caused less political frictions than the sometimes heated debate in legal circles suggested. My conclusion of limited conceptual relevance builds upon three related arguments.

First, equal access to social benefits is no novelty introduced by ECJ citizenship case law. From the very beginning, the Rome Treaty guaranteed the equal treatment of migrant workers with the twofold purpose of securing fair working conditions and preventing downward pressure upon the wage level in host states.[35] In 1968, the EU legislator stated without caveats that migrant workers 'shall enjoy the same social and tax advantages as national workers'.[36] In combination with generous ECJ case law, intra-European free movement soon transcended pure economic conceptualisations and turned the fundamental freedoms into the nucleus of 'social citizenship'.[37] Moreover, most national social security systems gradually embraced territoriality instead of nationality as the door-opener for various forms of social benefits after the Second World War.[38] Thus, the traditional linkage between nationality and access to social benefits had already been loosened when the ECJ embarked upon its citizenship case law. This conclusion does not question the dogmatic novelty of the judgments, but puts their conceptual implications into perspective.

[33] Case C-73/0 *Bressol and Chaverot* [2010] ECR I-2735, para 82; and, more recently, Case C-20/12, *Giersch et al* [2013] ECR I-0000, para 53 et seq.

[34] Indeed, the Belgian constitutional court reacted to the ECJ ruling by annulling six out of nine regional rules in question, since they did not meet to (strict) ECJ standards on proportionality; see Lenaerts, ch 1, section II.A in this volume.

[35] See Art 48(2) of the original EEC Treaty and the explanatory statements in the 'Spaak Report' (Rapport des Chefs de Délégation aux Ministres des Affaires Etrangères, 21 April 1956) section 3. III; for background information, consult the historic study by S Goedings, *Labor Migration in an Integrating Europe* (The Hague, Sdu, 2005) ch 2.

[36] Art 7(2) Regulation (EEC) No 1612/68 [1968] OJ L257/1 (which has, in the meantime, been replaced by Art 7(2) Regulation (EU) No 492/2011 [2011] OJ L141/1).

[37] The dogmatic and conceptual free movement pedigree of Union citizenship case law is emphasised by S O'Leary, 'Developing an Ever Closer Union between the Peoples of Europe?' (2008) 27 *YEL* 167, 174–77 and S Giubboni, 'Free Movement of Persons and European Solidarity' (2007) 13 *ELJ* 360, 363–68.

[38] For an overview, see T Kingreen, *Soziale Rechte und Migration* (Baden-Baden, Nomos, 2010).

Second, the Court was careful not to overstretch its case law. Although the limits of equal treatment became visible only gradually, we may, with the wisdom of hindsight, point to the 'real/genuine link'[39] or 'certain degree of integration'[40] criterion as being the crucial threshold. Economically inactive Union citizens who do not meet this criterion may be subjected to discrimination. The relevance of this criterion should not be underestimated. The ECJ breaks open the social security systems of the Member States, but only for those Union citizens with a genuine link who have integrated themselves into the host society to a certain degree. This is no abstract vision of transnational solidarity between the peoples of Europe.[41] On the contrary, the Court accepts that social benefits may be restricted to solidarity (national) communities, but at the same time ensures that these communities embrace Union citizens who have integrated themselves into host societies to a certain degree.[42]

Third, it is important to distinguish between the financial and constitutional effects of equal treatment obligations. The Court obliges the Member States to extend social benefits to most EU citizens living in their territory, but does not substitute its own vision of social justice for national policy preferences. ECJ judgments mandate equal treatment and may thus be costly in financial terms, but they do not force the Member States to alter their social security systems.[43] Britain, Sweden and Romania certainly have different levels of social protection, which the ECJ extends to most migrant Union citizens living in these countries, but it does not push Member States towards harmonisation (equal access to social benefits also needs to be distinguished from the functioning of mutual recognition in the internal market which often entails a neoliberal drift supporting competitive deregulation).[44] Some commentators criticise the inherent judicial lack of vision of social justice.[45] This conclusion

[39] Case C-224/98 *D'Hoop* [2002] ECR I-6191, para 38; Case C-138/02 *Collins* [2004] ECR I-2703, para 67; and Joined Cases C-22/08 and C-23/08 *Vatsouras* [2009] ECR I-4585, para 38, which both concern benefits for job-seekers.

[40] *Bidar* (n 32) para 57 and Case C-158/07 *Förster* [2008] ECR I-8507, para 49 in relation to Union citizens other than job-seekers.

[41] The Court is often criticised for disrespecting the link between (national/social) solidarity and access to social benefits; eg by F de Witte, 'The End of EU Citizenship and the Means of Non-Discrimination' (2011) 18 *Maastricht Journal of European and Comparative Law* 86.

[42] For further reflection, see C O'Brien, 'Real Links, Abstract Rights and False Alarms: The Relationship between the ECJ's "Real Link" Case Law and National Solidarity' (2008) 33 *ELRev* 643, 646–50 and the prospective plea by C Schönberger, *Unionsbürger* (Tübingen, Mohr Siebeck, 2005) 407–32; one may recognise this conceptual limitation of the case law even if one does not go as far as constructing a new type of citizenship based on residence, as propagated by D Kostakopoulou, *The Future Governance of Citizenship* (Cambridge, Cambridge University Press, 2008).

[43] For a differentiated evaluation, see A Somek, 'Solidarity Decomposed: Being and Time in European Citizenship' (2007) 32 *ELRev* 787, 806–18.

[44] See A Somek, 'The Argument from Transnational Effects I' (2010) 16 *ELJ* 315, 338–40 and T Kingreen, 'Fundamental Freedoms' in A von Bogdandy and J Bast (eds), *Principles of European Constitutional Law*, 2nd edn (Oxford, Hart Publishing, 2009) 515, 532–42.

[45] See D Kochenov, 'Citizenship without Respect: The EU's troubled Equality Ideal' (2010) Jean Monnet Working Paper No 08/10, 27–34, available at: centers.law.nyu.edu/jeanmonnet/papers/10/100801.pdf; and Ross (n 12) 286–87.

may also be presented in a positive light, since equal treatment respects economic and social policy choices of the Member States.

C Quality of the Court's Reasoning

Most academics working on the Court's citizenship case law have read Kay Hailbronner's sharp and intelligent critique of the dogmatic inconsistencies of early judgments. At the time, the material and personal scope of equal treatment (Article 18 TFEU) and the status of 'limitations and conditions laid down in' secondary law (Article 21 TFEU) were discussed controversially.[46] This early and radical phase of the case law came to an end, however, when the Court yielded to the legislator in *Förster*. But even if we accept the Court's basic assumptions for the purposes of our discussion, dogmatic irregularities persist today. Michael Dougan reminds us of the weak points: when it comes to social benefits, we are uncertain about the role of personal circumstances and indirect judicial review.[47] Recent judgments often lack coherence and clarity.

As a result, it has become difficult to predict the outcome of social benefits cases – and sometimes one cannot even be sure of the successful party after the ruling has been delivered. *Vatsouras* is a case in point: German courts still struggle to decide whether job-seekers qualify for social assistance. This is partly their fault, since the Federal Social Court hesitates to make the final assessment with which it was entrusted.[48] But Luxembourg also bears some responsibility, since the ECJ failed to provide clear standards.[49] This reflects a general tendency: while considerations of legal certainly may have guided the *Bidar* and *Förster* rulings,[50] recent judgments have lost orientation. The Court fluctuates between 'simple' interpretation of secondary law and (in)direct judicial review[51] and remains ambiguous about the relevance of individual circumstances.[52] Moreover, Luxembourg handles the cross-border yardstick generously, thereby extending free movement to situations with a marginal transnational dimension, which is often difficult to delineate.[53]

[46] See Hailbronner (n 8).

[47] See Dougan, ch 5, section IV in this volume.

[48] The ECJ explicitly asked the national court to assess the character of unemployment benefits in *Vatsouras* (n 39) para 41.

[49] It rendered its judgment in full awareness that German unemployment benefits cannot be neatly qualified as either social assistance (which in the light of *Förster* can, in principle, be declined for up to five years) or labour market reintegration measures (where the *Collins*-standard mandates payment at an earlier point); *cf* the brief description of the measure in,*Vatsouras* (n 39), paras 8 and 41–44.

[50] As argued by C Semmelmann, 'Die Grenzen der Unionsbürgerschaft im Urteil Förster' (2009) Europarecht 683, 689–91 and M Jesse, 'The Value of 'Integration' in European Law' (2011) 27 ELJ 172, 181.

[51] For a critical assessment, see Dougan, ch 5, section IV in this volume.

[52] On the role of personal circumstances see Ross (n 12) 289–93 and E Spaventa, 'Seeing the Wood despite the Trees? On the Scope of Union Citizenship and its Constitutional Effects' (2008) 45 *CML Rev* 13, 39–43.

[53] See Case C-34/09 *Ruiz Zambrano*, Opinion of AG Sharpston, paras 69–78 and N Nic Shuibhne, 'Free Movement of Persons and the Wholly Internal Rule' (2002) 39 *CML Rev* 731, 741–60.

Arguably, the Court delivered one of its most ambiguous judgments in *Ruiz Zambrano*, the constitutional implications of which will be discussed in the next section. The official reasoning was essentially limited to apodictic declarations of result. The Court postulated a new substance of rights test without distinguishing established case law, which had characterised all citizenship cases since *Bickel and Franz*. The 'substance of rights' standard is a new and independent category and the judges failed to explain its rationale, implications and limits.[54] The official reasoning was limited to six paragraphs.[55] Some of these deficits were remedied a few months later in the *Dereci* decision with a noticeable effort on the side of the Grand Chamber to explain the implications and limits of the new doctrine.[56] Nevertheless, this does not unmake the widespread confusion in the aftermath of *Ruiz Zambrano*.

In short: the outcome of individual citizenship cases occasionally resembles a game of chance. 'It is difficult to avoid a sense of unease at such an outcome. Lottery rather than logic would seem to be governing the exercise of EU citizenship rights'.[57] Across Europe, considerable intellectual resources have been spent in recent years, both by academics and judges, trying to decipher the proclamations from Luxembourg. That is disappointing. The Court should fulfil its primary mission under Article 19 TEU to 'ensure that in the interpretation and application of the Treaties the law is observed'. This is particularly relevant for a supranational legal order, which depends on decentralised adjudication. Yet, observance of EU law by national courts requires guidance.[58] In *Förster*, *Bidar* and *Dereci,* the Court met this challenge (irrespective of whether you like the outcome or not), but in *Vatsouras* and *Ruiz Zambrano*, the sense of direction is lost. A Supreme Court should behave more responsibly.

II. A NEW FRONTIER? THIRD-COUNTRY NATIONAL FAMILY MEMBERS

Times change and the focus of academic attention changes with them. Access to social benefits has been in the spotlight for more than a decade. Certainly, uncertainties persist, not least because the Court sometimes fails to provide clear guidance.[59] Nevertheless, the core battles about the reach and limits of

[54] For a more comprehensive critique, see K Hailbronner and D Thym, 'Annotion of Case C-34/09 *Ruiz Zambrano*' (2011) 48 *CML Rev* 1253.

[55] *cf* Case C-34/09 *Ruiz Zambrano* [2011] ECR I-1177, paras 39–44.

[56] See Case C-256/11 *Dereci* [2011] ECR I-0000, paras 44–101 (note that para 54 even points at the 'literal, teleological and contextual interpretation' of the Citizenship Directive); and the comments by Lenaerts, ch 1, sect II.B this volume.

[57] Opinion of AG Sharpston (n 53) para 88 with regard to cross-border yardstick triggering the application of Arts 18 and 21 TFEU.

[58] Guidance does not require the ECJ to decide each case; it should certainly leave discretion to national courts (thereby enhancing subsidiarity and fostering compliance with EU law, if national courts retain decision-making powers of their own). But guidance in the form of clear and abstract criteria should not be abandoned.

[59] See above, I.C.

equal treatment have been fought. Arguably, the main argument of the underlying constitutional dispute was settled when Article 24 of the Citizenship Directive established an explicit right to equal treatment, thereby vindicating the approach of the Court since 1998[60] – and when the Court accepted the legislator's central remaining caveat in *Förster*.[61] As indicated at the outset, I suggest that the centre of gravity has changed.

What then is the frontier of the future? If you consider the sequence of controversial citizenship cases of the past decade, a common thread besides social benefits stands out: the legal status of third-country national family members. The *Ruiz Zambrano* judgment, which concerned the residence status of Colombian parents of Union citizens of minor age who have never lived outside their home state of Belgium, is a prime example.[62] But I do not rely upon this case only. The line of judgments upon which I build my argument is much more extensive. Experts of the ECJ's citizenship case law are familiar with cases such as *Carpenter*, *Baumbast*, *Akrich*, *Zhu and Chen*, *Eind*, *Metock*, *Ibrahim*, *Teixeira*, *McCarthy* and *Dereci*.[63] Although these cases relate to different issues of primary and secondary law, they have one thing in common: they concern the interface between Union citizenship and the residence status of third-country national family members.

Generally speaking, it is not surprising that the legal status of third-country national family members has become the new battleground, since it raises formidable challenges for the ECJ. Third-country national family members cannot rely upon citizenship rights directly, but benefit from Union citizenship through 'derived rights acquired through their status as members of the beneficiary's family'.[64] This derivative character presents their status as a perfect test ground for citizenship rights beyond the transnational market paradigm (A). By extending Treaty rights with constitutional status to third-country nationals, the Court enters into conflict with both national regulatory claims (B) and legislative prerogatives of the EU legislator on migration law within the area of freedom, security and justice (C). It will be argued that these constitutional challenges defy easy resolution and require judicial choices about the meaning and limits of Union citizenship.

[60] When the Court extended equal treatment to all economically inactive Union citizens in other Member States; *cf* Case C-85/96 *Martínez Sala* [1998] ECR I-2691 and Case C-274/96 *Bickel and Franz* [1998] ECR I-7637.

[61] See, again, Dougan, ch 5, section V in this volume with a view to Art 24(2) Directive 2004/38.

[62] See *Ruiz Zambrano* (n 55) paras 39–44.

[63] See Case C-60/00 *Carpenter* [2002] ECR I-6279; Case C-413/99 *Baumbast* [2002] ECR I-7091; Case C-109/01 *Akrich* [2003] ECR I-9607; Case C-200/02 *Zhu and Chen* [2004] ECR I-9925; Case C-291/05 *Eind* [2007] ECR I-10719; *Metock* (n 22); *Ibrahim* (n 23); *Teixeira* (n 23); Case C-434/09 *McCarthy* [2011] ECR I-3375; *Dereci* (n 56).

[64] *Dereci* (n 56) para 55.

A Citizenship beyond the Market?

The Court has been accused by some[65] – and encouraged by others[66] – for sponsoring a functional understanding of 'market citizenship'[67] based on the transnational promotion of individual liberty. In order to benefit fully from the promises of Union citizenship, you need to be an active migrant in pursuit of (economic) happiness outside your home country.[68] Of course, that statement is true at a very abstract level only. The Court has always embraced a generous reading of the fundamental freedoms and later extended their benefits to economically inactive citizens on the basis of Articles 18 and 21 TFEU. Also, judgments such as *Carpenter* and *Metock* gradually abandoned the functional market integration logic.[69] But as a matter of principle, transnational mobility remained the backbone of citizenship cases – that is, until the Court crossed a crucial threshold in its *Ruiz Zambrano* judgment.

The facts of the case have little resonance with transnational market integration. The economically inactive *Ruiz Zambrano* family did not move across intra-European borders. Rather, the applicant father, a Colombian national, had been residing in Belgium as a failed asylum seeker for some years and was unemployed when the national court referred the case to Luxembourg. Attempts to regularise the residence status had been rejected in protracted administrative and judicial proceedings, although the Belgian authorities did not actively pursue coercive measures to deport the family to a third state.[70] The issue of Union citizenship arose when two children were born and the parents failed to register for their Colombian nationality. Based on Belgian legislation for the prevention of statelessness, they received Belgian nationality (and Union citizenship). On this basis, the third-country national father of the Union citizens claimed a residence permit, which the Court willingly conceded.

To cut a long story short: in the *Ruiz Zambrano* judgment, there is neither 'market' nor 'transnationalism'. The facts of *Ruiz Zambrano* are in essence about considerations of social justice. Should third-country national parents of minor citizens born in their country of residence receive legal residence status?

[65] See eg Spaventa, 'Seeing the Wood despite the Trees?' (n 52) 30–39 and D Kochenov, 'A Real European Citizenship' (2011) 18 *Columbia Journal of European Law* 56, 91–106.

[66] See A Somek, *Individualism* (Oxford, Oxford University Press, 2008) ch 10 and, on the basis of controversially existentialist suppositions, U Haltern, 'Pathos and Patina' (2003) 9 *ELJ* 14, 39–44.

[67] The term, '*Marktbürgerschaft*' has been coined by H-P Ipsen, *Europäisches Gemeinschaftsrecht* (Tübingen, Mohr Siebeck, 1972) 250–54: and was used first in H-P Ipsen and G Nicolaysen, 'Haager Konferenz für Europarecht und Bericht über die aktuelle Entwicklung des Gemeinschaftsrechts' (1965) *Neue Juristische Wochenschrift* 339, 340.

[68] For recent accounts how the Court's citizenship case law fits the transnational market paradigm, see N Nic Shuibhne, 'The Resilience of EU Market Citizenship' (2010) 47 *CML Rev* 1597 and Wollenschläger (n 6) 30–34.

[69] See the references below in n 95.

[70] In 2000, deportation to Colombia had been declared inadmissible by a Belgian court, although this conclusion might possibly have been revisited after the end of the civil war; *cf Ruiz Zambrano* (n 55) para 15.

This question does not concern transnational market integration and is traditionally discussed in a human rights framework.[71] The ECJ, however, is not bothered by this differentiation and extends Union citizenship beyond equal treatment and free movement, which had characterised all earlier citizenship judgments, to a purely internal situation without economic foundation, thereby leaving market citizenship behind. The main innovation of the judgment illustrates that the Court constructs Union citizenship as a free-standing guarantee in its own right – as one dogmatic and one methodological consideration substantiate:

First, the dogmatic consideration. The Court could possibly have constructed the case as a restriction to potential free movement and resolve it on the basis of Article 21 TFEU, arguing that non-regularisation of the father's residence status and the potential departure from Belgium hampers the children's capacity to exercise their intra-European free movement rights at a later point.[72] But it deliberately decided not to do so. Instead, the Grand Chamber states explicitly that all interveners had rejected the link with Community law and that the Citizenship Directive does not apply.[73] Luxembourg does not hide the change of paradigm; it establishes the 'substance of rights' test as a free-standing normative category which flows directly from the status of Union citizenship and does not require cross-border movement.[74] By granting unemployed third country national parents a legitimate right to stay in their children's home country, the Court moves beyond 'transnational market citizenship' for good.

Second, a methodological comment. As is often the case, the judgment builds upon a teleological argument, the 'fundamental status', in which the Court has identified Union citizenship as being 'destined to be'.[75] This is not a particularly strong dogmatic foundation for a new legal guarantee, but it should not come as a surprise against the background of the Court's traditional recourse to teleological interpretation ever since *Van Gend & Loos*.[76] Moreover, the new doctrine may possibly rely upon a subtle change in the language of Article 20 TFEU, which defines Union citizens to 'be additional to' (instead of 'complementing') nationality, thereby underlining its autonomous character.[77] All of these arguments are not

[71] On the approach of the ECtHR, see D Thym, 'Respect for Private and Family Life under Article 8 ECHR in Immigration Cases' (2008) 57 *ICLQ* 87, 95–102.

[72] See M Nettesheim, 'Der Kernbereich der Unionsbürgerschaft' (2011) *Juristenzeitung* 1030, 1031 and Kochenov, 'A Real European Citizenship' (n 65) 74–91.

[73] See *Ruiz Zambrano* (n 55) paras 37 and 39.

[74] For further reflection, see Hailbronner and Thym (n 54) 1255–57.

[75] Again, *Grzelczyk* (n 32) para 31; arguably, the French formulation 'a vocation à être' does at least hint at the inspirational, forward-looking intention, which in other language versions, such as German, is lost; it is not immediately clear why the Court changes its English translation to 'is intended to be' (*Ruiz Zambrano* (n 55) para 40) instead of the more stimulating 'is destined to be' in earlier judgments

[76] *cf* the general account by T Tridimas, 'The Court of Justice and Judicial Activism' (1996) 21 *ELRev* 199, 204–06.

[77] For this argument, which is not taken up by the Court, see A Schrauwen, 'European Citizenship in the Treaty of Lisbon: Any Change at All?' (2008) *Maastricht Journal of European and Comparative Law* 55, 59–60; J Shaw, 'Citizenship: Contrasting Dynamics at the Interface of Integration and Constitutionalism' in P Craig and G de Búrca (n 13) 575, 598–600 and H de Waele,

particularly strong, but they remain the only viable explanation for the 'substance of rights' standard. This telos may not have been in the mind of the drafters of the Treaties of Maastricht or Lisbon, but it would have been naïve to assume that Union citizenship would remain an empty normative shell.

B Federal Balance of Power

Although the Court positioned itself for a great leap forward in *Ruiz Zambrano*, for structural reasons it is bound to stop halfway. The new 'substance of rights' doctrine, which flows directly from the 'status' of Union citizenship, sounds appealing but it is no disguise for the structural impediments that hinder the realisation of a grand design. Presenting these limitations with a view to the federal (vertical) balance of power and the horizontal dialogue with the legislator(s) relates my argument back to the constitutional legitimacy of citizenship case law and its inherent limits. Indeed, the federal balance of power may have been one crucial reason why the Court opts for a new category in *Ruiz Zambrano*: the 'substance of rights' test. It would have been straightforward to activate human rights or end the uncertainty about reverse discrimination, but the Court rightly decided not to follow this path, which would have provoked resistance on the part of the Member States, including national constitutional courts. The ECJ certainly does not strive for such conflict.

My argument is best understood when we contrast the Court's *Ruiz Zambrano* judgment with the opinion of Advocate General Sharpston. Her opinion addressed both reverse discrimination and the scope of the Charter, proposing a rather complex combination of both issues.[78] But the Court evades these arguments. It does not alter its standpoint on reverse discrimination and eschews the thorny issue of the scope of the Charter. By establishing a new dogmatic category, which flows directly from the status of Union citizenship (instead of relying upon Articles 18 or 21 TFEU), the Court makes sure that its established case law on purely internal situations, which are not governed by the fundamental freedoms, is not directly affected by the 'substance of rights' test. Only this new category requires no cross-border element.[79] At the same time, the new standard is inherently flexible and requires later refinement, which allows the Court to take on board political and academic criticism.

Indeed, the Court reacted quickly. Only a few months after *Ruiz Zambrano*, the ECJ emphasised the limited impact of the new doctrine. When we read the 'substance of rights' test in the light of the McCarthy and *Dereci* judgments, it

'The Ever-Evolving Concept of EU Citizenship. Of Quantum Leaps, Paradigm Shifts and Copernican Revolutions' in L Talani (ed), *Globalisation, Migration and the Future of Europe* (London, Routledge, 2011) 191, 192–94.

[78] See Opinion of AG Sharpston (n 53).

[79] For further comments, see Hailbronner and Thym (n 54) 1257–58.

becomes plain that it only concerns extreme situations such as loss of nationality (*Rottmann*) or departure from EU territory (*Ruiz Zambrano*).[80] With its narrow field of application, it cannot be relied upon in regular circumstances. Unlike the fundamental freedoms, Article 20 TFEU does not prohibit national 'restrictions', which may deter Union citizens from exercising their rights or cause other serious inconvenience.[81] The 'substance of rights' test is much narrower and concerns legal-existential questions which 'deprive' Union citizens of their rights.[82] The new yardstick will resolve extreme cases only that concern matters of 'to be or not to be'. For other purposes, 'regular' fundamental rights take over[83] as the *Dereci* judgment states in welcome clarity.[84]

This conclusion is convincing. The 'substance of rights' criterion is too abstract to guide the adjudication of individual cases. Human rights are the adequate category to address these concerns. Why did the Court not choose this path from the beginning? The answer is simple: extending the Charter of Fundamental Rights to purely internal situations (such as the facts underlying the *Ruiz Zambrano* judgment, if you decide not to bring the case within the reach of the fundamental freedoms) is left to the Member States. This is dangerous territory for the Court, since Article 51 of the Charter deliberately limits the scope of EU fundamental rights and the corresponding ECJ prerogatives to the Member States 'when they are implementing Union law'.[85] Outside the scope of EU law, national courts should apply the ECHR (as interpreted by the ECtHR), not the Charter (as interpreted by the ECJ).[86] Disrespect for this rule would substantially alter the federal balance of power to the detriment of the Member States and might cause resistance by constitutional courts, including the (in)famously vigilant German one.[87] That is a risk that the ECJ does not want to take. In the long run, however, it cannot evade this choice. Citizenship and fundamental rights cannot be held apart permanently.

[80] See the (re)interpretation of the *Ruiz Zambrano* judgment by *Dereci* (n 56) para 66, which defines departure from the Union as the crucial yardstick; it should be noted that the return of the *Ruiz Zambrano* family to Colombia was not imminent in the original case, since Belgian courts had originally barred their forced return to this country (see n 70); such detail does not, however, prevent the Court from (re)constructing the abstract criteria of its new doctrine.

[81] For the (wider) definition of restriction with regard to Art 21 TFEU, see *Runevič-Vardyn and Wardyn* (n 31) paras 68–76.

[82] *cf* the distinction between 'restriction' and 'deprivation' (with the Court opting for the latter in *Dereci*) by K Lenaerts, 'Civis europaeus sum' (2011) No 3 FMW –http://ec.europa.eu/social/main.jsp?catId=737&langId=en&pubId=6193&type=1&furtherPubs=yes, online journal on free movement of workers 6, 15 and above n 80.

[83] For further comments, see Hailbronner and Thym (n 54) 1259–62.

[84] See *Dereci* (n 56) paras 70–73.

[85] A detailed analysis is presented by P Eeckhout, 'The EU Charter of Fundamental Rights and the Federal Question' (2002) 39 *CML Rev* 945–94; note also that the Court explicitly states in *Dereci* (n 56) that it respects Art 51 of the Charter.

[86] This distinction explains the double reference in *Dereci* (n 56) para 72.

[87] *cf* the threat of 'ultra vires' under explicit reference to Art 51 of the Charter in Decision of 6 July 2010, 2 BvR 2661/06 '*Honeywell*', para 78 (for a translation see: www.bverfg.de/entscheidungen/rs20100706_2bvr266106en.html).

C Interaction with the Legislator

In relation to third-country nationals, the interaction between the ECJ and the legislator differs from the constitutional framework of Union citizenship. Why? Whereas the fundamental freedoms and Articles 18–25 TFEU establish citizenship rights with constitutional status which bind the legislator, third-country nationals benefit from these rules only by means of a legal reflex as family members of Union citizens.[88] Other third-country nationals are subject to a different legal regime: primary law establishes distinct rules for migration policy towards third-country nationals within the area of freedom, security and justice. Within this framework, the Treaty leaves more leeway to the legislator – from both a legal–dogmatic and a conceptual perspective.[89] Unlike Union citizens, third-country nationals do not have quasi-constitutional free-movement rights.[90] Instead of relying upon citizenship rights, they may invoke human rights 'only' that, under regular circumstances, guarantee no right to entry and a lesser degree of security of residence.[91] In short: the Treaty grants more leeway to the Union legislator to design migration policy than citizenship status.

By discussing third-country national family members within the citizenship context only, the ECJ, by and large, ignored migration policy as an alternative point of reference in all cases up to *Ruiz Zambrano*. It gave little or no explanation as to why it gave priority to the citizenship framework over migration policy as the potential alternative frame of reference.[92] This is disappointing, since the delimitation of two competing constitutional frameworks should not be brushed aside without further reflection.[93] It should therefore be welcomed that the *Dereci* judgment makes an effort to be more responsive. It discusses both the Citizenship Directive 2004/38/EC and the Family Reunification Directive 2003/86/EC as alternative but seemingly equal frames of reference.[94] The Court should follow this path and pay more attention to the migration policy aspects of the legal status of third-country national family members, by considering similarities and differences between the fundamental freedoms of Union citizens and human rights of third-country nationals, and it should explain why it gives priority to one set of legal rules in specific cases.

[88] As stated by the Court in welcome clarity in *Dereci* (n 56) para 55.

[89] For further comments see D Thym, 'EU Migration Law and Its Constitutional Rationale' (2013) 50 *CML Rev* 709, 718–21.

[90] See Arts 77–79 TFEU.

[91] By way of example: contrast Arts 45(1) and 45(2) Charter of Fundamental Rights for Union citizens and third-country nationals.

[92] For a superfluous reference, see *Metock* (n 22), para 66.

[93] For a similar argument, see A Lansbergen and N Miller, 'European Citizenship Rights in Internal Situations: An Ambiguous Revolution?' (2011) 7 *European Constitutional Law Review* 287, 300–01.

[94] *cf Dereci* (n 56) paras 45–58; both directives did not apply *in casu*.

III. 'TRUE' CITIZENSHIP?

The *Ruiz Zambrano* judgment received much attention. Despite limited practical relevance in the light of later judgments, this is justified by the conceptual implications. Why? By embracing purely internal situations, the Court abandons the functional underpinning of free movement case law. Certainly, judgments such as *Carpenter* and *Metock* had transcended the functional logic of transnational integration before, since they were, in essence, about the protection of family life as a means to its own end. But these judgments were dogmatically constructed as unjustified restrictions to free movement rights.[95] They may have paved the way for a general reorientation of ECJ case law, which would overcome the tradition of the 'market citizen'. That is why the *Ruiz Zambrano* judgment with its 'substance of rights' doctrine is so important: it establishes novel dogmatic standards beyond the transnational market paradigm.

Instead of focusing on the promotion of transnational liberty, the Court protects human well-being as a means in itself. The new 'substance of rights' test emanates directly from the 'status' of Union citizenship and serves no ulterior purposes – or, generally speaking, it promotes the judicial vision of social justice.[96] The Court, for the first time, presents us with a judgment which embraces (at least implicitly) Union citizenship as a truly 'fundamental status'[97] within the traditional meaning of state theory, which conceives of citizenship 'status' as a permanent feature describing a person's character as an autonomous moral entity in its own right,[98] and not as a transitory disposition which is activated by crossing borders.[99] The Court no longer limits itself to the promotion of transnational movement, but declares its vision of social justice. Arguably, such visions about good society are what citizenship is about. While in judgments such as *Carpenter* and *Metock* the market continued to be the frame for such questions, the 'substance of rights' doctrine establishes citizenship status as an independent frame in its own right.

[95] See E Spaventa, 'From *Gebhard* to *Carpenter*: Towards a (Non-)Economic European Constitution' (2004) 41 *CML Rev* 743; A Epiney, 'Von *Akrich* bis *Metock*' (2008) *Europarecht* 840, 847–53; and A Tryfonidou, 'Family Reunification Rights of (Migrant) Union Citizens' (2009) 15 *ELJ* 634.

[96] It should be noted that a minor element of functionalism survives, since third-country national parents of the *Ruiz Zambrano* family are 'only' protected as caretakers, not as citizens (human rights have to assume that function for third-country nationals); *cf* also *Dereci* (n 56) para 55: 'derived rights'.

[97] *Grzelczyk* (n 32) para 31; it should be noted that the *Ruiz Zambrano* judgment maintains an inherent ambiguity between the protection of 'status' as an end in itself and deference to the 'effective enjoyment' of rights guaranteed elsewhere; see also P Van Elsuwege, 'European Union Citizenship and the Purely Internal Rule Revisited' (2011) 7 *European Constitutional Law Review* 308, 314.

[98] For a reappraisal of the classic perspective of Georg Jellinek, see W Brugger, 'Georg Jellineks Statuslehre' (2011) 136 *Archiv des öffentlichen Rechts* 1; one may in so far draw a line between citizen 'status' and (neo)Kantian conceptions of moral personhood.

[99] See Nettesheim (n 72) 1032.

Not surprisingly, the Court received much acclaim for bringing Union citizenship closer towards 'real' citizenship.[100] But what is 'real' citizenship? And is it correct that the need for citizenship beyond the market is 'crystal clear', even a 'natural and fitting conclusion'?[101]I doubt it. It is far from obvious what citizenship means. Citizenship has always been a projection sphere for different visions of social justice – even at the height of the nation-state. Back then, socialists propagated different visions of citizenship than liberals or conservatives did. In today's globalised world, transnational and supranational developments have further complicated the picture.[102] Also, the invocation of 'real' citizenship in English or French language contributions may partly result from linguistic intuition, since the term 'citizenship/citoyenneté' is fraught with meaning. In German, by contrast, *Bürger* is a much more profane word, which may mean both citoyen and bourgeois. It is usually qualified with a prefix, such as *Marktbürger* (market citizen), *Staatsbürger* (state citizen), *Weltbürger* (cosmopolitan citizenship) – or *Unionsbürger* (union citizen). With such linguistic background, there is no 'real' citizenship, since every usage requires qualification.

That is not to say that there are no overarching themes which we may rely upon to evaluate ECJ case law. The notion of citizenship certainly has a bias towards equality, political participation and the protection of civil liberties.[103] Beyond such normative minimum expectations, however, certainty comes to an end. Intellectually, it is perfectly legitimate to defend 'market citizenship' or criticise an (overtly) rights-centred approach which diminishes republican participation.[104] Also, we may of course argue in favour of including third-country nationals (ie, non-citizens), but this is certainly no foregone conclusion. Academics should play with open cards and discuss their citizenship concepts before chastising or supporting the ECJ for its approach. Invocation of 'real' citizenship does not suffice.

This appeal to openness, however, does not extend to the ECJ. It is certainly not the function of the Court to actively engage in debates about different visions of citizenship. We also cannot expect the Grand Chamber of 15 judges to have a uniform citizenship concept, let alone describe it in their judgments. However, the uncertainty about the 'real' meaning of citizenship has repercussions for Luxembourg. It helps us to identify three final limitations of the Court's citizenship case law.

[100] Such interpretation was given in early comments by Nettesheim (n 72) and Kochenov, 'A Real European Citizenship' (n 65) in particular.

[101] Terminology used by Kochenov, 'A Real European Citizenship' (n 65) 94, who continues that people criticising the new approach use arguments 'routed in a passionate adherence to a familiar tradition rather than in reasoned analysis' (p 93).

[102] See, among many, R Bellamy, *Citizenship. A Very Short Introduction* (Oxford, Oxford University Press, 2008); S Kadelbach, 'Union Citizenship' in A von Bogdandy and J Bast (eds), *Principles of European Constitutional Law*, 2nd edn (Oxford, Hart Publishing, 2009) 435, 461–66 and Kostakopoulou (n 42) chs 1–3.

[103] For a careful assessment, see Nettesheim (n 72) 1036 f.

[104] For an overview of pertinent themes, see S Besson and A Utzinger, 'Future Challenges of European Citizenship' (2007) 13 *ELJ* 573.

First, the judicial invocation of 'citizenship' as the 'fundamental status' hints at an underlying philosophical concept on the side of the Court, which quite simply might not exist. Other commentators have elaborated upon the Court's limited vision of social justice.[105] This does not prevent the gradual emergence of a meaningful institutional vision about the substance of Union citizenship, but there possibly may be little material behind judicial invocations of citizenship. In its citizenship cases, it may pretend to have a more theoretical superstructure than it actually has.

Second, the Court (and academic observers) should not fall into the trap of confusing the label with legal substance. There are plenty of examples in EU law of noticeable gaps between Treaty language and substance. Often the wording is more ambitious than the contents, and occasionally the hard legal rules outdo the denomination. After all, we have 'regulations' (not laws) which prevail over national Acts of Parliament instead of having an administrative character; conversely, the 'common defence policy' hardly deserves its name, since it requires unanimity. Maybe citizenship is a similar misnomer, bound to remain a normative shell.[106]

Third, even if the Treaty concept of Union citizenship can be filled with meaningful legal substance, that would not necessarily entail the creation of real-life citizenship based on shared feelings of a mutual belonging among the 'citizens' of Europe. Most social scientists agree that the legal construction of Union citizenship does not mirror the social construction of togetherness.[107] Even if the Court moves towards 'real' citizenship judgments, it may thus establish a virtual, legal reality.

IV. CONCLUSION

The ECJ's citizenship case law features among the most prominent judicial developments in Luxembourg during the past 15 years. This is hardly surprising, given that citizenship has always been a projection sphere for different visions of social justice. Moreover, the case law had significant constitutional repercussions for the vertical and horizontal balance of power in Europe, which lie behind much of the political and academic criticism with which the Court was confronted. Revisiting the classic dispute about access to social benefits demonstrates these structural impediments of the judicial construction of Union citizenship. When it comes to the legislator, the judges are quite dominant: Although they yielded to the legislator in *Förster*, the Court holds much

[105] See A Williams, *The Ethos of Europe* (Cambridge, Cambridge University Press, 2011) and D Kochenov, 'Citizenship without Respect' (n 45).

[106] *cf* the original critique by J Weiler, 'European Citizenship and Human Rights' in J Winter et al (eds), *Reforming the Treaty on European Union* (The Hague, TMC Asser, 1996) 57–86.

[107] See the (critical) assessment by G Delanty, 'European Citizenship: A Critical Assessment' (2007) 11 *Citizenship Studies* 63 and J Přibáň, 'The Juridification of Identity, its Limitations and the Search of EU Democratic Politics' (2009) 16 *Constellations* 44.

interpretative leeway in regular circumstances, watering down the impact of legislative amendments. By contrast, the impact on the federal balance of power continues to bind the hands of the Court. Luxembourg is careful not to prescribe a specific social or economic model via its citizenship case law. We should therefore not overstate the conceptual relevance of the social benefits dispute, since the Court respects national policy choices and stops short of promoting pan-European social standards.

When considering the controversial citizenship cases of the past decade, a common thread besides social benefits stands out – the legal status of third-country national family members, which arguably constitutes Union citizenship's new frontier. Although various judgments have discussed the theme during the past decade, the controversial *Ruiz Zambrano* ruling accentuated the underlying constitutional and conceptual challenges. When adjudicating the legal status of third-country national family members, the Court leaves the functional logic of transnational market integration behind, positioning itself instead on questions of social justice. The dogmatic innovation of the *Ruiz Zambrano* judgments illustrates the novelty of the judicial approach: by establishing Union citizenship as a free-standing guarantee in its own right, it embraces purely internal situations. Its novel 'substance of rights' test leaves transnational (market) integration behind and moves Union citizenship into a new era, which raises formidable challenges.

The delineation of citizenship's new frontier is far from certain. As in earlier disputes about social benefits, structural difficulties constrain the judicial expansion of Union citizenship. First, Member States and their constitutional courts resist the judicial expansion of citizenship into areas which have hitherto been left to national discretion in line with Article 51 of the Charter of Fundamental Rights. Second, the Union legislator may lose influence if the Court extends, to third-country nationals, citizenship rights with constitutional status for which the EU Treaty establishes a distinct legal framework within the Area of Freedom, Security and Justice that provides for some legislative discretion. Third, the telos and *finalité* of Union citizenship is far from certain. There is fundamental disagreement on how to construe 'true' citizenship, in particular with regard to the (indirect) inclusion of third-country nationals. Such conceptual ambiguities reinforce constitutional impediments that originate in the vertical and horizontal balance of power. When adjudicating Union citizenship's new frontier, the Court cannot evade tough judicial choices.

7

Placing the European Union in International Context: Legitimacy of the Case Law

EILEEN DENZA

I. THE MANDATE OF THE COURT OF JUSTICE

SUCCESSIVE TREATIES HAVE given the Court of Justice no mandate which clearly identifies the legal order for which it is ultimately responsible or its relationship with other courts and tribunals. The Court is required to 'ensure that in the interpretation and application of the Treaties the law is observed'. The 'law' is not limited to the legal system established by or deriving from the Treaties, but may also include national laws and public and private international law. So, the Court had a relatively free hand in defining the nature of the legal order established by the Communities and later by the Union. Unsurprisingly, it began by describing more precisely – or perhaps enlarging – the nature of the legal order established by the Treaties, then it began to define more precisely its relationship with national legal systems and courts and only after some considerable time did it turn to the relationship between European and international law and to its own relations with other international courts and tribunals.

Because of the compact style following from collegiate decisions and the evolutionary nature of the Court's pronouncements, commentators have often attributed great significance to small shifts in terminology. In *Van Gend en Loos*[1] in 1963, the Court described the Treaties as creating 'a new legal order of international law'. In *Costa v Enel* [2]a year later, the language used was more innovative: ' By contrast with ordinary international treaties, the EEC Treaty has created its own legal system which, on the entry into force of the Treaty, became an integral part of the legal systems of the Member States and which

[1] Case 26/62 NV *Algemene Transport-en Expeditie Onderneming Van Gend en Loos v Nederlandse Administratie der Belastigen* [1963] ECR 1.
[2] Case 6/64 *Costa v Enel* [1964] ECR 585.

their courts are bound to apply. In the First EEA Opinion[3] in 1991, the Court held that

> the EEC Treaty, albeit concluded in the form of an international agreement, none the less constitutes the constitutional charter of a Community based on the rule of law. As the ECJ has consistently held, the Community treaties established a new legal order for the benefit of which the States have limited their sovereign rights.

To some commentators, these shifts in language suggested that the Court had come to the view that the Community legal order had been established or mutated into a *sui generis* system, outside the constraints of public international law, or into some form of hybrid system midway between international and national legal orders. A majority of scholars in public international law appeared to accept that European law had drifted outside their own remit.[4] There were few cases which required the Court to pronounce in general terms on the relationship of European law and international law, and the Court – whether as a matter of deliberate policy or in order to conceal internal uncertainty – preserved reticence in the face of academic scrutiny and debate. Thym argues that 'the Court's case law demonstrates the desire to sustain the autonomy of the European legal order through its posture towards international law; analogies and differences between the effects of European law in the national legal systems and international law in the Community legal order are guided by the objective to preserve the latter's autonomy'.[5] Craig and de Burca stress that the Court's approach was teleological rather than textual and 'amounted to a bold step to support its own conception of the Community legal order'.[6]

National courts, and national governments and their legal advisers, however, had to keep their feet more firmly on the ground. There was no sign that they believed that European law had departed from its original character as a treaty-based international legal order, albeit one which displayed a number of intrusive and effective features which when taken cumulatively made it unique. In *Brunner*

[3] Opinion 1/91(First EEA Opinion) [1991] ECR 6079, para. 211.

[4] On the rift, and the recent rapprochement, see U Khaliq, 'Treaty Conflict and the European Union, or Conflicting Perspectives on the European Union' (2012) 37 *ELRev* 493.

[5] D Thym, 'Foreign Affairs' in A Von Bogdandy and J Bast (eds), *Principles of European Constitutional Law* (Oxford, Hart Publishing, 2009) 320–21.

[6] P Craig and G de Búrca (eds), *EU Law: Text, Cases and Materials* (Oxford, Oxford University Press, 2003) 279. See also, C Timmermans, 'The EU and Public International Law' (1999) 4 *European Foreign Affairs Review* 181: 'However, almost from the days the Communities started to operate, there has been a tendency amongst lawyers, dealing more specifically with Community law when analysing the institutional characteristics of the Communities, to detach the Communities from their international law sources'. For other specific ways in which the Court detached the Community legal order from general rules of international law, see F Hoffmeister, 'The Contribution of EU Practice to International Law' in M Cremona (ed), *Developments in EU External Relations Law* (Oxford, Oxford University Press, 2008) 37. For a general analysis of the differences between Community law and public international law, see E Denza, 'Two Legal Orders: Distinguishing Features of the Intergovernmental Pillars' in *The Intergovernmental Pillars of the European Union* (Oxford, Oxford University Press, 2002).

v European Union Treaty,[7] for example, the German Federal Constitutional Court emphasised that Germany was not only one of the 'Masters of the Treaties' but

> could also ultimately revoke that adherence by a contrary act. The validity and application of European law in Germany depend on the application-of-law instruction of the Accession Act. Germany thus preserves the quality of a sovereign State in its own right and the status of sovereign equality with other States within the meaning of Article 2(1) of the United Nations Charter of 26 June 1945.

It is also true that some at least of the special features of the European legal order have been retrospectively legitimised by later treaties among the expanding number of Member States – for example, primacy in the uniform terms laid down and elaborated by the Court of Justice was formally endorsed in Declaration 17 concerning Primacy attached to the Treaty of Lisbon.[8]

II. RECEPTION OF INTERNATIONAL LAW

Distinct from the question of whether the Treaties and the instruments adopted under Treaty powers themselves constituted regional international law was the manner in which international obligations created under treaty or under customary international law were accepted and given effect within the European legal order. On the question of treaties, the European Community was given an express mandate. The Community was endowed with international legal personality, procedures were laid down under which it might conclude international agreements with non-Member States and with international organisations and provision was made that 'Agreements concluded under these conditions shall be binding on the institutions of the Community and on Member States'.[9] But the European Community soon found that – like national legal orders – a general instruction of this kind did not resolve all of the practical questions which arose. The European Court soon had to determine, for example, the conditions under which an international agreement that was binding on all the Member States but not formally on the Community as such should be accepted

[7] *Brunner v European Union Treaty* (1994) 1 CMLR 57. The Federal Constitutional Court confirmed its approach in para 240 of its Judgment of 30 June 2009 on the Treaty of Lisbon: 2 BvE 2/08. For similarly realistic analysis, see A Orakhashvili, 'The Idea of European International Law' (2009) 17 *European Journal of International Law* 315, 343–47, especially at 346 'any understanding of "European law" as a free-standing legal system is a fiction; international law always plays an important role in the operation and development of this law'; H de Waele, 'The Role of the European Court of Justice in the Integration Process: A Contemporary and Normative Assessment'(2010) 6 *Hanse Law Review* 3, 8.

[8] On this, see Y Shany, 'Assessing the Effectiveness of International Courts: A Goal-Based Approach' (2012) 106 *AJIL* 225, 235.

[9] Treaty establishing the European Economic Community, Rome 1957, Art 228. The Court confirmed that agreements concluded by the EEC formed part of the Community legal order in Case 181/73 *Haegeman v Belgium* [1974] ECR 449, paras 3–6. See C Kaddous, 'Effects of International Agreements in the EU Legal Order' in M Cremona and B de Witte (eds), *EU Foreign Relations Law* (Oxford, Hart Publishing, 2008).

as binding on the Community, the conditions under which an agreement binding on the Community could be directly enforced by individuals or enterprises in national courts, and whether – in the event of conflict with treaty provisions, subordinate instruments or fundamental constitutional principles of the European legal order – the international obligation should ultimately prevail.

The second and third of these questions have been confronted by most national courts. International law does not prescribe the manner of its reception into national or into other international legal systems – expecting only the required legal result – and examination of cases turning on the relationship show that difficult questions are usually not conclusively answered either by constitutional rules or by legal theories. Each national court begins with its own constitutional mandate and then applies or safeguards international obligations to the greatest extent consistent with that mandate. The national mandate may be highly deferential towards international law – for example, in the Netherlands – but in a case of direct conflict, it is the mandate of the national court which prevails.[10] Analysis of the judgments of the Court of Justice shows that it has followed this same approach throughout with respect to reception of treaty obligations into European law. The Court will attempt to interpret international treaty obligations under applicable international legal rules and will give binding treaty obligations maximum and uniform effect within the European legal order. But where it has found a clear conflict between the international rule and fundamental principles of European law, it has upheld its own mandate.

III. TREATY OBLIGATIONS AND CONFLICT WITH COMMUNITY LEGISLATION

The Court of Justice developed its constitutional approach to conflict between treaty obligations and European Community legislation in the *International Fruit* case[11] in 1972 and has applied, generalised and circumscribed its approach in two recent cases, *Intertanko* and *Air Transport Association of America*. The *International Fruit* case set out a three-stage test compliance with which would enable the Court, on the application of an individual or enterprise before a national court, to strike down secondary legislation for incompatibility with an international treaty obligation – first, the Community must itself be bound by the international rule; second, it must be the case that the nature and broad logic of the international treaty do not preclude this; and third, the international treaty rules must themselves be unconditional and sufficiently precise.

[10] For general accounts of the position, see A Cassese, *International Law* (Oxford, Oxford University Press, 2001) ch 8; E Denza, 'The Relationship between International and National Law' in M Evans (ed), *International Law* (Oxford, Oxford University Press, 2010) ch 14.

[11] Joined Cases 21/72 to 24/72 *International Fruit Company NV and Others v Produktschap voor Groenten en Fruit* [1972] ECR 1219.

The Court held that the EC was itself bound by the obligations under the GATT of 1947 – originally assumed by all its Member States – by virtue of the transfer of all national functions relating to tariffs and trade to the EC within the framework of the common commercial policy at the end of the transitional period. By virtue of succession or substitution, therefore – as was broadly accepted by other treaty partners in the practice of the GATT – the EC was itself bound by the GATT.

A Intertanko

In the *Intertanko* case,[12] the Court of Justice was asked to determine the compatibility of a 2005 Council Directive on Ship Source Pollution with the international rules contained in the International Convention for the Prevention of Pollution from Ships (MARPOL) and the UN Convention on the Law of the Sea (UNLOSC). Shipping interests, led by the International Association of Tanker Owners (Intertanko), argued that the Directive imposed stricter liability than the international regime under MARPOL and so risked violating obligations to permit free passage through international straits, exclusive economic zones and on the high seas, which were guaranteed under UNLOSC. The Directive extended criminal liability for oil pollution to cover 'serious negligence', which could be found where discharges were accidental rather than deliberate, and also provided that penalties could be applied to wider categories of persons contributing to pollution from ships. While the EC, along with its Member States, was a Party to UNLOSC, it was not a Party to MARPOL. The Court held, in regard to MARPOL, that it did not follow from the fact that all Member States were Parties to MARPOL that the EC was itself bound. This was because, MARPOL, unlike GATT, did not cover an area in which the Community had exclusive competence and had progressively assumed the powers of the Member States in such a way as to take on their related international treaty obligations.[13] Although the Community was itself directly bound by rules of customary international law, the rules on pollution of the seas by oil and other harmful substances laid down in MARPOL did not have the character of customary international law. MARPOL therefore failed the first of the three hurdles described above, and could not be relied on to strike down the Council Directive under challenge.

The Court of Justice has, for the most part, developed the second and third elements of the three-stage test described above in the context of GATT and World Trade law and has sometimes been criticised for being less than wholly

[12] Case 308/06 R *(on the application of international Association of Tanker Owners (Intertanko)) v Secretary of State for Transport* [2008] ECR I-4057. See E Denza, 'A Note on Intertanko' (2008) 33 *ELRev* 870; 15 *Columbia Journal of Transnational Law* 143.

[13] Paras 30–35.

receptive to international trade law in its own legal order.[14] It has repeatedly characterised the nature of world trading rules as being both flexible and reciprocal in nature and therefore inappropriate for enforcement by individuals or enterprises within the national or European legal order. Although the application of international treaty rules within the European legal order is a constitutional matter,[15] the Court has always applied it through analysis of the character of the international agreement being invoked, as well as the specific terms relied on by the plaintiff. The Court confirmed its approach, even in the case of *FIAMM*, where the complaint was brought by enterprises affected by countermeasures against the EU and was based on failure by the EU institutions to comply, before expiry of the deadline, with a finding of illegality made by the World Trade Organisation Dispute Settlement Board. The Court in that case held that '[a] DSB decision which has no object other than to rule on whether a WTO member's conduct is consistent with [WTO obligations] cannot in principle be fundamentally distinguished from the substantive rules which convey such obligations', and re-emphasised the need to preserve the balance which was characteristic of the WTO agreements.[16]

In *Intertanko*, the Court took this same approach to the UN Convention on the Law of the Sea. It concluded that UNLOSC (with one possible exception not relevant to the case) created rights and obligations among the States Parties and did not create rights or freedoms regarding navigation or pollution which were capable of being invoked by individuals in national courts irrespective of the position of the flag State. Rights given under UNLOSC to 'ships' are, in reality, enforceable by the flag State whose nationality the ship possesses and not by the owner or master of the vessel or by associations of ship owners. It followed that the nature and broad logic of UNLOSC did not permit the Court to assess the validity of a Community measure in the light of its terms. Although there was a powerful case that the Directive could not be reconciled with the commitments of the Member States under MARPOL, or with commitments under UNLOSC binding the Community to permit innocent passage to vessels of other States Parties, the Court of Justice held that it was unable to address the conflict. The Council had long been aware of the challenge to the compatibility of the Directive with

[14] See eg G Gaja, 'Trends in Judicial Activism and Judicial Self-Restraint relating to Community Agreements' in E Cannizzaro (ed), *The European Union as an Actor in International Relations* (The Hague, Kluwer Law International, 2002) who describes the requirement as 'an instrument of judicial self-restraint that is designed to leave greater discretion to political institutions when implementing an agreement' (p 129) and complains that the approach 'does not contribute to enhancing the rule of law in international society' (p 134).

[15] On this see I Cheyne, 'International Instruments as a Source of Community Law' in A Dashwood and C Hillion (eds), *The General Law of EC External Relations* (London, Sweet & Maxwell, 2000) 258: 'The legal consequences of international legal rules and obligations depend entirely on domestic constitutional law'.

[16] Joined Cases C-120/06 P and C-121/06 P *Fabbrica Italiana Accumulatori Motocarri Montecchio SpA (FIAMM) and Others v Council and Commission* [2008] ECR I-6513, paras 116–34. See comment by M Bronckers, 'From Direct Effect to Muted Dialogue: Recent Developments in the European Court's Case Law on the WTO and Beyond' (2008) 11 *Journal of International Economic Law* 885, 886, 891–94.

international treaty rules, and provided that the international rules were correctly understood, it can hardly be argued that the Court had the proper responsibility for correcting the position. National courts too often deliver judgments which place their governments in breach of international obligations.

B Air Transport Association of America

The Court applied the same principles regarding the effects of international agreements within the European legal order in the case of *Air Transport Association of America, American Airlines Inc, Continental Airlines Inc, United Airlines Inc v Secretary of State for Transport*.[17] In this case, a challenge was mounted by a number of US or Canadian airlines regarding the lawfulness of a Council Directive which brought international aviation within the scope of the carbon trading system intended to reduce greenhouse gas emissions as envisaged by the Kyoto Protocol to the UN Framework Convention on Climate Change. The scheme established by the Directive would apply to any international flights which landed in or took off from the territory of the Member States of the EU and not merely to those segments of such flights which took place over the territory or territorial waters of the Member States. The Directive, it was claimed, by reason of this extensive jurisdiction, violated provisions in three international agreements – the Chicago Convention, the Open Skies Agreement and the Kyoto Protocol itself – as well as rules of customary international law (discussed below).

In the context of international aviation agreements, the Court followed the same approach as in the context of international shipping in *Intertanko*. The Chicago Convention on International Civil Aviation had been ratified by all Member States, but the European Union was not itself a party. The doctrine of functional succession could not apply so as to bind the Union, since all the powers of the Member States in the areas covered by the Convention had not been transferred to the Union; consequently, the Convention failed at the first hurdle of the three-stage test. As to the second and third hurdles, Advocate General Kokott emphasised that although the application of international agreements within the European legal order was a question of EU law, it was up to the Parties to the Open Skies Agreement and the Kyoto Protocol to determine whether they gave persons subject to the Union's legal order the right to rely on them in order to contest the validity of an internal act. EU law – like most domestic legal systems – gave protection to individuals only in so far as was necessary to safeguard their rights guaranteed under international agreements. The Court, following this analysis, concluded that the Kyoto Protocol (to which

[17] Case C-366/10 *Air Transport Association of America, American Airlines Inc, Continental Airlines Inc, United Airlines Inc v Secretary of State for Transport* (2012) 2 CMLR 4. See E Denza 'International Aviation and the EU Carbon Trading Scheme: Comment on *Air Transport Association of America*' (2012) 37 *ELRev* 314; B Mayer, '*Air Transport Association of America and Others v Secretary of State for Energy and Climate Change*' (2012) 49 *CML Rev* 1113 (note).

the Union is a Party) was characterised by great flexibility in the timing and manner of implementing the commitments of States Parties to reduce emissions of greenhouse gases, and that the obligations set out in the Protocol were not sufficiently unconditional or precise. Thus, the Kyoto Protocol failed both the second and the third of the tests and could not be relied on to challenge the validity of the Council Directive. Only the Open Skies Agreement (to which the Union is also a Party) gave direct rights to individuals and undertakings holding the nationality of a Party (in contrast to UNLOSC discussed above). In the event however, both the Advocate General and the Court – by somewhat different analyses of a complex carbon trading scheme by reference to the treaty provisions capable of being directly invoked – held that the Directive did not violate the Open Skies Agreement.

One argument not directly addressed by the Court – but relevant in terms of relations between legal orders as well as politically – was whether the Union was entitled to enact a unilateral measure, given that the Kyoto Protocol envisaged that multilateral agreement to bring international aviation within the constraints of the carbon trading scheme should be negotiated within the framework of the International Civil Aviation Organisation (ICAO). The EU had actively sought agreement within ICAO over a number of years, without success, and expressly acknowledged that if such agreement were reached, its own scheme would require modification. The Advocate General took the view that the Kyoto Protocol did not and could not confer exclusive competence on ICAO – particularly since the contrary view would open up the possibility that ICAO members not party to Kyoto could obstruct realisation of its objectives. Unilateral EU action had not been premature and the Union continued to seek agreement within the ICAO framework. It is difficult to imagine that this argument – advanced mainly by airlines based in a state which has categorically rejected the Kyoto Protocol – could have succeeded as a matter of construction of the Kyoto Protocol and its effects in international law.

IV. RECEPTION OF CUSTOMARY INTERNATIONAL LAW

While the *Air Transport Association of America* case did not break new ground in the context of reception of treaty obligations into the European legal order, but merely applied established principles in the field of international civil aviation, it did break new ground regarding reception of customary international law. Like all developed national legal orders, European law had always accepted that it was bound by customary international law without the need for any express mandate to that effect and had applied customary rules as a tool of interpretation of Community instruments in a number of cases. In the *Poulsen* case, for example, the Court stated that 'the European Community must respect international law in the exercise of its powers' so that a Community Regulation 'must be interpreted, and its scope limited, in the light of the relevant rules of the international law of the sea'.[18] In the *Racke* case, the Court accepted that 'the rules of customary international law concerning the termination and the suspension of treaty relations by reason of a fundamental change of circumstances are binding upon the Community institutions and form part of the Community legal order'. In the latter case, the plaintiff claimed that the suspension by the Community of its Cooperation Agreement with Yugoslavia (whose relevant provisions had direct effect) was invalid because of non-compliance with the requirements of customary international law on termination or suspension in consequence of fundamental change of circumstances. The Court held, however, that in carrying out a judicial review it was limited 'because of the complexity of the rules in question and the imprecision of some of the concepts to which they refer' to assessing whether the Council had made manifest errors of assessment in applying the rules.[19] It found, therefore, that the suspension by the Community of its Agreement with Yugoslavia was not unlawful.

In the *Air Transport Association of America* case, the Court set out for the first time general guidance to determine the circumstances in which customary international law may be relied on to challenge the validity of a Union measure. At the level of national courts, plaintiffs have often challenged the lawfulness of national measures – in particular criminal prosecutions – by reference to customary international law, but national courts have generally found a way of denying the international rule overriding effect, either because it is not accepted as giving individuals direct rights or is not capable of being applied at the national level without transposition. The Court began by determining whether a rule of customary international law had been established, using for this purpose the methods accepted and applied in international law and assuming – in line with the cases cited in the previous paragraph – that if established, the customary rule bound the Union. But for an individual to be able to invoke a binding customary rule so as to invalidate a Union measure, he must further show first that the rule is capable of calling into question the competence of the Union to adopt the measure, and second that the measure challenged might affect individual rights or create obligations under Union law. In addition, judicial review – following the *Racke* case – must be limited to determining whether the EU institutions made 'manifest errors of assessment' in applying the relevant principles.[20]

The Court proceeded on the basis of these criteria to assess whether the customary rules invoked by the plaintiff airlines were capable of meeting these tests, and if so, to evaluate the compatibility of the Council Directive against them. As listed in the questions referred by the UK court, these were:

(a) the principle of customary international law that each State has complete and exclusive sovereignty over its air space;

[18] Case C-286-90 *Anklagemyndigheden v Poulsen and Diva Navigation* [1992] ECR I-6019, para 9.

[19] Case C-162/96 *Racke v Hauptzollamt Mainz* [1998] ECR I-3655. See the analysis of these cases in P Koutrakos, *EU International Relations Law* (Oxford, Hart Publishing, 2006) 244–49.

[20] *Air Transport Association of America* (n 18 above) paras 101–10.

(b) the principle of customary international law that no State may validly purport to subject any part of the high seas to its sovereignty;
(c) the principle of customary international law of freedom to fly over the high seas;
(d) the principle of customary international law that aircraft overflying the high seas are subject to the exclusive jurisdiction of the country in which they are registered, save as expressly provided for by international treaty.

The first three of these were agreed by the Parties and accepted by the Court as constituting rules of customary international law. The Court found further that these rules were capable of being relied on in order to determine whether the Council had competence to adopt the disputed Directive whose application extended to airlines carrying out flights in part over the high seas and over the territory of non-Member States. On the substance, however, the Court held that the scheme established under the Council Directive did not contravene any of the three rules. The fourth principle advanced was controversial – since the essence of the plaintiff airlines case was an objection to being assessed under the scheme on the basis of their emissions throughout an international flight and not merely on the basis of the part of the flight taking place over Union territory. The Court did not accept that this fourth principle had been established as a rule of customary international law and it therefore made no assessment as to compliance by the Directive.

These rules for assessing the validity of Union instruments by reference to customary international law are innovative. National courts have not put forward general methods of assessment, but have usually limited themselves to determining specific claims of conflict – so the Court of Justice was breaking new ground internationally as well as in constitutional terms. The criteria are consistent with the Court's approach to alleged conflict with international treaty obligations, and they strike a convincing balance between deference to international customary law and the nature of the Union's own legal order. Of course, they leave the Court of Justice with the responsibility of determining the existence of an international customary rule and also whether the rule has, on the facts, been violated by Union action. The judges appointed to the Court are not, as a general rule, primarily experts in public international law, and the same is true of counsel appearing before them, so their findings may, in some cases, be open to reconsideration by other international courts or tribunals. The Court's conclusions in regard to the existence and application of the complex international rules on jurisdiction in the *Air Transport Association of America* may be faulted as excessively reliant on European principles and precedents. But, in this, the Court does not differ from national courts which also sometimes determine the existence and application of rules of customary international law, and in so doing, themselves contribute to the formation and development of that law. The Union was given an express mandate by the Treaty of Lisbon to contribute 'to the strict observance and the development of international law',[21] and the cases described above, which articulate more clearly the relationship between international law and European Union law, are consistent with that mandate.

Kadi

The primacy of its own mandate in a case of conflict with international law rules has been most clearly articulated in the judgment of the Grand Chamber of the Court of Justice in the *Kadi* case.[22] The case was brought by an individual challenging EC implementation of a binding UN Security Council sanctions resolution under which he was identified as being involved with terrorism and found his assets in Sweden indefinitely frozen. He had been shown no evidence of his involvement with terrorism and had been given no opportunity either at the UN or at the European level to challenge his inclusion on the list of persons subject to freezing. The Court of First Instance upheld the contested Community regulation on the basis that, as a result of the principles governing the relationship between the international legal order and the Community legal order, judicial review of its lawfulness was in principle excluded, even though such review was a constitutional guarantee forming part of the foundations of the Community.[23] The Court of Justice, however, reversed the Court of First Instance, taking a radically different approach to the extent of the duty imposed by the UN Charter where it conflicted with fundamental rights protected by the Community legal order.

In its analysis, the Court began by stressing that the Community must respect international law in the exercise of its powers and must interpret its own measures in the light of the relevant rules of international law.[24] Special deference was due to the resolutions of the Security Council, given its primary responsibility under the UN Charter for maintenance of peace and security at the global level. However, the Charter did not prescribe a particular model for implementing its resolutions within domestic legal orders, so it did not follow, from the principles of the UN legal order and its primacy at the international law level, that review of an implementing measure was precluded. Under the Community legal order, assuming that the UN Charter applied as a binding international agreement, it would take priority over acts of secondary Community law, but not over primary law or, in particular, the general principles of which fundamental rights formed part.[25]

[21] Treaty on European Union, Art 3(5).

[22] Joined Cases C-402/05 P and C-415/05 P *Kadi and Al Barakaat International Foundation v Council and Commission* [2008] ECR I-6351.

[23] Case T-306/01 *Yusuf v Council and Commission* [2005] ECR II-3353 and Case T-315/01 *Kadi v Council and Commission* [2005] ECR II-3649.

[24] Citing *Poulsen and Diva Navigation* (n 18 above) para 9, and *Racke* (n 19 above) para 45.

[25] Paras 291–309.

The Court considered the argument that deference to the UN institutions implied that it should forgo the exercise of its own review powers, given that, under the UN system as recently improved, fundamental rights were adequately protected. Nevertheless, it noted that the improvements had taken place after adoption of the contested regulation and still did not offer guarantees of judicial protection or opportunity for individuals to assert their rights. There was still no requirement for the Sanctions Committee to communicate to an applicant the evidence on which his inclusion in their list was based, and no right for him to assert his rights before the Committee or be given reasons for rejection of his appeal. The Court's conclusion was therefore

> that the Community judicature must, in accordance with the powers conferred on it by the EC Treaty, ensure the review, in principle the full review, of the lawfulness of all Community acts in the light of fundamental rights forming an integral part of the general principles of Community law, including review of Community measures which, like the contested regulation, are designed to give effect to the resolutions adopted by the Security Council under Chapter VII of the Charter of the United Nations.[26]

The *Kadi* judgment – unlike some of the innovative judgments described above – cannot be faulted for failing to clarify its reasoning in the most rigorous and transparent manner. It places the European legal order in what might be described as an intermediate or mezzanine level between the international legal order and national legal orders. The Court stressed that it had no competence to review the Security Council resolution itself, or to challenge its primacy in international law, even though it was fully aware that the effect of its ruling would, at least in the short term, place Member States in breach of their obligations under the UN Charter to comply with its terms. In this, it was more restrained than the Court of First Instance, which had asserted the right to review the UN resolution by reference to the principles of *ius cogens*. Its definition of the protection of fundamental rights as central to the Community legal order is carefully constructed with reference to earlier case law, and it concludes that this is central to its mandate under the European legal order. The Court in no way suggests that it is independent of the international legal order, but rather characterises itself in this context as a domestic court which gives effect to international legal obligations to the greatest extent possible consistent with its own mandate. On the facts of the *Kadi* case, it found a clear conflict between the international obligation and its own mandate, and it gave priority to that mandate while refusing to assert any jurisdiction to review the Security Council resolution as an international legal instrument. It may be said to be legitimate, in terms of being deferential to other legal orders (human rights as well as the United Nations) while protective of its own mandate.

In terms of its reception, the *Kadi* judgment had mixed success. In general, it was welcomed more enthusiastically by European lawyers than by international

[26] Paras 318–26.

lawyers. De Burca, analysing the contrasting approaches to the implementation of UN sanctions taken by the European Court of Human Rights, the European Court of First Instance and the Court of Justice, argues that the Court of Justice adopted a 'strongly pluralist approach, treating the UN system and the EU system as separate and parallel regimes, without any privileged status being accorded to UN Charter obligations or UN Security Council measures within EC law' and that this approach threatened the image of the EU as an actor committed to 'effective multilateralism'. [27] This criticism seems unfair if the judgment is taken, as suggested above, as an example of the tensions in the relationship between international law and national or domestic legal orders. Nor, in practice, could it be regarded as diminishing the UN system to review the effects of implementing its specific measures, since the immediate effect of the series judgments has been for improvements to be made in terms of accountability both by the Security Council and by the Council of the EU.[28] Since the *Kadi* case, a series of challenges through varied legal techniques have been issued by national courts regarding the lawfulness of the Security Council sanctions regime, and in the longer term, such systematic challenges have tended, at least to some extent, to strengthen its transparency and its legitimacy rather than to undermine it.[29]

V. RELATIONS WITH OTHER INTERNATIONAL COURTS

The longest and most intense relationship of the Court of Justice is with the European Court of Human Rights. Although, as shown above, the Court of Justice has been ready to incorporate international law into its own legal order only where it was directly binding on the Community or on the Union, it found a way to admit the European Convention on Human Rights and Fundamental Freedoms (ECHR) and the case law of the European Court of Human Rights into its own jurisprudence. The reasoning was set out most clearly and fully in the judgment of the Court of Justice in the *ERT* case, in the context of a preliminary reference on the effect of Article 10 of the ECHR on freedom of expression, in the context of determining the lawfulness of a national system of exclusive television rights. The Court said:

> It must first be pointed out that, as the Court has consistently held, fundamental rights form an integral part of the general principles of law, the observance of which it ensures. For that purpose the Court draws inspiration from the constitutional traditions common to the Member States and from the guidelines supplied by international

[27] G de Búrca, 'The European Court of Justice and the International Legal Order After *Kadi*' (2010) 51 *Harvard International Law Journal* 1, 48–49. For extensive analysis and criticism of *Kadi*, see the contributions by G de Búrca, A Nollkaemper and I Canor in (2009) 20 *EJIL* 853–87.

[28] *Kadi* (n 22 above) para 320.

[29] See A Tzanakopoulos: *Disobeying the Security Council – Countermeasures against Wrongful Sanctions* (Oxford, Oxford University Press, 2011) 100–02, 135–36, 195–96.

> treaties for the protection of human rights on which the Member States have collaborated or of which they are signatories . . . The European Convention on Human Rights has special significance in this respect . . . It follows that the Community cannot accept measures which are incompatible with the human rights thus recognized and guaranteed.[30]

This inclusive approach opened the way not only to using the ECHR to interpret Community instruments but to annulling, for incompatibility with Convention rights, not only Community instruments but national measures taken by Member States acting within the scope of the Treaty. [31] The Court of Justice has had consistent regard for the jurisprudence of the Court of Human Rights, and even in these very few cases where the Court of Human Rights construed the ECHR in a way different from an earlier finding by the Court of Justice, it has been difficult for critics to show that the outcome in these particular cases was markedly different or defective from the standpoint of practical protection of human rights.

In its first Opinion on the draft Agreement establishing a European Economic Area, the Court said expressly that the Community's

> competence in the field of international relations and its capacity to conclude international agreements necessarily entails the power to submit to the decisions of a court which is created or designated by such an agreement as regards the interpretation and application of its provisions.[32]

This statement suggested to some observers that the Court was preparing the way towards endorsing the proposition that the Community, under existing treaty powers, could accede to the ECHR. In the event the Court did not accept that the Community then had power to accede, but its reasons related to the constitutional powers of the Community and not to any unwillingness on its own part to submit to binding decisions of another international court regarding interpretation of an international treaty to which the Community might become a Party.[33]

The Member States clearly accepted the approach of the Court of Justice in regard to the need for amendment of the Treaties in order to integrate the Union into the legal order of the ECHR. Although the reluctance of some Member States meant that this was not done by the Treaty of Amsterdam, express provision for accession was made in Article 7 of the (never ratified) Treaty establishing a Constitution for Europe[34] and ultimately in Article 6(2) of the Treaty on

[30] Case C-260/89 *Elleniki Radiophonia Tileorassi (ERT) v Dimotiki Etairia Pliroforissis* [1991] ECR I-1759, para 41. For a full account of the development of the reasoning of the Court of Justice, see H-J Blanke, 'The Protection of Fundamental Rights in Europe' in H-J Blanke and S Mangiemeli (eds), *The European Union after Lisbon* (Heidelberg, Springer, 2011) 159, 161–63.

[31] See eg *The Queen v Ministry of Agriculture, Fisheries and Food ex parte Bostock* [1994] ECR I-955.

[32] Opinion 1/91 [1991] ECR I-6079, para 40.

[33] Opinion 2/94 [1996] ECR I-1759. See A Arnull, 'Left to its Own Devices? Opinion 2/94 and the Protection of Fundamental Rights in the European Union' in A Dashwood and C Hillion (eds), *The General Law of EC External Relations* (London, Sweet & Maxwell, 2000) ch 5.

[34] Cm 5897.

European Union as amended by the Treaty of Lisbon. Declaration 1 concerning the Charter of Fundamental Rights of the European Union, attached to the Treaty of Lisbon, confirmed the earlier jurisprudence of the Court of Justice in stating that:

> The Charter of Fundamental Rights of the European Union, which has legally binding force, confirms the fundamental rights protected by the European Convention for the Protection of Human Rights and Fundamental Freedoms and as they result from the constitutional traditions common to the Member States.

In Declaration 2 concerning Article 6(2) TEU, the Conference noted 'the existence of a regular dialogue between the Court of Justice of the European Union and the European Court of Human Rights; such dialogue could be reinforced when the Union accedes to that Convention'.

The Treaty of Lisbon may therefore be taken as explicit endorsement by the Member States of the approach taken by the Court of Justice to its relationship with the European Convention and Court of Human Rights, as well as of the political imperative of formally integrating the two legal orders.

VI. PROTECTION OF THE UNION'S OWN LEGAL SYSTEM

While the Court of Justice has shown itself receptive and even deferential to external courts mandated to interpret legal regimes outside the European Union's legal order, it has, by contrast, been fiercely protective of the system established under successive Treaties uniformly to interpret the law of the Union and to ensure that it is observed, and it has been defensive of its own place within that system. It has followed that attempts by the Member States to set up what might be described as hybrid courts in order to interpret agreements to which non-Member States as well as Member States are Parties – even where they have tried not to undermine the position of the Court of Justice – have been unsuccessful and have been abandoned. The Court first set out its protective attitude in Opinion 1/76[35] (most remembered in the different context of exclusive competence of the Community to conclude international agreements). The draft Agreement referred to the Court was to establish a system of financial compensation for the laying up of vessels that were surplus to the requirements for inland water transport in the Rhine–Moselle river basin, and the requirement for an external international agreement derived from the geographical need to include Switzerland as well as a number of EC Member States also involved in the arrangements. A tribunal was to be formed with six judges from the Court of Justice and one from Switzerland, and it would have been open to national courts to refer questions of interpretation of the Agreement or of implementing acts either to this hybrid tribunal or to the Court of Justice. The

[35] Opinion 1/76 *Laying-up Fund for Inland Waterways* [1977] ECR 741.

Court held that this system prejudiced its own standing to interpret agreements binding on the Community and risked undermining the autonomy of the Court should a question of interpretation come first before the tribunal and later before the Court of Justice. The Court concluded that the tribunal could be established only on condition that judges belonging to the Court of Justice were not called upon to serve on it, and that the proposed tribunal was therefore incompatible with the EEC Treaty.

The Court of Justice, on broadly similar grounds, in Opinion 1/91 vetoed the establishment of a Joint Court under the draft Agreement establishing a European Economic Area (EEA).[36] The EEA was originally intended to comprise, in addition to all the Members of the EU, the seven Members of the European Free Trade Association (EFTA): Austria, Finland, Sweden, Switzerland, Norway, Liechtenstein and Iceland. The objective of the EEA was to establish, in regard to the common areas of application (the single market, related rules such as competition and some other policies), maximum homogeneity between the legal orders of the EC and of the EEA. Provisions from the EC Treaty were reproduced exactly in the draft EEA Agreement and a joint court, composed of judges from the Court of Justice and from the EFTA Court, would have had jurisdiction to interpret the Agreement. The Court of Justice, when asked to rule on the draft Agreement, ruled that there were two problems. The EEA Court might find itself called to rule on the division of competence between the Community and its Member States – thereby prejudicing the requirement of the Community Treaties, so that disputes among Member States on the interpretation of the Treaties were assigned to the exclusive jurisdiction of the Court of Justice. The second objection was the same as in Opinion 1/76 described above. The Court of Justice would have jurisdiction to interpret the proposed EEA Agreement, and notwithstanding the identical wording of specific provisions, these provisions might in fact have different meanings, given the difference in the underlying purposes and fundamental nature of the legal order established under the Community Treaties and that envisaged under the draft EEA Agreement. The Court of Justice therefore held that the concept of a joint court conflicted with the very foundations of the Community. It would not be possible, even by amendment of the Treaties, to cure the fundamental incompatibility.

The attempt to establish a joint EEA court was thereafter abandoned and replaced by an EFTA court with more limited jurisdiction. The EFTA Court was composed only of judges from the EFTA States and would have no jurisdiction over disputes between Parties to the EEA Agreement. These could be referred to an EU/EFTA Joint Committee – but the Joint Committee was to be bound by decisions of the Court of Justice and was specifically instructed that its decisions were not to affect the case law of the European Court of Justice. If the dispute related to terms in the EEA Agreement identical to terms in the Community Treaties, and was not settled within three months by the Joint

[36] Opinion 1/91 [1991] ECR I-6079.

Committee, then the Court of Justice might also be asked to rule. In the absence of an agreed solution, Parties were entitled to take safeguard measures, which could be challenged through arbitration. In Opinion 1/92, the Court of Justice – having successfully defended its own position as ultimate arbiter of the Community Treaties – gave approval to the EEA Agreement as thus revised.[37]

The lessons from Opinion 1/91 were carefully taken on board a few years later, when the Community sought to negotiate an Agreement creating a European Common Aviation Area. The Parties would be all the Member States of the EU and candidate states for accession, as well as Norway and Iceland. The Agreement was to be concluded by the Community alone, without the Member States, and the provisions for settlement of disputes were modelled on the revised EEA Agreement. The Court of Justice confirmed that these arrangements did not threaten its own autonomy.[38]

Eeckhout points out that these cases, though constitutionally important, are of limited scope – relating only to proposed arrangements which would extend EU policies to neighbouring countries, with the risk of 'confusion as to the origin, nature and methods of interpretation of duplicated legal provisions'. They are not relevant to the possibility of EU accession to independent international organisations with their own system of dispute settlement. Such independent courts would have no competence to rule on relations between the Union and its Member States, or on provisions of the Union Treaties or legislation. Submission to decisions of such courts would not threaten the exclusive jurisdiction of the Court of Justice over the European legal order.[39]

VII. EUROPEAN AND COMMUNITY PATENT COURT

Opinion 1/09 on the draft Agreement on the European and Community Patents Court, however, showed that the difficulties in establishing a hybrid court had still not been delineated sufficiently clearly by these earlier cases. The background lay in the attempt to create a court with jurisdiction over the existing European patent issued under the European Patent Convention and the proposed Community patent. The European Patent Convention, signed at Munich in 1973, is a treaty to which all 27 EU Member States and 11 other States are Parties. Although the system for applying for a European patent is unitary, the patent consists of a bundle of national patents, each governed by the national law designated by the patent holder, and it must be enforced through the separate national legal systems (laborious, expensive and lacking uniformity). The

[37] Opinion 1/92 *Agreement on the European Economic Area* [1992] ECR I-2821. The final version of the EEA Agreement is at OJ 1992 L1/3.

[38] Opinion 1/00 *Agreement on a European Common Aviation Area* [2002] ECR I-3493. See M Bronckers, 'The Relationship of the EC Courts with other International Tribunals: Non-committal, Respectful or Submissive?' (2007) 44 *CML Rev* 601, 606–09.

[39] P Eeckhout, *External Relations of the European Union: Legal and Constitutional Foundations* (Oxford, Oxford University Press, 2004) 206–09.

proposed Community patent, by contrast, would be unitary, having equal effect throughout the territory of the EU, and could be granted, declared invalid or lapsed only in regard to that entire territory. In June 2011, political agreement was reached under the enhanced cooperation procedure (Spain and Italy not participating) on a European Union unitary patent Regulation. Parallel talks had taken place over some years on the concept of a single European patent court system – with primary jurisdiction over individual actions relating to both kinds of patent – widely thought desirable to simplify enforcement of patents across the area covered by the European Patent Convention.

The system devised for the proposed European and Community Patents Court tried to take account of the considerations set out by the Court of Justice in Opinion 1/91. In particular, it was provided that where a question of interpretation of the (EC Treaty) or validity or interpretation of acts of the EC arose before lower courts under the proposed system, they might request a Court of Justice to decide the question, while the Court of Appeal would be required to refer to the Court of Justice. The decision of the Court of Justice would be binding on all courts under the proposed system. Member States were however divided over the lawfulness of the draft Agreement, and in 2009, the Court of Justice was asked to rule. Its Opinion was delivered in March 2011, on the basis of the Treaties as amended by the Treaty of Lisbon.

The Court of Justice began by setting out the nature of the legal order established by the founding Treaties of the European Union, recalling the cases described above, but it then pointed out that 'As is evident from Article 19(1) TEU, the guardians of that legal order and the judicial system of the European Union are the Court of Justice and the courts and tribunals of the Member States'. Although the Court of Justice was to ensure respect for the autonomy of the European Union legal order, some important and complementary obligations were also laid on Member States and on national courts and tribunals to ensure that 'in the interpretation and application of the Treaties the law is observed'.[40]

The proposed Patents Court would be outside the institutional and judicial system of the EU and be an organisation with distinct legal personality. The exclusive jurisdiction to be vested in the Patent Court in a significant number of actions would deprive the courts of the Member States of that jurisdiction. Although international agreements might confer additional powers on the Court of Justice or affect its powers, it was a condition that they did not change the essential character of the Court or adversely affect its autonomy. But, the legal systems approved in the contexts of the EEA and of the European Common Aviation Area were essentially designed to resolve disputes over the international agreements concerned. The Patent Court, by contrast, would have jurisdiction over the Regulation on the (Union) patent as well as other instruments, fundamental rights and general principles of EU law relevant to its interpretation. In

[40] Opinion 1/09 *Draft Agreement on the European and Community Patents Court*, paras [64]–[70].

the field of its exclusive jurisdiction, it would take the place of national courts and tribunals and deprive them of the power to request preliminary rulings in that field from the Court of Justice. This direct cooperation between national courts and the Court of Justice, in the interpretation and application of EU law and in the protection of individual rights conferred under it, was 'indispensable to the preservation of the very nature of the law established by the Treaties'. There was a further problem in that if the Patent Court issued a decision in breach of EU law, the decision could not be the subject of infringement proceedings or give rise to financial liability on the part of Member States. It followed that the system under the draft Agreement was incompatible with the EU Treaty and the Treaty on the Functioning of the EU.[41]

In consequence of the Opinion of the Court, the attempt to set up a hybrid court was abandoned and discussions continued on the basis that only EU Member States would be Parties to what is now to be called the Unified Patent Court. The revised draft Agreement also contains provisions for joint Member State liability for any failure of the Patent Court correctly to apply EU law.

VIII. MOX PLANT

A further rule protecting the autonomy of the Court of Justice as primary guardian of the law of the EU Treaties is the requirement in Article 292 of the EC Treaty[42] under which 'Member States undertake not to submit a dispute concerning the interpretation or application of this Treaty to any method of settlement other than those provided for therein'. This provision has been generally respected by the Member States, so that it has not been necessary for the Court to enforce it. Ireland, however, complained about the operation of a plant to recycle plutonium from spent nuclear fuel in Sellafield on the coast of the Irish Sea, and in 2001 it instituted proceedings against the UK before the Arbitral Tribunal established under the UN Convention on the Law of the Sea (UNLOSC). Ireland complained of violations of UNLOSC by the UK in failing to carry out a proper environmental assessment, failing to cooperate with Ireland and failing to protect and preserve the marine environment. The European Commission then brought infraction proceedings against Ireland, claiming that Ireland had failed to respect the exclusive jurisdiction vested in the Court to rule on any dispute concerning the interpretation or application of Community law.[43]

The Court found that the provisions of UNLOSC relied on by Ireland were largely regulated by Community measures, several of which were listed in the appendix to the Declaration of Community competence submitted with the Community's instrument of conclusion of UNLOSC. Ireland had also relied on

[41] Paras 71–89.
[42] Now Art 344 TFEU.
[43] Case C-459/03 *Commission v Ireland* [2006] I-4635.

Community instruments in its statement of claim and pleadings before the Arbitral Tribunal. The UNLOSC provisions relied on by Ireland were rules that formed part of the Community legal order, and the Court of Justice had exclusive jurisdiction to determine a dispute between Member States over their application. The Court also noted, in the context of the allegation of failure in the duty of cooperation, that submitting the dispute to the UNLOSC Arbitral Tribunal involved the risk that a judicial forum other than the Court of Justice would rule on the scope of obligations under Community law.[44]

The Court's decision in the *Mox Plant* case did not give rise to conflict with the UNLOSC Tribunal because Article 282 of UNLOSC provides that if the parties to a dispute have agreed through a general, regional or bilateral agreement or otherwise, then a dispute should, at the request of one of them, be submitted to a procedure that entails a binding decision, and that procedure should apply in lieu of the UNLOSC provisions unless the parties to the dispute agree otherwise. The UNLOSC Tribunal, although it initially decided that it had jurisdiction, suspended proceedings once it was claimed that the dispute related to Community law, and it discontinued them following the Court's judgment.

It may be that the requirement for Member States to settle their disputes on EU law before the Court of Justice is now too inflexible – given the plethora of specialised tribunals now established under international agreements to which the Union, often together with its Member States, is a Party, so that their provisions form part of Union law. But it is not for the Court to apply discretion or comity where the Treaties have provided none, so it cannot be criticised for asserting exclusive jurisdiction over the interpretation and application of the Treaties on the facts of the *Mox Plant* case.[45]

IX. CONCLUSION

Recent judgments of the Court of Justice – even if they have not finally resolved the nature of the 'new legal order' – have resolved uncertainties and filled gaps in regard to the position of that legal order within the global system of international law and national laws. The European Union and its Court of Justice stand Janus-faced between the international legal order and the national legal systems. Towards the Member States and their courts, the EU and its Court behave as a treaty-based international legal order – one with characteristics which, taken together, are uniquely intrusive into national legal orders and uniquely effective within these legal orders – but these are not characteristics that are incompatible with an international legal system. Towards other inter-

[44] See M Cremona, 'Defending the Community Interest: The Duties of Cooperation and Compliance' in M Cremona and B de Witte (eds), *EU Foreign Relations Law* (Oxford, Hart Publishing, 2008) 149–51 and 166–69.

[45] For wider assessment of the judgment, see N Lavranos 'On the Need to Regulate Competing Jurisdictions between International Courts and Tribunals' EUI Working Paper MWP 2009/14, 9–17.

national legal orders, the Court is open and deferential to the extent compatible with its own mandate, as established in the Treaties and developed by its own jurisprudence. In the case of fundamental conflict with its own legal order, the Court will defend its own mandate. In this behaviour, it resembles national courts.

The cases placing the Union in its international context have been relatively few, but they are consistent, coherent and faithful to the mandate of the Court of Justice. Its delineation of the relationship between international and Union law is within the spectrum of constitutional relationships provided in national legal systems, and its construction of international agreements has had due regard to the terms and objectives of those international agreements. There is every indication that the Masters of the Treaties are ultimately content with this outcome.

8

Of Feasibility and Silent Elephants: The Legitimacy of the Court of Justice through the Eyes of National Courts

MICHAL BOBEK*

THERE HAS TRADITIONALLY been an intriguing disconnection in discussions concerning the legitimacy of the Court of Justice of the EU (the Court). On the one side, the most frequently invoked legitimising element for the evolution of the Court's creative case law over the years has been and remains national courts. Their ongoing support, their embracing of the EU law mandate and the thus created relationship of mutual trust and cooperation between them and the Court are said to fuel the entire EU law legal engine. On the other side, once national courts had been allowed to provide the initial fuel, their role in the legitimacy narrative and assessment appears to be terminated. Very little or nothing at all is known and accordingly used for examining the legitimacy of the Court's case law with respect to whether or not national courts are satisfied with the Court's decision(s) once they receive them, whether they consider them authoritative and whether the Court's case law is in fact followed by national courts in other cases. Which of the two sides is, however, in fact more important for the Court's overall legitimacy with respect to national courts? The few flashes of glamorous limelight of a case going to Luxembourg or the vast, unexplored spaces of normal day-to-day (non)application of EU law by national courts?

This contribution embarks on an expedition to the latter unexplored dark side. It critically examines the legitimacy of the Court and its case law against the needs and expectations of national courts and reasonable exercise of national judicial function. These expectations are introduced and discussed under the umbrella notion of functional legitimacy: is the judicial output of the

* I am much obliged to Henri de Waele, Jakub Camrda, Urszula Jaremba, Jan Komárek, Stephen Weatherill and Carsten Zatschler for their stimulating comments on the draft of this contribution. All opinions expressed are strictly personal to the author.

Court feasible in the eyes of national courts? Does it provide realist and reasonable guidance in EU law matters for the exercise of normal judicial function at the national level? Against this yardstick, three aspects of the judicial output of the Court are examined in turn: the Court's individual judgment and its reasoning; the case law of the Court more broadly, its reception by national courts and compliance; and finally the institution of the Court of Justice as such.[1]

I. INTRODUCTION: LEGITIMACY AS FEASIBILITY

In the realm of notions, legitimacy is one of the troubling ones. Desired by everyone, frequently discussed and invoked, yet difficult to define and virtually impossible to measure. When is an institution such as a court legitimate? A tentative reply might involve such notions as authority, credit and voluntary compliance, acceptance or willingness to follow. Often, a distinction between input and output legitimacy is drawn;[2] the former focusing on the process and way of reaching decisions, whereas the latter on the acceptance of substantive outcomes and results.[3]

Beyond such minimalist description, views and approaches start to differ considerably: who assesses what exactly with respect to what constituency or respondents (general public – professional public – other specific group or constituency)?[4] What precisely is being looked at (an institution as a whole –

[1] This contribution is not based on any large-scale primary research, but on personal experience and fieldwork of the author. The author has qualified as a judge in the Czech Republic. Following the Accession of the Czech Republic to the EU, he worked for four years as legal secretary to the Chief Justice at the Supreme Administrative Court of the Czech Republic, where he also headed the Research and Documentation Department of the Court, advising administrative judges on matters of EU law, and also collaborating with a number of colleagues in other national courts Europe-wide within the Association of the Councils of State and Supreme Administrative Jurisdictions of the EU. For eight years, he has also been lecturing on EU law and principles of its domestic application to judges, judicial trainees and other national practitioners in the Czech Republic, Slovakia and elsewhere, being, inter alia, external lecturer at both Czech as well as Slovak judicial academies. It is humbly suggested that one of the best sociological studies of genuine life of EU law in national courts is to be asked to explain certain decisions of the Court to average national judges, and then try to devise, together with them, how such a decision of the Court could be implemented in practice before national courts so as to provide a reasonable and workable result. It is from such ongoing work at the intersection between the Luxembourg 'will' and national 'won't' that the main arguments of this chapter emerged.

[2] See eg FW Scharpf, *Governing in Europe: Effective or Democratic?* (Oxford, Oxford University Press, 1999) 6–30 or FW Scharpf, 'Legitimacy in the Multilevel European Polity' (2009) 1 *European Political Science Review* 173.

[3] JHH Weiler, 'The Political and Legal Culture of European Integration: An Exploratory Essay' (2011) 9 *International Journal of Constitutional Law* 678, 682 adds to this traditional bi-polar division a third type of legitimacy 'rooted in the politically messianic'. Unless, however, the process of the journey into a promised land (and the hardship endured en route) is part of the messianic promise, it could be also suggested that political messianism is in fact a type of axiomatically postulated macro-result within the outcome/results type of legitimacy.

[4] See eg JL Gibson, GA Caldeira and VA Baird, 'On the Legitimacy of National High Courts' (1998) 92 *American Political Science Review* 343 or GA Caldeira and JL Gibson, 'The Legitimacy of the Court of Justice in the European Union: Models of Institutional Support' (1995) 89 *American Political Science Review* 356.

composition and staff – procedures – reasoning standards of written decisions etc)?[5] Against what criteria is the output of the institution measured (legal (textual) – sociological – moral)?[6] Finally, what level of legitimacy debate is one at precisely? Is it general or overall legitimacy or support for an actor or institution, or specific legitimacy or support for a concrete policy or decision? The former refers to institutional commitment or overall goodwill of an institution amongst the public. It differs from the support of, or disagreement with, a single decision of that institution, which is the object of the latter.[7]

Whatever parameters one chooses for defining a particular vision of legitimacy, it may be nonetheless suggested that the ultimate purpose of legitimacy assessment and debate will always lie in the realm of social interaction. Even if the chosen parameters are moral or purely normative, the legitimacy argument itself will eventually be used for justifying why certain actors should or should not behave in a certain manner.[8]

Over the years, the legitimacy of the Court of Justice of the EU has been addressed from various perspectives. Most of these discussions would use as their yardstick variously framed moral visions of what a court should or should not be doing, relying for instance on the Court's faithfulness to the text of the Treaties and the degree of departure from it (textual yardstick)[9] or on variously captured discussions of value impartiality/political engagement of the Court (moral ideal-centred yardstick).[10] The resulting spectrum would then typically

[5] *cf* the various approaches outlined in N Huls, 'Introduction: From Legitimacy to Leadership' in N Huls, M Adams and J Bomhoff (eds), *The Legitimacy of Highest Courts' Rulings: Judicial Deliberations and Beyond* (The Hague, TMC Asser Press, 2009) 3–30, 13–18, or MA Loth, 'Courts in a Quest for Legitimacy: A Comparative Approach', in Huls, Adams and Bomhoff (eds), ibid, 267–88, 269.

[6] See RH Fallon, 'Legitimacy and the Constitution' (2005) 118 *Harv L Rev* 1787, who helpfully distinguishes between legitimacy as a 'legal', 'sociological' and 'moral' concept, according to against which kind of criteria legitimacy is discussed.

[7] Although one intuitively assumes that there is a connection between these two types of legitimacy, the precise empirical nature is very far from clear. See further, Gibson, Caldeira and Baird, above n 4, 344, 348 and 356–57.

[8] See Weber's definition of legitimacy and legitimate order in M Weber, *Wirtschaft und Gesellschaft: Grundriss der verstehenden Soziologie*, 5th edn (Tübingen, Mohr Siebeck, 1980) 11–20 (in English translation *Economy and Society: An Outline of Interpretive Sociology* (Berkeley, University of California Press, 1978) 31–38).

[9] See especially TC Hartley, 'The European Court, Judicial Objectivity and the Constitution of the European Union' (1996) 112 *LQR* 95 (drawing the scale of Court's rulings within, outside and contrary to the text of the Treaties) or P Neill, 'The Constitutional Role of the European Court of Justice' in A Dashwood et al, *The Developing Role of the European Court of Justice* (London, European Policy Forum, 1995) 45–49.

[10] Can a court that has – as its (semi-declared) aim – the furthering of European integration be, by definition, an independent arbiter, in particular between the Union and Member States? See in particular M Cappelletti, 'Is the European Court of Justice "Running Wild"?' (1987) 12 *ELRev* 3, 8 and 9, reviewing H Rasmussen, *On Law and Policy in the European Court of Justice. A Comparative Study in Judicial Policy-Making* (Dordrecht, Martinus Nijhoff Publishers, 1986). The question keeps coming back: see more recently R Herzog and L Gerken in their joint article entitled 'Stoppt den Europäischen Gerichtshof!', ('Stop the European Court of Justice!') published in the *Frankfurter Allgemeine Zeitung* of 8 September 2008, accessible also online at: www.cep.eu. See also Editorial Comments: 'The Court of Justice in the Limelight – Again' (2008) 45 *CML Rev* 1571.

be one of an activist/self-restrained Court with reference to a subjectively conjured boundary. Such a boundary, however, can only be established against an abstract normative ideal of 'proper' exercise of judicial function. It is based on the author's personal, often culturally determined, convictions about what judges should and should not do.

As already mentioned above, EU law studies have traditionally shown an intriguing gap in legitimacy discussions relating to the Court. On the one hand, the perhaps most frequently invoked legitimising element for the Court's activity and its case law is national courts. This is the special relationship of mutual trust and cooperation, in which national courts request preliminary rulings, and the Court answers them. The Court is legitimised to answer because a national court asked. If, as the same narrative continues, national courts were not satisfied with the answers given by the Court, they would not keep making further requests for preliminary rulings in the future. The Court has thus been able to build a federal-like structure for Europe because national courts faithfully cooperate with the Court. They accepted and embraced their European mandate and act as Union courts.

If, however, the main source of legitimacy for the Court is references sent by national courts, should national courts not also be the main yardstick for measuring the legitimacy of the Court's judicial activity? There is no doubt that, in its case law, the Court engages with a number of other audiences,[11] vis-a-vis whose expectations and ideas its performance and/or legitimacy can be measured: Member States and their executives; national parliaments; other institutions of the Union, in particular the Union legislature; national and European academia; other international organisations and international community generally, etc. However, in spite of all these perceived or real other interlocutors, at least in proceedings on preliminary rulings, it is still national courts that are indeed the chief 'clients' of the Court. They are repeat players. Their ongoing support is crucial.

The obvious problem for such legitimacy assessment is one of knowledge: the genuine life of EU law at the national level generally is one huge black box. We know very little of what is actually going on in normal[12] national courts in terms of EU law application and enforcement, but also how the legitimacy of the Court's rulings is perceived and evaluated in national courts. The lack of knowledge is occasionally alleviated by national reports on domestic application of EU law in typically collective volumes[13] or sector or area-specific study of

[11] See eg JHH Weiler, 'A Quiet Revolution: The European Court of Justice and its Interlocutors' (1994) 26 *Comparative Political Studies* 510.

[12] 'Normal' refers to ordinary lower national courts (first instance and appellate); to some degree also to national supreme courts. On the other hand, for structural, procedural and also political reasons, national constitutional courts constitute a category on their own. See further M Bobek, 'The Impact of the European Mandate of Ordinary Courts on the Position of Constitutional Courts' in M Claes, M de Visser, P Popelier and C Van De Heyning (eds), *Constitutional Conversations in Europe* (Cambridge, Intersentia, 2012) 287–308.

[13] Notably AM Slaughter, A Stone Sweet and JHH Weiler (eds), *The European Court of Justice and National Courts: Doctrine and Jurisprudence* (Oxford, Hart Publishing, 1998); A Łazowski (ed), *The Application of EU Law in the New Member States: Brave New World* (The Hague, TMC

domestic application of EU law.[14] Such – by definition – limited 'dives' into national practice are nonetheless rather the exceptions confirming the rule of the black box. How do national judges solve normal EU law cases? What is the normal life of EU law in national courts? Normal life of the law is not defined by grand constitutional battles over primacy once every ten years or so when a new EU treaty is reviewed by national constitutional courts. Normal life of EU law is defined by thousands of dull tax cases, consumer protection actions, common customs tariff classification disputes, trans-border enforcement of small civil claims, companies' shareholder quarrels and so on. What is the genuine practice in such cases with respect to EU law? Do national courts follow the guidance of the Court? Or is the Court's case law silently neglected? What would this mean for the authority and legitimacy of the Court, if its case law in national courts was in fact by default disregarded?

Only large-scale comparative field research in national courts can give reliable answers to these questions. This contribution can at least demonstrate the importance of such questions for the legitimacy of the Court and outline some of main themes for such types of research, focusing in particular on two overreaching issues: first, what might be out there in the black box called national courts' application of EU law; and second what might it mean for the legitimacy of the Court and its case law?

However, before entering into the debate proper, it is essential to introduce the yardstick for assessing the legitimacy of the Court and its case law from the vantage point of the national judicial function. This yardstick could perhaps best be named *functional* legitimacy or legitimacy *as feasibility*. It is concerned with the practicability or feasibility of the Court's pronouncements on what national courts should do with respect to EU law in the national judicial domain. It accepts, as national courts arguably generally accept, that it is the Court's competence to issue guidance as far as *what* EU law is and *how* EU law is to be applied by national courts. At the same time, however, the chief interest of a normal national court is to do its own job properly: to deliver a decent decision within reasonable time and, if possible, with minimal effort. This does in no way suggest any laziness on the part of national judges, but normal constraints on judicial business or any human work. A national judge, in particular in a lower court, is typically obliged to dispose of dozens of cases every month. In such settings, an unreasonable increase in the amount of work and/or its complexity is not anything a judge would seek.

Asser Press, 2010); G Martinico and O Pollicino (eds), *The National Judicial Treatment of the ECHR and EU Laws* (Groningen, Europa Law Publishing, 2010).

[14] eg MA Jarvis, *The Application of EC Law by National Courts: The Free Movement of Goods* (Oxford, Clarendon Press, 1998); AJ Braakman, *The Application of Articles 85 and 86 of the EC Treaty by National Courts in Member States* (Luxembourg, Office for Official Publications, 1997); AP Dourado and R da Palma Borges, *The Acte Clair in EC Direct Tax Law* (Amsterdam, IBFD, 2008). An excellent category in itself is the Ius Commune Casebooks for a Common Law of Europe Series, published by Hart Publishing (www.iuscommune.eu).

It is at the cross-section of these two assumptions that the yardstick of functional legitimacy is born. In its *normative* (or moral) dimension, it is translated into the ideal of a clear, understandable, consistent and above all feasible guidance. From the point of view of national judges, only those decisions of the Court which can be applied by normal, mortal judges, and do not require judicial Euro-Hercules in terms of zeal, capacity and resources, tend to be accepted and followed. The same vision can then be translated and perhaps somewhat quantified in the *sociological* (or empirical) dimension of the same functional legitimacy: if and only if the Court is issuing such feasible guidance, will it be followed by national courts. The more feasible a decision or area of case law is, the more legitimate it appears and the more likely it is to be complied with. Conversely, unfeasible or impracticable decisions are hardly ever followed by national courts or are likely to be swept under the carpet. 'Unfeasible' eventually leads to 'irrelevant', because it is 'socially irresponsive'. Such case law is not able to predict and normatively capture the social reality and genuine life of EU law in national courts and becomes gradually, at least in the eyes of national judges, devoid of any legitimacy.

This contribution thus reverses the more traditional view of discussing the relationship between the Court and national courts: instead of looking at what national courts are obliged to do as Union courts, it looks at what the Court ought to be doing in order to enable the national courts to realistically function as Union courts. In the words of a judge at the Court of Appeal of England and Wales, Lady Justice Arden:

> The supranational courts [referring to the Court of Justice and the European Court of Human Rights – note author] are not slow to say what they expect of national courts. But I would argue that the question of how to achieve the most suitable form of supranational adjudication must be also considered from the perspective of national systems. It is time to turn the tables and ask what the national courts are entitled to expect of supranational courts.[15]

The ensuing parts of this contribution further elaborate upon this notion of functional legitimacy and examine the legitimacy of the Court from the point of view of national courts with respect to three key issues: the judgment of the Court (individual decision and its support); the case law of the Court (general or diffuse support); and the institution of the Court of Justice itself.

[15] Lady Justice Arden, 'Peaceful or Problematic? The Relationship between National Supreme Courts and Supranational Courts in Europe' (2010) 29 *YEL* 3, 5.

II. THE JUDGMENT

Today,[16] substantive reasons stated in the decision itself tend to be considered as the key legitimising element of an individual judicial decision.[17] A decision, while being responsive to the parties and potentially also to broader societal interests in the case, compels obedience by being clear and well reasoned, resting on solid grounds of argument, being logical and consistent, employing acceptable method and arguments. Such a decision encapsulates the modernist belief in impersonal and rational authority. It is authoritative and thus legitimate.

It can hardly be the ambition of this contribution to enter into any deep-level debates on proper judicial reasoning of individual decisions of the Court of Justice.[18] The focus shall be, instead, on one particular aspect of the legitimacy of the Court's reasoning; namely, the frequently invoked (and reproached) 'cryptic, Cartesian style' of the Court. The argument, put forward notably by Joseph Weiler some ten years ago,[19] and since then picked up and repeated by other authors, goes essentially as follows: the Court should abandon its cryptic style and move towards a more discursive, analytical and conversational style, in order to demonstrate that it takes into account national sensibilities. The key-words are 'openness' and 'discursive transparency', in particular in constitutional cases, which should lead to greater authority and legitimacy of the Court's decisions in the eyes of national courts. The same applies, by analogy, to dissenting opinions: they should also be introduced, as they are in the end beneficial for the quality of the majority judgment. They force the majority to deal with arguments running against the solution eventually adopted by the Court in a more nuanced, responsive way. Finally, dissenting opinions ultimately enhance the legitimacy of the entire process of judicial decision-making, as it is apparent that other views were also duly considered but rejected.

[16] As opposed to pre-modern visions of judicial and administrative authority, where legitimacy was derived from inherited personal status and/or transcendent sources. A judicial decision was a legitimate decision because it was adopted by the right person, who represented the will of the God or that of the sovereign. EV Heyen, for instance, re-construed on the basis of Lutheran funeral sermons from the late 17th century a set of virtues an administrator ought to have in order to be a good official and pass equitable decisions. The most important one was godliness [*Gottesfurcht*], from which other virtues were derived: fairness, graciousness, persistence, diligence, cleverness and fidelity. See EV Heyen, 'Metaphern für "Ampts-Person" und "Ampts-Tugend" in lutherischen Regentenpredigten des späten 17. Jahrhunderts' in P Becker and R Von Krosigk (eds), *Figures of Authority: Contributions towards a Cultural History of Governance from the Seventeenth to the Twentieth Century* (Brussels, Peter Lang, 2008) 29–50.

[17] With, however, considerable variations in a number of legal cultures, which may extensively rely or even substitute the substantive legitimacy by institutional legitimacy – see notably with respect to the French legal culture M Lasser, *Judicial Deliberations: A Comparative Analysis of Judicial Transparency and Legitimacy* (Oxford, Oxford University Press, 2004) 60 and 179–202.

[18] See in particular J Bengoetxea, *The Legal Reasoning of the European Court of Justice: Towards a European Jurisprudence* (Oxford, Clarendon Press, 1993) and recently G Beck, *The Legal Reasoning of the Court of Justice of the EU* (Oxford, Hart 2013).

[19] JHH Weiler, 'Epilogue: The Judicial Après Nice' in G de Búrca and JHH Weiler (eds), *The European Court of Justice* (Oxford, Oxford University Press, 2001) 225.

Are judgments of the Court of today indeed still cryptic? Compared with the Court's overall style in the 1980s and the beginning of 1990s, on which the above quoted suggestion was most likely based, the style of the Court of the last decade or two has changed. Looking at decisions of the Court from the early 1990s and contrasting them with decisions issued in the early 2010s, it appears that the length of reasoning in judgments rendered on preliminary rulings has almost doubled. Is this still cryptic, Cartesian? The mere length of a decision has naturally very little to do with its discursiveness. At the same time, however, today's Court's decisions are quite different from those rendered, say, 20 years ago. Is this the moment at which the cryptic Cartesian can be said to have disappeared? Is there such a moment? What is the yardstick?

It may be accepted that, normatively speaking, a more explicit and open drafting style is no doubt always compelling in the form of a general ideal. However, it is questionable whether all the ensuing practical implications of such an ideal are equally appealing to all the other cultures and audiences apart from the internationally minded (and Anglo-American dominated) legal academia. Three aspects are worth highlighting with respect to the current format of decisions of the Court and the EU legal system: culture, audience and function.

Culturally, today's Court is embedded in civilian (or Continental) legal systems. There naturally is a considerably diversity in national judicial styles across Europe.[20] One may, however, still suggest that even within such a diverse context, lengthy intimate discursive confessions of what individual 'learned and noble friends' or 'judicial brethren' think are the odd exception, and the concise, impersonal style of an anonymous court the rule.[21] This is not a normative argument. It is just an empirical observation as to the mainstream expected format of the Court's decisions. In the eyes of the vast majority of national courts in today's EU, what is likely to be perceived as more acceptable: a decision which looks roughly similar to the standard national supreme judicial 'product' or a strange bundle of individual judicial opinions, which one has to disentangle first, and which has no parallel in the national system?

This leads to the second element: the audience. If the audience and legitimacy yardsticks are to be indeed national courts, then it may be suggested that

[20] See generally H Kötz, *Die Begründung höchstrichterlicher Urteile* (Deventer, Kluwer and Nederlandse Vereniging voor Rechtsvergelijking, 1982); H Kötz, 'Die Zitierpraxis der Gerichte: Eine vergleichende Skizze' (1988) 52 *RabelsZ* 644; or C Perelman and P Foriers (eds), *La motivation des décisions de justice* (Brussels, Bruylant, 1978).

[21] Weiler (above n 19) 255 argued that the 'more discursive, analytic, and conversational style' is also practised by other than common law courts. The example he mentioned in this respect is the German Constitutional Court. It might be suggested, however, that producing lengthy judgments with numerous citation strings is something quite different from being discursive and conversational. Reading through a normal decision of a German supreme jurisdiction (the Federal Constitutional Court or one of the five supreme federal jurisdictions), one fails to see the typical common law style of genuinely engaging with the quoted authorities, displaying alternatives, canvassing various options, etc. Instead, one finds quite authoritative style, in its abrupt way adjudicating rather on disputes amongst the various strands of *Schriftum* than real life parties, hardly famous for its discursive openness. Further on this difference, see eg B Markesinis, 'Judicial Style and Judicial Reasoning in England and Germany' (2000) 59 *CLJ* 294.

the national judicial dreams of an ideal court's judgment may somewhat differ from the academic ones. A more explicit discursive style, abundant reasons, a true account of judicial mentalities, allowing for dissent – all of these are the dreams of people who have the time, energy and appetite to spend hours analysing one case in depth. Judges, practitioners as well as other mortals, who, unlike academics, have to apply the case law as well, may not necessarily share the same dream. Their dream, on the other hand, rather includes hopes of being able to find the applicable law within a reasonable time, within a line of case law which speaks concisely and in one voice and which is relatively stable.[22] In short, different audiences naturally have different expectations from a decision of the Court. It is somewhat questionable to claim that the wishes of one audience are 'universal'.

Third, systemically speaking, full disclosure of all arguments, coupled with the introduction of concurring/dissenting opinions, enhances the complexity and thus the maintenance costs of the running of a legal system. Lengthy and complex judicial opinions, dissenting in three parts and concurring in the other four,[23] are, from the point of view of accessibility of the law, a luxury affordable only in systems where supreme judicial opinions are counted in tens – not thousands – every year.[24] The functional argument within the EU legal order from the point of view of national courts[25] is who should, in practical terms, 'digest' and 'explain', for the benefit of legal practice, the ensuing discursive diversity? It is one situation when up to approximately one hundred decisions on merits rendered annually by a national supreme jurisdiction[26] and containing some dissonant voices are immediately jumped upon, systemised and interpreted by a

[22] Stable in the sense of the absence or minimal amount of open and above all hidden reversals in the case law. See further E Carpano (ed), *Le revirement de jurisprudence en droit européen* (Brussels, Bruylant, 2012).

[23] One may only wonder at which stage the blessing of the individual judicial opinion becomes a burden. See, by the way of illustration, the judgment of the US Supreme Court in *Williams v Taylor*, 529 U.S. 362 (2000), the heading of which reads: 'Stevens, J, announced the judgment of the Court and delivered the opinion of the Court with respect to Parts I, III, and IV, in which O'Connor, Kennedy, Souter, Ginsburg, and Breyer, JJ, joined, and an opinion with respect to Parts II and V, in which Souter, Ginsburg, and Breyer, JJ, joined. O'Connor, J, delivered the opinion of the Court with respect to Part II (except as to the footnote), in which Rehnquist, CJ, and Kennedy and Thomas, JJ, joined, and in which Scalia, J joined, except as to the footnote, and an opinion concurring in part and concurring in the judgment, in which Kennedy, J, joined. Rehnquist, CJ, filed an opinion concurring in part and dissenting in part, in which Scalia and Thomas, JJ, joined'. There is no doubt that discursive premium sharply increases with the amount of dissents with respect to footnotes.

[24] And perhaps not even in those – for critical voices from within the English system, see eg A Samuels, 'Those Multiple Long Judgments' (2005) 24 *Civil Justice Quarterly* 279. But see also R Munday, 'Reasoning without Dissent: Dissenting without Reason' (2004) 168 *Justice of the Peace* 968 (Part I) and 991 (Part II).

[25] Which is different from the argument against dissenting opinions relating to the internal function and decision-making within the Court and the principle of collegiality – see section II.B of Koen Lenaerts' contribution to this volume.

[26] As is indeed the case with respect to, eg, the US Supreme Court or the UK Supreme Court. One may only contrast this with the sheer amount of cases supreme Continental jurisdictions would typically deal with. Further see M Bobek, 'Quantity or Quality? Reassessing the Role of Supreme Jurisdictions in Central Europe' (2009) 57 *American Journal of Comparative Law* 33.

number of law professors and practitioners, supported by reliable and detailed databases, journals and the fabric of national scholarship. It is something very different should the same element be introduced in quite a complex and multi-level system, in which the supreme jurisdiction decides hundreds of cases annually (and rising),[27] and which is not able to rely on much genuine trans-European debate and practice-oriented scholarship. If such a system still wishes to achieve a decent consistency of results in, say, Slovenian Maribor, Portuguese Porto or Finnish Oulu,[28] then the imperative is decreasing and not enhancing the overall systemic complexity, access and intelligibility.

It may be suggested that a national judge values reasonable conciseness and the constant structure of the Court's decisions. They enable easy access, orientation and reading. It is little things that matter: each part of the decision following in clear and constant order (opening with a short summary of the case; legal framework of the Union; national law; facts, procedure and questions referred; arguments of the parties; the Court's appraisal; all neatly packed in paragraphs and numbered). Immutability of a structured collegiate decision allows navigating within decisions quickly and relatively easily, surely more easily than in an only moderately (if at all) structured format of a bundle of individual judicial opinions. It is like shopping in one's favourite supermarket: one is happy that the goods can be found quickly in their usual places and hates to see the shelf contents rearranged every second week.

Seen in such perspective, and tied to a clear audience of national courts and their expectations, it may be suggested that the current style of individual decisions of the Court is in fact being appreciated. General appreciation obviously does not mean agreeing with the style of reasoning in each individual case. There have been and are problematic cases in which the Court offers hardly any reasons at all,[29] where it becomes too irresponsive to the parties[30] or where the reasoning itself is simply bad by whatever standards.[31] Still, the current

[27] The Court decided 638 cases in 2011; 574 in 2010; 588 in 2009; 567 in 2008; and 570 in 2007, out of which references for a preliminary ruling represented in each year 423; 385; 302; 288; and 265 cases respectively. In *Court of Justice Annual Report 2011* (Luxembourg, Publications Office of the European Union, 2012) 96.

[28] Examples of smaller EU Member States are chosen deliberatively: in contrast to the larger EU Member States (Germany, UK, France, Spain, Italy, Poland), where such 'digestion' and 'service' function for the benefit of national courts might be carried out by national scholarship, in the majority of the other smaller EU Member States, such national scholarship tends to be very small.

[29] See eg Case C-273/04 *Poland v Council* [2007] ECR I-8925. In this case, the most hotly debated issue focused not on the merits of the case, but on the admissibility of the action. In his Opinion of 21 June 2007, AG Poiares Maduro spent 48 paragraphs (out of a 76 paragraphs-long Opinion) discussing, similarly as the Member States in their submissions, the issue of admissibility of the action. The Court did not address this issue at all. It simply stated, in paragraph 33 of its judgment, that '[i]n the present case, the Court considers it necessary to rule at the outset on the substance of the case'.

[30] See, with respect to arguments advanced by the Member States, examples mentioned in J Komárek, '"In the Court(s) We Trust?" On the Need for Hierarchy and Differentiation in the Preliminary Ruling Procedure' (2007) 32 *ELRev* 467, 482–83.

[31] An example might be provided by a three paragraph 'reasoning' together with a reference to an impertinent previous decision, while completely omitting to mention a number of other, pertinent previous decision, but saying actually the contrary, in Case C-302/04 *Ynos* [2006] ECR I-71.

usual Luxemburg 'product' arguably meets the expectations of its mainstream European judicial 'clients' better than the academically advocated alternative.

To put the same point differently: what is being expected, and against what the Court's individual decisions are being measured by national courts in terms of functional legitimacy, is judicial *reason*, not necessarily abundance of *reasons*. National judicial reason is tied to the national judicial function. It hopes for clear, understandable and feasible solutions, which can be reasonably implemented at the national level by Member States' courts. This is something different from providing for abundance of reasons in the decision itself.

To illustrate the contrast: the Grand Chamber judgment in *Ruiz Zambrano*[32] has recently been pilloried as the epitome of an illegitimate decision, expanding the scope of EU law through citizenship while giving no substantive reasons. True, the reasoning of the Grand Chamber is at its best limited to six paragraphs.[33] This rather 'modest' reasoning can thus no doubt be challenged from various angles.[34] At the same time, however, from the vantage point of national courts, the decisions is not devoid of an understandable reason, giving clear and transposable guidance to them (*EU law prevents the deportation of third-country nationals on whom minor children who are Union's citizens are dependent*).

An example from the other side of the spectrum is a Grand Chamber decision in *Cartesio*,[35] with respect to the question concerning the possibility of appeals against national decisions submitting requests for preliminary rulings. In the decision itself, extensive reasons are given,[36] in which, however, it is difficult to find any judicial reason in the sense of clear and above all transposable guidance for national courts (*Appeals against orders submitting requests for a preliminary ruling are not incompatible with EU law as such, the decision of the appellate court on such an appeal however lacks any binding force on the lower court if it wishes not to be bound? Lower courts are free to selectively disregard the binding force of a decision of your superior court as they please?*).

Arguments presented in this part in no way suggest that the best decisions of the Court or any supreme court are those reduced to a series of brusque executive commands, which do not need to provide any reasons as long as they can be implemented. Quite the contrary: every decision needs to secure its legitimacy by giving substantive reasons. The power of the normative ideals of openness, transparency and discourse is readily acknowledged. What has been nonetheless attempted was to challenge academic claims that a more discursive and conversational style in the Court's decisions, including dissenting opinions, is *the* desire of *national courts*. It might be the (legitimate) desire of parts of the European legal academia. It might also be the wish of one individual judge or a

[32] Case C-34/09 *Ruiz Zambrano*, Judgment of 8 March 2011, not yet reported.

[33] ibid, paras 39–44.

[34] From amongst the first reactions, see eg case notes by K Hailbronner and D Thym in (2011) 48 *CML Rev* 1253 or by N Nic Shuibhne in (2012) 49 *CML Rev* 349. See also Stephen Weatherill's contribution to this volume, section V.

[35] Case C-210/06 *Cartesio* [2008] ECR I-9641.

[36] ibid, paras 80–98.

court as far as the Court's reply to its particular arguments is concerned. Such wishes should, however, be weighed against the wishes and needs of other audiences as well as systemic requirements of a reasonable function of the EU legal order in its present shape and form, in order to achieve a reasonable balance. Seen in this perspective, it might be concluded that the current reasoning style of the Court does not perhaps have such a bad reputation in the eyes of national judges.

III. THE CASE LAW

Functional legitimacy can also be employed in assessing the case law of the Court in general terms. The yardstick (feasibility and reasonable exercise of national judicial function) as well as the constituency (national courts) remain the same. What changes is the focus, which shifts from questions of understanding, acceptance and concrete support for an individual decision to a more diffuse support and overall sociological acceptance of the Court's case law or its specific areas.

A The Silent Elephant

Is the case law of the Court accepted and followed by national courts? The frank answer is that no one knows, at least at the overall European level, ie, considering the majority of Member States. What is known is the Luxembourg orthodoxy of what EU law in Member States ought to be, coupled with and in a way backed-up by the mainstream EU-centred and EU-optimist constructionist scholarly writings, typically dealing with the issue of national acceptance of primacy of EU law. Scratching the surface in the form of a few selected national constitutional cases in such studies, the results and narratives presented on their basis appear to be so unanimously optimistic as to be almost scary: initial resistance (mostly due to lack of knowledge or information on the part of national courts or false national pride), gradual seepage and/or hesitation, but, in the end, the national courts have seen the light and embraced their 'European mandate'. They became 'Union courts'. Some national differences might still persist, but these are marginal issues of national doctrinal or constitutional construction, which are just of academic interest (aka united in diversity).[37]

[37] A good overview of the approaches, in particular the 'Euro-Legalism', offers KJ Alter, 'Explaining National Court Acceptance of European Court Jurisprudence: A Critical Evaluation of Theories of Legal Integration' in AM Slaughter, A Stone Sweet and JHH Weiler (eds), *The European Court of Justice and National Courts: Doctrine and Jurisprudence* (Oxford, Hart Publishing, 1998) 227 ff, or M Claes, *The National Courts' Mandate in the European Constitution* (Oxford, Hart Publishing, 2006) 246 ff.

Is this indeed a faithful account of the practice of national courts? Or might the reality be somewhat different? One of the major fallacies of the mainstream optimist narratives is the interpretation of *silence* on the part of national courts. True, the fact that national courts do not openly revolt against the guidance given in the case law of the Court of Justice could mean that they do agree with it. It can, however, also mean something quite different: that they do not know EU law and case law of the Court or, more problematically, that they do not care about it, or, in the worst case scenario, that they know it but for whatever reason they do intentionally not care about it. In all these cases, a national judge will also be silent and not question the case law of the Court of Justice. Does it mean that such a judge has 'embraced her European mandate'?

In EU law, the question of genuine compliance by national courts with their 'European mandate' has been and remains the proverbial elephant in the room. More precisely: the problem is to assume compliance on the basis of lacking data and equal absence of open revolt with acceptance. This contribution can hardly push the elephant – nourished over decades and by now firmly established in the mainstream of EU legal studies – out of the room. As of today, there are no large-scale empirical studies which could shed any reliable light on what is the reality in application of EU law in national courts. What can be attempted, however, is to describe the size and shape of the silent elephant plus make few suggestions about how it could be measured. Furthermore, what does its existence mean for the legitimacy of the Court of Justice's case law?

Every year, national courts in the European Union decide tens of millions of cases. There are hundreds of thousands of appellate court decisions and tens of thousands of decisions by national supreme courts.[38] All supreme courts are, by definition, courts of last instance.[39] In how many of these national court cases EU law issues are raised is impossible to state. What can be estimated, however, is two other figures, which indirectly suggest that there is a considerably discrepancy between when national courts should take EU law into account according to the Court of Justice and when they actually do. First, what portion of national judicial decisions these days is being rendered materially within the scope of EU law? Second (and in contrast), how many requests for a preliminary ruling does this mass of national cases generate?

[38] These order of magnitude figures have been obtained by adding up data from national judicial statistics supplied by the EU Member States for the purpose of the biannual evaluation report of the Council of Europe Commission for the Efficiency of Justice (2009 Scheme for Evaluating Judicial Systems), accessible online at: www.coe.int/t/dghl/cooperation/cepej, heading 4.2.2., points 90–92 in each of the national reports. With respect to Germany, data from the 2007 Report were used, as Germany did not supply any statistics in 2009.

[39] In the sense of Art 267(3) TFEU. It is, however, clear that the set of national courts, against whose decision there is no judicial remedy under national law in the concrete case in the meaning of Art 267(3) TFEU, is considerably greater. It many also include first or second instance courts if, in the particular proceedings, no further appeal is possible. See further M Broberg and N Fenger, *Preliminary Reference to the European Court of Justice* (Oxford, Oxford University Press, 2010) 224–30.

In how many of the cases decided every year by national courts is EU law applicable? A rough indicator might be provided by the fact that much of the national law today is nothing more than domestic implementation of EU law. If the applicable national law is just implementing EU legislation, then the case is materially within the scope of EU law.[40] Moreover, in the views of the Court of Justice, even if the Member State has implemented EU legislation, national courts are still bound to take the original piece of EU legislation as well as any new Court's case law into account for the purpose of conform interpretation (indirect effect).[41]

Estimates with respect to how much of the national legislation today is nothing but implementation of EU law differ considerably according to the computing method used by the respective author and data sets taken into account on either side – EU as well as national. They may lie anywhere between 10 per cent and 70 per cent or even 80 per cent.[42] Whatever figure one takes as a starting point, it needs to be adapted with respect to judicial application of EU law in the Member States. On the one hand, one has to downgrade the potential figure for the purpose of real life cases: in any national legal system, there are obviously far more national judicial decisions applying, for instance, the national criminal code (largely outside EU law)[43] than there are instances of judicial application of provisions falling within the scope of EU legislation in the area of, for instance, fisheries[44] (exclusive EU law competence and a considerable amount of EU legislation in the area). Thus, the percentage for judicial application of EU law is likely to be lower than the percentage of the overall amount of implementing legislation. On the other hand, the above named potential percentage span of national implementing measures includes only implementation of directives and other EU legislation in need of implementation into the national legal system. It does not reflect the national judicial application of regulations and potentially other sources of EU law which need not be implemented. At the same time, some of

[40] Case 5/88 *Wachauf* [1989] ECR 2609 or Case C-260/89 *ERT* [1991] ECR I-2925, recently restated in, eg, Case C-27/11 *Vinkov*, Judgment of 7 June 2012, not yet reported.

[41] Case C-106/89 *Marleasing SA* [1990] ECR I-4135 or Joined Cases C-240/98 to C-244/98 *Océano Grupo Editorial SA* [2000] ECR I-4941; more recently, eg Case C-555/07 *Kücükdeveci* [2010] ECR I-365, paras 47–48.

[42] From the more recent debates, see eg A Töller, 'Mythen und Methoden: Zur Messung der Europäisierung der Gesetzgebung des Deutschen Bundestages jenseits des 80%-Mythos' (2008) *Zeitschrift für Parlamentsfragen* 8; T Hoppe, 'Die Europäisierung der Gesetzgebung: Der 80-Prozent-Mythos lebt' (2009) 20 *Europäische Zeitschrift für Wirtschaftsrecht* 168; Y Bertoncini, *What is the Impact of EU Interventions at the National Level?* (Paris, Notre Europe, 2009). A discussion with respect to Denmark, Austria and the Netherlands provide contributions in the first issue of (2010) 88 *Public Administration*. Comparative discussion with respect to the new Member States offers R Zbíral, 'Analýza míry vlivu EU na vnitrostátní legislativu: Srovnání situace v ČR s jinými členskými státy' ('An Analysis of the Degree of Influence of EU Law on National Legislation: Comparison of the Czech Situation with Other Member States') (2011) 150 *Právník* 1049.

[43] Ie, with respect to just 'normal', purely 'national' crimes and offences, not involving any of the EU legislation in area of criminal law or any other aspect of EU law (in whatever of its incidental forms – eg Case C-226/97 *Lemmens* [1998] ECR I-3711).

[44] More precisely, 'the conservation of marine biological resources under the common fisheries policy', which is EU exclusive competence – Art 3(1)(d) TFEU.

these regulations, especially those relating the judicial cooperation in civil and commercial matters,[45] tend to be applied quite frequently by national courts.

What then can be the final estimate? If one were to take as a starting point the lowest available percentages suggested, which would lie around 10 per cent, thus also accounting for the sector-specific differentiation in legislative versus judicial use of national implementing laws, and were to slightly increase this figure to account for instances of direct application of regulations and potentially other sources of EU law at the national level, then even on a very, very sober estimate, one still lands in the area of approximately 10 to 15 per cent.[46] In other words, it is suggested that, roughly, at least one in eight cases decided at national level is a case in which EU law is applicable.[47] In all these instances, the case is materially within the scope of national application of EU law, and EU law – including the case law of the Court of Justice – should be taken into account, directly or indirectly.

Let us therefore assume that EU law is applicable in at least one in every eight cases decided at the national level. In terms of the figures already mentioned relating to the number of cases decided annually by national courts in the Member States, this amounts to several millions of cases in all the courts of Member States and tens of thousands of decisions in courts of last instance. The former have the opportunity to submit requests for preliminary rulings to the Court of Justice, the latter are under an obligation to do so, provided none of the exceptions to the duty to make a reference under Article 267(3) TFEU are applicable.[48] Against such assumptions, a look at the annual statistics of the

[45] The quantitative champion in this respect is most likely the Council Regulation No 44/2001 of 22 December 2000 on jurisdiction and the recognition and enforcement of judgments in civil and commercial matters [2001] OJ L12/1, followed by other regulations on civil, commercial and family matters. Regulation No 44/2001 itself would be applied, even in relatively small jurisdiction like the Czech Republic, in hundreds of cases annually. *cf* survey provided in H Bončková and M Žondra, *Souhrnná zpráva o rozhodovací praxi českých civilních soudů v případech s evropským prvkem (2004–2008)* (*Summary Report of Practice of Czech Civil Courts in Matters with European Element (2004–2008)*) (Brno, Nejvyšší soud, 2010) 10–13.

[46] One might even add that in contrast to these figures based on computation for 1990s and early 2000s, the EU's legislative spree of the last decade has considerably expanded further into civil, commercial and criminal law and thus multiplied its own application in the areas of 'normal' judicial business. It can therefore be suggested that the final figure used (10–15%) is with respect to the year 2012 in fact considerably under-valued. Yet again, what is sought here is just the overall order of magnitude, not exact units.

[47] *cf* the very varying estimates made by the national supreme administrative courts with respect to the amount of cases involving EU law in their proceedings every year in Annex II to the General Report to the colloquium 'The Preliminary Reference to the Court of Justice of the European Communities', organised by the Association of the Councils of State and Supreme Administrative Jurisdictions of the European Union on 20 and 21 May 2002 in Helsinki (online at: www.juradmin.eu), including figures like 20% (Germany); 25% (Sweden); or even 33% (Finland) of all cases, on the one hand, and figures like 15 out of 5000 cases (Greece) or 20–40 out of 3500 cases (Portugal) decided annually, on the other. In the personal opinion of the author of this chapter (and with all due respect to the data provided by some member jurisdictions to the colloquium), for a national supreme *administrative* jurisdiction, the figure is in fact rather likely to lie in the realm of 20% and more.

[48] Case 283/81 *CILFIT* [1982] ECR 3415 or Case C-461/03 *Gaston Schul* [2005] ECR I-10513.

Court of Justice tells us that, in 2007, the Court received 265 requests for a preliminary ruling submitted by national courts; in 2008 it was 288; in 2009 it was 302; in 2010 it was 385; and in 2011 it was 423.[49]

Where are the zeros behind the figures for preliminary rulings? Even when allowing for the (very unlikely) assumption that the existing EU legislation and previous case law of the Court are both absolutely clear and understandable, providing seamless guidance in all areas and issues already adjudicated upon, so that national courts are well able to apply it flawlessly by themselves, and also accepting an extremely generous understanding of when an issue of interpretation of EU law is clear and obvious, there still remains a sheer discrepancy in the order of magnitude of the numbers presented. Millions of EU cases in all national courts, and tens of thousands of cases in courts of last instance, generate two or three hundred requests for preliminary rulings annually.

Two approaches can be taken to interpreting these numbers. First, continuing on the more traditional constructionist wave of institutional optimism, a number of weak spots in the very rough calculation just carried out may be easily identified in order to discard it as mistaken and reaffirm the orthodoxy: national courts have fully embraced their mandate as Union courts and the flourishing dialogue within the preliminary ruling procedure is the evidence of this success. The long overdue explanation within the orthodoxy is, however, how it is possible amongst other things that such an unremitting success has generated such a meagre docket for the Court of Justice over the years and that a considerable number of these docket cases essentially come from the same 'usual suspects' within just some Member States.[50] To push the same line of institutional optimism even further, it could even be suggested that it is in fact because national courts have mastered EU law and understand the special character of the preliminary ruling procedure that they refrain from using it with respect to interpretative problems of lesser importance. However, a quick look at the types of cases submitted to the Court renders such a position untenable, not to speak of a skim through national decisions involving EU law.

Second, one might accept that although such an illustrative calculation has a number of flaws, it nevertheless, in a way, reflects a genuine problem: namely, that silence on the part of national courts may not mean only 'acceptance' and 'embracing', but also or above all 'ignorance' and 'disregard'. If the preliminary rulings system in particular and EU legal system generally indeed functioned as they predict they ought to function, ie, the national courts followed the guidance of the Court genuinely and in full and sent preliminary rulings to Luxembourg when they applied EU law at the national level and they come under the obligation to submit a request for a preliminary ruling, then the num-

[49] *Court of Justice Annual Report 2011* (Luxembourg, Publications Office of the European Union, 2012) 96.

[50] *cf* ibid, tables 19 and 20 (pp 117–21). For a discussion with references to previous articles concerning the (in)equal distribution of requests for preliminary rulings amongst the Member States, see also Broberg and Fenger, above n 39, 37–58.

ber of preliminary rulings submitted annually to the Court would be bound to have one or more zeros attached to the end of the current figure.

The 'field' experience of the author of this contribution[51] confirms the second version. It could be claimed that this professional experience is limited to a handful of new Member States of the EU and thus is not genuinely representative of the entire Union. This objection is true, with two counter-objections: first, due to the pre and post-EU enlargement euphoria (and, more significantly, funding), judges and other practitioners in the new Member States have, over the last ten years or so, received in total considerably more additional education in EU law than their counterparts in the old Member States. Thus, paradoxically perhaps, it could be suggested that the likelihood of a judge in a new Member State going out and applying EU law where appropriate might be even slightly higher than in some of the old Member States, where disregard for EU law could be said to be 'business as usual'. Second, from a number of Euro-wide comparative projects on judicial education in EU law as well as discussions with a number of colleagues from the old Member States, it would appear that the general knowledge of EU law amongst judges is generally low, with two exceptions: specialised jurisdictions dealing more with EU law cases (for example, matters of competition law, trade law, customs and tax, trademarks, international protection etc) and the overall 'positive deviation' in the Benelux countries, in particular the Netherlands. However, even with respect to the very open Dutch judiciary, illustrious authors despair once they face reality in national courts. For instance, Sacha Prechal recently opined:

> [O]n the basis of some scarce and stray publications – where often some cautious allusions are made on the matter – personal experience and contacts with the national judiciary, one comes to a somewhat perplexing conclusion, namely that the quality and capacity of the national courts to apply EC law and to do so correctly is a matter for serious concern. It seems that after several decades of EC membership national judges, even the 'younger' generation, are rather still struggling with EC law than smoothly applying it.[52]

To sum up, national courts are, in the above outlined one in eight cases, or in reality perhaps even more frequently, deciding within the scope of EU law. They should thus take EU law into account. In the courts of the Member States, however, EU law is not daily bread, in spite of the baker saying it ought to be, especially if the Court's doctrines as to the application of EU law in national courts, such as ex officio application of EU law and indirect effect of directives, were to be taken seriously. EU law is more of a rare cherry which will be put on the cake typically only if one of the party guests brings it along. To state the same more clearly: in the majority of cases in which EU law ought to be considered and applied, EU law angles are either not recognised or intentionally neglected.

[51] Described above, n 1.

[52] S Prechal, 'National Courts in EU Judicial Structures' (2006) 25 *YEL* 429, 432–33.

B The Matter of Feasibility

The sweeping brush of the big numbers presented above ought to be considerably readjusted qualitatively. Not engaging with EU law and the Court's case law need not necessarily mean ignorance or disregard. It may also mean that EU law, even in spite of the case finding itself in its scope of application, indeed does not need to be applied in the particular case, and the decision will be made on different grounds. Thus, the motives for the missing zeros and the huge discrepancy in numbers are highly relevant. However, as already mentioned, empirical studies of this type are lacking in EU law scholarship. It is thus impossible to verify how well the above presented estimated figures correspond with reality.

What can be offered at this stage instead is at least the (re)introduction of qualitative considerations for national judicial acceptance of the case law of the Court of Justice. A good sample for a glimpse at qualitative aspects of national judicial practice provides principles of domestic application of EU law, such as direct effect, primacy, state liability, ex officio knowledge and application of EU law, national practice on preliminary rulings, remedies, language regime of national application of EU law etc. Principles of domestic application of EU law are good test cases as they allow assessment of how (un)successful the norm-setting body (ie, largely the case law of the Court of Justice in these areas) is in regulating how national courts should approach and apply EU law.

The yardstick for assessing the legitimacy of the Court's case law in this area is yet again the already introduced notion of functional legitimacy with respect to national courts. Feasible, understandable guidance, which is at least somewhat compatible with the work and function of a normal, mortal national judge, can be considered legitimate. Conversely, case law setting impossible requirements, uselessly upsetting or completely atomising national procedures, disregarding Member States' courts interests in the name of full effectiveness of EU law will be, in the eyes of national judges, devoid of such functional legitimacy.

The notion of functional legitimacy is largely apolitical. The dividing line is one of exercise of reasonable judicial function in national courts, not (at least not primarily) political or constitutional concerns of Member States' interests, national sovereignties, the keeping of the last word, etc.[53] Thus, for instance, the Court's constitutionally heavy case law on primacy,[54] which requires national courts to disapply even national constitutional provisions if incompatible with EU law, can be said to be functionally legitimate. It provides perhaps politically

[53] Again, all this applies to 'ordinary' national courts, not national constitutional courts, which in this respect are institutions with political agenda. Equally, it is readily acknowledged that the nation of 'ordinary national courts' is very far from a homogenous group, as it in fact includes a number of various courts (general, area-specific, subject-matter specialised etc) at various levels in various states, which are likely to differ in their particular agendas.

[54] Case 106/77 *Simmenthal* [1978] ECR 629, or Case C-285/98 *Kreil* [2000] ECR I-69.

difficult, but functionally feasible and clear, guidance to national courts: in case of conflict, apply EU law and disregard national law. There are obviously further technical aspects to such a simply stated rule, such as temporal issues or questions of parallel disapplication,[55] or the precise procedural fleshing out of the principle.[56] These nonetheless do not change the fact that the original guidance is feasible.

Conversely, there are areas of the Court's guidance relating to principles of national application of EU law that are in themselves politically 'marginal' and, from this point of view, perhaps even uninteresting, but in national judicial practice unfeasible. Examples might include the Court's case law on comparative language interpretation of EU law in the Member States; the way in which a national court of last instance should ascertain that a question which it does not wish to submit on request for a preliminary ruling is an *acte clair*;[57] the discerning of whether or not there is a general principle of EU law at stake in the case;[58] but also Member States' liability for judicial breaches of EU law.[59]

To these areas of unfeasible guidance – which has been impractical from its very inception – may be added other areas of originally perhaps feasible guidance, which as a consequence of contradictory case law assembled over time, however, became a minefield in which not many national judges dare to tread. Mentioned in this aspect can be the questionable status of *res iudicata* of a national decision incompatible with EU law;[60] assessing whether or not a national procedural rule is equivalent and/or (in)effective and thus in compliance with EU case law on national remedies;[61] or the EU law ever green in the

[55] Recently Case C-314/08 *Filipiak* [2009] ECR I-11049 or Case C-409/06 *Winner Wetten* [2010] ECR I-8015.

[56] *cf* eg Joined Cases C-10/97 to C-22/97 *IN.CO.GE.'90* [1998] ECR I-6307 or *Kücükdeveci*, above n 41.

[57] Both of these critically discussed with further references in M Bobek, 'On the Application of European Law in (Not Only) the Courts of the New Member States: "Don't Do as I Say"?' (2007–08) 10 *CYELS* 1.

[58] A curious reader is invited to read in turn decisions in Cases C-144/04 *Mangold* [2005] ECR I-9981; Case C-13/05 *Chacón Navas* [2006] ECR I-6467; Case C-101/08 *Audiolux* [2009] ECR I-9823; and *Kücükdeveci*, above n 41 and on the basis of guidance provided in these cases by the Court decide whether for instance prohibition of retroactivity, protection of good faith or prohibition of abuse of rights are (still?) general principles of EU law.

[59] Case C-224/01 *Köbler* [2003] ECR I-10239 and Case C-173/03 *Traghetti del Mediterraneo* [2006] ECR I-5177.

[60] From the more recent decision on finality of judicial decisions, see eg Case C-234/04 *Kapferer* [2006] ECR I-2585; Case C-119/05 *Lucchini* [2007] ECR I-6199; or Case C-2/08 *Fallimento Olimpiclub* [2009] ECR I-7501. For a comparative discussion of problems in complying with Court's guidance in this area from the point of view of national administrative courts, see the proceedings and national reports for the 21st Colloquium of the Association of the Councils of State and the Supreme Administrative Jurisdictions of the European Union, published as S Biernat et al (eds), *Consequences of Incompatibility with EC Law for Final Administrative Decisions and Final Judgments of Administrative Courts in the Member States* (Warsaw, Naczelny Sąd Administracyjny, 2008).

[61] Further see M Bobek, 'Why There is no Principle of 'Procedural Autonomy' of Member States' in H-W Micklitz and B de Witte (eds), *The European Court of Justice and the Autonomy of the Member States* (Cambridge, Intersentia, 2012) 305, 312–18.

form of simultaneous formal absence but factual existence of horizontal direct effect of directives.[62]

In all these areas, the interests and aims that led the Court to establishing given sets of requirements can be identified. A national judge, however, may wonder whether the Court has also genuinely thought through the consequences, impact and the potential life of its case law in national courts. For instance, ever since the 1980s, the *CILFIT* decision and the requirements stipulated therein with respect to the *acte clair* exception to the duty to refer have had a prominent place in the Court's case law as well as textbooks of EU law. A decision of a national court of last instance – which would have indeed faithfully and in full followed the guidance of the Court in *CILFIT* – is impossible to find.[63] *Köbler* and state liability for judicial breaches of EU law have been a firm part of the Luxembourg orthodoxy and EU law textbooks since 2003. Almost ten years later, there is, at least to the knowledge of the author of this chapter, not a single decision in any of the Member States which would have indeed awarded damages following the *Köbler* guidance.[64]

In both of these, as well as other lines of the Court's case law just mentioned, the guidance given by the Court is difficult, if not impossible, to follow in national courts. The first requires a national judicial Hercules, who reads in a number (or all?) official languages of the Union, closely follows all decisions issued by the Court of Justice as well as decisions in other Member States courts, is well aware of the particular Union law concepts and methodology and is able to discern (the not always entirely manifest, to say the least) *telos* of Union legislation. The second one either directs the individual applicant towards a non-existent institution, as there is no competent court to decide the case, or towards the same institutions which decided the case in the first round of judicial proceedings on merits, to now decide on state liability caused by their own previous decision.

The answer to both of these and other problematic lines of case law of course can be (selective) deference. For instance, the Court stated in *Köbler*, with nonchalant lightness, that the application of the principle of state liability 'cannot be compromised by the absence of a competent court'[65] in national legal systems. Thus, there is no doubt that from the point of view of the Court, it is the

[62] Re-launched yet again after the *Mangold* decision: see eg 'Editorial Comments: Horizontal Direct Effect – A Law of Diminishing Coherence' (2006) 43 *CML Rev* 1, or A Dashwood, 'From *Van Duyn* to *Mangold* via *Marshall*: Reducing Direct Effect to Absurdity?' (2006–07) 9 *CYELS* 81.

[63] It is surely not a problem finding national last instance decisions which quote *CILFIT*. That is, however, something quite different from finding a decision which genuinely carries out the test for '*acte clair*' established in *CILFIT* (above n 48) in paras 16–20 of the decision. The genuine test applied by national courts is, if applied at all, very different – for examples see Bobek, 'On the Application of European Law', above n 57, 16–18.

[64] Moreover, if *Köbler* were indeed applied in the Member States' courts, how is it possible that such a highly contentious issue, which is new and surely very far from clear, almost an entire decade since its enunciation in 2003, would generate only one other request for a preliminary ruling from all the Member States, namely the already quoted *Traghetti del Mediterraneo* (above n 59) in 2006?

[65] *Köbler*, above n 59, para 45.

failure of the Member States for not by now having established a supra-supreme court to decide on claims for damages against national supreme jurisdictions, followed perhaps by a supra-supra-supreme court and so on. Such a repartition of tasks, however, hardly reminds one of a true 'relationship of cooperation', unless obviously such a relationship means cooperating only in good and problem-free times and being abandoned at the very first moment a problem arises (which, by the way, happens to be caused by requirements set by the partner himself).

Such unfeasible guidance and, consequently, dysfunctional decisions in the eyes of national courts, over time create areas of virtual case law. It is 'virtual' because it, in fact, exists only in a few pronouncements of the Court and in EU law textbooks recounting the Luxembourg orthodoxy. In the national practice, however, most of the judges are blissfully ignorant of its existence.Those who are not, and know the requirements set by the Court of Justice, may eventually be forced to disregard them anyway, because they cannot reasonably comply with them.

Thus, when adding to the purely quantitative assessment presented in the previous section, a qualitative aspect and looking at a selected area of Court's case law in a qualitative way, it may also be suggested that one eventually bumps again into the same elephant silently sitting in the room: in practice, absence of open revolt can hardly be equated with acceptance and embracing of an EU mandate.

Where does this leave the legitimacy of the Court of Justice and its case law? If the legitimacy of the Court is to be assessed normatively as against (typically) an integration-centred value ideal, then the fact that there are areas of unfeasible or virtual case law which exist in EU law textbooks only and are disregarded by national courts, is no reason to worry. The case law of the Court is legitimate as long as it complies with the normative ideal: in a legalistic world, reality is of little importance. Conversely, if the legitimacy of the Court's case law is evaluated in more sociological terms, as has been repeatedly suggested in this contribution, then reality matters. Compliance is essential for authority and legitimacy. The inability to reasonably regulate how EU law is applied in national courts leads to irresponsiveness and irrelevance, which in turn result in loss of legitimacy.

In every legal system, there will no doubt be certain leeway between what the supreme jurisdiction says the law is and what the law genuinely is on the ground, in lower courts and the courts of first instance. As Fred Bruinsma metaphorically puts it, supreme jurisdictions will frequently be just lighthouses in symbolic fields, mostly relying on the persuasive power of their judgments.[66] There will thus always be a gap between the judicial pronouncements of the supreme jurisdiction and day-to-day practice in lower courts. The question becomes,

[66] F Bruinsma, 'A Socio-Legal Analysis of the Legitimacy of Highest Courts' in N Huls, M Adams and J Bomhoff (eds), *The Legitimacy of Highest Courts' Rulings: Judicial Deliberations and Beyond* (The Hague, TMC Asser Press, 2009) 73.

however, how broad the gap can be in order to still be able to claim that there is a functioning system. How far can the 'sein' be allowed to deviate from the 'sollen'? Again, it is clear that with respect to positivistic and state-centred normative systems, in EU law translated into the already mentioned 'EU-legalism',[67] these two levels are disconnected. Even if 'sollen' says A and 'sein' is in fact non-A, the social reality does not affect the validity of the norm. It can, however, considerably affect its social legitimacy and acceptance. If the norm-setting authority keeps enacting rules which are, for whatever reason, not able to regulate social reality to any reasonable degree, it becomes irrelevant and consequently may be perceived as illegitimate.

IV. THE INSTITUTION

If arguments articulated in the previous parts of this contribution are at least partly accepted, then there is a gap or disconnect between the national courts and the Court of Justice. From the point of view of national courts, this substance-related disconnection may eventually also become translated into questions relating to the Court itself and its composition. Do those people in that Luxembourg ivory tower/glass house/sky castle understand what is going on down here? Do they see and take into account our concerns? Do they listen to us before rendering their decisions? Do they consider our interests as well, or does full effectiveness of EU law trump everything, no questions asked? Do they think about the consequences and impact of their decisions on our work?

For any high jurisdiction, a certain degree of disconnection is natural and inevitable. Even national supreme or constitutional courts are often considerably disconnected from real life and the ongoing concerns of lower courts and ordinary judges. A fortiori, the same is true of a European or international court. At the same time, however, the effort of any sensible national supreme jurisdiction is to keep this disconnect as narrow as possible. A number of institutional and procedural measures are typically put in place in order for the supreme and lower jurisdictions to better understand the concerns, interests and the work of the other. Such measures, through the participation, voice and knowledge transfer, not only lead to more advised and acceptable decisions issued by the supreme jurisdiction, but, pragmatically speaking, also to greater legitimacy of the supreme jurisdiction and its decisions amongst lower courts and eventually to enhanced overall compliance.

There is no reason why the same considerations should not apply to the Court of Justice. The Court certainly seeks to emulate a similar type of support and legitimacy amongst Member States courts, not only by restating at any opportune occasion the special relationship of cooperation and mutual trust there is between itself and national courts, but also through a number of social,

[67] See above, n 37.

professional and academic occasions (ranging from judicial group visits in Luxembourg to stages, seminars, conference, participation in the works and proceedings of various association, networks etc). Relying on the same yardstick of functional legitimacy and the vantage point of national judges, three interrelated issues concerning the legitimacy of the Court as an institution will be discussed in this section, relating to *information* accessibility and exchange, *procedure* and finally the *composition* of the Court and its staff.

A Information

Partners share information. Mutual trust means information flow in both directions. Looking at the preliminary rulings procedure through the eyes of national judges, this is not entirely the case. Two aspects are worth highlighting here with respect to national judicial access to information and materials in the procedure on preliminary rulings: access to information in pending proceedings and access to documents after the case is finished.

First, when a national court submits a request for a preliminary ruling, it is obliged to provide all the information the Court needs to decide the case. Otherwise, the question may be declared inadmissible.[68] This is entirely justified: it is the duty of the national court to provide the Court of Justice with the factual and legal issues of the case, explained succinctly but in sufficient detail. However, once a national court has submitted a request for a preliminary ruling, the Court falls silent. This may yet again be fully understandable from the point of view of the Court: the written procedure is under way, with parties to the original proceedings before the national court as well as EU institutions or Member States submitting their observations. However, with the exception of a short notice published in the C series of the Official Journal, which contains only the name of the submitting court and the questions asked, the outside world has no knowledge of the case for the next year or two, before the Opinion of the Advocate General is issued, or, more and more frequently today, until the judgment of the Court itself.[69]

At the same time, however, to the outside world and especially to other national courts, the fact there is a case pending before the Court concerning certain questions may be highly relevant in other proceedings, concerning the same or similar questions of EU law. There are frequently similar cases pending

[68] *cf* Joined Cases C-320/90, C-321/90 and C-322/90 *Telemarsicabruzzo* [1993] ECR I-393; more recently, eg Order of the Court of 8 September 2011 in Case C-144/11 *Abdallah*, not yet reported, or Order of the Court of 15 April 2011 in Case C-613/10 *Debiasi*, not yet reported.

[69] According to the Court of Justice Annual Reports from last few years, about 46% of judgments delivered in 2011 were delivered without AG's Opinion (compared with 50% in 2010; 52% in 2009; 41% in 2008; 43% in 2007; 33% in 2006; 35% in 2005; and 30% in 2004). These figures, however, do not include cases that were disposed of by a reasoned order pursuant to Art 104(3) of the Rules of Procedure or disposed of otherwise. The frequency of the involvement of AGs if calculated against the *number of cases filed* with the Court of Justice would thus naturally be lower.

before other national courts across the Union. If other national courts knew that an already pending case is indeed similar, which is on the basis of the very short notice published in the Official Journal difficult if not impossible to assess, they could adapt the management of the cases before them to that fact and start genuinely cooperating with the Court. They might perhaps wait a little and then incorporate the Court's decision into their own judgment and not go ahead and decide their national case without addressing any EU law at all. They can suspend national proceedings with reference to the already pending case without submitting their own questions and await the decision of the Court in the other proceedings. National courts could thus save the Court's resources by not submitting their own requests which will, in the horizons of a few months or even weeks after they were submitted, become devoid of content anyway and ultimately disposed of by the Court by a reasoned order, which in turn does not necessarily please the referring judge.[70]

In all these cases, access to information for national courts concerning pending requests for preliminary rulings would eventually mean greater compliance on their part and less time and resources spent in terms of costs for the Court of Justice. All that would be required would be to make references in pending cases accessible – if not in full, then at least in the form of a summary, giving key facts, reference to relevant legislation and questions asked and reasons for them.

Second, once the national court's decision applying the guidance given to it by the Court of Justice in the individual case becomes final, the national court is invited by the Court to send it a copy of the final decision.[71] In this way, the Court has assembled a remarkable collection of national decisions applying EU law over the years. To have access to these final national decisions would no doubt be of considerable informative as well as didactic value to national courts, as well as to the academic community. From the point of view of national courts, there are frequently issues which the Court does not answer in its reply to a preliminary ruling, either because it cannot or does not wish to. The national judge, however, is obliged to deal with them anyway, in order to resolve the pending case. Thus, there is frequently considerable 'added value' in the final decision of a national judicial colleague when applying EU law. In order to make this added value accessible for other national courts, would adding one more entry into the electronic case information sheet entitled 'final decision of the national court', at least for the newest case law, constitute such a burden for the Court?

[70] Although the fact that the case was not decided by a judgment of the Court but by a reasoned order pursuant to Art 104(3) of the Rules of Procedure does not per se imply any sense of 'inferiority' of the question asked, it might be quite difficult to explain this fact to an embarrassed national judge, who is being told that the answer to her question is obvious and can be clearly inferred from existing case law of the Court, which the Court has issued *after* the national judge submitted her original request for a preliminary ruling.

[71] Point 32 in 'Information note on references from national courts for a preliminary ruling' [2011] OJ C160/1.

It is not the obligation of the Court to make national case law accessible. That is certainly true. However, sticking to the mere compulsory and necessary simply misses out on the idea of partnership and of inviting compliance by providing useful help and sharing information. It is not suggested that the Court should build up databases of national case law, but just make accessible one piece of information it receives in any case which could be beneficial to its national partners and the knowledge of EU law generally. Eventually, making the data from this collection accessible would necessitate initiative from outside the Court, through the Association of Councils of State and the Supreme Administrative Jurisdictions.[72]

To sum up, with respect to information access, the Court does not score very well. The information exchange between partners in the vision of the Court is somewhat one-sided: national courts are obliged to provide all the necessary information relating to the case they submit; they are obliged to keep the Court up-to-date during the course of the procedure; and they are asked to provide the Court with their final decision. Apart from its decision, however, the Court does not appear to be ready to provide much in return, for the benefit of its partners.

This information vacuum is being felt. Over the last few years, therefore, the same type of information started to be shared nationally or horizontally, through various channels. First, some national courts with more flexible and open national public administrations were able to receive information relating to pending cases before the Court through their national agents or ministries, which have established databases of cases pending before the Court for the benefit of the judiciary and the public service.[73] Second, a bottom-up exchange of national decisions applying EU law is emerging. The exchange is horizontally driven, established either by national-based judicial networks,[74] or by commercial enterprises[75] or, sometimes, by judicial 'self-posting', ie, information provided by the submitting jurisdictions themselves freely on their websites.[76] The

[72] The Association developed, in agreement with the Research and Documentation Department of the Court, a database of national decisions applying EU law. The database is called Dec.Nat. and is accessible at the website of the Association (www.juradmin.eu). Unfortunately, the database is not interlinked with the Court's own database (CVRIA).

[73] This leads to a procedurally somewhat intriguing situation when information about the ongoing judicial business before the Court is in fact supplied to the national court by one of the parties to the proceedings before the Court (the Member State and its representatives), which may often also be a party in the original proceedings before the national court.

[74] For instance, the already mentioned Association of Councils of State and the Supreme Administrative Jurisdictions runs apart from the Dec.Nat. (above n 72) also the JuriFast database. The latter provides information on cases in which national supreme administrative jurisdictions applied EU law or in which they submitted requests for a preliminary ruling for the benefit of other members of the Association. The data and case summaries are provided directly by the member courts.

[75] Notably CASELEX and other databases.

[76] For example the Czech Supreme Administrative Court (www.nssoud.cz) or the Polish Supreme Administrative Court (www.nsa.gov.pl) publish on their websites all requests for preliminary rulings submitted by national administrative courts, together with referring questions and final national decisions.

Court itself, which has the natural position and potential for becoming the genuine information hub in this respect, is conspicuously silent, or even rather ideologically hostile to access and information exchange in relation to its judicial work.[77]

This situation is regrettable. The question is whether the issue of access to information and its exchange could be at least generalised to provide a broader picture of the current balance in initiative in between European courts, ie, the Court and national courts. In a contribution written six years ago, Hjalte Rasmussen pointed out that, in contrast to its pro-active and rich reports producing activities before and after the Nice Treaty, in more recent years the Court has fallen silent. He traced this development back to what he called a post-2005 crisis, where 'a major cause for the Court's silence could in fact be that its internal culture has been severely affected by the ideological and enlargement stalemate'.[78] The suggestions made by the author of this chapter in reply played down the ideological element and stressed the practical difficulties resulting from the changes in the Court's structure following the Nice Treaty and in particular the large personnel intake following the 2004 and 2007 enlargements.[79] Can, however, such an explanation still be valid eight years after the 2004 enlargement? Or was Rasmussen right in suggesting that the reasons for the change in attitude are ideological, not practical?

Whatever the reasons might eventually be determined to be, it is suggested that the initiative and activity void created by the Court turning silent on reforms and further evolution of the EU legal system[80] has been gradually and partially perhaps filled by other actors, inter alia, also by a number of national judicial associations and networks.[81] In such networks and settings, however, the

[77] By the way of analogy, contrast the ideological approaches chosen in relation to the public access to pleadings already submitted to a court by, on the one hand, the Court in Joined Cases C-514/07 P and C-528/07 P *Sweden and API v Commission* [2010] ECR I-8533, and on the other, the European Court of Human Rights in *Társaság a Szabadságjogokért v Hungary*, Judgment of 14 April 2009, App No 37374/05.

[78] H Rasmussen, 'Present and Future European Judicial Problems after Enlargement and the Post-2005 Ideological Revolt' (2007) 44 *CML Rev* 1661, 1665.

[79] M Bobek, 'Learning to Talk: Preliminary Rulings, the Courts of the New Member States and the Court of Justice' (2008) 45 *CML Rev* 1611, 1636–37.

[80] Or rather just defensive, with the only public contribution over the last few years prompted by the need to define (and defend) its own position vis-a-vis the proposed accession of the EU to the European Convention – *cf* the 'Discussion document of the Court of Justice of the European Union on certain aspects of the accession of the European Union to the European Convention for the Protection of Human Rights and Fundamental Freedoms' of 5 May 2010, accessible at: curia.europa.eu.

[81] Three key judicial associations should be mentioned in this respect. For administrative justice, it is the (already several times mentioned) Association of the Councils of State and Supreme Administrative Jurisdictions of the European Union (www.juradmin.eu); the European association for supreme courts of general jurisdiction is the Network of Presidents of the Supreme Judicial Courts of the Member States of the European Union (www.network-presidents.eu); the organisational platform for the cooperation of the European constitutional jurisdictions is the Conference of the European Constitutional Courts (www.confcoconsteu.org). An additional forum for constitutional matters is also provided by the Venice Commission (www.venice.coe.int). Further, see eg M Claes and M de Visser, 'Are You Networked Yet? On Dialogues in European Judicial Networks' (2012) 8 *Utrecht Law Review* 100.

Court is not the agent, but just an observer or perhaps a privileged participator. This may, in itself, not be a bad thing; quite the contrary: suggestions for changes in the EU legal landscape will surely enjoy greater national legitimacy if coming from national courts and not simply being ordained from the top down. At the same time, however, they may also demonstrate certain shifts in the position of the Court and its perception amongst national courts.[82]

B The Procedure

The *procedure* on preliminary rulings is in general one of the strong legitimising elements of the Court and its case law from the point of view of national courts. Their voice, or more precisely the voice of the submitting court itself, is determinative. It is the national court that frames and submits the question, having the decisive say in what the Court will be deciding upon. Even if it is open to the Court to occasionally reformulate the question asked (aka '*what the national court is essentially asking is*'), the Court will always be bound by the facts and the way in which these are interpreted by the national court, as well as the picture it receives from the national court about the interpretation of national law.

There are, however, two finer points concerning national courts' participation in the procedure on preliminary ruling which should be mentioned. First, once the national court submits its question, it loses contact with the case, as well as the Court of Justice itself, unless the Court asks later on for clarification with respect to the question submitted. The fact that the voice of national court(s) is not heard later on in further stages of the preliminary rulings procedure has sometimes been mentioned as a problem. This was the case in particular with respect to the hearing before the Court or even deliberations of the Court, in which knowing a little more about national law or factual situation in the original case could be beneficial. Moreover, there would also be the pedagogical and legitimacy-enhancing element. In this way, the Court could have reached its decision with direct assistance from the national judge. The national courts and judges would thus obtain direct voice and participation in the Court's decision-making.

With the ever increasing case load of the Court, the idea that a national judge would be asked to come along and present views to the Court, in whatever form, became gradually unfeasible. Today, it is not even mentioned any more as one of the options for the potential future preliminary rulings procedure reforms.[83] Perhaps rightly so; apart from the indeed considerable logistic difficulties, one may also doubt whether such reform would be constitutionally

[82] Further see also AWH Meij, 'Circles of Coherence: On Unity of Case-Law in the Context of Globalisation' (2010) 6 *European Constitutional Law Review* 84, 93 and 98–99.

[83] Overview of the recent debates provided by, eg, Broberg and Fenger, above n 39, 25–36. See also Editorial Comments: 'Delivering Justice – Small and Bigger Steps at the ECJ' (2011) 48 *CML Rev* 987.

sound. The national court has had its (quite considerable) opportunity to shape the opinion of the Court through its framing of the preliminary ruling question. If, in addition to that, the same judge were allowed to further influence the opinion of the Court in person, the preliminary ruling procedure might be running the danger of becoming too much of individual national judges seeking to rubber stamp their particular views and causes, instead of a way of finding a more universally acceptable solution, applicable and transferable to all the other courts in the Union, detached from the particularities of national solutions, disputes and contexts. On the other hand, the overall legitimacy-enhancing potential of national judicial participation in the decision-making of the Court is surely relevant. It could, however, be realised in a somewhat different way.[84]

Second, the fact that the voice of one national court submitting the original request for a preliminary ruling was amply listened to does not necessarily mean that other national courts also have the impression that their voices are being heard. This problem emerges in a particular setting, ie, in cases in which the preliminary ruling procedure is used as a tool for lower courts to voice their disagreement with decisions of their superior courts.

Disagreement of a similar sort can be voiced in a number of ways. In the more polished and stable cultural environments, such disagreement is only occasional and limited to substantive questions. If strongly compelled, a lower court may submit a request for a preliminary ruling, raising the substantive issue on which it disagrees with its superior court, but framing it as a general question of interpretation of EU law, not primarily as a way of disagreeing with its superior court. Once the decision of the Court arrives, it is implemented and all courts will silently agree on modifying their case law accordingly. There is thus no open, direct attack on the authority of the national superior court.

In the less polished and stable environments, the preliminary ruling procedure may become the tool for direct and open attack on the authority of the superior courts, and the Court an unfortunate hostage to national judicial feuds. Sadly, a number of requests for preliminary rulings coming from the new Member States which joined the Union in 2004 and 2007 fall rather into the second category.[85] Such cases, irrespective of their outcome, might pose a problem in terms of procedure and its overall legitimacy amongst other national courts: the request for a preliminary ruling will be submitted by a lower court seeking to challenge the case law of its superior court. In doing so, the referring court will present the facts and national law to the Court in a way favouring the outcome it wishes the Court to reach. There might also, however, be other

[84] Discussed below in IV.C.

[85] An illustrative list might include: Case C-328/04 *Vajnai* [2005] ECR I-8577; Case C-302/06 *Koval'ský* [2007] ECR I-11; Case C-173/09 *Elchinov*, Judgment of 5 October 2010, not yet reported; Case C-399/09 *Landtová*, Judgment of 22 June 2011, not yet reported; Case C-17/10 *Toshiba*, Judgment of 14 February 2012, not yet reported; Case C-416/10 *Křižan*, Judgment of 15 January 2013, not yet reported. Case C-210/06 *Cartesio*, above n 35, could also be more broadly included into this category.

possible interpretation of the same facts and national law, which the superior court might offer if given the chance to do so.

There are two significant recent cases in which this problem became apparent: *Melki and Abdeli*[86] and *Landtová*.[87] Both cases were launched by national supreme jurisdictions as a way of voicing their disagreement. In the first case, the French *Cour de cassation* (Court of Cassation) essentially disagreed with new French legislation giving the *Conseil constitutionnel* (Constitutional Council) the power to hear priority questions on constitutionality. In the second case, the Czech *Nejvyšší správní soud* (Supreme Administrative Court) challenged the established case law of the *Ústavní soud* (Constitutional Court) making the payment of a pension supplement for workers conditional upon the Czech citizenship and residency requirement. Both national supreme courts presented their case to the Court in certain way, so as to arguably favour the outcome they wished the Court to reach. However, in *Melki and Abdeli,* the original interpretation offered by the *Cour de cassation* was somewhat corrected by the observation submitted by the French and Belgian Governments, who relied on the position taken in the meantime by the *Conseil constitutionnel*.[88] Thus, the *Conseil constitutionnel*, although not being entitled to submit observations to the Court in a question which directly concerned it, was heard indirectly, through the observations submitted by national governments.

The second case, *Landtová*, had a somewhat less lucky course of procedure and outcome. The Czech Agent submitting observations on behalf of the Czech Government had been clearly instructed to defend the position of the government, which was the same as that of the Czech administrative courts and the *Nejvyšší správní soud* which submitted the request for a preliminary ruling: that the pension supplement based on nationality in question was indeed in violation of EU law. Thus, the opinion of the *Ústavní soud*, which was in fact under direct and open attack in proceedings before the Court, was not represented. After becoming aware of this fact, especially through the Opinion of AG Cruz Villalón,[89] the *Ústavní soud* wished to communicate its views to the Court of Justice. It believed that the AG's Opinion contained a number of inaccuracies and mistakes due to the way in which the reference by the *Nejvyšší správní soud* was framed. The *Ústavní soud* thus drafted a statement reproducing its position and arguments, put it into a letter and sent it to the Court. The registry of the Court, instructed by the president of the chamber deciding the case, put the letter into an envelope and sent it straight back to the *Ústavní soud*, noting in its reply that 'members of the Court do not correspond with third persons regarding cases that have been submitted to the Court'.[90] In reaction to the ensuing

[86] Joined Cases C-188/10 and C-189/10 *Melki and Abdeli* [2010] ECR I-5667.

[87] *Landtová*, above n 85.

[88] *Melki and Abdeli*, above n 86, paras 33–36 and 48–51.

[89] Opinion of AG Cruz Villalón of 3 March 2011 in *Landtová*, above n 85.

[90] Quoted from the decision of the Ústavní soud in case Pl. ÚS 5/12 of 31 January 2012, not yet reported, point VII in fine. An English translation of the decision is available at the website of the Ústavní soud at: www.usoud.cz.

decision of the Court in *Landtová*, the *Ústavní soud* declared in its next judgment (on the same matter but in relation to a different person) the decision of the Court as to be ultra vires and not to be followed by Czech courts and public authorities.[91]

On its merits, the decision of the Czech *Ústavní soud* is plainly wrong. The *Ústavní soud* demonstrated a very peculiar (mis)understanding of the procedure before the Court and its role in it. It believed, inter alia, that it was a party with a right to be heard in the Court and that by not hearing it, the Court of Justice violated the *Ústavní soud*'s right to a fair trial [sic!]. There is an ongoing debate about the extent to which moral persons benefit from human rights protection; to state that a constitutional court, ie, an organ of the state, has constitutionally guaranteed rights, is quite a groundbreaking novelty. The *Ústavní soud* also assumed that, in the procedure on preliminary rulings, the European Commission appears as amicus curiae before the Court.[92] At the same time, the *Ústavní soud* somewhat forgot that nothing prevented it from submitting a request for a preliminary ruling itself, explaining to the Court the situation in full and inviting it to reconsider.[93] Beyond all these obvious misconceptions, there emerges a subtext picture of a vexed court, which reacts bluntly and entirely disproportionately to a very undiplomatic step by the Court. With unassailable kindergarten logic, the *Ústavní soud*, which allowed its judicial ego to take over any sense or reason, is essentially saying: if you do not want to talk to us, we will not talk to you either and this is what we will do to you.

The lesson to be learned from this comedy of errors for the legitimacy of the preliminary ruling procedure is perhaps the following. There is little doubt that the Court will continue to atomise national judicial hierarchies by stating that lower national courts are not bound by the case law of national superior courts if they deem it incompatible with EU law (the *Elchinov* scenario)[94] and that they cannot in any way be prevented from referring to the Court by their national superior courts (the *Cartesio* scenario).[95] This follows from the way in which the Court currently perceives its function: as a genuine European supreme jurisdiction, still in the 'construction stage', thus allowing for direct access from any echelon of national judicial hierarchy, unfiltered by national hierarchies or remedies. Whether or not this is wise, especially in the longer

[91] Decision of plenary court in case Pl. ÚS 5/12 of 31 January 2012, not yet reported.

[92] ibid, point VII in fine.

[93] Which would be by the way in line with the position taken by the German *Bundesverfassungsgericht* [Federal Constitutional Court] in BVerfG, 2 BvR 2661/06 of 6 July 2010, para 60, whom the Czech *Ústavní soud* otherwise likes to quote extensively, including in the present decision. The *Ústavní soud* has, however, strangely missed this point.

[94] Every lower national court can disapply national law based on its own assessment, ie, it is under no obligation to submit a request for a preliminary ruling on this issue first – see *Kücükdeveci*, above n 41, paras 54–55, or *Elchinov*, above n 85, para 28.

[95] Even if there appeared to be hardly any evidence that this would indeed be the case. See critically M Bobek, '*Cartesio* – Appeals against an Order to Refer under Article 234 (2) EC Treaty Revisited' (2010) 29 *Civil Justice Quarterly* 307.

term, might be open to debate,[96] but there is no doubt that the current system and its policy are set in this direction. If that is indeed the case, then the Court should also allow – either by amending its Rules of Procedure or by a mere change in policy regarding amicus curiae briefs – for national dissenting voices to be heard in such situations. Current Rules of Procedure, essentially designed for intergovernmental types of disputes, are no longer appropriate once the preliminary rulings procedure has moved on to adjudicate more and more on intra-state judicial quarrels. If it is clear that a request for a preliminary ruling submitted by a national court is nothing other than a challenge to a position of national superior courts, would it be such a problem to simply invite the national superior court to submit observations as well? A lot, in terms of support, acceptance and overall legitimacy from the side of the other national courts, can be potentially achieved by modifying just a little. Failing to do so, the Court is likely to encounter more unnecessary resistance or even open defiance in the future, especially taking into account that the number of cases (in)directly challenging national judicial hierarchies does not appear to be diminishing.

C Composition and Appointment

There is no doubt that, from whatever point of view, including that of national courts, members of the Court of Justice in general enjoy a high degree of recognition and expertise-derived legitimacy. There are, however, two aspects which are worth elaborating upon in greater detail with respect to the composition of the Court. First is the recurring theme of disconnection from national judicial practice and reality and ways in which such disconnection could be bridged. Second is the question of whether institutional changes in judicial appointments to the Court of Justice and the work of the Panel established pursuant to Article 255 TFEU, introduced by the Lisbon Treaty, might change anything in national judicial perception of the legitimacy of the entire process.

The disconnect between the Court and national courts could be said to include two elements: distance and, to some extent, professional background. The distance-related element of this disconnection has already been discussed above: a supranational European jurisdiction will, by definition, perceive issues differently from national courts trapped in their national perceptions, dogmas and routines. As far as the professional background-related disconnection is concerned – seen from the vantage point of national courts – the Court of Justice is largely an 'academic' court. It is composed of high profile quality

[96] Critically Komárek, above n 30. Questioning this policy with respect to special position of national constitutional courts see Bobek, 'The Impact of the European Mandate', above n 12, 287–308.

experts with, however, chiefly academic rather than judicial professional backgrounds.[97]

Analytical academic minds that are able to rise above the narrow national routine and to see a broader European picture are no doubt essential for the work of the Court. At the same time, however, the rising above should not amount to losing touch with the ground. Metaphorically speaking, a good court, as with any other working place, should ideally have a sensible portion of both stonemasons as well as master builders.[98] Although our natural preference is to venerate the latter and omit the contribution of the former, both are essential for building a cathedral. Stonemasons without master builders will not be able to construe much more than a plain stone church. Conversely, blueprint dreams of master builders are very likely to remain on paper only if not being continuously checked by a critical and realistic eye, which knows what can currently and feasibly be built.

If academic lawyers are equated with master builders and professional judges with stonemasons, the meaning of the metaphor becomes plain. National judges, faced with unfeasible decisions of the Court and frustrated by the fact that they cannot reasonably comply, start making connections between the composition of the Court and the decisions it passes, often coming to the conclusion that such an unrealistic and impossible decision could only have been passed by someone who lives in an ivory tower and has never seen a normal (national) court from the inside. Questions start being asked. Do they actually know how a normal court works? Have they thought through the consequences and the ways in which this could be reasonably implemented? Or are the dreams of master builders not to be tainted with gravity and basic laws of physics?

This is obviously a one-sided perception. Frequently, the national judicial grumbling fails to discriminate between what is indeed unfeasible and what is just new and/or inconvenient to the established national judicial routines. This does not mean, at the same time, that such opinions would not be voiced at the national level, typically rather informally, in closed judicial discussions or seminars. Open disagreement is quite rare, at least at the European level.[99] The fact that very little open national opposition can be detected might yet again serve as an indirect confirmation of the size of the silent elephant. Only those who know

[97] Amongst the present 35 members of the Court of Justice (27 Judges and 8 Advocates General combined), 11 mention in their official biographies online (curia.europa.eu) at least some judicial experience in national ordinary courts prior to their appointment. A further three members of the Court, although having primarily academic professional backgrounds, have prior judicial experience from national constitutional courts. The majority of current Court members, however, have no prior national judicial experience. They have either an academic or civil service background, or frequently both.

[98] There is the possibility of a master builder who is at the same time also an excellent stonemason, ie, of an architect being a good craftsman as well. Unfortunately, the incidence of this species tends to be quite rare.

[99] For an exception confirming the rule in English, see notably PJ Wattel, 'Köbler, CILFIT and Welthgrove: We Can't Go On Meeting Like This' (2004) 41 *CML Rev* 177 or, in much more diplomatic and balanced tone, Lady Justice Arden, above n 15.

and who care about EU law are ever likely to openly disagree. The silent masses have no need to openly voice their disagreement. The silent judicial masses just do not care.

There are ways in which the personal legitimacy of a distant high jurisdiction perceived as disconnected might be increased. To require that any candidate for appointment to the Court must have a national judicial experience is surely not the way. First, it has no foundation in the Treaties themselves.[100] Second, the selection and appointment to the Court is first nation-specific and secondly Euro-political in the Council, thus very unlikely to embrace one set of requirements and vision for the suitable candidates. Third and foremost, however, a good court should be a mixture of people from various professional backgrounds: again, it is only in the symbiotic cooperation between stonemasons as well as master builders that elegant cathedrals come to life.

If a greater connection to national judiciaries is unlikely to be realised at the level of members of the Court, an alternative could be the Court's staff, in particular at the level of legal secretaries (*référendaires*). Looking at the practice of a number of Continental national highest jurisdictions, this indeed appears to be a way of bridging, at least to some extent, the disconnection. In a number of Continental judicial systems, lower court judges can, for certain period of time (months, up to several years) be seconded to the national high jurisdiction in order to work as legal secretaries.[101] Their work with and for the higher jurisdiction serves two purposes: those of the receiving institution as well as of the individual judge. First and foremost, both parties mutually socialise: in the decision-making of the high jurisdiction, the voice, views and concerns of those 'down there' are listened to and considered when making decisions. The high jurisdiction thus receives necessary feedback on what it is doing and how it is perceived. At the same time, by taking part in the decision-making process and seeing the problem from the point of view of the higher jurisdiction, the individual judge also learns that there might be (understandable) reasons for which the view of the high jurisdiction differs, following broader and more general aims. This knowledge and experience transfer not only increases the quality of the decision-making of the institution, but also enhances its legitimacy amongst the lower court judges. Not only did they 'listen to one of us', 'we' also, to some extent, participated in the decision-making.

Unfortunately, this type of personal exchange between the Court and national courts is currently little used.[102] This fact is quite striking in comparison to other Union institutions, in particular the Commission, but also the Council

[100] *cf* the minimalist requirements in Art 253 TFEU.

[101] Named differently in different systems, for instance, '*wissenschaftliche Mitarbeiter*'; '*juges référendaires*'; stagiaires, seconded magistrates or judges etc.

[102] The very parameter of such exchange is its length; the occasional shorter (typically in terms of days or weeks) stage or visit of national judges to the Court are thus, useful and helpful as they are, something different from the more lasting (in terms of months or rather years) type of judicial exchange described here.

and the Parliament, which rely on national seconded civil servants.[103] True, to examine the professional background of current legal secretaries at the Court in a representative and comprehensive way is impossible. No biographical data is openly accessible and very little past research appears to have been done on *référendaires* in the Court and their contribution to the formation of the case law.[104] From the personal knowledge of the author of this contribution, however, there appear to be only few *référendaires* with a judicial (or any national practitioner's, for that matter) background.[105] The typical profile of a *référendaire* at the Court is either a junior academic lawyer or a civil servant, coming from within other departments of the Court itself or other Union institutions. The currently prevailing professional background of *référendaires* at the Court thus hardly helps in bridging the disconnection with national courts and judicial realities in the Member States.

Taking into account the positive experience and enhanced legitimacy for the supreme jurisdiction of such judicial secondments at the national levels, could it perhaps not be helpful to proactively look for greater involvement of national judges as *référendaires* at the Court in the future? True, implementation of this suggestion would be difficult,[106] but the benefits would be considerable. Apart from all the other legitimacy enhancing consequences in national judiciaries such development would have, one stands out with respect to the main motif of

[103] According to the May 2012 issue of the *Clenad* newsletter (*Clenad* is *Comité de Liaison des Experts Nationaux Détachés*), there are approximately 1100 seconded national experts currently working in the European Commission alone (available online at: www.clenad.eu).

[104] In contrast with, for instance, by now a number of studies carried out with respect to US Supreme Court law clerks in, eg, TC Peppers, *Courtiers of the Marble Palace: The Rise and Influence of the Supreme Court Law Clerk* (Stanford, Stanford University Press, 2006); A Ward and DL Weiden, *Sorcerers' Apprentices: 100 Years of Law Clerks at the United States Supreme Court* (New York, NYU Press, 2006).

[105] With the few exceptions confirming the rule coming, for linguistic reasons, almost exclusively from France or Belgium.

[106] It is clear that within the set of all the practical difficulties, there is one which stands out: the question of language. The Court maintains, as the last EU institution today, French as its only internal working and drafting language. Over the last decade, however, and in particular as a consequence of the 2004 enlargement, the French language started having difficulty in maintaining its position as a second foreign language within the European Union. The second foreign language in Central and Eastern European new Member States is in fact German. This became gradually reflected also within other EU institutions: an illustration of the shift might be provided by the work statistics of Commission's DG for Translation. Whereas in 1997, 45.4% of texts translated by the DG for Translation were originally drafted in English and 40.4% in French (the remaining 14.2% in other languages), in 2008, 72.5% of texts were drafted in English and only 11.8% in French (with the remaining 15.7% drafted in other languages, in particular German and Dutch) – in Information Booklet *Translating for a Multilingual Community* (Luxembourg, Office for Official Publications, 2009) 6.

Within such settings, it might be indeed difficult to find appropriately qualified national judges from outside France and Belgium who would be able to draft decisions in French. Today, exclusivity of French within the Court leads to certain institutional isolation, as it considerably narrows the pool of suitable *référendaires* candidates. On the other hand, this is just a speculation, as the Court advertises vacancies for positions of *référendaires* internally only, if at all. It can therefore hardly be categorically stated that 'there are no suitable candidates in national judiciaries' if no one has ever openly tried to get some.

this contribution: an ongoing and in-built feasibility and reality check for the Court's case law, a critical feedback on practicability of a solution and the possibility of its implementation in normal day-to-day judicial business in a Member State's court.

Finally, since the entry into force of the Treaty of Lisbon, Article 255 TFEU has modified the appointment process to the Court. A Panel has been set up, whose task is to 'give an opinion on candidates' suitability to perform the duties of Judge and Advocate-General of the Court of Justice and the General Court before the governments of the Member States make the appointments' (Article 255 TFEU). The second indent of the same Article foresees that 'the panel shall comprise seven persons chosen from among former members of the Court of Justice and the General Court, members of national supreme courts and lawyers of recognised competence, one of whom shall be proposed by the European Parliament'.

Taking into account that the provision of Article 255 TFEU foresees composition of the Panel of candidates from three potential sets of backgrounds (former EU judges; judges of national supreme courts; other lawyers of recognised competence) it might have been believed that the Panel will chiefly be composed of former EU judges, who are also mentioned as the first potential set of members. In exercising his power under Article 255 TFEU, last sentence, the President of the Court of Justice, however, suggested a composition of the Panel in which four out of seven judges are senior national judges[107] and the other two are former EU judges. The remaining member of the Panel is a former member of the European Parliament, currently a lawyer in Madrid, put forward by the President of the European Parliament.[108]

From the point of view of the legitimacy of the selection process to the Union courts in the eyes of national judges, such a step can only be commended. Strong participation of representatives of national judiciaries in the confirmation process also creates a sensible counterbalance to the political appointment process in the Council. It furthermore adds a unifying element to the rather varied selection mechanism in the individual Member States. It may be expected that such participation could increase the legitimacy of entire process in the eyes of national judges.

Whether or not the activity of the Panel will eventually meet these expectations is to some extent too early to state. In the first three years of the functioning of the Panel, two slightly different questions concerning its institutional design nonetheless became apparent. First, the hearings of the Panel are not

[107] Respectively: the Vice-President of the French Council of State; a Member of the Supreme Court of the UK; the President of the Supreme Court of Denmark; and the President of the Hungarian Constitutional Court.

[108] See, 'Recommendation concerning the composition of the panel provided for in Article 255 TFEU', document of the Council No 5932/10 of 2 February 2010. The composition of the Panel was approved as suggested by the President of the Court by a Council Decision of 25 February 2010, published in [2010] OJ L50/20.

public and the opinion given on the suitability of the candidate is confidential, communicated only to the representatives of the Member States' governments.[109] On the one hand, it is not difficult to understand such confidentiality based on the concerns for the protection of the personal reputations of the candidates. No one would wish to read a public indictment of one's unsuitability for a high office, put in whatever diplomatic terms, especially after being already selected at the national level. On the other hand, however, in being secretive, the Panel fails to fulfil its arguably basic role in publicly setting quality standards for EU courts and thus enhancing their standing and legitimacy. With the exception of few national high civil servants who see confidential Council documents, no one has any idea why a national candidate received a negative opinion. Thus, with tongue-in-cheek, one could suggest that the style of the work of the Panel represents the traditional quintessence of the Union's executive decision-making: absence of public debate, transparency, accountability and ensuing lacking democratic legitimacy are substituted with high quality expert composition of the decision-making body and technocratic legitimacy.

The Panel sought to counter these problems by publishing general reports of its activity.[110] The reports set out, in an abstract and general way, the Panel's expectations and requirements, based on past decisions, from which no individual information is discernible, but which should provide future guidance for candidates and the public.

By laying down more detailed criteria by which it evaluates the candidates, the Panel appears to have presently run into a second type of problem; namely, the reproaches that it is adding, at its will, new criteria that are not provided for anywhere in the Treaties. It is true that, when contrasting the very general criteria in the Treaty itself[111] with the elaborate set of requirements set by the Panel,[112] the Panel went way beyond the Treaties. On the other hand, was not the very purpose of establishing the Panel the fleshing out of further and more stringent requirements for the function of judges and Advocates General in Union courts,

[109] See Arts 7 and 8 of the 'Operating rules of the panel provided for in Article 255 TFEU', published as Annex to the Council Decision No 2010/124/EU relating to the operating rules of the panel provided for in Art 255 of the Treaty on the Functioning of the European Union [2010] OJ L50/18.

[110] 'Activity Report of the Panel Provided for by Article 255 of the Treaty on the Functioning of the European Union', document of the Council No 6509/11 of 17 February 2011 and (Second) 'Activity Report of the Panel Provided for by Article 255 of the Treaty on the Functioning of the European Union', document of the Council No 5091/13 of 22 January 2013. See also J-M Sauvé, 'Le rôle du comité 255 dans la sélection du juge de l'Union' in *The Court of Justice and the Construction of Europe: Analyses and Perspectives on Sixty Years of Case-law* (Berlin, Springer, 2013) 99–119.

[111] Art 253 TFEU: 'The Judges and Advocates-General of the Court of Justice shall be chosen from persons whose independence is beyond doubt and who possess the qualifications required for appointment to the highest judicial offices in their respective countries or who are jurisconsults of recognised competence'.

[112] See, in particular, point III in the First Activity Report, which sets out six elements of evaluation of candidates for first term of office: legal competence, including basic knowledge of EU law; professional experience; ability to exercise judicial office; guarantees as to impartiality and independence; linguistic capacity; ability to work in an international environment where more legal traditions are present.

so as to avoid past negative experience with Member States appointing candidates with not only no knowledge of EU law, and/or very little capacity to work in an international environment, but even without any decent knowledge of French and English?

V. CONCLUSION: MINDING THE GAP AND THE VALUE OF DISAGREEMENT

This contribution examined three aspects of the legitimacy of the Court of Justice of the EU and its case law as to their feasibility from the vantage point of national courts. First, with respect to individual decisions of the Court, it was suggested that, perhaps contrary to academic beliefs, when assessed against the needs and expectations of national judges, the current standard of reasoning of the Court does not generally raise too much cause for concern. What national judges expect from the Court in terms of output is not an abundance of reasons, but feasible and practical judicial reasons, clearly discernible, free of contradictions and reversals, which can be implemented at the national level.

Second, as far as the overall acceptance and compliance with case law of the Court in national courts is concerned, this contribution strongly cautioned against mistaking overall silence and absence of open revolts for compliance and the national judicial embracing of the European mandate. It further explained why such assumed but hardly proven belief of compliance is dangerous for the viability of the European judicial project. Disconnection and irresponsiveness lead to social irrelevance. Irrelevance and inability to predict and govern behaviour of addresses of regulation lead to loss of legitimacy.

Third, three aspects of the institutional design and procedure of the Court were examined, yet again, from the point of view of national judges. Both the Court as well as national courts could certainly perform better if the Court shared more of the available information with its national counterparts. Furthermore, if the Court wishes to remain on its current atomising-national-judicial-hierarchies-course, it should become more accommodating and be ready to listen to opposing national judicial voices within the preliminary rulings procedure. Finally, the Court could try to bridge some of its distance from national judiciaries and ensuing disconnection by better integrating national judges into its staff, who could provide experience, relevant practice-oriented feedback on some of its constructs and endeavours and, in the end, also greater legitimacy to its decision-making in the eyes of national judges.

On the whole, in spite of being critical of some aspects of the Court's case law, the overall conclusion of this contribution is far from stating that the Court's case law would be considered illegitimate by national courts. When it provides clear, feasible and non-contradictory guidance, at least those national judges who care are happy to follow the Court. Problems emerge when the Court starts disregarding the limits of any reasonable national judicial potential and allows sweeping and inconsiderate one-sided assertion of dominance of EU interest. Shapeless, all-leading *effet utile* trumps any legitimate national courts' interests, judicial potential, as well as feasibility and practical reason. In such instances, the Court's case law is driven into social irrelevance and is typically not followed.

Lastly, in addition to the suggestions made in the previous parts of this contribution, problems of a similar sort can also be avoided, or at least kept to a minimum, with the help of critical EU scholarship that does not limit itself to restating the Luxembourg orthodoxy in a legalistic manner, but is ready and able to comparatively engage with the practice and reality of national systems. For this purpose, critical voices, academic as well as (or especially) judicial, are indispensable. They should not be condescendingly discarded as those who are just uninformed, mistaken or have not 'yet seen the light', but should be attentively listened to. They may help in redefining and reshaping the case law of the Court and its approach for the future, to render it more relevant, responsive to national judicial concerns and thus narrow the disconnection gap. Only those who care speak up. They may disagree with a particular point, but the overall European project is dear to them, so they take pains to disagree openly. The danger (and the genuine opponent) is the silent masses that could not care less.

However, in contrast to earlier stages of EU law scholarship, it is perhaps no longer believed that being critical of some aspects of EU law or the Court and its case law automatically means being 'against the EU'. For most of the younger generations of lawyers in Europe today, certainly those on the European Continent, the relevant question is arguably no longer 'EU or not EU' but 'what type of EU'. It is a choice within, not either/or. In such settings, paraphrasing immortal dialogues between Jim Hacker MP and Sir Humphrey Appleby in 'Yes, Minister', one might be 'pro-Europe' but occasionally 'against Brussels' (or 'against Luxembourg', for that matter). Conversely, those who are always 'pro-Brussels' (or 'pro-Luxembourg') might, in the end, in fact be 'against Europe'.[113]

[113] '*Yes, Minister*', series 2, episode 5, '*The Devil You Know*', first airing on the BBC on 23 March 1981.

Epilogue: Judging the Judges – Apology and Critique

JHH WEILER

I

IF WE ADOPT a sociological approach to legitimacy, an approach which tries to gauge empirically the measure of acceptability of institutions and regimes, there is no legitimacy crisis in the European Court of Justice. It is widely respected, and rightly so, and its decisions are, we tend to believe, mostly followed – or at least open revolt is rare.[1] If we adopt a normative approach, the picture might be somewhat more complex, but certainly not approaching any measure of crisis. And yet, the very notion of 'legitimacy' – one of the most underspecified concepts in political theory and social science – is most problematic in this context. A bit like sovereignty there is simply not enough agreement to be able to use it in a broadly and meaningfully accepted way.

Yet, this volume is still timely and important. First, for what it is worth, authors using diverse definitions still come out with the same result. The Court is not 'illegitimate'. But more interestingly, for all the loose use of the term legitimacy, it is often a proxy to something no less important: a proxy for factors which enhance or detract from the authority and authoritativeness of judicial decisions and of the Court as an institution or to its normative compliance with our understanding of the proper province of judicial decision making. Indeed, on the normative side, we should be concerned with the appropriateness of the conduct of our principal institutions of governance, of which the Court is one, regardless of its acceptability or popularity. The most evil and normatively illegitimate regimes can be, and in the course of history often have been, wildly popular and acceptable.

What this book is really about, then, is not the grand issue of 'illegitimacy', but rather a more painstaking enquiry into factors which impact authority and authoritativeness and normative hermeneutic propriety. And the question is how complacent we can be in relation to these more modest yet more realistic yardsticks for 'judging' the Court.

[1] See Michal Bobek, ch 8 in this volume, 208 et seq.

The first chapter of this volume, which follows from the editors' general introduction, is authored by Koen Lenaerts, Judge and Vice-President of the European Court of Justice. It is entitled *The Court's Outer and Inner Selves – Exploring the External and Internal Legitimacy of the European Court of Justice.*

The circumstances of this opening chapter are emblematic.

This was a conference to which a broad range of eminent scholars of different jurisdictions were invited to present papers critically examining the Court and its jurisprudence. The idea was not to identify this or that questionable decision, but to examine the case law which might go to the 'legitimacy' of the ECJ. It was no doubt gratifying to the organisers that one of the most brilliant and respected judges on the Court would come to participate and engage with the participants. Lenaerts was, he said, aware of criticisms of the Court. But these, he opined, were based on misunderstandings. He thus wanted to explain. Once he explained, the misunderstandings would be removed and, presumably, with them the criticism. It was, he said, important that we hear this before we engaged in our work. If there was a whiff of condescension in this framing it could be set aside, for this was to be an auspicious beginning for what could be a day and a half of engagement between a prominent sitting judge and some of the keenest scholars of the new generations of European law.

The engagement did not take place. Due to personal circumstances, Judge Lenaerts unfortunately had to leave after the first day of the conference. There could thus not be a sustained discussion of his own paper, nor could he fully engage with the various issues which were raised by this broad array of careful and respectful critics in the subsequent presentations.

This is a pity. I was there as an auditor, keen to hear what a new generation of scholars would have to say on a topic that had not been revisited for some time. The chapters presented and published in this volume do not deal with trivia. As stated, all are rightly dismissive of sweeping 'illegitimacy' talk. But, they do not pick this or that case in which one might not agree with the analysis or result of a decision; they raise, instead, questions which go to the hermeneutics of the Court, its implicit *Weltanschauung*, its method and style of reasoning.

One talks a lot about the importance of dialogue between the ECJ and Member State courts. Here, then, was a chance for a dialogue between a member of the Court and a different interpretative community. Instead, the judge and the critics of the Court ended speaking not so much with each other but mainly at each other, even in this book.[2]

I thought that it might be a good idea to offer at least a partial remedy. If Lenaerts' piece stands as one bookend to this volume, I offer this epilogue as the other bookend, in which I engage directly with his remarkable chapter.[3]

[2] Lenaerts was evidently unable to avail himself of the various chapters reflecting the work of the conference when he revised his chapter for publication.

[3] Only a fool would look for any personal animosity in this exchange. I would not like, however, any mistake to be made about the spirit in which this response is written. It is best captured in the

It is remarkable for at least three reasons.

First and most obviously, it is so because of the author. Lenaerts is rightly respected as one of the truly great scholars of European law. His prowess, where he is second to none and better than most, is his encyclopedic knowledge coupled with a most ingenious synthetic talent. Take any disparate group of cases in any area and put it through the Lenaerts mill, and an illuminating doctrinal map will emerge, often with novel categories and a systemic narrative. He does it with great effect when dealing with the meta-narrative, the EU legal order as a whole as with its arcane minutiae. It is a prowess on display in this chapter. In particular, there is, in this chapter, one specific dimension to his synthetic prowess which is on display – his harmonising skill. It is reminiscent of the great New Testament scholars whose task and skill was to harmonise the disparate accounts, often contradictory, or seemingly contradictory, to be found notably among the Gospel accounts. In the Synoptic Gospels Jesus is put on trial before the Sanhedrin. In John there is no trial, just an interrogation before the Chief Priest. Which account is right? Which is wrong? Enter the harmonising scholars – no one is ever wrong! Read more carefully, think more deeply and there is a way to harmonise the disparate accounts. Lenaerts has a similar facility with the case law of the European Court, as noted on display in his chapter. Contradictions? Read more carefully, think more deeply and they all fit together.

Lenaerts' chapter explores external and internal legitimacy. He sets up the most exacting criteria. External legitimacy turns on the requirement that the Court only interprets and applies the law, saying what the law (already) is. There is a line between law and politics, the crossing over of which renders the decision and the Court illegitimate. Just so.[4]

Internal legitimacy looks, in his words, at the quality of the judicial process. In the EU, where judicial power is shared by the ECJ and national courts, the Court must never encroach on the prerogatives of national courts. Internal legitimacy also turns on the need for judgments to be 'sound' in their legal reasoning; their need to be 'transparent' and easy to understand rather than 'cryptic'. The grounds of the judgment must be strong and convincing and meet the arguments put by the parties. Decisions must be coherent with the rest of the jurisprudence, and based on criteria known in advance.[5]

words of the illustrious medieval commentator of the Bible, a son of Gerona in the Kingdom of Aragon, Nachmanides – a scholar, poet and physician, who was also a great orator and attained fame by his role in the celebrated 1263 *Barcelona Disputatio*. In his introductory verses to his interpretation of Genesis he anticipates an ongoing conflict of views he will have with one of his illustrious predecessors. 'And with Abraham the son of Ezra, We shall have open rebuke and hidden love' writes Nachmanides, which is classically interpreted as indicating that, while he will criticise Ibn Ezra openly, his admiration for his work will not be lessened. I am no Nachmanides, but these beautiful words are apt. Disagreement notwithstanding, among European law scholars Lenaerts remains in my eyes second to none. See the annotation by CB Chavel in Nachmanides, *Commentary on the Torah – Genesis* (New York, Shilo Publishing, 1971) 5, fn 19.

[4] See Koen Lenaerts, ch 1 in this volume, at 13.

[5] See Koen Lenaerts, ch 1 in this volume, at 14.

I have many problems with these criteria, both conceptual and pragmatic, but will state just a few. That line between law and politics begs more questions than it resolves, to state the most obvious. Soundness of legal reasoning is often like beauty, in the eye of the beholder,not an easy tool for meaningful objective assessment.

Be all that as it may, Lenaerts can only be commended for adopting these most exacting criteria. You would think that no court would get a clean bill of health on these criteria, not least the Court of Justice. The ECJ *never* crossed the line between law and politics? Transparent, non-cryptic, soundly reasoned decisions?

Here, then, is the second remarkable thing about the first chapter of this volume. To read Lenaerts, the Court is, well, perfect. It is not simply that it has no major legitimacy problems in the big sense I have discarded at the outset; in said chapter you will not find any factors which might compromise its authority or authoritativeness as an institution. You will not find a single criticism of a single decision of the Court. You will not find a shade of any other criticism of the Court.

Lenaerts tells the meta-story of the legal order – the well narrated tale from *Van Gend & Loos* to fundamental rights – and the Court comes out unblemished. Lenaerts addresses some of the more delicate decisions which have at a minimum raised some eyebrows. There is an answer to everything. Lenaerts addresses explicitly some systemic critique of what he calls internal criticism – all a misunderstanding based on a failure to understand how the Court really works. I hope I am forgiven if I suggest that it has at least the whiff of old style Marxist 'false consciousness'. If you think the Court is less than perfect, it is because we have not explained it well enough, because you do not understand it well enough. This is a truly remarkable apologia.

The third remarkable thing about this chapter is something I have never encountered before. Lenaerts' chapter serves as the substantial opening of this volume. And yet, almost all other contributions in one respect or another refute at least some aspects of the Lenaerts story.

You may read Ján Mazák and Martin Moser's piece on *Adjudication by Reference to General Principles of EU Law*,[6] and wonder about the soundness of legal reasoning, the transparency of the judgments and whether the grounds of the judgment are strong enough to be convincing – all criteria set out by Lenaerts in his explanation of internal legitimacy. Stephen Weatherill's rather devastating analysis of the Court's case law on the internal market[7] says it all in the subtitle: *A Circumloquacious Statement of the Result, Rather than a Reason for Arriving at It?* Jukka Snell in his examination of the Legitimacy of Free Movement Case Law[8] is kind in his final analysis – as one should be. I already indicated that the question of legitimacy is the wrong one to ask. But along the

[6] See Ján Mazák and Martin Moser, ch 2 in this volume.
[7] See Stephen Weatherill, ch 3 in this volume.
[8] See Jukka Snell, ch 4 in this volume.

way he adds plenty to Weatherill's list. Michael Dougan[9] swats off the crass charges of illegitimacy in the field of social welfare and citizenship, but it is doubtful if the Court would pass Lenaerts' criteria on his analysis. Daniel Thym, in an interesting sociological and political analysis of Citizenship, rather than a doctrinal dogmatic one, is nuanced – but also has this to say: 'When it comes to the legislator, the judges are quite dominant: Although they yielded to the legislator in *Förster*, the Court holds much interpretative leeway in regular circumstances, watering down the impact of legislative amendments'.[10] Michal Bobek is entirely sociological and not normative at all. He follows the trend: there is no legitimacy crisis. If one takes the relationship with national courts as one's yardstick, it is a workmanlike relationship where national courts, once they have made a preliminary reference, are happy to follow any clear guidance from the ECJ. But there are interesting words of caution:

> [A]s far as the overall acceptance and compliance with case law of the Court in national courts is concerned, this contribution strongly cautioned against mistaking overall silence and absence of open revolts for compliance and the national judicial embracing of the European mandate. It further explained why such assumed but hardly proven belief of compliance is dangerous for the viability of the European judicial project. Disconnection and irresponsiveness lead to social irrelevance. Irrelevance and inability to predict and govern behaviour of addresses of regulation lead to loss of legitimacy.
>
> [T]hree aspects of the institutional design and procedure of the Court were examined, yet again from the point of view of national judges. Both, the Court as well as national courts could certainly perform better if the Court shared more of the available information with its national counterparts. Furthermore, if the Court wishes to remain on its current atomizing-national-judicial-hierarchies-course, it should become more accommodating in being ready to listen to opposing national judicial voices within the preliminary rulings procedure. Finally, the Court could try to bridge some of its distance from national judiciaries and ensuing disconnection by better integrating into its staff national judges, who could provide experience, relevant practice-oriented feedback on some of its constructs and endeavours and, in the end, also greater legitimacy to its decision-making in the eyes of national judges.[11]

I have never come across an opening chapter to a book which stands so at odds with the book's actual content. And yet, as stated above, there is no direct engagement between the two, in either direction. It is for this reason that I decided to respond to Lenaerts' chapter directly.

I want to make clear two things about my approach. My purpose is not to show that Lenaerts is necessarily wrong in any given argument he makes. And it is certainly not to argue about the correctness or otherwise of the cases discussed in his chapter. In an exploration such as this, the outcomes are mostly beyond the point, as will become clear.

[9] See Michael Dougan, ch 5 in this volume.
[10] See Daniel Thym, ch 6 in this volume, 173–74.
[11] See Michal Bobek, ch 8 in this volume, 233.

What I do hope to show is that on the substance of the arguments many of his explanations raise more questions than they give answers; that the issues, both analytic and normative, are far more complex in almost every instance discussed. No less important is the overall tonality of his piece. He is, as always, hugely courteous and respectful. But the overall complacency of the peace is both breathtaking and demoralising. What are we to make – given the topic of this volume and the original conference – of a chapter which cannot even hint at a single issue on which the Court might do better?

I am sensitive to the constraints of a sitting judge. A judge may decide that, once on the bench, the only engagement with the interpretative communities of his or her jurisdiction is to be through his or her judicial decisions. Many do. Some may think that even if a judge need not eschew altogether extrajudicial engagement in the general area of European law, if a conference is about 'judging the judges', that would be one arena in which one should seize pole position – an arena in which one might not go, at least initially, beyond careful listening, respectful of the maxim *nemo judex in causa sua*.

But if a judge enters the arena of academic discourse generally, dedicated no less than the judicial arena to critical pursuit of the truth, and especially to this arena specifically, I think the discussion about the Court and, indeed, the Court itself, would be better served by an approach more searching, and institutionally a tad more self-sceptical.

Lenaerts' chapter is divided into three parts. He first gives a rapid potted version of the constitutional history of the Union in his characteristically masterful way. He then addresses issues of what he calls external legitimacy by discussing a series of cases touching the relationship between the Court and the legislature and the Member States. He concludes with an analysis of internal legitimacy.

I do not plan to work my way *mano-a-mano* through the piece, but to focus on a few examples, the main purpose of which would be to show that, by his very own criteria, the 'legitimacy' issue is at a minimum far more complex than his text and conclusions would suggest.

II

What is most striking about the historical survey is precisely this very point – the absence of hardly any indications that some of the developments he describes raise complicated issues of legitimacy by his own criteria. The text speaks for itself.

Here is the narrative about external legitimacy at the start of the opening chapter:

> If courts go beyond their duty of saying 'what the law is', they lack legitimacy as they intrude into the political process. By drawing the borderline between law and politics, courts are in fact drawing the contours of their own legitimacy. The imperative need

> for courts to stand behind that line is, by no means, a novel question, but it has accompanied them ever since constitutionalism was born. As Chief Justice Marshall famously articulated more than two hundred years ago, in *Marbury v Madison*, whilst '[i]t is emphatically the province and duty of the Judicial Department to say what the law is', acts of a political nature 'can never be examinable by the Courts'. Drawing the line between law and politics may be seen as a manifestation of the principle of separation of powers which seeks to prevent courts from undermining the prerogatives of the political branches of government and thus, to preserve the 'check and balances' set out by the Founding Fathers. [12]

Now let me contrast this statement with the following centrepiece in the historical analysis:

> [T]he ECJ aimed to safeguard the core of European integration set out in the Treaty by providing solutions to problems that were expected to be tackled by the EU political institutions but were not in practice as the latter could not reach the then necessary consensus. It thus allowed interest-driven litigation to overcome the political deadlock that prevented the completion of the internal market, as free movers sought to tear down barriers to trade that could have been eliminated by EU harmonisation. The principle of mutual recognition defined in *Cassis de Dijon* best encapsulates this line of jurisprudence. It set in turn the stage for the Commission's action plan adopting a 'new approach' to remove obstacles to interstate trade, which, with the adoption of the Single European Act (the 'SEA'), was no longer governed by intergovernmental dynamics given that Member States gave up their right to veto (ex Article 100a EEC, now Article 114 TFEU).[13]

At a minimum there is a tension between these two quotes. It is not an automatic public good, when 'problems which were expected to be tackled by the EU political institutions but were not in practice' are solved by the judicial branch. On its face, at least, it seems to be the kind of intrusion which is frowned upon earlier. In terms of hermeneutic audacity I might not focus so much on parallel functionalism (aka inaccurately mutual recognition) in *Cassis* (which in some respects is a by-product of the principle of proportionality), but on the Rule of Reason which, de facto at least, rewrote then Article 36.

In the same vein Lenaerts deals with the *Francovich* cluster:

> Hence, in a further development of its case-law, the ECJ decided to enhance the effective protection of EU rights by creating new remedies, this time grounded in EU law itself (with cites to Case C-213/89 *Factortame I* [1990] ECR I-2433; Joined Cases C-6/90 and C-9/90 *Francovich and Others* [1991] ECR I-5357; Joined Cases C-46/93 and C-48/93 *Brasserie du Pêcheur and Factortame III* [1996] ECR I-1029).[14]

These cases have probably ended up having far less practical importance than might have been originally thought, hoped or feared. But the hermeneutic credibility of the Court was widely called into question. This passes with no comment in Lenaerts' chapter.

[12] See Koen Lenaerts, ch 1 in this volume, 13 (fns omitted).
[13] ibid, 15–16 (fns omitted).
[14] ibid, 15 (fns omitted).

Undoubtedly, I can live comfortably with the hermeneutics of *Cassis* and even *Francovich*. And I would not make too much of Lenaerts' silence. In fact, he is not so silent since there is a kind of implicit admission about that past line between law and politics when he describes the present. It is part of Lenaerts' thesis that there has been a shift to a 'new paradigm' where the Court is

> less assertive as to the substantive development of EU law. It sees its role primarily as one of upholding the 'check and balances' built into the EU constitutional legal order of States and peoples . . . Overall it displays greater deference to the preferences of the EU legislator or, as the case may be, to those of the Member States.[15]

It does not take too much re-engineering backwards to understand the 'old paradigm' which has now allegedly been replaced. But how really new is the existing paradigm?

III

Lenaerts uses *Test-Achats*[16] and *Sturgeon*[17] as major planks to outline his defence of the contemporary external legitimacy of the Court. In *Test-Achats*, the Court held, against the view of the Council, that allowing some Member States to maintain without temporal limitation an exemption from the rule of unisex premiums and benefits in certain insurance policies was incompatible with the objective of equal treatment between men and women, which was the purpose of the directive in question, and would be incompatible with Articles 21 and 23 of the Charter. In *Sturgeon*, the Court famously held that although the regulation in question awarded compensation only to passengers whose flight was cancelled and as a result of which they suffered a delay of three hours or more, a similar right under similar conditions (three hours' delay or more) would be awarded to passengers whose flight was delayed rather than cancelled.

For Lenaerts, 'a close reading of *Sturgeon* and *Test-Achats* reveals that the ECJ limited itself to applying the principle of equal treatment so as to enhance the objectives pursued by the EU legislator'.[18] This legitimated in his view terminating, against the view of the legislator, a provision unlimited in time according to which Member States could allow differing actuarial assessments of men and women in one case, and writing into the Regulation on passenger compensation, against the views of the Council and the Advocate General a provision protecting passengers in case of delay with the same three-hour delay as in the case of cancellation.

[15] ibid, 16.

[16] Case C-236/09 *Association Belge des Consommateurs Test-Achats ASBL and Others v Conseil des Ministres*, Judgment of 1 March 2011, not yet reported.

[17] Joined Cases C-402/07 and C-432/07 *Sturgeon and Others and Böck v Air France* [2009] ECR I-10923.

[18] See Koen Lenaerts, ch 1 in this volume, 25.

It is not surprising that Lenaerts chose these cases since they seem to call into question his 'new paradigm'.

I want to contexualise both cases in a somewhat different way which might at least call into question the very categorical and confident way in which Lenaerts presents both reasoning and result.

Test-Achats takes us to the territory of gender equality. We understand discrimination as treating the like in an unlike manner and treating the unlike in a like manner. Of course, critical in any analysis of discrimination will be the comparator chosen to define likeness. Through history and in all cultures women have suffered discrimination oftentimes of a profound and harmful manner. Even the Enlightenment and the French Revolution made only little mark on such. Since men and women are biologically different in many ways, and thus 'unlike', it was easy to justify consciously and subconsciously differing treatment, mostly detrimental and harmful to women. Given this history, it is a matter of prudential judgement to treat with great suspicion any instance where gender is the selected comparator for likeness with consequent justification of different treatment of women. In the United States, for example, gender, like race, is treated as a 'suspect class' of comparator, requiring the strictest scrutiny by the courts. This strategy is not without some dangers. Simply to remove gender as a comparator typically results in treating women in the same way as men are treated. But then it is maleness and male sensibilities which define the norm. Women are treated mostly like men, not men like women. It works in most cases, but can be detrimental to women in others. And second, sometimes simply to disregard the biological and other differences may lead to palpable discrimination, by treating the unlike as if they were like. We have separate male and female tennis and soccer and basketball sport competitions for obvious reasons. There gender is legitimately used as comparator. (It is not so clear to me why there are separate male and female chess championships.) Our default, thus, may well be for 'unisex' regulation, but with awareness to these two potential countervailing 'side effects' which might, in the very interest of equality, justify using gender as comparator.

Both health and life insurance are particularly sensitive cases. In different societies and cultures there are statistically marked differences in life expectation between men and women as a class. Typically, women live longer, which in fact for certain policies would result in lower premiums. This is not dispositive as to the question whether we should allow gender to be a comparator in writing insurance. We might, for example, find that working class men live shorter lives than middle or upper middle class; or that whites live longer than blacks, and yet as a matter of normative social policy we may forbid the usage of class or race as insurance comparators. Note that in these two examples to allow the use of race or class as comparators would result in a detriment to socially disadvantaged categories in many societies.

This is what makes the issue of gender in insurance so tricky. Our basic default suspicion of gender as comparator may justify a presumption in favour of unisex insurance regulation. And the requirement that empirical studies be conducted to correlate differences in, say, insurance premiums and veritable actuarial predictions is also fully justified. But should these substantiate a correlation between verifiable actuarial predictions and differing treatment of men and women, there is a hugely delicate and fraught normative question to be taken, especially given the fact that a wholesale shift to unisex regulation may in certain circumstances be to the detriment of women (and the delight of insurers). I think the more plausible reading of the Regulation is that this question was left open, deferred for a later date, because of its delicacy and consequentiality, or even left indefinitely at the discretion of Member States so far as empirical data rather than prejudice informed the actuarial practices.

Lenaerts cites with approval Recital 32 of the *Test-Achats* decision whereby Article 5(2) of Directive 2004/113,

> which enables the Member States in question to maintain without temporal limitation an exemption from the rule of unisex premiums and benefits, works against the achievement of the objective of equal treatment between men and women, which is the purpose of Directive 2004/113, and is incompatible with Articles 21 and 23 of the Charter.

And yet in my humble opinion, this is a colossal *non-sequitur*. For it begs the question whether empirically verified actuarial gender differences should or should not, as a matter of policy, be allowed to serve as comparators. Articles 21 and 23 do not and cannot help in this matter. In fact, depending on how that difficult question is resolved, and normative arguments can be made one way or another, to annul Article 5(2) could have the effect of working against the objective of equal treatment and would violate Articles 21 and 23. Treating the unlike in a like manner is as inimical to equal treatment as treating the like in an unlike manner. There are differences between men and women and it is a deep moral question when we should take them into account in allowing different treatment as in allowing pre-natal leave.

At worst it was highly inappropriate for the Court to arrogate to itself the decision in this matter, the proper forum for which ought to have been democratically accountable politicians. At best, it is unfortunate that this decision was taken by the Court without it would seem, from its decision and from the gloss given to it by Lenaerts, fully grasping the depth of issue involved. To present the decision as simply implementing the teleology of the legislator I find less than convincing, even sad.

There is in this case and others like it a second underlying assumption in Lenaerts' various analyses of the relationship between Court and legislator. It comes into sharp relief in his explanation of the *Sturgeon* decision. The reader will be well advised to re-read the magnificent Opinion of AG Sharpston in comparison with the characteristically cryptic decision of the Court. One does not have to agree with every move, or conclusion, the Advocate General makes to note how much closer she comes to the criteria Lenaerts sets out in his opening paragraphs on the characteristics a judicial decision should have to enjoy legitimacy.

But for present purposes what is more important is the final decision. The Advocate General holds that it should fall to the legislator to decide on the number of waiting hours which would justify compensation in the case of delay rather than cancellation. The Court as we know decided this itself, equating delay with cancellation.

Let me say a word on the merits. From a consumer rights perspective, the reasoning of the Court (and Lenaerts) makes perfect sense. If you are entitled to compensation after three hours in case of cancellation, would it not stand to reason that the same relief will be given in case of a 'merely' delayed flight? What difference does the cause of waiting make? Three stressful hours in a crowded airport are three stressful hours regardless of the cause.

This, of course, is only so if as is so often the case today, we succumb to the enthralment of the culture of rights and look at the legislation through that prism alone. But if the perspective is one of responsibility and duty (of the airlines) – and the 'compensation' to the traveller has as a primary objective, or at least a major objective, the penalisation and deterrence of derelict airlines, it is possible at least to imagine that delay and cancellation might be regarded as involving different degrees of dereliction and thus meriting different degrees of sanction and deterrence – in which case the consumer equivalence perspective loses its determinant force and becomes, at best, one factor to be considered. And if there is any merit in this, and even if there is at least some question that this might be at the source of the differentiation, should not this alone point in the direction of the Advocate General rather than the Court? I come to the same conclusion as above. At worst, this decision should certainly have been left to politically accountable bodies; at best, it would be more reassuring if one had the impression that the Court examined the issue in its true complexity.

But my dissatisfaction with Lenaerts' theorem as regards the relationship between Court and legislator runs deeper. Let us assume that in relation to these two cases my substantive contextualisation and critique are wholly misconceived, as might well be the case.

I think it is fair to say that Lenaerts believes that if the Court can detect 'spot on' what Council (and Parliament) truly intended in any given piece of legislation, and if the solution adopted in this or that facet violated, say, a general principle of law such as equality, then the Court would be doing its duty, rather to 'interpret' it – effectively to amend it – as it did in *Sturgeon*, rather than annul it in whole or in part. After all, what is the harm? If they do not like the judicial decision they can amend it (provided, of course, they do not violate primary Union law).

He does not seem to grasp, or at least does not mention in his chapter, the major impact such decisions have on the political process, given the rules on majority voting (as well as unanimity, where relevant). It is not fanciful to imagine that in a situation such as *Sturgeon* you may have mustered the necessary majority for a regulation which compensated for cancellations but not delays, and would not have had the requisite majority for a regulation which compensated for both. If the Court follows the Lenaerts path rather than the Sharpston path, you may not get the necessary majority to change or even discard the legislation altogether. To put it bluntly, judicial amendment of the type so carefully explained and justified by Lenaerts may result in legislation for which there might not have been a majority at the time of enactment. This could result in very crass interference in political decision-making. There really is a fundamental difference between the following two situations: [A] A court saying to the legislature: for legal reasons you cannot do X, but you can do Y. So X is annulled and you decide if you want to do Y instead; [B] A court saying to the legislature: for legal reasons you cannot do X, but you can do Y. So we will do Y because we think that is what you intended; or because this will cure the legal defect of X.

I would not wish to exclude circumstances in which the strategy advocated by Lenaerts might be justified or at least not harmful, but I would certainly regard it as the exception, and do not share his enthusiasm for it.

I tried to explain above the real and present danger that this type of judicial intervention, even if hermeneutically defensible on some teleological assumption, might end up affecting the actual political process, shifting the burden of majority-voting and thus constituting a major judicial encroachment into the very heart of political decision-making. But even in instances where this is not the case, it is not clear to me that the *political process* is enhanced by the Court mopping up after the legislator creating a moral hazard – a little bit like diligent cite-checkers inadvertently encouraging sloppiness in the principal author of an article. It also shifts responsibility to the Court for activity which should really be in the political province.

In dealing with external legitimacy and the cases he cites,[19] Lenaerts, to use his own words, was focused 'on examining whether the ECJ is committed to standing behind the line that divides "law" from "politics"'. What I think he manages to demonstrate is that the ECJ (and on occasion he himself in his chapter) draws the line that divides 'law' from 'politics'. Once drawn, the Court does indeed stand firmly behind it. Whether that is helpful to an analysis of the kind attempted in this volume is uncertain.

IV

In dealing under this heading with the ECJ and national courts, Lenaerts uses as his centrepiece the *Bressol*[20] case. I can be brief. It is an exemplary case and it makes Lenaerts' point very well – the kind of division of tasks which ensures

[19] As I explained, I see no purpose in walking through every case explained by Lenaerts. A close reading of almost all of them shows considerable complexity.

[20] Case C-73/08 *Bressol and Others v Gouvernement de la Communauté française* [2010] ECR I-2735.

respect and compliance with European Union law, but does not encroach on, for example, the fact finding function of Member State courts.

The question here is: how typical is the case? Is it the rule or the exception? In the much celebrated *Baumbast* case[21] the Court had to decide, inter alia, whether the fact that Mr Baumbast did not have emergency medical insurance was of such a nature as to constitute an unreasonable burden on the public finances of the State (United Kingdom) and thus permit his exclusion seeing that he was no longer a migrant worker. Answering this question would require an empirical analysis no less complex than *Bressol* and the answer could differ from one Member State to another. Some of the parameters which might have to be thrown into the mix would be the average cost of each emergency case; the statistical likelihood of requiring emergency medical assistance; the number of migrant workers who would potentially benefit from such a ruling as well as the state of public finance. What might be not unreasonable for Germany might be unreasonable for Portugal or Greece. A *Bressol* type instruction to the national court would seem to be indicated. Instead, the European Court decided the issue itself (where at least certain elements should have been the province of the national court) and did so in a breathtaking 'guesstimate' with no reference to any hard data.

I would always bow to Lenaerts' encyclopedic knowledge of the case law. Which is the more typical case: *Bressol* or *Baumbast*?

V

The second part of the 'internal legitimacy' concerns '[t]he persuasiveness of the ECJ's reasoning'. Lenaerts here engages with a critique which is 'often argued' regarding the quality of reasoning and style of judgment.[22]

The central case in this section is the 'landmark case'[23] *Ruiz Zambrano*.[24] Lenaerts concedes that the essential reasoning of the decision is to be found in a mere six paragraphs, and understands that this may be considered a problem to his very own criteria for 'internal legitimacy'. The solution he proposes is the stone-by-stone approach.[25]

[21] Case C-413/99 *Baumbast and R v Secretary of State for the Home Department* [2002] ECR I-709. The *Garcia Avello* case (Case C-148/02 *Garcia Avello v Belgium* [2003] ECR I-11613) may be given as a striking example of the Court's failure to respond to arguments of the parties. Denmark raised what was probably the most profound objection to the ruling sought by the claimant, namely that it hinders integration of migrant communities into host countries which seek their integration. The objection is dismissed in one brief paragraph (Recital 43 of the Judgment).

[22] I am assuming that all readers of this piece will have read Lenaerts' chapter, and will know that he engages specifically with a piece by me (see his text to fn 152).

[23] See Koen Lenaerts, ch 1 in this volume, 46.

[24] Case C-34/09 *Gerardo Ruiz Zambrano v Office national de l'emploi (ONEm)*, Judgment of 8 March 2011.

[25] See Koen Lenaerts, ch 1 in this volume, 47.

The stone-by-stone metaphor used by Lenaerts is interesting. What he really describes in his chapter is a step-by-step approach, whereby the reasoning of the Court, cryptic and uncommunicative in any single case, supposedly expands into a fully reasoned and dialogical narrative when read over a number of cases. Stone-by-stone adds gravitas to the process. It is not simply a communicative process but one built on a 'founding stone',[26] rock solid in its reasoning, and the entire edifice thus cannot be blown away by, say, a mischievous wolf as would be the case with an edifice built with straw or sticks.

Rottmann[27] is the foundation on the basis of which one is to read and understand *Ruiz Zambrano*. How solid are the stones, how clarifying does the reasoning become if the cases are to be read in sequence?

The founding stone of the founding stone, the legal premise on which the Court in *Rottmann* reached its conclusion was to stress 'once again that "citizenship of the Union is intended to be the fundamental status of nationals of the Member States" '.[28]

This is, indeed, the hermeneutic founding stone of that decision. And the Court does stress it again and again in its Citizenship jurisprudence. And being so, it should not surprise us that in evenly balanced cases the Court would tilt in favour of the fundamental status. But the epistemic status of this foundational statement is rather problematic. Intended by whom? And what does 'fundamental status' actually mean, and from where does it derive as a legal concept?

The innocent reader might come to believe that it is to be found in the Treaty itself. But at least on one reading of the language of the Treaty it would seem to be in tension with text, teleology and legislative history.

In the original Maastricht Treaty one simply found: 'Every person holding the nationality of a Member State shall be a citizen of the Union'.

Amsterdam and Nice introduced a significant amendment: 'Citizenship of the Union shall complement and not replace national citizenship'.

Article 20 of the TFEU has finally settled on the following: 'Every person holding the nationality of a Member State shall be a citizen of the Union. Citizenship of the Union shall be additional to and not replace national citizenship'.

The fact that the limiting phrase was added to the Citizenship clause in response to some serious criticism and public reaction to the initial formulation may, at least to some, argue for a limiting rather than an expansive reading, especially when at stake are issues as in *Rottmann*, which precisely pit national and European Citizenship somewhat in opposition to each other.

I would like to repeat that my beef here is not with the actual decision in *Rottmann* or *Ruiz Zambrano*; it is with the reasoning and communicative quality of the internal steps within the decision. In no case to my knowledge has the Court ever explained how it arrives from a Treaty which was amended to include

[26] ibid, 47 et seq.
[27] Case C-135/08 *Janko Rottmann v Freistaat Bayern* [2010] ECR I-1449.
[28] See Koen Lenaerts, ch 1 in this volume, 48 (fn omitted).

the statement that European Citizenship complements or is additional to national citizenship to its iconic statement about European Citizenship being the fundamental status of nationals of the Member States. And, in the same vein, I am unaware of any case in which the Court has explained what it actually means when its talks about the 'fundamental status' of Citizenship.

And yet the Court uses this formula as the basis for some of its most important and path breaking decisions, such as *Rottmann/Ruiz Zambrano* (which Lenaerts invites us to read as part of the same reasoning chain) and Lenaerts uses too as the basis for his stone-by-stone explanation.

This, it is respectfully submitted, is a striking example not of judicial reasoning but of oracular statement. It is so, because we say it is so. And what it means – well you will find out.

The second 'stone' in the *Rottmann* decision is paragraph 42 of the judgment cited by Lenaerts, in which the Court explains that, since the decision of the German authorities to annul his naturalisation because of the fraudulent behaviour of Mr Rottmann at the time of his application would render him stateless, and thus deprived of his European citizenship, the matter becomes one of European law and subject to review by the Court.

I have some sympathy with the Court's approach, and it is certainly less oracular than the 'fundamental status' on which it is based. But this too, as a matter of reasoning, could profit from being, well, more profuse. At one level it begs the question given the language of the Citizenship clause and the priority it seems to give to Member State nationality. In cases such as *Collins*,[29] an American who had never set foot in Ireland and whose connection to the Union was the result of what might only be called the profligate Irish nationality rules, was treated as enjoying all rights without the Court seeming to be concerned at the manner in which nationality is granted, even though such grant is what bestows on the individual the status of European citizen with all the attendant rights to him or her and, significantly, the attendant duties on all other Member States. That case is predicated on total sovereign discretion of the Member State at the entry gate to European citizenship. Of course, one may distinguish entry and exit, but it would not require particularly creative lawyering to have taken the opposite tack in *Rottmann*. This hugely complex issue involving Member States, Union and individuals, sovereign state rights, third countries, responsibilities of individuals weighed against their rights is disposed of in fewer than a hundred words. I have seen longer letters to *Le Monde* or *FAZ*.

Yes, as Lenaerts argues, *Rottmann* did foreshadow *Ruiz Zambrano* – one apodictic stone after another. It does very little in my opinion to substantially improve the quality of reasoning and communication.

And, indeed, it seems that at a certain point Lenaerts ceases to claim that. For there is a gentle sleight of hand in Lenaerts' use of the stone-by-stone argument

[29] Case C-138/02 *Brian Francis Collins v Secretary of State for Work and Pensions* ECR [2004] I-2703.

to defend the apodictic style of many of the ECJ's decisions including important ones such as *Ruiz Zambrano*.

After taking the reader through *Rottmann* and *Ruiz Zambrano*, Lenaerts reconceptualises the Court's approach:

> [T]he fact that the argumentative discourse in *Ruiz Zambrano* left important questions unanswered is no less no more than a sign of judicial prudence. It is not that the ECJ decided to avoid answering difficult, complex and politically sensitive questions. On the contrary, it is simply that those questions would only be addressed when the cases at hand required it. This is actually what the ECJ did in *McCarthy* and subsequently in *Dereci*.[30]

That indeed is how prudent courts should, in most cases, act. But this is precisely where one notices the gentle sleight of hand: the critique of the Court is not that in this or that case it leaves important questions unanswered, the critique is that all too often the reasoning in the questions it does answer is cryptic and apodictic. Lenaerts himself seems to accept that. The authoritative tracking by Lenaerts of the answers the Court gives to the questions left open in *Ruiz Zambrano* in *McCarthy* and *Dereci*, as well as the masterly harmonising with *Zhu and Chen*[31] is interesting, but sidesteps the critical issue of the quality of the reasoning and its communicative efficiency and effectiveness.

There is another interesting evolution in the way Lenaerts deals with this issue. He starts off by acknowledging in his characteristically gracious manner that there is 'great merit' in the critique of the Court's legal reasoning,[32] but goes on to explain that these deficiencies are caused by institutional constraints in the organisation of the Court, namely that it operates under the principle of collegiality, the absence of separate or dissenting opinions and the need for consensus building. The absence of dissenting opinions means, for example, that the decisions cannot be 'as profuse' as would be otherwise the case. Consensus building requires bringing on board 'as many' opinions as possible. The result is an argumentative discourse limited to the very essential.[33] There is a distinct feel to that part of the analysis which acknowledges a problem, tries to explain why it comes about (principle of collegiality) and then offers an analysis of how in the face of these constraints the Court does its best to deal with the issue (stone-by-stone). And yet at the end of the stone-by-stone analysis, Lenaerts' perception of the problem and solution seem to have changed. I think even an attentive reader might have understood the step-by-step approach as an attempt by Lenaerts to show how the Court is creatively struggling with a less than optimal situation created by the institutional constraint of the principle of collegiality which prevents it from issuing fully reasoned, less apodictic, more discursive decisions – important for what Lenaerts calls internal legitimacy.

[30] See Koen Lenaerts, ch 1 in this volume, 49–50 (fns omitted).
[31] Case C-200/02 *Zhu and Chen* ECR [2004] I-9925.
[32] See Koen Lenaerts, ch 1 in this volume, 46.
[33] ibid.

And yet when he sums up, we find this:

> [T]he 'stone-by stone' approach followed by the ECJ is not only the right way of building a solid edifice to the rights attaching to the status of citizen of the Union, but is also entirely consistent with the dynamics of Article 267 TFEU ... The inter-judicial dialogue that takes place under Article 267 TFEU is deeply intertwined with the way in which the ECJ builds up its argumentative discourse.[34]

What, it seems, started off as a way to deal with a real problem which Lenaerts seemed to acknowledge, has morphed into the best possible way of conducting the dialogue so that presumably, even if the Court were not under the constraints of the principle of collegiality, it should not change a thing in its manner and style of reasoning and drafting its judgments. Of course, this entire paragraph is predicated on the shift from a real concern with the quality of reasoning and communicating what it does decide, to the separate and mostly distinct question of whether and when the court (any court) should answer questions not before it, and with regard to which I largely agree with Lenaerts. So at the end of the day, here too, all is perfect. Not even a hint that anything at all might be even slightly sub-par.

In conclusion, Lenaerts simply has not answered the 'oft argued' critique against the quality of legal reasoning and the communicative style of the Court. What he demonstrated effectively is that the Court, like many prudent common law courts, moves from one question to another as they present themselves to the Court and does not give abstract answers. But as regards the quality of reasoning and communicative effect, all the cases he brings demonstrate the piling of one apodictic stone on top of another. In a way, what these cases prove is how a hugely important line of cases can be built on shifting sands when it comes to legal reasoning.

VI

The contributors to this volume focused on the jurisprudence of the Court in discrete areas of EU law.

Perhaps by way of conclusion I may briefly mention some structural issues which potentially compromise the institutional authority of the Court and the authoritativeness of its jurisprudence.

1. The possibility of reappointing judges and advocates general at the end of their term of office is an ongoing scandal unknown in all respectable jurisdictions. It compromises the appearance of independence of the judges (since their reappointment would depend on their own government), and it has been argued over the years that in some instances it was not only the appearance of independence that has been compromised. What is worrying

[34] ibid, 59.

is that in several IGCs, proposals were brought forward which would have limited the term of ECJ judges to one term of, say, 9 or 12 years. They were always rejected by the Member States. I cannot find a benign explanation for such rejection.

2. I do not wish to labour any more on the question of the quality of reasoning and the style of judgment. I do believe the system is mature enough to tolerate dissenting opinions and, perhaps, separate opinions. It would remove one of the reasons Lenaerts cites for the extremely economical style of the Court. So long, however, as the judges may be reappointed the possibility of dissenting opinions would be inimical. The Court may, however, explore other forms of indicating divisions in arriving at a decision – most common in many high courts – without necessarily divulging the names.[35]
3. The European Court is a human institution. It cannot be perfect. Occasional reform has always been considered advisable. But to date, such reform has typically been dominated by the Court itself, with the assistance at times of former judges. It is hard to imagine good reform which would exclude an important voice of former and present judges. But the domination of the reform agenda by the European Court itself compromises the critical foundation of any reform agenda.
4. Lenaerts refers to the Court as the constitutional umpire of the Union. Rightly so. Especially in those countries where there is a specialised constitutional court it would improve the credibility and the dialogical potential if judges coming from those jurisdictions tended to be constitutionalists or even constitutional court judges.
5. A Cato's Cry: the Court should abandon its fetishistic attachment to the preliminary reference procedure. It is detrimental to its authority and authoritativeness in at least two fundamental ways. In all preliminary reference cases, it sits as court of first and last instance. True, a national court may resubmit a question, but it will be decided by the same court. Important decisions should be appealable, and potentially subject to review by a higher court. The situation in the EU is more acute than in those Member States which have a similar internal preliminary reference procedure. In the EU it is not only the strictly constitutional which reaches the Court by way of preliminary reference, but just about any question of European law, many very critical. To have these decided by a court of last instance is neither necessary nor justifiable. Additionally, insisting on a monopoly over the preliminary references continues to clog the docket of the Court. The current President of the ECJ has done wonders to streamline the Court's work. But the docket still runs at an average of more than one decision per working day. It is inimical to the administration of justice for two reasons. First, want it or not, it limits the time available for thinking, deliberating and drafting. It cannot

[35] *cf* WTO Appellate Body Report, *European Communities – Measures Affecting Asbestos and Asbestos Containing Products*, WT/DS135/AB/R, 12 March 2001.

but compromise the quality of the judgment. Second, it reduces the specific gravity of the case law; it 'inflationises' the value of ECJ decisions.

The role the European Court has played in the process of Union building and European integration has been second to none. There is nothing so good that it cannot be better. That is, I believe, the common wish of all those who are parties to this volume.

Index

adjudication:
  decentralised adjudication, 164
  dynamic adjudication, 1–4
  general principles of EU law, 61–4
    legal certainty and, 66, 70
    legal integration, 71
    limits, 70, 85
  jurisprudence, 7
  procedural legitimacy, 5
  substantive legitimacy, 5
adjudicators, 1
Agafi ei and others, 85
age discrimination, 61, 72–9
  equal treatment in employment, 77
    Council Directive 2000/78/EC, 72–3, 78, 81–5
Air Transport Association of America case:
  conflict with EC/EU legislation, 181–3
  customary international law, 182–5
Aklagaren v Mickelsson and Roos, 104, 114–15
Audiolux case, 71, 84

Bartsch case, 76
Baumbast case, 133–5, 147–8, 247
Bidar case, 140, 148, 163–4
Blanco Perez case, 34–5
Bonnarde case, 96
Bressol case, 42–3, 124, 161, 246–7
Brüstle case, 70

Carpenter case, 99, 166, 171
Cartesio case, 207
case law, 145–53
  activism v self-restraint, 16–17
  conflict with community legislation, 178–9
    Air Transport Association of America, 181–9
    Intertanko case, 179–81
  constitutional implications, 156
    EU legislator, impact of, 156
    member states, impact of, 156
  consistency, 32–40
  controversial nature, 3
  customary international law, 182–5
    Kadi case, 185–7
  equivalence and effectiveness, 15
  EU in an international context, 177– 8
    customary international law, 182–5
    mandate of the ECJ, 175–7
    Mox Plant case, 193–4
    treaty obligations, 178–9
  free movement, 127–54
    legitimacy, 109
  general principles of EU law:
    Kücükdeveci case, 72–6, 81–5
    legal effects, 79–81
    Mangold case, 61–4, 72–6, 81–5
    non-discrimination on the grounds of age, 76–9
    source of interpretation, as a, 67–72
  indirect judicial review, 147–8
  internal market, 87–108, 109–26
  legitimacy, 8
    citizenship, 132–40, 145–53
    feasibility, 198–202
      case law, 208–18, 233
      functional legitimacy, 202, 208–18
      judicial reasoning, 203–4, 233
    interpretation, 132–40
    primary Treaty provisions, 137–9
    real link principle, 135
    welfare rights, 135–7
  personal circumstances assessment, 142–4, 148
  safeguarding European integration, 15–16
  'substance of rights' doctrine, 169, 171
  treaty obligations, 178–9
    Air Transport Association of America, 181–9
    Intertanko case, 179–81
  Treaty provisions on EU citizenship, 46
  Union citizenship, 127–54, 155–74
  upholding EU constitutional legal order, 16
Cassis de Dijon case, 93, 96, 105
  mutual recognition, 16, 241
Charter of Fundamental Rights of the European Union, 78, 122, 136n52, 151n115, 169, 174, 189
Chicago Convention on International Civil Aviation, 181
CILFIT case, 216
Citizen's Rights Directive (CRD), 18–19
citizenship:
  access to welfare provision, 156–64
  case law:
    1998–2008 interpretation133–40
    developments since 2008, 140–53
  classic disputes:
    third-country relatives, 164–70

citizenship (*cont*):
'true' citizenship, 171–3
welfare provision, 156–64
cross-border solidarity, 151
dependency, 56–8
deprivation effect, 50–2
developing concept, 133–45
dual nationality, 50–1, 152–3
emancipation, 47
free movement, 47, 53–5, 127–8, 153–4
1998–2008 interpretation of case law, 133–40
developments since 2008, 140–53
fundamental rights, 50–8
impact of Eurozone debt crisis, 151
impeding effect, 50–2
internal legitimacy, 46
interpretation, 133
judicial activism, 128–33
judicial construction, 155–6, 173–4
Ruiz Zambrano, 5, 46–7, 48–9
'substance of rights' doctrine, 100–1, 169, 171
third-country relatives, 164–5
'true' citizenship, 171–3
third-country relatives, 164–70
see also welfare provision
Citizenship Directive (2004/38/EC), 140–1, 145, 148–9, 157, 170
Collins case, 18–20, 148
Commission v Austria, 124
Commission v Ireland, 193–4
Commission v Italy, 114
Commission v Spain, 26–9
'considerable influence' test, 9, 91–5, 101, 114
consistency of rulings, 17, 32–40, 88, 114
export of goods, 116
free movement of goods, 114–15
treatment of regulatory and fiscal barriers, 115–16
Costa v Enel, 175
courts, *see* European Court of Human Rights; European Court of Justice; national courts; Unified Patent Court
Council Directive 2000/78/EC (equal treatment in employment Directive), 72–6, 81–5
Council Directive 2006/123/EC (Services Directive), 113, 126
customary international law, 11, 182
Air Transport Association of America, 181, 182–5
assessing validity of EU instruments, 184–5
EU law and, 182

De Agostini case, 39
Dereci case, 52–3
dependency, 56–8
direct effect, principle of, 15, 40, 68, 72, 75, 128, 214
Directive 2004/38 *see* Citizenship Directive
discrimination, 32, 35, 76
age discrimination, 9, 61–2, 72–6, 82–3
commercial freedom, 94, 116
equal treatment, 61
gender equality, 243–5
reverse discrimination, 47n157, 168
see also non-discrimination, principle of
dual nationality, 50–1, 152–3
dynamic adjudication, 1–4

education:
limited EU powers, 122, 137–8
non-discrimination, 124
Environmental Crimes case, 139
equal treatment:
constitutional effects, 162
financial effects, 162
harmonisation, 162
minority shareholders, 84–5
principle of, 61
minority shareholders, 84
students, 42–3
third-country relatives, 164–5
welfare provision, 161, 164–5
see also discrimination; non–discrimination, principle of
EU law:
breach:
'inherent in the system of the Treaty', 89
ECJ interpretation of legislation, 17, 68–9
legal certainty, principle of, 23–4
primary EU law, 20–3
proportionality, principle of, 24–5
reconciliatory interpretation, 18–20, 59–60
secondary EU law, 26–9, 59
value diversity, 60
foundations, 85
general principles, 67–72, 85
case law, 70–2
interaction between judicial and political institutions, 131–2, 245–6
regulatory conflicts, 132
nature, 64
role of ECJ, 64–6
defining the law, 66
standards:
demarcations of responsibility, 2
good governances, 2
proper administration, 2
European and Community Patent Court *see* Unified Patent Court
European Coal and Steel Community, 2
European Court of Justice:
authority, 235, 251–3
authoritativeness, 235, 251–3
case law, 145–53
citizenship, 132–40, 145–53, 173–4

interpretation, 132–40
primary Treaty provisions, 137–9
real link principle, 135
welfare rights, 135–7
citizenship:
indirect judicial review, 140–2
interpretation of EU law, 147
personal circumstance assessments, 142–4
real link principle, 135, 152
rights to equal treatment, 146–7
rights to residency, 146–7
uni-lateral policy making, 133
consistency of rulings, 114–17
dependency, 56–8
deprivation effect, 50–2
dissenting opinions, 7
dynamic adjudication, 2–4
EU institution, as an, 117–24, 218–33
appointment, 231–3
composition, 227–31
information sharing, 219–23
mutual trust, 219
procedure, 223–7, 233
European Court of Human Rights and, 187–9
external legitimacy, 240, 242
ECJ and the EU legislator, 17–29
harmonisation of law, 29–40
free movement, 47, 53–5, 134–5, 140
fundamental human rights, 52–3
second order rights, 133–4, 136
impeding effect, 50–2
indirect judicial review, 140–2
internal legitimacy, 40, 237–8
citizenship, 46–7, 48–9, 249
ECJ's legal reasoning, 45–7, 60–1, 249–51
endorsement of national courts, 40, 247–51
European integration, 40–5
interpretation of EU legislation, 17, 235
principle of legal certainty, 23–4
principle of proportionality, 24–5
primary EU law, 20–3
reconciliatory interpretation, 18–20
judicial institution, as a, 110–17
judicial output:
case law, 208–18
feasibility, 198–202
judgments and reasoning, 203–8
reasoning, 203–8
legitimacy, 4–6, 14, 197–8, 238
case law, 87–90, 119
national courts, support from, 197–8
procedural legitimacy, 5, 6
substantive legitimacy, 5, 6
mandate, 194–5
Mox Plant case, 193–4
primacy of, 185–7
protection of, 189–91, 193–4
Unified Patent Court, 191–3
Member States and, 29
harmonisation of laws, 29–40
national interest, 29
minimum standards, 110
consistent case law, 110, 114–16
normal judicial methods, 110, 111–14
reasoned judgments, 110
primary EU law:
interpretation of, 20–3, 26
procedure, 128, 223–7
preliminary rulings, 223–5
role, 60
protection of mandate, 189–91, 193–4
relations with other international courts, 187–9
secondary EU law:
interpretation of, 26–9, 59
separation of powers, 13, 59
separation of law and politics, 1, 245–6
Union citizenship:
'substance of rights' doctrine, 169, 171
third-country relatives, 164–5
'true' citizenship, 171–3
see also case law; citizenship; legitimacy
European Convention on Human Rights (ECHR), 70, 187–9
ECJ and, 189
mandate of national courts, 53, 98
European Court of Human Rights:
ECJ and, 11, 187–9
enforcement of ECHR, 53
interpretation of ECHR, 53
Treaty of Lisbon, 189
European Union:
constitutional framework, 131
interaction with ECJ, 131
ECJ as an EU institution, 117–24
ECJ interpretation of legislation, 17
principle of legal certainty, 23–4
principle of proportionality, 24–5
primary EU law, 20–3
reconciliatory interpretation, 18–20, 59–60
secondary EU law, 26–9, 59
value diversity, 60
integration of functions, 14, 155–6
judicial function, 14
judicial process, 14
national courts, 14, 60, 126
export of goods:
consistency of law, 4, 116

Family Reunification Directive (2003/86/EC), 170
Fidium Finanz case, 113
fiscal barriers to free movement, 115–16
Förster case, 140–5, 149, 155, 157–9, 163–4, 239

free movement, 153–4
  citizenship, 47, 53–5
  Citizenship Directive, 170
  compliance with minimum standards, 111–13
  controversial nature, 120
  economically active citizens, 150
  effective judicial protection, 131
  EU context, 125–6
  fiscal barriers to free movement, 115–16
  free movement of goods, 114–15
  free movement of services, 113
  law, 110, 124–6
    United States, 109–10
  legitimacy of case law, 109–10, 124–6
    ECJ as a judicial institution, 110–17
    ECJ as an EU institution, 117–24
  market economies, 120
  mutual recognition, 113
  regulatory barriers to free movement, 115–16
  scope, 92
  Union citizens, 127–8, 153–4
    case law, 133–53
    judicial activism, 128–33
fundamental rights, *see* human rights

Garcia Avello case, 50
GATT, 179
Germany v Parliament and Council, 102, 139
gender equality, 243
  insurance, 243–4
Grunkin and Paul case, 142–3
Grzelczyk case, 147–8, 155
Gysbrechts case, 116

harmonisation of law, 1, 9, 29–37, 92
  absence of, 29–37
  constitutional principles in national law, 29–32, 60
  consistency, 32–7
  ECJ role, 29–40, 60
  internal market, 105
  presence of, 37–40
  principle of proportionality, 24–5, 30
    consistency, 32, 34–7
  regulatory powers and, 138
  scope, 101–4
  trade laws, 16, 241
Hartlauer case, 33–4, 36
healthcare, 27–9, 112
  consistency, 32–7, 137–8
  limited EU powers, 122, 137–8
  free movement of services, 114
  non–discrimination, 124
  public health, 43–5
human rights, 7, 15, 49, 70–2, 80, 128, 169
  citizenship and, 169
  civil rights, 136
  economic rights, 107
  entitlement to welfare, 136–7
  Lisbon Treaty, 100
  political rights, 107, 136
  protection of, 16, 186
  scope of application:
    Dereci case, 52–3, 55
  'substance of rights' doctrine, 168–9
  social rights, 107, 136
  third-country relatives, 170–1, 171n96
  see also Charter of Fundamental Rights of the European Union; European Court of Human Rights

Iida case, 53–6
import of goods:
  consistency of law, 4, 116
indirect judicial review, 10, 135, 154, 163
  citizenship, 140–7
  secondary legislation, 148
Inter-Environnement Wallonie case, 73–4
internal market:
  case law, 90–3
  definitions, 90
  free movement law:
    scope, 92
  harmonisation:
    scope, 92, 101–4
  individual nations and, 92
    regulatory autonomy, 92
  justification for creation, 104–7
  regulatory homogeneity, 91
  restrictions on use, 94–6
  serious inconvenience, 96–8
  structure of internal market law, 106–7
  substance of rights, 92, 98–101
  see also Treaty on the Functioning of the European Union
International Association of Tanker Owners (Intertanko):
  conflict with EC/EU legislation, 178–81
International Civil Aviation Organisation, 182
International Convention for the Prevention of Pollution from Ships (MARPOL):
  conflict with EC/EU legislation, 178–81
International Fruit case, 178
Intertanko case, 179–81

judges, 5, 64, 200, 229, 233
  adjudication, 64
  appointment, 184, 231, 251–2
  function, 232
  independence, 88, 158, 251
  legislators and, 149, 153, 173
  quality of reasoning, 252
  separation of powers, 149, 153
judicial activism, 2n4, 128–33, 153–4
  expansionist tendencies, 128–9

overriding member state autonomy, 129–30
judicial legitimacy, 127–8
quality of judicial process, 14
role in democratic societies, 13
separation of law and politics, 13, 245–6
see also legitimacy
judicial reasoning, 7–12, 14, 37, 40, 58–9, 66–7, 70, 88, 101, 163–4, 233–4, 236–8, 243
ECJ as a judicial institution, 110–17
free movement of EU citizens, 130, 136, 145
Kadi case, 186–7
legitimacy of judicial decision-making, 198–9, 203–8
Mangold and *Kücükdevici* cases, 72–6, 85
non-discrimination principle, 76–81
persuasiveness, 45–7, 247–51
quality of reasoning, 163–4

Kadi case, 185–7
Keck and Mithouard case, 93, 115, 118
Kerckhaert case, 115
Köbler case, 216
Konsumentombudsmannen *v Gourmet International Products*, 94
Kücükdeveci v Swedex, 61–4
Council Directive 2000/78/EC, 74–6
principle of direct effect, 72, 79–81
principle of non-discrimination, 72, 76–9
rulings, 81–5
see also Mangold v Helm
Kyoto Protocol, 181–2

Landtova case, 225
legal certainty, 84
principle of, 23–4
legal reasoning, 14, 40, 58, 238, 250–1
consistency test, 37,
persuasiveness, 45–7
legitimacy:
acceptability, 235
assessment of:
acquiescence, 5
obedience, 5–6
popular support, 6
case law, 87–90
conflict with EC/EU legislation, 178–82
free movement law, 109–26
international law, 177–8
mandate of the ECJ, 175–7
Treaty obligations, 178–82
external legitimacy, 17–40, 240–2
functional legitimacy, 202, 208–18
compliance, 209–13
feasibility, 214–18
implementation of judgments in national courts, 208
input perspective, 4
internal legitimacy, 14, 40–59, 237–40, 247
judicial activity, 5
meaning, 4, 235–40
external legitimacy, 17–40, 240–2
internal legitimacy, 14, 40–59, 237–40, 247
output perspective, 4–5, 6
procedural legitimacy, 5, 6, 63, 87
substantive legitimacy distinguished, 87–90
substantive legitimacy, 5, 6, 63, 87, 203, 207
see also case law; judicial legitimacy
Lisbon Treaty, 2, 78, 100, 122–3, 125, 227

McCarthy case, 50–2, 152–3
Maastricht Treaty, 131, 134, 146, 248
Mangold v Helm, 61–4
age discrimination, 72
Council Directive 2000/78/EC, 72–6
equal treatment in employment, 72
legal certainty, 70
legal reasoning, 83–4
principle of direct effect, 72, 79–81
principle of non–discrimination, 72, 76–9
rulings, 81–5
Marbury v Madison, 13, 241
market access, 33
free movement of goods, 114–15
market regimes, 120–4, 125
Melki and Abdeli case, 225
Mesopotamia Broadcast case, 37–40, 60
Metock case, 166, 171
Mox Plant case, 193–4
mutual recognition, 16, 94n8, 112, 113–14, 162, 241

national courts:
access to ECJ information, 219–23
application of ECJ judgments, 122–4
application of the European Convention on Human Rights, 169
compliant interpretation of ECJ judgements, 89–90
disconnect with the ECJ, 218–19, 227–30
guidance from the ECJ, 164, 164n58
international law and, 177–8, 181, 184
judicial activism, 128, 130
judicial institutions, as, 110–11
legitimacy of the ECJ, 197–8, 200–2, 207–8, 217–18
domestic application of ECJ judgments, 208–13
procedure on preliminary ruling, 223–7
relationship with the ECJ, 14, 34, 40–5, 59–60, 156, 175–7, 236
interpretation of ECJ judgments, 89–90
human rights, 53, 169
role in the EU system, 126, 164
separation of functions, 2, 53n178, 125n110

national courts (*cont*):
standards:
demarcations of responsibility, 2
good governances, 2
proper administration, 2
state liability, 89–90
see also European Court of Human Rights; European Court of Justice; Unified Patent Court
NCC Construction Danmark case, 71
Nelson case, 23–5
see also legal certainty; proportionality
Nerkowska case, 142–3
Nice Treaty, 222, 248
non-discrimination, principle of, 4, 82–4
advertising, 93
age discrimination, 9, 72, 74, 76–9, 81–5
Council Directive 2000/78/EC, 72–4
distinguished, 82
education cases, 124
foundations, 76–9
legal effects, 79–81
legal source, as a, 81
restrictions on use, 93–6
scope, 82–3

O & S case, 56–8
Omega case, 29–30, 32, 35, 60, 70

Parliament v Council, 78
personal circumstances assessments, 144, 148
citizenship, 142
indirect judicial review and, 144, 147, 163
proportionality principle, 140
Placanica case, 32–4, 36
Poiares Maduro, 111
primacy, principle of, 15, 40, 63, 68, 177, 185–6, 201, 208, 214
see also supremacy, principle of
procedure, 128, 233
conflict of law, 137–8
preliminary rulings procedure, 212, 223–7
proportionality, principle of, 24–5, 30
consistency, 32, 34–7
see also personal circumstances assessments

Racke case, 183
real link principle, 18–19, 134–5, 141–2, 147, 148, 152
Regulation 883/2004 (coordination of social security systems), 27, 148–9
Regulation 1408/71 (application of social security systems to people moving within the Community), 27, 132, 148–9
regulatory barriers to free movement, 115–16
remedies, 15, 16n14, 214
compliance, 215, 226, 241
jurisprudence, 128
Residency Directives, 146–7
restrictions on use of products, 93–6
Rottmann case, 47–8, 247–9
Ruiz Zambrano case, 5, 46–7, 48–9, 58–9, 98–101, 163–4, 166–70, 207, 247–50
Runevic-Vardyn case, 97, 160

Sala case, 127, 132–3, 155
Sayn-Wittgenstein case, 29, 30–2, 35, 60, 160
proportionality, 32
serious inconvenience, 96–8
separation of powers, 59
courts' application of, 13
definition, 13
judges, 149, 153
judicial v legislative processes, 92
law and politics, 1, 13–17, 245–6
'serious inconvenience' test, 96–8, 101
Simmenthal case, 74, 80
social security, 137–8
Regulation 883/2004 (coordination of social security systems), 27, 148–9
Regulation 1408/71 (application of social security systems to people moving within the Community), 27, 132, 148–9
see also welfare provision
Smits-Peerbooms case, 112
Sturgeon and others case, 20, 22–6, 59, 242, 244
'substance of rights' doctrine, 5, 98–101, 144–5
third-country relatives, 169
supremacy, principle of, 63, 68, 71, 128, 177, 201
ECJ and national courts, 40
exclusionary effect and, 81n103
Kadi case, 185–7
national acceptance of, 208, 214

Test-Achats case, 20–1, 25–6, 59–60, 82, 242–4
third-country relatives:
equal treatment, 164–5
EU legislator and, 170
federal balance of power, 168–9
residency, 166–8
substance of rights, 169
traité-cadre, 67
Treaty on Stability, Coordination and Governance 2012, 151
Treaty on the Functioning of the European Union, 90–3, 108, 150
conflict of law, 137–8
harmonisation:
scope, 101–4
internal market, 90
justification for internal market, 104–7
obligations, 107
restrictions on use, 94–6
scope, 105, 137–8

serious inconvenience, 96–8
'substance of rights' doctrine, 98–101

Uberseering case, 116
UN Convention on the Law of the Sea (UNCLOSC), 193
conflict with EC/EU legislation, 179–81
Unified Patent Court, 191–3
Union citizenship, 10
free movement, 127–8, 153–4
case law, 133–53
judicial activism, 128–33
judicial construction, 155–6, 173–4
access to welfare provision, 156–64
third-country relatives, 164–70
'true' citizenship, 171–3
'substance of rights' doctrine, 169, 171
third-country relatives, 164–5
'true' citizenship, 171–3
see also citizenship
United States:
free movement law, 109–10
Marbury v Madison, 13, 241
Ustavni soud case, 225–6

Van Gend & Loos case, 79, 167, 175
'Vanbraekel reimbursement', 27–9
Vatsouras case, 18, 59, 140, 149, 157–9, 163–4
Viking Line case, 106
Vodafone, O2 et al v Secretary of State, 102–4

welfare provision, 153–4
access to, 156–7
EU legislator and, 157–9
federal balance of power, 159–63
economically inactive citizens, 155–6
entitlement, 136–7
equal treatment, 161, 164–5
EU legislator and, 157–9
continuity, 159
extended interpretative autonomy, 157–8
federal balance of power, 159–63
burden of proof, 160
justification, 160
national economic or social models, 161–3
public policy considerations, 160–1
national economic or social models, 161–3
constitutional effects, 162
equal access, 161
financial effects, 162
real link, 162
quality of reasoning, 163–4
real link principle, 18–19, 134–5, 141–2, 147, 148, 152
social security, 137–8
Regulation 883/2004 (coordination of social security systems), 27, 148–9
Regulation 1408/71 (application of social security systems to people moving within the Community), 27, 132, 148–9
Wolzenburg case, 143
World Trade Organisation (WTO), 180

Zhu and Chen case, 51–2, 250

www.ingramcontent.com/pod-product-compliance
Ingram Content Group UK Ltd.
Pitfield, Milton Keynes, MK11 3LW, UK
UKHW020832290926
15470UKWH00009B/1857/J

9 781849 463355